STUDIES OF THE MIND AND ART

OF

ROBERT BROWNING

STUDIES OF THE MIND AND ART

OF

ROBERT BROWNING

BY

JAMES FOTHERINGHAM

FOURTH EDITION, REVISED

LONDON

HORACE MARSHALL & SON

1900

Truth, truth, that's the gold! And all the good
I find in fancy is, it serves to set
Gold's inmost glint free.
The Two Poets of Croisic.

What's poetry except a power that makes,
And, speaking to one sense, inspires the rest,
Pressing them all into its service?
Balaustion's Adventure.

To the motive, the endeavour, the heart's self,
His quick sense looks: he crowns and calls aright
The soul o' the purpose, ere 'tis shaped as act,
Takes flesh i' the world, and clothes itself a king.
Luria.

In the facts of modern life—in the often unknown growth of souls in and thro' any form [of experience] there is an infinity of what men should be told, and what none but a poet can tell.—RUSKIN.

The experience of each new age requires new interpreters, and the world seems always waiting for its poets.—EMERSON.

The intellectual and moral must be co-ordinate with the æsthetic part of poetry to give it strength and worth—Truth must go with Beauty.

His noblest characteristic . . . I call his simultaneous perception of Power and Love in the absolute, and of Beauty and Good in the concrete.—BROWNING, *Essay on Shelley.*

If there be any quality more perceptible than another in Browning's mind it is his decisive and incisive faculty of thought, his sureness and intensity of perception, his rapid and trenchant resolution of aim.—SWINBURNE, *Essay on Chapman.*

PREFACE TO THIRD EDITION

———◆———

THESE Studies were published some years ago, and soon went through two editions. For various reasons they were not reissued at that time. They are issued now because many inquiries for them, since they went out of print, and other considerations, seem to show that there is still room for them in the literature of their subject.

The book has been carefully revised, in many parts rewritten, three chapters are new, five others largely so, and many additions have been made, with the view of making it more complete within its plan as a study of Browning's work. More space has been allowed me than in the former editions, and I have been glad to avail myself of it, though the longer and more important of the later poems are still excluded. In " The Ring and the Book," the "Dramatic Idyls," "Fifine," "Ferishtah," and some others of these later poems there is matter for a further group of studies.

Since this book was first issued some important events bearing on its subject have happened. The poet, who seemed to write with much of his old nervous force as late as 1889, submitted at the close of that year to mortal fate, and was laid, with impressive recognition of his services to English life and literature, in the great Abbey where he rests. In 1891 his *Life and Letters*, by Mrs. Orr, was published. And last autumn the *Letters of Elizabeth Barrett Browning*, fitly edited by Mr. F. G. Kenyon, were published. And a fairly cheap and complete edition of Browning's *Poems* has been issued at length.

Those parts of the book affected by Mrs. Orr's *Life*, and by Mr. Kenyon's volumes, have been rewritten. One is grateful for both. The sweet, ardent, brave spirit of the wife is the main matter of Mr. Kenyon's book, and there is less of the husband and his work than one might have expected. And Mrs. Orr leaves us longing for more matter bringing us into direct touch with the poet himself. For such matter we could have spared a good many pages at the beginning of her book, and all the " astrological hints."

The number of Browning readers has, I infer, considerably increased during the last ten years. One judges that the attitude of these readers is at once free and cordial, recognising the poet's vigour, his individuality, his wealth of poetry and thought, though by no means accepting all parts of his work. Such readers I would help, if I may.

Mr. Ernest E. Speight, B.A., has kindly done a short index, chiefly of poems dealt with, and a few leading matters.

JAMES FOTHERINGHAM.

BRADFORD, *April* 1898.

PREFACE TO SECOND EDITION

———+———

THE last two chapters of this edition are new, and other chapters have been revised. My wish has been to make the book complete as a survey of all sections of Browning's work, though it has not been possible on the scale and plan of the book to make it a survey of all the poet's works. Space has kept me from adding to what was said, in the first edition, of " The Ring and the Book," and others of the more interesting and important of the later poems.

The issue of this edition gives me a chance of noticing a few points suggested by revision, or by criticism of these " Studies "—points I notice simply to make clearer the design of the book, and its estimate of the poetry under review.

One difficulty of Browning study for some time appears very curiously to have been the impression that Browning readers were a sect, holding a poetic creed of their own, and even insisting on a sort of cult in relation to the poet. They are thought to make too much of the poet, and too much of his kind of poetry, and to take him too seriously. Nothing pleases them—such

is the theory—so much as a problem, nothing
excites them like a search for hidden meanings,
and poetry with nothing to puzzle over is worth
nothing. There may have been, there may be,
Browning students of this sort. Other good poets
besides Browning have attracted such disciples.
They bring heat if not light to the study. I may,
perhaps, be allowed here to say in view of such
amusing impressions that I hold none of the
heresies in art they are thought to hold, unless it
be heresy to think that poetry must have essential,
and not merely formal value, beauty, and interest;
and that the poetry of man's thought, passion,
and effort is the highest, not any poetry of the
triviality, sentimentality, or self-indulgence of men,
however fair the forms these may take through
the sympathy of genius. And a poet who
requires and repays deliberate study may surely
be so studied, without implying that he is the
only poet worth such study. The specialisation
of study is for certain ends, and for a time—a
distinct advantage, and need not, except in the
case of narrow minds, lead to narrow judgments.
I should certainly and strongly wish to be of the
" party " of *all* true poets, yet avoid partisanship
even in the case of the greatest. No writer can
be understood merely in his own circle. And so,
while putting a high and earnest value on the
poet and poetry here reviewed, it has been my
aim to study both with frank esteem for other
ideals, in the free world and among the varied
interests of literature.

But a larger and more obstinate objection remains—the poet and his manner. He is hard, rugged, a lover of paradox and tangled problems; occupied with questions no way pertinent to the living interests of men, with psychological puzzles and vain investigations of the soul; dealing with matters that belong to the thinker rather than the poet, and dealing with them obscurely, casuistically, as the "dramatic apologist" of all sorts of odd folks and quaint beliefs. He brings neither pleasure nor tranquillity such as art ought to bring, but only toil and turmoil of verse and thought. He has range and energy of mind, spiritual power, and much force of style. But he is over intellectual, aggressive, emphatic, without sympathy, or charm of spirit or of art.

Browning is not for all hours or minds, and he has not all the virtues and graces of man and of poet. There are powers and beauties in other poets of his century most grateful and delightful to us, that we do not find in and do not expect from him. We take him for what he is, for the hours he belongs to, and we find his qualities and virtues good and great, his gifts ample and precious, his influence high and cordial.

Our poet has not all the interests he might have had to commend him to the spirit of his time. He has little of that yearning towards the greatness of Nature, that care for her sympathy and for all her beauty which so many of us have. He has little lyrical tenderness, grace, or sentiment—that play of "the heart within the mind" about the themes of human life, which so many like, and which makes art, not indeed a triumph of the spirit, but a consolation and a rest. He has little political or social zeal. The passion of humanity that he has takes other forms and concerns itself with other objects than those of the time. When I seek expressive utterance or fine enforcement of social hopes and principles, a quickening zeal for practical aims and for the immediate good of men, a passionate belief in all that ameliorates or brightens at any point human labours and lives, I find these in other writers.

But have those who blame our poet for his "defects" at such points a wide enough scope themselves? I judge not. The fervid politician is too apt to be heedless and impatient of everything not in his field and on his lines. But a true poet and fine writer, just lost to us, spent much labour impressing a truth politicians often forget—that there is an inner life, a "kingdom" within, and that that too is important to us all. It may be the old word is yet vital and true, that "the kingdom of God"—the realm and sphere of all great and finally important things for men and for mankind—is within. If the fact be so, Browning has done well to exemplify the interest and worth of this sphere, and has served us all by doing so.

And there is much more to be said for him even at this point. Since the days of "Paracelsus" and "Sordello," he has grasped the social idea with great force, and, though his work has done little to advance it directly, his spirit and *morale* are well on the side of all earnest life and work.   His poetry is full of a " sense of substance and purpose," and has a " core of common sense." In this and other ways it is a " school of life," and keeps well in touch with the living world.   His ethical principles have much that is nobly practical and pertinent for our life to-day.   And the poet is not only inquisitive and speculative, he is active strenuous, enjoying.   He lives and thinks, he does not dream, evade, postpone, or doubt.   And if he has never written as if the *summum bonum* of poetry and life were to be found in the aims and ideas of zealous philanthropy and liberalism, it has been that he is a poet, and could not forget that, though social justice and progress are a great part of human good, " politics " are on a lower plane and of less value than poetry.

Two other classes of critics are hard to please when such work as Browning's is in question. One says the poet is not, and ought not to be, a thinker.   Another finds fault with him for not speaking explicitly and directly, but always as a dramatist.   And anon both objections are thrown together.   To take the second first—dramatic statements and moral principles may tease those who, for reasons of their own, are set upon doctrines or rules ; but the poet must be true to his genius and his art, and his method rests on a large and just conception of the nature of moral truth.

Yet for some the poet has spoken too definitely,

having mixed his poetry with theology, and involved his art in the trammels of Christian dogma.
I trust I have shown that such is not the fact.   I
do not find dogma, as I do not wish to find it.
What I find is a free recognition of the value of
certain great religious principles.   As I read him,
the poet has illustrated, through dramatic interpretation of the mind of man, the bearing and
truth of what men have affirmed in and sought
through religion.

And because I have taken this principle as a
clue to the meaning and scope of the poet's work,
some think that I have given an improper value
and bearing to it—a value and reference poetry
as such cannot have.   The question raised is
deeply involved in much of what follows in this
book, and is otherwise important, so I should like
to have it clear.   The poet as poet is not a philosopher, and poetry as such is not philosophy.
And I have no kind of wish to offer even the
most " philosophic poetry " in place of philosophy
on any of the great questions, and certainly no
wish to avoid or hasten the just investigation of
those questions on their proper grounds.   The
contrary has long been my desire and is my aim.
And when I compare the principles and scope of
Spencer with the ideas and spirit of Browning, it
is not to offer a royal road of poetry for the hard
ways of science; it is to ascertain and estimate
their relations to realities that belong to the cog-
nisance of both.   The poet, who is a spiritual
thinker, and profound observer of man and life,

has a right to be heard on the matters in question. The true philosopher would be the first to allow that the facts and principles such a poet is master of are not only pertinent, but are of high and peculiar value for our conclusions on the final moral questions.

The breadth of Browning's "statement" of these matters may be judged by the fact that his readers include men of very varied schools of thought, from orthodox Christians to the advocates of "philosophic ignorance." Indeed, all who seek a serious and spiritual "reading" of man's mind and life will find much in his work with which they can agree. In this spirit, and with this hope, all that is written here of the matters now in question has been written.

BRADFORD, *July* 1888.

PREFACE TO FIRST EDITION

———◆———

THE following chapters are an essay towards a study of the mind and art of Robert Browning. They are critical and expository, literary and ethical. They are studies of life and thought as presented by the poet, and of the poet's work as tested by these; studies of the poet's art, and expositions of the matter as well as the bearing of his work. This seems the right way to present this poet.

A poet who reads the life and thought of his age has strong claims on its deliberate attention; and if it be too much to say that the best poets of our own time concern most readers more than any other poets, it is the fact that they have much to give no others can give, and that without them we do not know ourselves.

This kind of "criticism" is thought to be the forte and the foible of Browning. His significance in this respect I have tried to show; I trust it has been shown on grounds proper to literature.

But it will be said that one who serves such a function ought not himself to need explanation. That will depend on other things besides the

value of his work.   In the present case, anyhow,
the need seems to be a fact.   The reasons for it
I have tried to explain.   The great reason lies,
however, in the matter and significance of the
work.   The poet must be read from the inside,
and as a whole.   To be put in a position to do
that is to be put in a position to understand
the poet.

One scarcely expects all who read good poetry
to read Browning.   But I would gladly commend
the poet to those readers who have a genial yet
serious care for poetry, and who have a serious
yet genial care for life.   And if one can show
the beauty and worth of the poet's work, and
place it rightly in the field of life and thought,
more of those to whom he really belongs may
read Browning.

These studies were in part, and in the first
instance, lectures read to literary societies and
classes during the past six years.   Their use
and their acceptance in that form has been one
reason for offering them to a wider public.   But
this book is not those lectures.   Besides new
chapters and much new matter, the whole has
been worked out afresh with a view to the
design above described, and with a strong sense
of the difference between the two forms.

In writing these studies I have used only the
poet's works and the excellent Browning Bibliography of Dr. Furnivall.   But, as I have read at
their dates of issue most of the best critical essays
on Browning, it is quite likely that I owe sugges-

tions and qualifications to some of these, which I would thus acknowledge. All who touch the life and early writings of the poet are indebted to an essay by Mr. E. Gosse. So far as the estimate of ideas goes less has been done, except in essays of Mrs. Orr, Miss West, Professor Dowden, and Mr. R. H. Hutton, and in some of the papers of the Browning Society.

I hoped when I began this book to have made it a practically complete survey of the poet's work, and especially to have given the more important of the later poems. Those who know the many volumes of the poet's writings, and the matter they contain, will see why I have had to omit these. And it seemed better, with the space I had at command, to seek completeness within my plan, and up to an important date, than to reduce exposition to bare analysis and critical study to illegible condensation, in order to include all the poems intended. I am convinced that a mastery of the method and ideas of the poet in the poems here dealt with will afford a discipline and a clue for the later poems, while I may be permitted to say that in love for the poet, and with a desire still further to extend the study of his work, I should be glad, if opportunity offer, to include the poems now omitted.

BRADFORD, *September* 1887.

CONTENTS

CHRONOLOGICAL LIST

OF

BROWNING'S POEMS

IN ORDER, AND WITH DATES, OF PUBLICATION

1833. PAULINE.

1834. Sonnet, EYES CALM BESIDE THEE, LADY, *Monthly Repository* (reprinted in *Browning Society's Papers*, part 12).

1835. PARACELSUS.

1835–6. THE KING (given later as song in part 3 of "Pippa Passes," revised, with six lines added); PORPHYRIA; JOHANNES AGRICOLA (given later as "Madhouse Cells," in the "Dramatic Lyrics"); LINES (given later as song quoted in part 6 of "James Lee's Wife"). These four poems were printed in the *Monthly Repository*, edited by the young poet's friend, W. J. Fox.

1837. STRAFFORD.

1840. SORDELLO.

1841. BELLS AND POMEGRANATES, No. I. (Price 6d. pp. 16), "Pippa Passes."

1842. BELLS AND POMEGRANATES, No. II. (Price 1s. pp. 20), "King Victor and King Charles."

1842. BELLS AND POMEGRANATES, No. III. (Price 1s. pp. 16).
DRAMATIC LYRICS. Contents :—
Cavalier Tunes—1. "Marching Along"; 2. "Give a Rouse"; 3. "My Wife Gertrude." "Italy" and "France" ("Italy" given later as "My Last Duchess," "France" later, as "Count Gismond"). "Camp" and "Cloister" (later, 1. "Incident of French Camp";

1852. INTRODUCTORY ESSAY by Browning to certain (spurious) Letters of Shelley.

1854. THE TWINS (done in aid of a Bazaar for a "Girls' Refuge" founded and promoted by his wife's sister).

1855. MEN AND WOMEN.   Two vols.

Vol. i.—Contents: "Love among the Ruins"; "A Lovers' Quarrel;" "Evelyn Hope"; "Up at a Villa —Down in the City"; "A Woman's Last Word"; "Fra Lippo Lippi"; "A Toccata of Galuppi's"; "By the Fireside"; "Any Wife to Any Husband"; "An Epistle containing the Strange Experience of Karshish, the Arab Physician"; "Mesmerism"; "A Serenade at the Villa"; "My Star"; "Instans Tyrannus"; "A Pretty Woman"; "Childe Roland to the Dark Tower came"; "Respectability"; "A Light Woman"; "The Statue and the Bust"; "Love in a Life"; "Life in a Love"; "How it Strikes a Contemporary"; "The Last Ride To- gether"; "The Patriot: An Old Story"; "Master Hugues of Saxe - Gotha"; "Bishop Blougram's Apology"; "Memorabilia."

MEN AND WOMEN.

Vol. ii.—Contents: "Andrea del Sarto"; "Before"; "After"; "In Three Days"; "In a Year"; "Old Pictures in Florence"; "In a Balcony"; "Saul" (whole of it); "De Gustibus——"; "Women and Roses"; "Protus"; "Holy Cross Day"; "The Guardian Angel"; "Cleon"; "The Twins" (as above); "Popularity"; "The Heretic's Tragedy: A Middle Age Interlude"; "Two in the Campagna"; "A Grammarian's Funeral"; "One Way of Love"; "Another Way of Love"; "Transcendentalism: A Poem in Twelve Books"; "Misconceptions"; "One Word More: To E. B. B."

1856. BEN KARSHOOK'S WISDOM (written at Rome, 1854, pub- lished in *The Keepsake* of this year).

1857. MAY AND DEATH, published in *The Keepsake* of this date, and then in "Dramatis Personæ," with some changes.

1862. Dedication of *Last Poems*, by E. B. Browning, "To Grateful Florence." The volume, edited by R. Browning, had besides a Preface by him.

1863. POETICAL WORKS OF ROBERT BROWNING. Third Edition. Three Vols. (In these volumes no new work is given, but "Sordello" is given as last poem of vol. iii., and the poems made up to date were arranged in the order they kept in all editions until the final edition, and there very little changed—the arrangement being into "Lyrics," and "Romances," and "Men and Women," afterwards "Dramatic Lyrics," etc. "Johannes Agricola," then put as a romance, is now put among "Men and Women." The "Soliloquy of the Spanish Cloister," then named such, and "Porphyria," became "Porphyria's Lover." The shorter poems were all put first, and in the last two vols. the plays and the longer poems, "Paracelsus," etc.)

1864. GOLD HAIR: A LEGEND OF PORNIC, *Atlantic Monthly*, May. Given in "Dramatis Personæ," and in the second edition of that volume, with three fresh stanzas put between 20 and 21.

1864. PROSPICE, in *Atlantic Monthly* for June; then in "Dramatis Personæ."

1864. DRAMATIS PERSONÆ. Contents of this series same as now, with these points of difference—(1) "James Lee" became "James Lee's Wife," 1868; (2) "Deaf and Dumb," written in 1862, was put in the series in 1868; (3) and so was "Orpheus and Eurydice" (printed in Royal Academy Catalogue of 1864).

1868. POETICAL WORKS OF ROBERT BROWNING, 6 vols. (This edition gave "Pauline" and all up to its date except "Karshook's Wisdom," which was not reproduced. It remained until 1888 the standard edition.)

1868-9. THE RING AND THE BOOK, 4 vols.

1871. HERVÉ RIEL, printed in *Cornhill Magazine* for March (reprinted in "Pacchiarotto," etc., 1876).

1871. BALAUSTION'S ADVENTURE.

1871. PRINCE HOHENSTIEL-SCHWANGAU.

1872. FIFINE AT THE FAIR.

1873. RED COTTON NIGHT-CAP COUNTRY.

1875. ARISTOPHANES' APOLOGY.

1875. THE INN ALBUM.

1876. PACCHIAROTTO AND OTHER POEMS. (Contents as in final edition.)

1877. AGAMEMNON OF ÆSCHYLUS. Transcribed by Robert Browning.

1878. LA SAISIAZ and THE TWO POETS OF CROISIC " (with Prologue and Epilogue).

1879. O LOVE, LOVE, THAT FROM THE EYES DIFFUSEST YEARNING. A version of two stanzas of a Choral Ode from the " Hippolytus" of Euripides, done for Professor Mahaffy's little book on that dramatist in Macmillan's series of " Classical Writers," to give its readers an idea of the music and spirit of the original, *vide* p. 116.

1879. DRAMATIC IDYLS. First Series. (Contents as in final edition).

1880. DRAMATIC IDYLS. Second Series. (Contents as in final edition.)

1883. JOCOSERIA. (Contents again same.)

1883. SONNET TO GOLDONI—

> Goldoni, good, gay, sunniest of souls.

Done for Album of Committee of Monument at Venice. Given in *Pall Mall Gazette* for December 8th, but dated November 27th (reprinted in *Browning Society's Papers*, part 5).

1883. Paraphrase from Horace, ALL SINGERS, TRUST ME, HAVE THIS COMMON VICE, *Pall Mall Gazette*, 13th December (*Browning Society's Papers*, part 5).

1883. THE BLIND MAN TO THE MAIDEN SAID. A version of a German song, found in a translation of Wilhelmine von Hillern's novel, *The Hour will Come*, by Mrs. C. Bell, and done by Mr. Browning (vide *Browning Society's Papers*, part 4, p. 410).

1883. HELEN'S TOWER. Sonnet, written for Lord Dufferin, as inscription for a tower raised in memory of his mother. Published in *Pall Mall Gazette*, 28th December 1883, but dated 26th April 1870, given part 5, *Browning Society's Papers*. Tennyson's lines for the same purpose, done in 1861, are given, *Memoir*, vol. i. p. 478, with Lord Dufferin's description of the memorial tower and its site—" An old world tower on the summit of a high hill, looking over the Irish Sea to a long blue line of Scotch coast."

1884. SONNET ON RAWDON BROWN, printed in *Century Magazine*, February 1884, dated 28th November 1883 (vide *Browning Society's Papers*, part 5).

1884. THE NAMES. Sonnet.

> Shakespeare !—to such name's sounding, what succeeds ?

Dated 12th March 1884, given in *Shakspere Show-Book*, May 1884 (vide *Browning Society's Papers*, part 5).

1884. THE FOUNDER OF THE FEAST. A Sonnet done for album given to Mr. A. Chappell, director of Saturday and Monday Popular Concerts at St. James's Hall, printed in *World*, 16th April 1884, and in *Browning Society's Papers*, part 7.

1884. FERISHTAH'S FANCIES.

1885. WHY I AM A LIBERAL. Sonnet, for book with same title, edited by A. Reid, and published by Cassell & Co. (vide *Browning Society's Papers*, part 7).

1886. SPRING SONG.

> Dance, yellows and whites and reds !

Printed in *The New Amphion, the Book of the Edinburgh University Union Fancy Fair*. Given now in "Parleyings," vi.

1887. PARLEYINGS WITH CERTAIN PEOPLE OF IMPORTANCE IN THEIR DAY.

1887. MEMORIAL LINES.

> Fifty years' flight ! wherein should he rejoice.

Done for Queen's Jubilee Memorial in St. Margaret's Church (given in *Browning Society's Papers*, part 10).

1889. ASOLANDO.

NOTE.—In compiling the above List, Dr. Furnivall's Bibliography has been used, and certain sections of the valuable Bibliography of Mr. T. J. Wise, given in the *Athenæum*, 1894-96.

STUDIES OF THE MIND AND ART

OF

ROBERT BROWNING

———♦———

INTRODUCTION

BROWNING'S WORK IN RELATION TO THE
THOUGHT AND ART OF HIS AGE—HIS
PLACE IN VICTORIAN POETRY—CERTAIN
QUALITIES OF HIS WORK, AND THE QUES-
TIONS THEY RAISE

IT was feared by some at the opening of the
Victorian era that science and machinery were
fast bringing us, if they had not already brought
us, to an age in which poetry could not live.
This was the assurance of Carlyle, and the fear
of Fitzgerald. And there were reasons for the
fear, as it then seemed. Both the facts of literature and of life seemed to bear it out. For
some twenty years after the deaths of Shelley
and Byron there did not appear to be much
promise of a new or a strong poetry. And many

I

circumstances of the time, many things in its bias and temper, were little favourable to that art which is the pure and disinterested yet passionate expression of man's mind and man's life.

And others since that time have seen in our occupation with political and economic reforms and with material advances, and also in our occupation with knowledge for its own sake or its uses simply, conditions little favourable to poetic art, or even antagonistic to it. Busy men are apt, indeed, to be out of tune for poetry, and men who care for affairs only, or for knowledge only, or who by the daily custom and bent of their lives are set restlessly on the " uses " of things rather than the natural or the human joy and beauty of them,—such men, by force of their very virtues, are little capable of sympathy with an art that seems to serve none of their ends, and to belong, indeed, to another world than that in which their lives are almost wholly spent.

Yet though these, and other things too, in the life and spirit of our century have been unfavourable to a general and cordial regard for literary art, we find that a new spirit and a fresh power declared themselves pretty clearly and very soon, both in prose and in poetry. Early in the forties both Tennyson and Browning had done strong and distinctive work, while in prose Carlyle had done this in the thirties. The work thus begun was nobly maintained. And now in surveying the Victorian era as a whole we can see that it must be accounted one of the great ages of our litera-

ture, and especially of our poetry, " in spite of
democracy, materialism, and the reviews," to sum
up the fears of the prophet of the era.

Carlyle himself was the first to lead off the
" revival," and he remained a great and significant
force for many years of the era. But confining
ourselves to poetry (for which Carlyle saw no
future) it has long been clear that the two poets
who had most definitely proved their power by
1845, Tennyson and Browning, were and are the
leading poets of the era. And it would now,
perhaps, be generally allowed that, of the poets of
the Victorian age, Browning brought the strongest,
richest, and most active mind to poetry, and was
for that and other reasons the keenest and most
powerful poetic force of his time. In certain
respects he is not the equal of other good poets
of his age, of one great poet especially. In sense
of form and colour, in the eye for beauty and the
ear for music, in sense of fitness, and of the
structural and other limits of the art and medium
of poetry, in fine mastery of certain of its powers
and effects—though his powers in some of these
are great, greater than have often been recognised
—other poets of his age have equalled him, one
poet certainly surpassed him. But in wealth and
force of life and passion and thought, in variety
and energy of nature as of interest, and in a
certain Shakespearean play, breadth, and vitality of
mind, none of the Victorians have equalled him.
His lyrical and his dramatic powers, allowing
of course for differences of form and purpose,

place him with the Elizabethans; his reflective
and critical powers put him with the best in that
kind of verse; and his subtlety and force as a
humorist are also great.

We have said that this, or something like this,
would now be fairly allowed. But it took a long
time to get this seen and allowed. Tennyson
and Browning had a very different experience in
the matters of critical estimate and popularity.
From the issue of the "Poems" of 1842, and
certainly from the issue of "In Memoriam,"
Tennyson was the favourite and the fashion of
the Victorian age. Browning did strong and
clear work as early as 1845, but not until 1870
was his quality and power as a poet broadly
recognised. For years his work remained unread
or misread—read by a few only of those who
read poetry, misunderstood by many of those who
looked into it. No small part even of the critical
opinion of the country was offended or puzzled
by it. For some thirty years this was the general
judgment and temper in regard to much of
Browning's work. Only after 1870 his work
began to find fair appreciation and acceptance.

Browning himself could never quite understand
why his work proved difficult and even bewildering to many for a long time. He did not wish
it to be so, of course, and did not see why it was
so. He made some efforts to approach the
"public" and bring it to "like" him even. In
the main, however, he kept his path. He did the
work his genius chose and inspired, in the way he

felt to be true and fit. He made that work
clearer, stronger, fuller; and waited for that
audience without which the singer sings in vain.
After the better part of a lifetime of work and
song he found his " audience " a growing number,
and generously appreciative of and grateful for
his song. After years of work it must have
been, and indeed we know it was, a high
pleasure to the poet to find his work understood
and heartily valued. This is the reality of fame,
that fame which for many has been but a hope,
and for some but a voice and a shadow—esteem
and use rewarding the integrity and fidelity of
genius. In some respects it may well have
seemed to the poet—bountiful, cheerful, and
strong as he was—like the judgment of posterity
itself. Only a long life enabled him to do this.
Wisdom and genius are always essentially " justified " of their works. But it is in such cases as
this only, when power, persistence, and truth are
well helped by time, that the thinker or the poet
finds himself at length approved, and his work
duly taking its place in that " hierarchy of powers "
by which the thought and passion of man will be
ruled beneficially for long years to come.

To some, of course, this slow growth of appreciation and regard will seem in itself an objection
and proof of defect. They will look at the long
time it took to win fame, rather than at the fame
won in the end; and they urge that, of all
writing, poetry ought to appeal most readily and
quickly to those whom it concerns. But it has

not been so, nor is it in the nature of all poetry
that it should be so.   There are, in fact, two
kinds of literature in this respect—the literature
that from a fine simplicity and generality meets
with immediate acceptance; and the literature
which because it is more original or deeper, or
because it is more complex or more intellectual,
meets with a slower, or it may even be a somewhat
remote, acceptance.   The work of many good
poets has had to pass through a time of waiting.
The simplest work may be the best, as they tell
us, but simplicity is not a matter of words only.
And there are facts of emotion and character, as
of action and belief, that are not simple; and
truth and adequacy must count in art as well as
simplicity.   It has besides been found to be part
of the poet's function to lead in new developments
of mind and fresh constructions of experience.
And then the new experience, the freer and fuller
passion or thought, and the style framed to
express or suggest these, must be known and
mastered through the writings themselves before
the poet can be rightly appreciated.   And the work
that meets acceptance only after a certain period
of waiting and preparation is by that assured of a
fuller significance.

In any case a generation passed between
Browning's first work and his due appreciation.
Now this means that his work has a pertinence
and fulness of interest for the later Victorian time,
such as it had not for the readers of the earlier
time.   And what, we must ask, is the significance

of this as regards the time? as regards the poetry? change of literary taste and fashion? persistence of the poet? or some coincidence of interests, as between the poet and the later time of a literary sort?

By such phrases it is often sought to explain, or rather it must be said to set aside explanation of, such facts as those just referred to. But we can never understand such facts, unless we bear in mind that the facts of literature are vital facts, in the full sense of the term. The roots of all literature are to be found in life. It is originated and maintained, not merely touched and modified, by the passions and beliefs, by the principles, interests, and hopes of men. To regard literature therefore as casual, or decorative only, as ethically superfluous and without essential relations to the life it expresses or reflects, is to take it, not only superficially, but falsely.

Like other vital facts, even when they seem to lie apart, and to have merely special relations, the facts of literature are in wide relations, are animated by the larger forces and borne upon the greater currents of man's work and life. And the more alive literature is with passion and thought, the more sensitive it is to every touch of man's experience, the greater must be the vital significance it carries. Of no part or kind of literature, then, can this be so true as of the greater poetry. There especially may be found, by such as can read them, those "open secrets" of the lives of men which go far to help us to understand the spirit of those lives and of the life of man.

And so it happens that the poetry that an age, or any important section of an age, cares for, finds really expressive and true, must tell much of the age itself. There are significant relations and correspondences between such poetry and the age for which it has vital interest—relations that explain the interest of the poetry, and throw light on the elements and conditions of the secular life. That poetry is, in fact, a better clue to the emotions and beliefs, to the dominant and deeper passions and ideas, of the age than anything else in its records. Since, then, the poetry of Robert Browning has greater interest and fuller pertinence to-day than it had forty years ago, it must be because the time and phase of life upon which we have come have closer relations with this poet and his work than obtained between him and the earlier years of the century. That decade through which we are being borne rapidly is more responsive to, and puts a higher value on, the convictions and principles, the interests and ideals, of this poetry than earlier decades of the century did. Regarded in this way, the wider appreciation and increasing value for Browning's poetry acquire what may seem an unexpected, but is surely a real significance as an index of changes and movements greater and deeper than any changes of literary fashion as such. From this point of view, then, let us try to reach the significance and ascertain the relations of the poetry in question; and to do this it may be best to go straight to the heart of matters.

Our age has been constantly called *the Age of Science*, and by that has been mostly meant physical or natural science. Our greatest advances were there, our ruling ideas were determined, and, in the case of many minds, exhausted by the generalisations of that science. Our whole bent of mind was fixed by scientific curiosity, our standard of belief by the methods, conceptions, and hypotheses of modern physics. Our image of the whole was formed of the matter, and bounded by the scope, of physical ideas. That was the state of things as regards the mode and measure of thought for fully a quarter of the century, say from 1850 to 1880. But that is no longer a fair, not to say a sufficient or complete, description of the temper and thought of our time. Many still hold, no doubt, by physical science as the ruling factor and only legitimate sovereign of the world of thought, and by them our characteristics are drawn from that point of view. They are such as these—our interest in and regard for facts; our bias to what is real; our demand for exactness of knowledge, for stringency of reasoning; our distaste for hypotheses, except those of physics—these are our qualities and virtues. And as art-work and theories about art always in time take their colour and scope from the larger ideas that are governing the age—from its view of the world and life—so our art-work in its various kinds and media has reflected this ruling spirit. And those who argue from the scientific basis of thought—content and even resolved to

make it the measure of things every way—have
set forth, in regard to art, that imagination and
beauty, in the old senses, and all spiritual elements, have practically gone out of art, because
out of belief and life, and ought even to be
excluded deliberately and completely, that we
may have art rest sincerely on knowledge. They
would tell us that now we are to have, and in the
future can only have, a literature of fact, not a
literature of emotions and ideals any more.

Such, then, was the mode, and thus it was
argued by those who were ruled by the dominant
ideas of the years above mentioned, and much of
it continues still. But, looking at the matter in
a historic and not at all in a dogmatic way or
spirit, have we not got a good deal beyond that
time and phase of thought? To many of the
most active and representative minds of those
years, it did seem as if we had reached the final
phase of human culture and belief. Can that
mode of thought be now regarded as an ex-
haustive and final philosophy of man? Rather
what is it we see by help of the test above given
and from that point of view—that is, by taking
our higher and more vital literature as a clue to
the inner life and intimate thought of the present
time? Is it not the fact, in the terms of philosophy, that a sensational and virtually physical
philosophy is giving way before an idealistic and
spiritual philosophy?—a mode of thought, deriving from Hume and concluding on Comte
on Mill and Spencer, is giving place to a mode

thought deriving from Kant and Hegel, and as
yet without conclusion, but profoundly convinced
that the only conclusions that can be agreeable to
experience and adequate to the nature of man
must be sought on that ground, found at that
level and in that direction? The oracle speaks
there, though no philosophy has yet been able to
interpret its whole message; the great problems
are thinkable and soluble there, though no
" system " has yet adequately resolved them.

Or the matter may be put in other terms and
from another side—in the terms and on the
grounds of literature purely. Looking at it thus,
what does the record show? We find that our
century's literature began with the *transcendentalism* of Wordsworth and the *idealism* of Shelley.
Neither of these, it is true, rested on quite definite
grounds of thought, on philosophic grounds. But
that does not affect their value as regards our
inquiry, or it may be that it adds to their value,
as implying a deeper grasp and a more vital
impulse. But those impulses, with their ideas,
seemed for a time to have been exhausted, and
to have been replaced by work involving no transcendental ideas, carrying no ideal impulses, but
resting on positive ideas and physical conceptions.
Yet now is it not the fact that the idealism of the
earlier years of the century is coming back into
our literature—not in the old ideas, certainly, but
ll the more for that in a truly romantic spirit
nd scope? And this idealism has come upon
s again, in part out of the old, old depths of

spiritual thought and passion ; in part out of our
science, and what may be called our realistic
passion, our concentration upon fact and law outside us ; and a new sense thus won of the ultimate
things always come upon by man's mind, whatever line it may take.   Thus it happens that the
new idealism comes enlarged, because informed by
the results and expanded by the ideas of modern
knowledge, by its great conception of the history,
order, and extent of the universe.   It comes,
therefore, with fresh sense of the mystery, and a
deeper sense of the greatness, of the system in
which we have our part.   It comes also with
fresh conviction that the great things of man's
own mind and history, the poetry and religion
of the race, nobly interpreted and spiritually
affirmed, provide, not indeed a key to the great
secret, yet a clue guiding us among the questions
that arise at the end of all knowledge, and among
the things that wait at the end of all experience.

Browning's relations, as poet and thinker, to the
course of things thus generally described, and to
the movements upon which it is set, is a matter
of so much importance in the study of his poetry
that it must be early and frankly considered.   I
may of course be said, it has been said, that they
do poetry a disservice who involve it in such
matters and movements as those we have de
scribed, or connect it with changes such as thes
in the course of thought.   Poetry, as a transcri
of life, and almost a substantive part of it, shou
spring from more general sources, and deal wi

simpler matters than these. And if Browning
has much to do with these things, then the difficulty and peculiarity of his work is quite explained. We must meet the questions thus raised
at a later point. Here it may be said that a poet
who deals, as Browning does, with human motive
and passion, and with the "inner life" of men,
must work on some intuition of the life and
nature of man, on some basis of thought in
regard to these; must hold some positive relation
to the great ideas that have divided and distinguished minds on those points ever since men
have had interest in and thoughts concerning them.

And Browning's relations here, the motive and
quality of his work in this regard, are, it seems to
us, at once strongly distinctive and very significant. Broadly, we may say his work, in the
aspect in which we are now considering it, is in
real and deep sympathy, and agreement even,
with the spiritual and ideal return of thought in
our time; and as this return has put many in
touch with his mind and work, who would scarcely
have been so twenty years ago, so his sympathy
and scope put him, partially at least, out of touch
with the years when art renaissance, physical
science, doubt, and criticism were the prevailing
moods and the ruling powers of the time. As
regards the poet, his relations here are as characteristic of his genius as of his mode of thought. As
regards his readers, those relations are in good
measure the reason why the mind and the work
of this poet attract and satisfy, as they did not in

earlier decades of our century. And surely the
strength, balance, and fulness of the humanities
of the work, as of the mind of the poet, are tested
and disclosed by his position and relations here.

And Browning's relations in this matter, which
we have said are as distinctive of his art as of his
point of view and mode of thought, may be come
at on several lines, and chiefly through the principles of his work, and comparison of his work in
its principles and quality with other works of his
time. Let us consider the matter on these lines
—(1) Through the early affinities of his art;
(2) through certain qualities and principles of
his work as a whole; (3) through certain qualities and principles of his mind, and his own relations to certain great matters.

The fact that Browning began with Shelley,
not with Keats, has much meaning here. It
meant, let us say, idealism, and a romanticism
that struck its roots thus early into passion and
life. The themes he then chose will be found to
show the same sympathy and scope. They may
be described as spiritual and passionate, and both
strongly. The mediæval return, which in Keats
may seem chiefly imaginative, æsthetic, is in
Browning also ethical and vital. It is for him a
return to the age when, and to the types through
which, thought and passion boldly grasped the fact
and dared the depths of life. Carlyle resumed and
continued the Romantic Revival, and Tennyson
took up from Keats the Art Revival, early in the
thirties of our century. Browning is with the form-

rather than the latter in the scope and spirit of his work. He is more set on truth and adequacy than on finish and beauty of expression, more on worthy and strongly human themes than on music or facility of utterance. "Paracelsus" has more in common with "Sartor Resartus" than with "The Lady of Shalott" or the "Dream of Fair Women," and "Sordello" struggles in part with the problem of Teufelsdröckh.

Nor is Browning romantic only, as frankly so as Carlyle, though with many differences, rooted in the strong thoughts and passions of men, and seeking in poetry a medium for their frank and ample expression, he is what, for critical distinction simply, we call "Christian," and his art has that quality. This is, of course, a matter to be developed later, and in connection particularly with certain parts of his work. Here and on this point we must be satisfied to say that in certain principles and qualities of his work, Browning is the strongest and most eminent master of Christian art during the Victorian era—of Christian art in the sense defined by himself in "Old Pictures," and elsewhere. He held from the first, and from the first he wrought on the principle, that the art that is to represent human life must recognise the mystic greatness of thought and passion, of effort and aspiration in man, and must find ways to make itself the medium of this greatness. We are not here concerned as to whether this is a sound theory of art, but only with the fact that it was a constant principle of

Browning's art. It bewilders readers of " Paracelsus " and " Sordello," and much later of " Fifine."
It also consummates many a fine poem of the poet's
maturity. It stimulates the poet with a sense of
the greatness of his true subject, and it affects, of
course, his standard of truth and adequacy of expression, giving him, in fact, the standard indicated
in " Andrea del Sarto," and praised in " Old
Pictures," and in " A Grammarian's Funeral "—a
standard which even in art values ideality, fulness
of life, and a divine suggestiveness as more than
easy definiteness or technical perfection.

When we try this matter on the third of the
lines above named, we find the same results. It
has often been a question with Browning's readers,
in what relation he stood to the course of the
higher thought of his time—to that great discussion always proceeding, never complete, which
affects the grounds of all thought, and how he
was affected by the discussion. Nor has the
answer to the question, when put and tried by
reference to his works, seemed clear or certain.
Browning spent a long life in a century much and
deeply moved by debate of great questions. There
were great changes in many minds and much
movement of the mind of the age in his lifetime ;
and he took deep interest in the questions and
their discussion, but scarcely, so far as appears, an
interest that can be called personal. The debate
does not seem to have really affected his greate
convictions, or to have disturbed his centra
position. His principles, broad and deeply placed

almost from the days of " Sordello," remained the same. A man of strong nature and strong intellect, he seemed to maintain a marked independence, and occupied a significant position amid the controversies of his time. The great points only of its debate appear in his work. The many doubts of Clough, the spiritual regret and trouble of Arnold, the scepticism and pain of a dozen writers and singers—his work is clear of these— above them, it may be, but somehow remote from them ; while at the same time he showed, from " Paracelsus " onwards, a clear grasp and deep interest in whatever is general and permanent in the efforts men have made to harmonise experience and belief. He kept throughout a sure and sound sympathy with essential things. It results from this, we think, that many writers who spoke to the earlier years of his time, and who were more heard then than he was, have less pertinence now, because they have a narrower hold of life, and the modes of thought they expressed and emphasised have more or less faded into that past which so soon comes for all that is partial ; while Browning, with his freer and stronger touch both on the doubts and the beliefs, on the hopes and fears, that do not pass away, but stay with the heart of man, because their sources are always present in man's life, is more heard and far better understood now than he was then.

The same breadth and hold upon *essential things*, which Browning has thus shown in regard to less important controversies, he has shown in regard to

2

the grand controversy of our century—that controversy above described as between the realism of /
physical science and the idealism of faith, imagination, and philosophy. The present, we have said,
may be described as an age of science, tending to
a deeper thought of things, and seeking a larger
interpretation of experience. Our higher poetry,
to be adequate, must unite the tendencies and
combine the principles of both. It is peculiarly
distinctive of Browning that he combines and
harmonises those principles. He has the scientific
interest, the critical observant temper and power
of eye and mind, the love of facts, the respect for
experience, the perfectly free search after truth
which mark the faculty and make the virtues on
which we have set such value of late; and his
work has those qualities and interests so strongly
marked that many of its readers have been drawn
to it by these powers, and are only aware of these.
His habit is not to pass over facts or refine or
dream them away, but most distinctly to see and
grasp and interpret them within his scope. He
seeks the world of facts and events, the world
of men; but it is not to remain and rest there
He seeks a way through the world of facts and
experience, frankly and entirely faced and accepted
to an order and a world beyond—the world of th
mind and the heart at their best. From Plato h
learned (*cf.* " Pauline ") the reality of " the worl
of ideas." By the vivid energy of his own mir
he has maintained his sense of that " unsee
universe." But his way of reaching and maki

solid to himself whatever may be known or guessed of that "ideal world" is through the facts of man's mind, and the facts of experience exactly known. He has no belief in any simple intuition of thinker or poet. As against such thinking, and as against all vague abstractions, he is scientific, inductive if you will. His humour is realistic; his dramatic method is personal, particular. In a phrase he himself uses, he is at once objective and subjective, and both intensely. He has a strong hold on fact, a resolute aversion from fancies and illusions, however arising, from whatever part of man's nature they spring, by whatever interests encouraged; keen and hardy thought and care for reality are constant elements of his work. His energetic curiosity has in it something of Bacon; his vigorous research and intellectual exploration something of Aristotle. Science, in its large and thorough sense, though no "pursuit" of his, is in complete sympathy with the habit and operation of his mind. But with this quality and these powers he is also a thinker, and, above all, a poet. He is, therefore, not mastered by his practical bent nor by the world of facts, and he is certainly not absorbed or over-impressed by recent aspects of knowledge, or by the results of modern science. He knows how "mere facts" neither exhaust the world nor satisfy the mind. He knows the "infinite significances" that facts have for thought, and how this significance comes of the mind's own laws and depths. He is, in a word, an idealist in the last resort.

Behind the energetic realism and strong grip on facts is a " visionary power," and sense of ideas—convictions and passions that claim and affirm a world more real because ideal. Every fact—and the body of experience is seen upon this ground—is illumined and transfigured by this principle. He has the poet's " ulterior, intellectual perception," the artist's sense of the reality of the ideal, the thinker's conviction of its spirituality. Aware of both sides of experience, and keenly aware of its real side, he yet seeks on its ideal side the clue to experience and to the ultimate elements of man's own nature. Of all worlds, to him the most real is the world of man's thought and passion ; and this world of man's mind and spirit has far greater interest for him than any world of things and forces. The beliefs and emotions, the characters and actions, of men, the expression of man through religion and art, the revelation of man in literature and history,—here indeed is a realm of facts of most curious and profound interest, facts requiring and rewarding interpretation more than any other facts, and throwing more light than the whole body of physical knowledge on all that i of most value for us to know. With the strongl positive quality of nature that has been described Browning has bent his mind upon those fact above all others, and in his study and commar of them gives assurance both of solidity and dept In an age of science mainly physical, he has mai tained and illustrated the supreme interest a most real significance of man, not only to hims and with reference to every " use " of life, but with reference to knowledge too. To this ground he has kept; from this standpoint and with this outlook all his work has been made.

And yet it must not be supposed that the poet is a theorist or a dogmatist at all, either as respects philosophy or religion. Dealing with life and the grand facts that concern both religion and thought, he must involve results touching both, but as a poet. No formal conclusions may stand between him and life. According to a famous phrase, all formulas must be set aside that life may be seen truly, that the poet may use his qualifications for the mastery, frankly and totally, of all facts that concern him. With this freedom, and with his powers, the poet becomes a spiritual thinker of high value and pertinence at present. By sight of a clear, strong mind, by energy and depth of nature, he affirms the truths of man's mind in its integrity—the actual significance and scope of man as life and consciousness present him.

And now, having considered the question before us, as it regards the mind of the poet and certain principles of his work, let us consider it rather as it touches his readers, that we may see more closely the things that make this poetry so significant to them, putting them in tune with it and with its ideas. On the side of philosophy, we have found what has been called an " idealistic reaction " in progress among us; and that, as respects both thought and religion, is a good key to most other things and tendencies of the time present.

The life and passion of a people are fairly one.
And what is known as philosophy, though a
matter strictly or explicitly concerning a few, yet
gives the drift and sense of all the more earnest
and distinctive thought of the time.   And so it is
here.   After some years, during which a restricted
and partial creed, type of culture, and mode of life
had on the whole their way with us—with many
of us, at least—we have come to feel that they are
too narrow for us.   We have become aware of
elements ignored, of powers unsatisfied.   We have
felt the need, in other terms, for some transfigura-
tion of the world of real knowledge and real
interests; for some great expansion and idealisation of life.   Old conceptions and interpretations
were no more available.   They had become dreams
or incredibilities.   We were then as pilgrims out
in search of new shrines and homes.   For a time
we had thought that the " higher ideas " of physical
and cosmical knowledge would serve us.   They
seemed for a time capable of that development
and application which should satisfy all our reasonable wants, reconcile the soul to experience, the
mind to " the burden of an unintelligible world,'
and the heart to the sorrows and limits of life
But for not a few that appears no longer possible
The glow and promise of the dawn has " faded
into the light of day, the " common day " of rea
life, and many things are seen more truly withi
as without.   And so many, sanguine or resigne
once, now seek the escape of some fuller solutic
of questions.   They seek to breathe again " t

larger, the diviner air" of the great and faithful
spirits of the past. They seek the power that
made these great and generous. They see that
such power flows from great convictions, and from
the free and sublime affirmations of the "soul."
There is a higher thoughtfulness, a finer earnestness, and greater breadth of nature. Deeper
interest is taken in the history and problems of
man's mind; far deeper interest in the great
questions arising out of man's beliefs. The old
troublesome questions and longings, hopes and
fears, are seen to be part of the nature, not part
only of the delusions and superstitions, of man.
Culture and the heart have become more spiritual.
And so, whether it be in philosophy or art, the
history or the poetry of man's life, what we seek
is a vital affirmative interpretation of the mind
and the word. The new appreciation of Hegel,
and the increased and continued interest in
Browning, both spring from the same causes and
point in the same direction. We are no more
satisfied with a negative philosophy, with critical
studies. We seek a truth that shall sincerely
justify and carry forward the whole thought and
passion and power of man as they come to us out
of the past; as we find them around us in the
faith and work and art of the past; as we carry
them within us in that present which is not only
the memory but the soul of the past. From that
external nature which was over-ruling, from that
cosmical nature which was overpowering us, we
turn again to human nature and the full free mind.

We see again that the realities of mind have a
substance and significance all their own. Man's
own mind must be true. Man's proper nature
must be our best guide to the higher truth. The
higher truths—that is, true views of the highest
matters — must be spiritual views. And our
highest truth, that truth which must give the test
of belief, the measure of hope, the direction of
effort, and the symbol of faith, that must be built,
not only on natural knowledge, but on man's spirit,
must be not only a scientific but a philosophic
truth. It must be not rational and real only, it
must also be spiritual and infinite. It must give
credible interpretation of the world, it must interpret man to himself. And it now seems possible
to do this only at the height and on the ground of
some great spiritual philosophy.

After what has above been said, it is hardly
necessary now to say that with the spirit and
ideas of this movement, of this religious reaction,
as it might be called, the temper and work of
Browning are in generous and frank agreement.
No work of the time is more so. Just when
many minds suspect or have proved the inadequacy of a certain type of culture and view of
life, and are looking for a freer and fuller ideal,
his poetry has gained wider attention and new
interest. During the years when physical science
and philosophical scepticism were the ruling belief
and fashion, another poetry and another poetic
ideal had their way with the representative minds
of the time. A poetry deriving from Keats, not

from Shelley or Wordsworth, was the mode—a
poetry delightful and beautiful in many ways,
and, as art, worthy of the praise some good
critics have given it, but without the substance
and vital power of the greater work, because
without the beliefs and ideals of that work.
That poetry has less hold now, Browning more;
and the two facts should be seen to appreciate
the change. Browning's intense and profound
humanity, his larger thoughtfulness, his reality
and regard for facts, his spiritual quality and
depth, his regard for ideas and the great principles
of man's nature,—these qualities, indifferent or
objectionable before, are felt now to offer the
notes of the fuller ideals that are desired. He
kept his own course, and made work of his own
kind, through years that were out of sympathy
with him. By bent of genius, as by force and
breadth of nature, he had hold of a surer ground
and a larger thought than other writers of his
time. While these accepted the secular basis of
thought, he took life and history, the nature and
spirit of man in its whole scope, as his field and
ground. With frank acceptance and confidence,
nay with a positive delight, in whatever is real in
man, and with the most entire freedom as to all
doctrines about these realities, his test of faith has
been what best agrees with man as we know man,
—above all what best unfolds every sincere passion
and power of man's mind and will. The soul is the
sovereign fact; and the true ideal, resting vitally
in that, and respecting experience and knowledge,

must transfigure both in a spiritual sense, and carry the life and mind of man onward to those things that the spirit of man has always been aware of, but the fulness of which is beyond the grasp and even beyond the imagination of man.

The pertinence and import of our poet's work, in this aspect, and in these relations of it, have now, we trust, become clear on the broad ground above taken. We have deliberately kept the discussion to the points thus raised, reserving further points of this order to the chapters properly concerned with them, and to the close of our study. We may be allowed to add here that in the present state of things, with much futile belief and futile doubt, and much unreality in both kinds, with that shift in the centre of thought, and that reconstruction of belief, which are in process in our midst, it is good to have the grand moral facts and their human bearings made clear by one who has kept just and equal hold on the mind and spirit of man, and who regards the matters in question in the ways above described. For thus in the light of a large and free interpretation of life we regain the depth and sincerity of the mind ; we recover through life and the soul those truths that many have not yet recovered through thought; and see that the great truths though they change in form, abide in their substance for ever, and grow for man with man's growth.

But all this we feel brings up at the outset one of the offences of Browning's poetry

rtain good readers. That he should deal with
ch matters of "belief and life" in and through
etry is his offence for them. These matters, so
nstantly interesting to some, may be for prose,
r philosophy perhaps, but they are not for
etry. And it scarcely meets their objection to
y that Browning is never didactic, that he is
ways dramatic, and presents these matters as
rt of life. He is dramatic, and he presents the
atters objected to as vital parts of his studies of
rticular minds in given situations. But his
fence is that he brings these matters up so
xplicitly and so often. And it may well be
gued that since he selects and develops his
rsonæ and his situations in the way and on the
es he adopts, these matters must belong to his
wn mind, to his intuition of man, and his inter-
retation of life. They surely do so belong, and
seems therefore better to take the question on
s merits, and as readers to reckon quite frankly
ith this quality of the poet's work and all it
rries. On the critical side of it we take the
uestion up at a later point. Apart, as it seems
us, from the preferences of certain readers, and
e one-sided theory of a certain school of critics,
e question whether poetry as such may deal
ith criticism of life and with the great interests
f belief requires little discussion. All poets
eply interested in man and in life do it. Shake-
eare does it as well as Milton; and Dryden and
ope do it even more; and Tennyson does it as
ell as Browning. And the great poets of Greece

did it long ago. And we all gain, on matters of
deep and permanent interest to us, through the
high function and human quality of poetry.

Much will of course depend on how these matters
are treated in poetry, and on the aspects of them
selected. And readers, who find the easy handling of familiar aspects poetic and interesting, are
apt to say, when less obvious aspects are presented under more strenuous treatment, that the
matter is unpoetic. But the principle is the same.
And it may be argued for Browning that his very
mode of presentment is such as to secure life and
reality for his approach to and treatment of these
matters. It is vain to say that he is *never*
didactic. It is fair to say that he is always
dramatic—that these matters are parts of life with
and for him, and are as we may say studied in the
place and at their worth in life. But the fact is, and
it is best to see it at once, that on these matters
our poet breaks fresh ground, and is independent
as well as strenuous in his handling. As a thinker
he is alert to see their meaning, as a poet quick
to feel their interest, while as an artist he broadly
holds that art not only may but must preserve
what belongs to the best interests and makes for
the larger good of men. And on this, as on other
points concerning poetry, let us not be misled by
the easy dictum that art must be the minister of
pleasure. It should unfold the life and serve the
joy of men, as we venture to argue at a later point,
by giving the world of man's life in that higher
reality which reveals both its beauty and its good.

CHAPTER I

LIFE OF THE POET—HISTORY OF HIS WRITINGS
—PERIODS OF WORK—AND GROWTH OF ART

It is matter of commonplace that the life of a man of letters is to be found rather in the content and history of his writings than in the events of his life. But the facts of a writer's life are helpful always, often essential, in the study of those writings. If the inward activity and experience be more than all outward circumstances, yet those circumstances have often close and important, and always suggestive, relations to the life of the mind. We propose here to set forth only such facts of the life of Robert Browning as seem to us to have these relations.

He was born May 7th, 1812, at Camberwell. It is well to know the stock from which an original and highly endowed nature comes. It helps us to trace his qualities, and understand, or at least to define, his powers. In this case the matter is certainly interesting. The main stock of the Brownings was, it seems, West Saxon, but through his mother the poet was German and Scotch as well. And the wise in these matters of heredity see much in this descent—English realism

29

and strong sense, a turn for German metaphysic and idealism, and on the Scotch side an interest in theology and a taste for argument.

The poet's father and grandfather were both of them clerks in the Bank of England, well-esteemed and successful. The grandfather was, we infer, a somewhat hard, worldly, and wholly practical man. The father was a man of finer nature and better gifts, more generous, a lover of letters, a lifelong reader and collector of books, who put the best things of that sort about the poet from his boyhood. He had some turn for verse, and for grotesque rhymes especially. He was a careful reader, and many of his books were old and rare. He was, besides, a man of simple tastes and much kindness. Both father and grandfather were finely healthy men, living to be eighty-four years, and of the father it was said that "he was never old." But the poet's mother, described by Carlyle as a "true Scotch gentlewoman," was of a delicate and nervous constitution ; and Mrs. Orr thinks that the mother's temperament was traceable in the son, with not a little of the energy and physique of his father.

Browning was educated at private schools near his home; but studied for a short time, Greek chiefly, at University College, London, and French with a tutor at home. It may seem curious that his father did not send him to one of the universities, except so far as the fact of the Brownings being dissenters may explain that, but he certainly encouraged and generously supported his son in all intellectual tastes and pursuits.

As a boy Browning was active, restless, quick,
keenly intelligent. His feelings were both sensitive and strong. He was and remained always
tenderly and warmly devoted to his mother, and
he showed as a child a fondness for and interest
in the life of animals, and a power to draw them
to him.

He was early a rhymer, and soon made verses.
He was a busy reader of books, not of the hour,
but those older masters of English of the sixteenth
and seventeenth centuries, when passion and
thought had scope. Yet his first verses naturally
show the influence of Byron, for the Byronic
fashion was then in its strength. Mr. Gosse has
told how he had " a volume of verses " made the
year of Byron's death. But next year he found
some of Shelley's poetry, and was so struck by
what he found, that he sought out that poet's
publisher, and got the rest of his works. At the
suggestion of Mr. Ollier, the publisher, he got
Keats also ; and it is a sure test of the poetic
sensibility of young Browning that he felt the
genius of these poets long before they had taken
their place in English poetry.

He passed, it seems, through a time of disturbance and restlessness, both moral and intellectual,
both as to choice of work and place in life, and as
to the questions the revolutionary temper and
discussions had raised in minds like those of
Byron and Shelley, and many others of that time.
There are traces of this in " Pauline," surely. But
it is pretty clear that this period was not of long

duration, and, though it modified the poet's creed
and way of viewing life, it left him as "Pauline"
implies, and "Paracelsus" makes clear, with a deep
religious emotion and conviction.

In the matter of profession he chose literature
—or, we may say, poetry chose him and held
him.   Other lines were thought of, it appears, but
his father honourably let him follow the true bent
and higher purpose of his mind.   It was a noble,
if also, with moderate means, an ascetic choice,
and he kept to it for years with little encourage-
ment, and with no "gains" that may be "posted"
in any ledger yet devised.   He lived for poetry
when there was no hope of living by it, and to
poetry he gave his whole life.

Mrs. Orr has a story about his "reading and
digesting the whole of Johnson's Dictionary" by
way of preparation for literature.   It scarcely
seems a sound or vital way of preparation, and
one must think that his study of the Elizabethans
shown in "Pippa Passes," and of Shelley and
Keats shown in all the early work, were much
more pertinent and fruitful.   To literature, anyhow, from this time, he gave himself, and not to
"study" the "British public," but to give what he
felt and saw, and to wait results.

His first schemes were characteristic, ambitious
we may say, with that ambition which is the
promise of accomplishment, because it is the
instinct of power.   He planned a series of monodramas about 1831–2, whose object was to depict
certain leading types of men and women.   His

scheme does not seem to have got much beyond
conception and outlines, and only a fragment of
it remains in "Pauline," printed early in 1833,
and reprinted in 1868. The poem keeps its
place among his works, not for the value he sets
on it, but simply because he could not keep it
from being published; and yet it shows more than
his bias and leading interest. One critic felt the
poet in it, and spoke rightly of its vivid, spiritual
power; and, as John Mill valued and Dante G.
Rossetti copied it, the poem is certified of a degree
of power and beauty.

"Paracelsus," published in the spring of 1835,
was his next poem. It was printed at his father's
cost, and its reception justified the caution of the
publishers, though it could not settle the merits of
the work. Its energy and abundance of style and
thought and passion, and the splendour of many
of its passages, ought to have made readers of it
aware of the poet and glad of his power. But it
found few readers, though Forster and Macready
saw its worth. The author is still moving on the
lines of monodrama, but his aim is more definite,
and his resources are far greater than they were
in "Pauline." The work, we are told, is "a poem,
not a drama," and "not a dramatic poem." The
author is not sure of the form, but it is clear that
he is seeking some sort of dramatic expression.

It was after the issue of "Paracelsus" that the
young poet, then living with his parents at
Hatcham, began to be known by other men of
letters. Talfourd, Hunt, Milnes, Dickens, Words-

3

worth, and Landor are some of those whose acquaintance was made by the author of " Paracelsus,'
as a poet of some distinction and of promise.

And among others to whom he became known
was Macready, the great actor, and Forster.
There was talk of a tragedy which Browning
might write. Macready, who wished to improve
the stage, and thought the young poet had
dramatic power, suggested a play. The subject
of Strafford was afterwards chosen. The result
was that the drama of that title was written, and
played at Covent Garden, May 1837, the chief
parts being taken by Miss Faucit and Macready
himself. It was a success, but had only a run of
five nights.

In the preface to "Strafford," the poet speaks
of other work with which he was busy, and from
which the drama was a pleasant escape. That
other work was "Sordello," with which, we infer,
the poet was occupied from 1837–1840, when it
was published by Moxon. Few read, very few
understood, and perhaps none approved. Into it
the poet had poured, without stint or flagging,
the wealth of thought, of self-observation, of
experience, of poetic study so far gained, as if
to prove himself, and compel attention by the
fit, however few. He counted on more sympathy
than he found. And it was natural that, dedi-
cating the poem twenty-three years later to his
friend, M. Milsand, the poet should acknowledge
disappointment; and very natural that the public
failed to read his poem.

With readers, so far, it is clear he had made
very little way. "Strafford" had been his most
successful work in that respect, and as by that he
had found a "pit audience" from the boards of
Covent Garden, he now sought a "pit audience"
through the press. Moxon suggested short works
in a cheap style. The poet agreed, and the plan
was carried out. His poems were issued in
pamphlet form, yellow paper covers, double
columns, at prices varying from 6d. to 2s. 6d.
That was the series known as "Bells and Pomegranates." There were eight parts, the first issued
in 1841, the last in 1846; the first began with
"Pippa Passes," the last had "Luria" and a
"Soul's Tragedy." In these were issued the
dramas, except the first, the "Dramatic Lyrics"
and the "Dramatic Romances"—the first work
by which the poet became known to the wider
public. The name of the series was explained in
Part viii.—"Bells" to denote the music, "Pomegranates" to signify the matter it was meant should
go with the music; "sound with sense, poetry
with thought," was the aim of the series and the
meaning of the title.

But here we have come to the romance of the
poet's life. In 1839 he was introduced to Mr.
Kenyon, a lover of art and a friend of good men,
and through him he was introduced to a very
dear relative, Elizabeth Barrett. The early parts
of the "Bells and Pomegranates" had drawn her
attention, and won her warm approval. And in
her "Lady Geraldine's Courtship" she spoke of

their author as one of the poets read to the Lady
Geraldine.

' Or from Browning some "Pomegranate," which, if cut deep
    down the middle,
  Shows a heart within, blood-tinctured, of a veined humanity.'

The phrase was happy and true, and showed that
finest sympathy which touches the heart of a poet
through his work. The lady had proved her powers
in works of her own, and by culture, as by genius,
she was well qualified for a true and even perfect
response to the mind of this poet. He saw the
poem and the reference, told Mr. Kenyon warmly
of his appreciation. Kenyon asked him to write
her. He did so, it seems, in January 1845. A
correspondence thus arose, and then personal
intercourse. Through some accident and a great
sorrow Miss Barrett was, as is well known, an
invalid, with no great hope of ever being anything else, in spite of keen and happy activities
of mind, and "with nothing," she said, "to interest any one." But Browning was interested and
strongly attracted at once. Heart whole till then,
he gave his whole heart then and for ever to this
bright, gentle, delicate yet ardent woman. They
saw each other often, though she had seen almost
no one for years. Her own words are that she
was "caught up into love, and taught the whole
of life in a new rhythm." And her "Sonnets
from the Portuguese" (a disguise, of course), the
vital record of her love, so intense and frank and
beautiful, so full of sweet surprise and passion

and joy at the strong love that had come to her, when death seemed the likelier visitant,—these sonnets are perhaps the most perfect of her works, and certainly one of the finest series of love poems in the literature of the world. Scarcely more ardent, never purer, notes were struck from love's lyre.

She grew slowly stronger. The doctor ordered a more genial climate for the winter. Her father, in a way he had, opposed. There was only one way to carry out that and other hopes, by ending her engagement with Browning in marriage. They were married, 12th September 1846, in the Church of St. Marylebone, without her father's consent. It was a romantic proceeding. It was her way, not to health only, but to all that was best in life; and though her father's attitude in the matter was always a sorrow to her, she never doubted that she did right to act on her own conviction and decision.

Just a week after the marriage they left for Italy, by way of Paris. They spent the winter in Pisa, but moved to Florence in April 1847, and soon settled there in the Palazzo Guidi. For the rest of Mrs. Browning's life they lived in Italy, mostly in Florence, with occasional visits to other parts of Italy, which were a keen pleasure to her, and visits to England and France. It was a new life for her, bright, interesting, supported by a perfect friendship and a cordial love. Some of her best work was done during those years, not so much of his, though some also of his best. " Christmas

Eve " and " Easter Day " belong to this time, and also the series of " Men and Women."

In the words of Mr. F. G. Kenyon (in his recently published " Letters of Mrs. Browning," vol. i. p. 395), " her already happy life was crowned by the birth, 9th March 1849, of her son," Robert Barrett Browning. Their home and life in Florence were fit and beautiful. She revived wonderfully in the stimulus of it, and in the mild climate. She loved Florence and Italy. Her love of the land, her delight in its memories and beauties, her interest in its affairs, were almost those of a patriot. She lived fifteen years there, and the " Casa Guidi Windows " and other poems, and her letters of this time, show her interest and the brightness of her life. Fragile, and something angelic in look and expression, she had a nature full of vivid and subtle force ; and she put herself, with a fire and enjoyment that those writings help us to measure, into her life and tasks. There are quite a number of descriptions of their Florentine home and its gracious happiness by those who then saw the poet and his wife in the Casa Guidi ; the poet robust, active, friendly ; the wife with slight figure, pale face, large brow, dark hair, and deep eyes, " half angel and half bird," full of quick enthusiasm, yet cordially human and brave.

But she was not and never could have been strong, and in spite of all favourable conditions, after a short illness and somewhat suddenly, she died, 29th June 1861,—died, as Browning touchingly says, with the assurance that she was well,

and would be better, unwitting of death. And so
" ended on earth," to quote Mr. F. Kenyon again,
" the most perfect example of wedded happiness
in the history of literature," regard being had both
to the life and its poetic expression.

The sorrow and surprise, we may say, of his
wife's death were deeply felt by Browning. For
the time her loss seemed to take the heart out of
his heart, and his dearest motive out of life. He
stayed in Florence only to see all due arrange-
ments made in regard to his affairs there. And
though his wife is buried there he never, Mrs. Orr
tells us, visited Florence again. " Why should
I come ? " he said to a friend who asked him, " I
can *see* it all in my head," a remark and attitude
uncommon and very characteristic.

The influence of his marriage on Browning's
work, though it must have been very real, is not,
we think, very marked. He did less work between
1849 and 1861 than was usual with him. Mrs.
Browning speaks of his requiring quiet and seclusion, of his only writing when the mood was on
him, and of the mood not coming for months
at this period (" Letters," vol. ii. pp. 434–35).
She says again that they worked apart and did
not read their work to each other until it was
finished.

And yet, in the work done by Browning at
Florence, there are surely traces of his wife's
influence. The work of that time has always
been, by many readers, highly valued, for themes
and style. In the former we may find his wife's

interest. Then it was, perhaps, owing to his wife, that in preparing an edition of his poems in 1849, containing the " Bells and Pomegranates" and " Paracelsus," he " revised with a view to remove obscurities." And the new poems of the next years, " Christmas Eve" and " Easter Day," in 1850, and " Men and Women," 1855, speak not only of the new interests of the life in Florence, but also of the influence of that " Audience of One " beside whom the work was made. " Men and Women " is a series which, for clearness and balance of matter and style, it would be impossible to surpass in the list of his poems, whether it was owing to the period of his mind then reached, or to circumstances.

But the years of fellowship passed, and the love which delayed death rose above it, spiritual and consummate. Browning is lyrical whenever he touches this theme, and, whether in the dedication of " Men and Women," or in the invocation of " The Ring and the Book," the poet sings with keenest passion—looking still, " despite the distance and the dark," to her whose presence, though unseen, was unwithdrawn, and whose power to help was greater and more essential than it had been in the past.

After his wife's death Browning devoted himself to his son and to his work, to the education of his son, to work that might be good for and bring good to the boy, to that song, moreover, which he felt to be his due " to England " and " to God who best taught song by the gift " of his wife.

He settled in London. It offended and depressed him at first, but with his interest in men and women it was good for him, and in time he saw not a little of the best of London society. Now, it seems, more deliberately and regularly than in the past, he set himself to the day's task of poetry. His many volumes after 1861 are the fruit of this, and their subjects and quality are partly, at least, a result of it. His home for the rest of his life was in the great city. His holidays for a series of years were spent in France, mostly at certain quiet little places on the north-western coast. And these visits gave him not a few of the themes of his later poems. He visited Switzerland too, and that has left its traces. Latterly he went back again to Italy, to simple old Asolo, an early visit to which had given him the "scenery" of "Pippa Passes"; to Venice, which years before he had visited with his wife; and to certain spots in the Alpine country of Northern Italy, that proved good for him, Sainte Pierre la Chartreuse, and Gressoney St. Jean, and later to Primiero. It was on one of these Italian visits, in the autumn of 1889, that he fell ill and died at Venice on Dec. 12. He had been failing for some time, but maintained his mental vigour and clearness to the very end. He was buried in Westminster Abbey on the last day of 1889 among the great poets of his country, and there beside him Tennyson also rests now.

And here it will be well for the interest of the matter in itself, and for its relation to the poetry, to consider and draw out the personal qualities

and characteristics of the poet. He spent, we
have seen, most of his years in London; and
this seems fit. There, where man and his problems
and ways touched and interested him. He was a
man with men, mixing with the life of his fellows;
friendly and manly, taking his part in conversation
frankly, and in fit circles an able and interesting
talker. In a certain way he was a man of the
world, measuring men and their affairs at their
due value in the world, yet independent and
unworldly at the heart of him. Observant, practical, common-sensible, but with a core of passion
and ideality. His nature was, in fact, richly
passioned, on a ground of strong intellect, with
manly control and even reserve of emotion. But
in his love for his mother and for his wife, and in
the disturbance of feeling roused by the deaths of
these, or by whatever touched the memory of the
latter, we see the depth and force, we feel the fire
and tenderness of his mind. His strong sensibility
to music is another test of his emotional quality.
He had, owing to this, a marked tenacity and
constancy of affection. He had a keen memory
for suffering and a certain shrinking from it. He
was thus an optimist by temper and habit, forced
by bias and energy of the brain, and by dramatic
observation and sympathy, to weigh his optimism,
yet inclined to make the best of things. He was
not on the surface sympathetic, and never sentimental. His centre was not in the emotions any
more than it was in the sphere of facts. With
the core of passion went a power of " abstraction,"

a life of thought and imagination. He was, we may say, very real and down upon the earth, but aware, too, and all the time, of the "world unseen," that world of principles, laws, ideals, souls, which seems shadowy and remote to many, but is life of life to the true and sure discerner.

We now resume the thread of the literary history. Between 1855 and 1864 is the poet's longest interval of silence; only in 1863 came a new and collected edition of his works, giving "Sordello," which had not been given before. This edition was dedicated to John Forster, and, with that fine cordiality which Browning often uses, he expresses himself "glad and grateful" that he who, thirty years ago, had been so "prompt and staunch a helper," should seem "even nearer now" than then. In "Dramatis Personæ" (1864) he gave new work, sustaining the strength, subtlety, and passion of his best, and discovering new phases of his power as a poet dealing with the mind, conscience, and spirit of man. Growth of argumentative and psychological subtlety and rapidity, a deepening of spiritual thought, a mellow, vital wisdom, and in some of the work a tender, meditative tone,—these are the notes of his first volume, published after the death of his wife.

He had now drawn a good degree of attention to his work; this volume confirmed it. Critical opinion, which in the best minds had long discerned his genius, was now in other cases also clearer as to his powers. The sense of these things, or evidences still more tangible, led to the issue, in 1868, of that edition of his works in six volumes, which, containing all published up to date, remained for twenty years the leading edition.

In the same year was published the first part of " The Ring and the Book," completed next year (1869). In the first section of that work the poet was still aware of a " British public that liked him not." He bore it no grudge for this, rather he hoped it might yet like and understand him. The " Ring and the Book " scarcely seems the kind of work to win the public, which will hardly read four consecutive pages of serious poetry, not to speak of four volumes. Long poems, whether Spenser's, Milton's, or Browning's, are seldom read as wholes; and there was a joke at the time that only the poet, the reader for the press, and a learned bishop who read everything, read " The Ring and the Book " through. Yet the poem is in many points and most parts read-able—more so than some that preceded and a few that have followed. And this is clear, that " The Ring and the Book," as it proved the vigour and fulness of the poet's mind, finally established his position. The poem was received as the poet's masterpiece, and as possibly the greatest poetical work of our time. Its fame and accept-ance certainly initiated, though they did not for some years bring, that wider interest which is the last period in the external history of the poet's writings. His subsequent works were among the

literary events of their years of issue, and most of
them went through several editions.

After 1870 Browning continued to provide his
readers with new works, with a fertility and constancy that were noteworthy—at times yearly,
and sometimes two in one year. But, having
followed the history up to the time of the poet's
fullest work, and the time when his genius met
with secure recognition, we need only, as to the
later works, notice the direction they have taken
and any new elements or interests they discover.

There is one new group, beginning with
" Balaustion's Adventure" (1871), going on to
" Aristophanes' Apology" (1875), and the " Agamemnon" of Æschylus in 1877. These represent
the learning of the poet, his care for Greek art,
and his pains to reproduce finely one Greek
dramatist at least. They were also suggested by
the scholarship, and quickened by the memory
and by the work of his wife (*cf.* close of
" Balaustion "). In " Balaustion " he has given a
" transcript " of the " Alkestis "; and in " Aristophanes' Apology," of the " Heracles " of Euripides ;
and in the " Agamemnon " a literal and not very
legible version of that drama of Æschylus. This
is not the place to enter into the merits of
" transcription " *versus* " poetic translation," nor
into the soundness of his estimates of the Greek
dramatists. He prefers Euripides, and if that
poet be read in his versions, or from his point of
view, the reader will no doubt agree with him.

In another group we may take " Prince Hohen-

stiel-Schwangau" (1871), harsh and hard as its
name, many readers think; " Fifine at the Fair "
(1872); and the original parts of " Aristophanes'
Apology" (1875). The first deals with the career
of Louis Napoleon, and presents what may have
been the motives and ideas of that singular
"saviour of society." The second, through
imaginary circumstance and argument of a
dramatic kind, deals with love's uses, rights, and
duties; the use of love, as of all experience, in
giving life, motion, and development to the soul.
The third deals with the dispute between tragedy
of a thoughtful, rational, and moral kind, and a
comedy which accepts life and the social order
for use and enjoyment. There is casuistic subtlety,
breadth, and impartiality, and there is dramatic
appreciation in these poems, but they are " hard
reading." They are full, ingenious, argumentative
to excess, and their dramatic method complicates
and obscures the argument.

In another group we may put " Red-Cotton
Nightcap Country" (1873), and " The Inn Album "
(1875). These poems rest on stories, presenting
and interpreting them by the poet's special method.
They were a surprise to some readers, and not a
pleasure. There is more " story " in these poems.
They use facts of that kind more, and are painful,
not to say " sensational," in theme. They show
courage and freedom in exploring man's deed and
man's heart. Do they also show a pathological
rather than an æsthetic or ethical curiosity and
development ?

"The Two Poets of Croisic" (1878) belongs to the same class, in so far as it tells, and construes in telling, the stories of two lives that had interested the poet, and set him thinking over those secrets of feeling and character that would enact and so explain them.

And the "Dramatic Idyls" (1st and 2nd series, 1879, 1880) and "Jocoseria" (1883) follow the same method as those poems that rest on and reconstruct stories. In such cases the poet draws more on actual life. The work is simpler in materials and problems than earlier works, more rapid and objective. But his treatment of these stories is most characteristic. They show a curious interest in all facts that throw light on human nature and the problems of passion or will, and they show what may be called his "criticism" of fact. They bring out the use of facts for this poet. "A story for the story's sake" is not his way. He thinks very simple stories may be very wrongly told—all the facts given and their meaning missed, because the *essential fact* has been left out. Nothing is so misleading as the facts of human life to those who are without a clue to their meaning, nothing more suggestive than those facts rightly seen and vitally placed. And our dramatist of the soul uses his genius and his method upon facts so as to suggest truths that go much beyond any mere narration of them. It is not merely to give them animation that he tells his stories dramatically, it is the better to get at their life and vital meaning, at

their sources and substance. It is a new application of his method, and yet with the old interest
and purpose, the "study of the souls" of men
through the matter of these stories; very different
work from "Paracelsus" and "Sordello," yet
animated by the same purpose that guided those
works forty-five years before.

"Ferishtah's Fancies" (1885) and "Parleyings
with Certain People" (1887) are didactic and
meditative. In dramatic form, they "discuss"
certain themes of life and art; "Ferishtah" being
wholly occupied with the "criticism of life," while
the later volume is more occupied with certain
questions of art about which the poet has never
spoken so forcibly. Both volumes were very
notable, especially at the point in the poet's life
at which they were done—the first for mellow
wisdom; the second for intellectual vigour, descriptive power, and a freshness and energy that
recall those of earlier periods. The poet was still
writing with a degree of vigour and freshness of
lyrical and reflective power in the year of his
death. His last volume was published on the
day of his death, and though some of the poems
of "Asolando" seem to be earlier work, much of
it is no doubt work of 1888–89. His activity
and zest lived with his life.

And so we raise the questions of the sequence
and changes of Browning's work, the *growth of his
mind and art*, the *periods of his work*. Between
"Paracelsus" in 1835, and "Asolando" in 1889
—an interval of fifty-four years—what changes

do we find? And has there been growth of mind and art as shown in the list of works? Can Browning's works be divided into periods, and, if so, what are their characteristics?

The *classification* of a poet's work on this principle has been much in fashion of late, and is certainly helpful, where it really generalises the facts of a poet's career; useful when it even approximates such generalisation of the order of a poet's works and the growth of his mind. Can we do anything of the kind exactly or even approximately for the works and for the art of Browning? The first impression of most readers will almost certainly be that it cannot be done in his case. Browning has been very much the man and the poet his readers know throughout his career, only, according to subjects, varying in difficulty and obscurity, not in vital characteristics or in the qualities and force of his genius. And there is so much truth in this view that one of the poet's ablest critics has expressed her judgment as to the uniformity and equality of the poet's work without qualification. "As a poet he has had no visible growth; he shows no divisions into youth, manhood, and age; no phases particularly marked by the predominance of an aim, a manner, or a conviction." His genius is thought to have "reached its zenith in 'The Ring and the Book' only because that gives the largest illustration of it"; but, according to this critic, no reason can be given for his writing it in 1868–9 rather than in 1840, except the external cause that led to its

4

production then; and "Fifine" might change places with "Paracelsus" without any discoverable incongruity.

Now, there must be a fairly good case for such a view when so careful a reader as Mrs. Orr not only thinks thus, but is so clear about it. And yet this is not likely to be the whole truth about the mind, the man, or the work. That it can even seem true proves exceptional balance and early fulness of growth; but a mind that did not grow, that was not enriched or changed by experience, and an artist who learned nothing from the practice of his art, would be above or against all laws. And, indeed, the work, when closely considered, shows that what is probable is also more or less actual. It is not easy to fix the lines of change or define the elements of it, to mark dates, separate works, and specify characteristics; and we may allow that in no case can that be done upon "hard and fast lines," such as are used at times. The division at best can only be made general and suggestive. Let us try what in that sense we can make of it.

Regarding the matter in view of the chronology of the poet's works, we must be careful to distinguish the question of form, and his definite choice of that, from the question of subject and his power over that. And as to the question of form, it will be found that the poet did not for some time settle that, while his mastery over the resources of his subject, and a certain maturity of expression were early reached. We shall find that for a time he seems to be seeking a form through which most fitly and congenially to develop and present his subject and the resources of his mind. This time extends from 1832 to 1846. During this time he was using, with greater or less felicity and success, several forms ; before its close he had proved his true power to lie in the use of a certain form, and at the close of it he concluded on that as his chief form. This is the form he calls the dramatic-lyric. And we may regard that as his first period, on the above grounds. It is the time of youth and prelude, 1832–1840. It is also the time of early manhood, 1841–46. During the first part of the time he was ascertaining the nature and compass of his theme and field of work, and using the forms of art he employed in " Pauline," " Paracelsus," and " Sordello." The second part of this time is that of the dramas and early dramatic-lyrics. During this time he was finding his standpoint and method as a poet—the way in which he could best deal with his theme and his genius. All the dramas, save " Strafford," are of this time, and the poems called dramatic-lyrics and romances —at first of a more lyrical, afterwards of a more dramatic quality.

Then in the same relation, that is as to the method and form of his work, the years from 1846–1869 would be a second period. During those years he was using the dramatic-lyric form with its full power, and giving, through it his knowledge and mastery of man and life, with a due balance of the elements of his genius, the argumentative and intellectual, the dramatic and the emotional. This was the time of his manhood and married life, and of the early London years after his wife's death. During this time some of the finest and most perfect of his dramatic lyrics, and some of the best of his dramatic monologues were made— the first in " Men and Women " and " Dramatis Personæ," the second in " The Ring and the Book," with fine lyrical work too. At first, indeed, the argumentative power is prominent in " Christmas Eve " and " Easter Day," then the dramatic and lyrical power in the " Men and Women " series ; then all his gifts, lyrical, argumentative, ethical, dramatic, are found in the " Dramatis Personæ " ; and anon in " The Ring and the Book," the dramatic and argumentative powers reach a fulness and energy that took the world by storm.

There would then be a third period, from 1870–76, testing the work by the same tests. During this time that balance of the powers of the poet's genius, and of the elements of his work which we spoke of as characteristic of the second period was disturbed. The argumentative and casuistic power and interest are, on the whole, dominant more pronounced than the dramatic, and the style and energy developed for dramatic-argumentative uses seems too strong for the poetic and dramatic interests. This is the time of his " hardest " and " least poetic " work, the time when he is most idiosyncratic in subjects, treatment, and style. It is the time of " Hohenstiel-Schwangau " and

" Fifine at the Fair," and "Aristophanes' Apology."
It is also the time of " Red Cotton Night-Cap
Country " and " The Inn Album," which, with
all their ability and interest, are certainly " too
characteristic."

And there is, we think, a fourth period, when the
balance is kept again in much, certainly, of the work
then made.   That is the time of the latest works,
from 1876 to 1889.   It is the time of the lyrics
in " Pacchiarotto," of the three series of " Dramatic
Idyls," of " Ferishtah's Fancies," and of the " Parleyings."   The work is on the whole simpler and
more dramatic, while the dramatic idyl, a fresh
development of the dramatic lyric, is by its very
aim more active, outward.   And even where the
work is " criticism " of life, art, or thought, as in
" Ferishtah " and the " Parleyings," it is simpler,
and the lyrics of the time have often a fine freshness and point.

But what conclusions may be justly drawn
from this survey as to the mind and art of the
poet?   As to the poet's mind, and his poetic
energy, there has been less of change than is
usually found over so long a period of years.
The change has been in the balance and proper
subordination of his powers and qualities, rather
than in their character and activity; much the
same mind, the same quality, the same ideals,
only a fuller mastery of resources and a surer
grasp of life.   The maturity and force of some
of the early work is surprising.   Some of the
dramatic lyrics that show well his mastery are

early work. The poems he called at first " Madhouse Cells " are as early as 1836. The " Spanish
Cloister " is of 1841, and so is " Pippa Passes,"
with its fine poetry and dramatic interest, and
" The Tomb at St. Praxed's," with its dramatic
skill and delineative wealth and accuracy, belongs
to 1845.

The art of the poet has, however, varied more
than the poet's mind and power. The elements
of interest, and his skill in the matter of form and
utterance, have varied in the way above described.
And there have been changes of method and
growth of art, such as have been thus far indicated.
These will afterwards be more fully analysed and
illustrated. But if any reader will refer to the
chronological list of the poems, and note how
many of the finest of the poems fall after the close
of the series of " Bells and Pomegranates," he will
have one means at least of testing the general
position above taken.

Our survey of the work as a whole suggests
also the question of *classification* of the poems
and one or two ingenious schemes have been
drawn. Mr. Nettleship has classified the poems
in relation to the poet's central idea of the progress or arrest of the soul. And his scheme is
interesting from that point of view, but surely too
narrow. Mrs. Orr, who regards the poems as
really one great group, has arranged them (in
part) according to their leading quality or main
matter, but does not consider her scheme as more
than suggestive. And the poet has himse

classed the poems up to 1864 by their form or principle. The matter is always hard, and neither poets nor critics make more than a partial success in most cases, it may be. Browning as well as Wordsworth exemplifies the difficulty, his distinction between the "dramatic lyric" and the "dramatic romance" being in not a few cases somewhat obscure. Yet this is to be expected when classification is attempted of complex facts. We offer only the arrangement made in the groups that follow, though we think this grouping will be found useful in regard of the matter of the poems and the art of the poet.

CHAPTER II

LITERARY RELATIONS——THE AGE AND ITS IDEAS
—— MODERN HUMANISM —— MATTER AND
FORM OF BROWNING'S POETRY——HIS DRA-
MATIC METHOD AND POWER

WITH the facts of the poet's life and literary
course before us, we now come upon certain
questions of much interest in regard to the poet
and the work, especially when we look at both in
due relation to the time through which the poet
lived.

We have spoken of his long waiting and the
slow acceptance of his work; a recent critic
speaks as if that acceptance were still to come.
During nearly forty years the poet, in the
strength and fidelity of genius, kept his aim and
maintained his work. The qualities of the man,
as of the artist, are in that; self-reliance and conviction are in every line of his work; the assurance and sincerity of genius and of truth.

But, with such independence, what have been
the poet's relations to his predecessors and contemporaries in literature? Under what influences did his mind ripen and his art take form?
Who have been his teachers? and whence have

his impulses come? On the face of matters, it
may seem as if he stood alone, with an energy
that required no outside influences, and an individuality that resisted them; so bent on speaking
his own mind in his own way, that he has stood
apart from his contemporaries in their interests
and forms of art. It seems impossible to place
him among them, or to classify his work with
theirs. And the intense way in which he has set
himself on matter rather than form, his emphatic
care for primary and direct expression,—these
also make his relations less apparent.

But there are such relations, though they are
not only less apparent, but freer and slighter than
in the case of others. Let us trace the chief of
them. Mr. Gosse has told us two things on this
matter—that the poet's first models were some
of his father's favourites in eighteenth century
literature, and that early compositions of the poet
were Byronic. It goes without saying that Byron
soon passed. As soon as the sentiment, the intellectual and moral basis, of the Byronic poetry
were felt, they must by this poet have been put
aside. But some things in Byron possibly made
a stronger impression. His energy and flow, his
general force and courage of nature, and his
manliness may have stimulated like qualities in
the younger poet, who has them on his own
account.

But he soon found work much more to his
mind, at once in its inspiration and its style.
This work, we have seen, was that of Shelley

and of Keats, work of memorable interest to him.
Many traces of his care for these poets are found
in his own works. Naturally, Shelley made the
deeper impression, and of him we find most. He
is the " sun-treader " of " Pauline," whose renown,
like sunlight, is to visit all the world, and he
has three pages of fine admiration in that poem.
Aprile in " Paracelsus " is a reminiscence of Shelley,
and depicts the defect and weakness easily arising
in that type. In the opening of " Sordello " we
find Shelley as chief among those to whom our
poet looks as he begins his high task, though he
feels Shelley's " pure face " fit rather for Athens
than for mediæval Italy. And the " Memorabilia "
speaks the honour of Shelley; while his " Essay "
on Shelley is the critical but cordial statement of
Browning's thoughts as to the place of that poet
in modern poetry, and his principles and aims,
his work being esteemed as a " sublime though
fragmentary effort towards a presentment of the
correspondency of the universe to Deity," of the
natural to the spiritual, of the actual to the ideal.
It is characteristic that to Keats the references
are fewer. His care for Keats is less, but he is
aware of the genius and pure value of the poet.
" Popularity " recognises these.

These references notwithstanding, it may seem
that neither Shelley nor Keats throws light on the
matter or the manner of Browning's work. The
music of the one and the beauty of the other
the lyrical intensity and ideal passion of the first
and the artistic sense and joy of the second, do

not seem Browning's way. Yet he has learned
from both, and been quickened in the very spirit
of his mind by Shelley. Browning regards Shelley
as the poet of the real-ideal; that is the effort and ✓
goal of his poetry, the meaning of every fact, and
of all passion, all life, and beauty is in that. And
this, we have seen, is the spirit of Browning, and
the goal of his art. It is true that the real is
more apparent in the one, and the ideal in the
other; the dramatic in the one, the typical in the
other; but the principle is the same in both—
what a critic and friend of Browning described as
the power to "see in everything an epitome of
creation," the power to see and feel the ideality of
the real.

And so in style, in a quality of natural, intense,
and immediate expression, he is in sympathy with
Shelley. He has rarely, if ever, Shelley's melody,
never his spontaneity and divine freedom of utterance; but he seeks, as Shelley did, the truest
statement within his reach without ulterior cares.
To Shelley poetry was life rather than art, and
that fine fire and singleness of soul which blent
truth and beauty and duty into one, and made
song its voice and minister—that is the high and
real meaning of poetry to Browning; and he first
found such song in Shelley.

But Keats? what affinities are there between
Browning and Keats? Tennyson and others
derive from Keats clearly, but not Browning.
But Keats had fine impulses for Browning. The
care for beauty, the love of things Greek, and the

power to enter into them, the sympathy with Mediæval and Renaissance things, and a keen passion for art,—these he shares with Keats, and if they have long since taken the quality of his own mind, he found them first in our verse in Keats.

Wordsworth, one of the great poetic influences of our century, and, however limited, one of its most original and forcible poetic minds, was slowly growing into fame and influence during Browning's early poetic years, and, in spite of great differences of temper and scope, some of Wordsworth's principles are part of Browning's mind. The radical humanity, the transcendent faith, the belief in simple things and duties, the high purpose and spiritual basis of his poetry, bring him into important agreement with the great idealist of nature and of natural life.

There are other poets one can trace—Shakespeare, of course—yet not without need to be named. That idea of man, and curiosity about human nature, and power to put the mind at so many points of view, which make the dramatic conception,—these come to every modern mind through Shakespeare. And Dante has given inwardness and intensity to this conception. It is clear from "Sordello" that the austere nature and thought of Dante, with its heart and crown of passion and tenderness, early made impression on Browning, and that his profound delineation of the "soul," and sense of the grandeur of spiritual results in man, gave direction and quality to the modern poet's studies.

And if we seek farther afield for sources of Browning's work, we find two fields wide enough —Greek literature and a field of much curious learning. Greek has been a lifelong interest. As early as "Pauline" are proofs of this knowledge and insight—passages that speak of the power of Keats. There are references to Plato as one who, "calm as beauty," held "the key of life," and the fine description of Agamemnon, and the passage that speaks in fit words of the impression made on him by the classic stories in youth. And his Greek translations are accepted by Greek scholars as vital and true.

The other field, fields rather, of curious learning—rabbinical, mediæval, mystical, artistic—in which he has gathered, it is only possible to name. The chief interest of these has been for facts or stories throwing light, often quaint and curious, on the passions and beliefs of men. "Pauline" was prefaced by an extract from a book of Cornelius Agrippa on the "Occult Philosophy." "Paracelsus" and "Sordello" both show the fields in which the young poet was roaming, and a hundred poems since show the same interests and research.

There is an inference suggested by this reading, and the use to which it is put, that, if accurate, is noteworthy; it is that the poet has cared more for the literature of fact than of form ; more for the curious and suggestive, because vital, records of man's mind than for "letters" as such—for life in every form and all its fields.

What has now been said of Browning's culture
may seem to imply that it has been remote from
his own time, and it has been so in part, and not
without bearing on his work. But his work and
ideas are to be understood in important points,
only in relation to his age with its principles and
motives——motives and principles that gave new
depth and direction, new interests and ideals, to
English life and letters between 1830 and 1850.
Keats, Shelley, and Byron all died early, and the
period and movement they interpreted closed with
their work. The new period, with the literature
that should express it, thus had the ground to
itself. This new period dates from 1832–33.
From that time we find a literature more or less
distinctly marked by the new interests and ideas
arising. Between 1815 and 1824 we find the
free and fervid impulses of the modern spirit and
the ideas of the great Revolution in the works of
Byron and Shelley. Between 1824 and 1833
there was almost no poetry of value; it was the
time of Moore and Montgomery. But in 1833
the new time made its voices heard; Carlyle,
Tennyson, and Browning had all spoken by that
date.

And what, as we now see them, and as they
grew during the years following, embodied in
action and expressed in literature——what were
the characteristics and distinctive ideas of this
period? We might answer the question by
simply bringing into view, in their order, the
books of the years from 1830–1860——works of

Carlyle, Faraday, Newman, Mill, Ruskin, Tennyson, Clough, Arnold, Strauss, Froude, Mansel, and Darwin; and the mere list of names, with the works they suggest, indicates the mental history and interests of those years, social and political, religious and scientific. The life of the time was deeply and fruitfully moved on all these great lines; the impulses and ideas of the great Revolution were developed and applied in political and social reform, in science and in belief. The political discussion and social advance have been, perhaps, the greatest in our history, resulting in what has been justly described as our greatest revolution—the enfranchisement of the people. The growth of science in knowledge, method, and ideas has been so great that many sciences seem new-made, and man's image of the physical universe and its order appears largely a product of the past fifty years, while the historical sciences have made in important parts as great advances; and the religious discussion has had, in the spheres both of history and doctrine, as great and critical an influence on the matter and spirit of belief, and on the ideal of religion itself.

The age has been earnest, rational, humane. It has been much occupied with the deeper questions arising out of society, and out of human life. It has, in fact, set itself more frankly to these questions, and to all problems of knowledge and of faith, than any former time, and if its curiosity has been largely physical, it has also directed much thoughtful investigation upon the nature and history of man. And its treatment of human nature, like its sense of social justice, has been truer and better considered than at any past time.

Now, some of these movements and ideas have not, so far as his work shows, been much to Browning. Of political and social interests there is slight trace. His interest has been in man's nature and history, and in the great points of ethics and of belief; and in these respects, though even here he has been less affected by the secular changes than many, his work is historically intelligible only amid the influences of such an age as has been described. The great theme of his poetry, indeed, implies this relation, though it is not governed by it. His conception of that theme, his breadth and freedom, his curious impartiality and research in exploring and presenting it, are in real agreement with the deeper spirit of the century, though not with certain sections or years of it, and, we take it, with certain great spiritual ideas that it is the effort of modern thought to unfold.

And so we come here closely upon a question of much importance in the study of modern literature, and nowhere of greater point than in the study of Browning—the question as to *the source and factors of the modern interest in human nature.* It is a large question, on which a good deal has yet to be said. We take it here chiefly as it bears on Browning. A care for and sympathy with man as man is one of the vital ideas of

modern literature. In its modern sense this care
and sympathy became explicit and deliberate in
the writers that in France preceded and promoted the Revolution. It is true that a spirit
of this kind, and sentiments involving it, are
found implicitly before the Revolution. They
were precipitated and applied by that, and
though the failure of the Revolution and the
wars following arrested the growth of the new
principles, that was only for a time. They soon
began to act through literature and upon life.
In England, where there had been much fear of
the Revolution, this took place most and best.
Between 1820 and 1845 this is plainly seen.
Polity, law, government, and society were re-
formed by those ideas and in their spirit; a new
conscience and a new humanity began to act,
and before long with great results. We had, in
fact, come upon the era of humanity, and were
coming to realised democracy; this was the
meaning and this the result of our reforms. And
intellectual as much as social movements gave a
new importance to man, not only by giving greater
scope and importance to reason, but by a vast
extension of our knowledge of and interest in
man's history. The revival of religious earnestness, followed by the rise of criticism, also gave
a time a deeper interest to man's mind, and to
every question of man's life. While, as new
questions arose in the life of the time, and
deeper questions both of knowledge and faith
were pressed home, and as the desire for justice

5

and for truth grew, the humanity itself gained in character and depth, as our literature between 1840 and 1870 proves almost painfully at times.

Two great interests, it has been said, have been given to modern literature by the growth of modern life and knowledge—nature and man. Browning has taken man as his part of "nature's infinite book of secrecy," and this bent and interest has been singularly clear and strong in his mind from the very beginning of his work. His first plan was a bold scheme in this field, and his first poems are studies of this kind. In the preface to " Sordello," he says, " The stress of the poem lay in the incidents in the development of a soul; little else is worth study. I always thought so." The words are strong and narrow, it may seem; but they are not so strong as our poet's conviction of their truth, nor so emphatic as his devotion to their view of the poet's work. These words give the aim and theme of all his work. There is growth of knowledge, power, and means in the work, but the interest is essentially the same. From the first he has aimed at the spiritual study and expression of man through the medium of his art.

But if the poet's subject has remained essentially the same, how about *his method* and *the form* of his work? There has been change and development in his choice of form and method. After a time of some uncertainty, if not experiment, he found his right point of view, his proper method as a poet whose aim was to present certain great views of man. Reviewing his career as an artist, and the forms he has used, let us see how this stands. He began with monologue in "Pauline"; then subdramatic poetry in "Paracelsus"; then the epic of a soul in "Sordello," where the poet himself speaks, because he thinks in that way to find freer expression for all he has to say of Sordello. He felt his theme and aims to be unsuitable for drama, where he must simply present and watch the play, no whit more in the secret of it than if a listener only; that is, no more free to express his mind about those secrets. But as a form of art, fitted to its theme and legible, that poem is very unsatisfactory. It has been less read than any of his works, and its form is a good part of the reason. He then made drama, and after that he put forth a little book of "dramatic pieces"; that is, poems lyrical in form, but dramatic in principle. Then came three more dramas, and next another little book of poems, lyrical and dramatic. In 1846 he returned to drama, and gave "Luria" and "A Soul's Tragedy." Now, the question being, Which of these works is most adequate to the poet and his subjects? there can be no doubt as to the answer—the dramatic lyrics are most vivid and sufficient. And the poet thought so himself clearly, for after 1846 this is the form he uses, whether for argument or narrative, or for more strictly dramatic purposes; whether in "Christmas Eve," "Men and Women," "The Ring and the Book," that being the fullest instance and capital test of his method of presentation as a poet.

Clearly, then, this poet, in the expression of whatever he knows about man, has tended to some dramatic form, to some dramatic or subdramatic method—for a time to set drama, but always to some kind of dramatic expression. The bent of his mind, whether from its own qualities or from its interest, is towards dramatic statement, whatever be the exact principle of his work in this kind.

And so no question in the criticism of this poetry is more necessary than the question, What kind of dramatic work does this poet make, and *what kind of dramatic power has he*? Is it really dramatic, or only akin to the dramatic? and if his proper form of art be, as was said, the "dramatic lyric," what exactly is that, and is it a legitimate and accurate form of art? There is much difference and some confusion as to the right answers to these questions, but, as they involve the core of the whole question of Browning's character and power as a poet, and as his poetry cannot be read fairly until his standpoint is reached and his method understood, we must make as clear as we can our answers to these questions regarding his art.

It has been shown that Browning's bent is to dramatic conception and statement. Even in "Sordello," where the form is least dramatic, the tendency comes clearly out. Browning made so many plays that it is plain he had a liking for

And this has been called " *dramatic thinking,*"
or " *dramatic apology,*" as if the primary and final
interest were intellectual, or as if the poems were
only cases of special pleading, only thought, stating itself in terms and combinations of life, or
argument so vivid that it has dramatic force and
a voice like the voice of life, though the work all
the same is intellectual, not vital; abstract, not
concrete. And we admit that some of the lyrics
have that look, and some of them that quality
mainly. But almost everywhere the work has
true dramatic quality, and involves the person, not
the mind only; character, not thoughts about man
and life only. The conception is dramatic, the
statement vital, and even in work where the leading
matter is argument there is a body of dramatic
detail and suggestion that gives you the man or
the type as a dramatic image.

In the old sense, then, Browning's work is not
dramatic; in the above sense it is distinctly so.
Action and active relations are not its sphere, but
the mind itself. Its aim is to represent the man,
not merely what he did or would do in given
circumstances, nor merely what he said or would
have said in active life. Its scope is thought and
passion, not speech and conduct. Its field is the
soul and its forces, not the world and its actions.

And this is its charm and its worth for us. The
new dramatic poetry cannot be as the old drama.
A new spirit and view of man and a new aim
animate and command it—a more subtle and
searching spirit, a deeper curiosity, a fuller effort.

The art that deals with man in our time must, in fact, express the modern interest and thought. You may, of course, prefer a simpler, a more unconscious and outward presentation of life; but at this time, and amid its science and philosophy and spiritual debate, you are not likely to get it, except, it may be, by forcible suppression or by languor and weakness. The same thoughtful and inward quality is in all our work dealing with human life—in George Eliot as in Robert Browning. The great novelist, in her interest and in her way of looking at men and human life shows the same tendency and presents similar results. As compared with earlier novelists, there is the same kind of difference between their work and hers that there is between the older drama and Browning's poetry, while George Meredith shows still closer affinities of aim and result. In fact, such art is the fit exponent of the modern spirit in its human interests and insight, and Shakespeare, in whom, indeed, all things of the modern world of man seem to be expressed or implicit, made much of " Hamlet " and " Lear " in this quality.

But, granting the dramatic quality of the poetry, and its relation to modern life, we have then to ask, What is it we get through such poetry, and how is it done ? The very " souls " of men, it is said. That is easily said, but has it solid meaning ? Can this poetry by its form and method give the minds of men ? To do this would seem to ask a subtler mastery and a more intimate knowledge than were demanded by the form and

aim of the older drama. The distinction between
the two must not be stressed. And we have
above implied that that drama, in the Master's
use of it, found scope for " all the things of man,"
yet the aim of the new form is more spiritual, and
in a sense more exacting. How is it achieved,
then ? Let it be frankly said that we make no
mystery of the matter. If it be done, it is done
within the laws and by the means of art. And
how ? It is done from the new point of view and
with the new field of vision, as Shakespeare did his
work from the older standpoint. Through his own
humanity and resources of nature and knowledge,
through vital sympathy and identifying imagination, the poet takes his stand within his *dramatis
personæ*, and feels with and thinks for them. He
animates and moves them so that they present
themselves. He takes some critical moment or
situation, and from that point the character is set
in action, that keenest action of the mind within
and on itself, and so the man is given with an
intimacy and vital truth the drama of " action "
could hardly use or reach by its own proper
means.

We have said the *man* is presented. But, looking closely at many of these dramatic lyrics, *is it
so ?* The poet speaks of the " soul," but that, you
will say, is only part of the man ; and in dramatic
art, which must be audible, if not visible, it is a
smaller part of the man in action than some appear
to think. And again, you say, many of these
poems are strictly " lyrical," dealing with purely

imaginary persons and situations, and only conceived to express some part of the poet's own
mind; while many of the poems are even worse,
regarded from our present point of view, for they
are simply meditations in character, or arguments
from an assumed dramatic standpoint. And all
you can have in such work, it may be thought, is
dramatic form without dramatic truth or reality.
It is only the poet's mind, and his view of what
may be said of and for certain "persons." His
soul animates and overflows the men and women
presented. And as in part proof of this, it is
urged that you cannot imagine any one save
Browning talking as all his men and women talk.
The poet is not only behind them; he is through
them and before them.

And yet the *men* and *women* are there in some
sense, and their "cases" are put with vital fulness.
That seems to be the fact; but for greater clearness on an important matter let us meet the points
just stated. The men given us in these poems
would not, and in many cases could not, have said
the things here said for them; but were such
things in them, do such things express them, even
if consciousness and thought must have been raised
to higher powers ere they could have uttered them
—for if these things and this speech of our poet
rightly interpret them in that inner sense, then
his method is justified and its results are vital.
But around all the *personæ* and in all the style
you are aware of the poet—his mind runs through
and qualifies all; or, in other words, his dramatic

expression is not purely objective.   You have the
men and women always plus Browning.   It is so.
And so it is in Shakespeare also, is it not?

But is not that part of the charm and value, and
part of the means, is it not the necessary medium,
of such work?   You could not have such dramatic
studies without this.   The men and women and
the questions of their lives are seen in the light
and amid the spaces of the poet's mind.

It may not be easy to say what it is you have in
this matter, what this " subjective medium " quite
exactly is.   It is not a judgment passed on the
" persons," nor a deliverance of the opinions or
preferences of the poet.   It is the sense of a large
free mind and personality identified in feeling and
thought for the time with the " persons " presented,
and working through them, but clear of their bias
and free of their limits.

But, further, it is said that, allowing for this
quality of characterisation, what is it you have in
Browning's *personæ*?   Not men in Shakespeare's
or Scott's sense?   It is not so clear what that
sense exactly is, while the nature of personality,
and its relations to those more general as well as
universal elements that belong to all minds are
very far from being clear.   But Browning certainly
gives types and generalisations in some of his
studies, and it results from his more spiritual and
inward dramatic poetry that his " persons " should
be less objective than those of Shakespeare or Scott.
Subject, however, to the conditions and design
of his art, he is a master of dramatic detail, and

has the quickest eye for essential circumstances or quality. To require the same embodiment of character from Browning that you have in great drama or novels, is to forget the difference both of means and of design. The poet would violate his principle to give it. But he has known how to define and embody with a vital precision, on the whole adequate to his kind of dramatic poetry. And if we do not maintain the critical perfection and æsthetic purity of Browning's work, considered as dramatic art; if we allow it to be in the nature of his mind, as of his purpose, that his work should involve much of himself, and that the spiritual should shadow the dramatic interest — we hold it not only clear that his power is dramatic, but his poetry is alive with the evidence and energy of it, and his very thought works itself out in that way, not in abstractions, but in terms of character and life. Through all he knows of them, through all he knows of man and man's mind, he animates and reveals his *personæ*, each one by himself, in situations best adapted to test and bring them out, and with a frankness and spirituality of statement only possible under the conditions he selects, so that the statement itself becomes the expressive image of the mind and will of the given " person," whether Duke or Bishop, whether painter or Pope.

CHAPTER III

CRITICAL OBJECTIONS — OBSCURITY AND ITS
CAUSES—FURTHER ANALYSIS OF DRAMATIC
METHOD, WITH REFERENCE TO IT—STYLE
AND ITS QUALITIES—CHARACTERISTICS

WE have seen Browning's theme, his conception
of his subject, and his method in the development
and expression of that subject. It remains to
consider the *characteristics* of the genius with
which he has illustrated his theme, and certain
qualities and ideas that have helped him to unfold
his subject with the power he has shown. Nor
would our purposes of introduction be served if
nothing were said of the poet's *style*, and of that
obscurity which is often supposed to be its chief
note, and a leading reason for the objections many
take to his work, and for the difficulties they find
in so much of it.

It may be best to take the last points first.
The objections to Browning, on the part of good
and careful readers of poetry, are understood to
be numerous and reasonable. By some they are
thought to spring from the nature of poetry, and
certainly from the theory and practice of the art
as always hitherto understood; while all their

difficulties are thought to arise from the faults of the poet, and his obscurity is assumed to be not in the nature of his subjects, but only in his way of treating them, and most of all in his way of setting forth whatever he has to say of them. It is still worth while to correct these mistakes, not only in justice to the poet, but in the hope of preparing a way of approach to him on the part of some who could read him if they would, and who, since they might, certainly ought, and lose by not doing so. The work of Browning is still received by some with a smile, and those who read him are expected to offer to culture and good taste some account of their peculiarity, if not some apology for their conduct. It is a pity people are often proud of their narrowness—that they emphasise their limits, and keep themselves from the larger experience and the true judgment by presuppositions that fall to the ground as soon as they grasp the facts and give their minds fair play in their appreciation.

And what are the pre-judgments that have kept good readers from Browning's poetry? We said that some of them arise from what is thought to be the nature of poetry and its primary laws as an art. Art, like other parts of the progressive life of man, has often suffered from two causes. People like what they have got used to, and erect their taste and the works of the past into laws to govern, and not into impulses and principles to stimulate and guide the works of the future, which is what they ought to do. So the standard of pleasure and the restraints of theory have operated to conventionalise art. But in proportion as it is strong and sincere art is vital, and should follow its own principles and instincts in the last resort. And so, if new work should require a revision of theories, before it can be understood or classified, then it may be the worse for the theories, not for the work. If Browning's work should require a fresh consideration of the laws of poetic art, there is nothing to complain of. We really gain by enlargement of art and its ideal. For what is the function of criticism in regard to original work in art? To judge and control art by some abstract and fixed standard? To test the creations of genius by some absolute theory of beauty and expression? To deliver decisions according to "law and precedent" and induction of "all previous instances," and so settle what is valuable and ought to be enjoyed? Is this the right relation of criticism to art? Or is its proper task simpler and greater—to follow, note, and generalise the facts of art, and so interpret its works freely and vitally; not to legislate for art, but to learn and understand and test art by frank appeal to the facts of experience and of the mind in its relation to art? That is, in truth, the right and fruitful task of criticism. For is not every work of genius, pure and distinct, in a real sense a work of nature, a product of the free spirit, yet also a complex result of natural qualities and forces working to rational issues under natural laws? And so

wisdom, not modesty alone, requires us, in dealing
with the works of the freest and strongest minds,
to know, enjoy, and explain rather than pass
judgment.

But, allowing these principles in regard to the
rights of readers and the business of critics, we
may seem no nearer agreement in regard to
poetry like Browning's. It will still be said,
" Poetry should respect form, this does not; verse
should have beauty, and often this has none.
Art, having to do with beauty, should give
pleasure; this has other effects. In its themes,
and in its handling of them, this poetry constantly
mistakes art's province. This poetry is intellectual
and abstruse, at the cost of readers and of art.
It expresses the mind and humour of its author
with a disregard of principle, not of convenience
only." Now, though none of these objections are
exact or quite pertinent, they represent common
impressions and have apparent truth, and we shall
do well to get at the right point of view as to
the matters they touch. It is many years since
Carlyle insisted with his emphasis that poetry has
a right to as much attention as any other serious
work. But still many seem far from clear about
the matter, and some of Browning's advocates
have made things worse by talking as if poetry
might be anything as to form if only its matter
were valuable and noble; as if the only thing to
be asked of a poet, as of a thinker, were that he
should have thought, and get it well out. Now
poetry has a right to give that degree and kind

of thought that is adequate to the mastery and treatment of its proper themes, and it has a right to require that amount of thought on the reader's part that shall be adequate to their full comprehension. And the poet must be a thinker as well as a poet, if his themes have weight and greatness. Every poet of high significance, every great poet certainly is so, and much of his truth and value must depend on his quality and power as a thinker. And yet the poet, as a poet, is not a thinker. His great qualities are depth, energy, sensibility of the heart and vivid force of mind; power to see and to say; power of realisation and power of song—that, seeing and feeling, he may make others feel and see. If these be wanting the man is not a poet, whatever other force and grasp of mind he may have. In other words, though intellectual quality and power in the highest degree will serve the poet, and the highest degree of poetic power is impossible without rich and strong intellectual power, yet of itself such power makes no man a poet and no work poetic. The poet must be a poet first and last, if not also midst and without end.

If, then, it be said that Browning is a thinker, and that very much of his value depends on that, it is not meant that that makes him a poet, or that thought is to be taken in place of poetry. The method, medium, and aim of the thinker all differ from those of the poet, though results reached by thought and authenticated by passion may be incorporated by the poet. With the endowment

6

of the poet, and through the medium proper to
poetry, he may give the results of keen, sagacious,
and powerful thinking, the vital process of it even
through "character in action." And Browning
shows a greater activity and prominence of intellectual faculty and result than is usually shown
by men of high and distinct poetic power, in part
from his method, in part from his personal qualities and his frank expression of them. At times
there may even be a preponderance of these in
his work; but in most of his work, and certainly
in his best, he is poet first and thinker second;
and the body of thought is given in an element
of passion and imagination, and with a force and
fitness of utterance, that are strongly poetic; and,
looking at it from the dramatic point of view,
which is nearly always the poet's, the thinking is
dramatic and vital.

Still, the poet is not to be read lightly or
fluently, and if the thought be vital or poetic it is
there, and requires serious and sustained attention; and it may be that the dramatic point and
energy of the thinking is often an element in the
difficulty. Is it not, then, a mistake to ask so
much attention? and a still greater mistake to
leave many parts such that, after the best attention
many readers can give, they remain obscure? As
to the attention asked, there are, one judges, two
questions about that—whether, having given due
attention, you are repaid for your trouble; whether
of all arts and studies, poetry only may not as
pains to master it? When frankly put, these

questions imply their own answers. And then, it may be, the objection is shifted, and is put, perhaps, thus: Art that is truly such and rightly made ought to give and will give pleasure. It will, but to whom, and when? To those capable of understanding it when they have given the pains necessary to do so. Its pleasure is not simple and immediate. Enjoyment of true and deep art does not precede, it may not accompany, it results from and follows real study of it. For, however much trouble the artist may save you by the vivid power of his work with reference to the field or subject in its original state, he can never save you the trouble requisite to master the theme as it stands in his work, or to comprehend his treatment of it.

And then the objection to this poetry is put in another way. It is said that the trouble it gives arises from its want of form, its disregard of beauty and harmony. As to the technical point of form, we leave that so far as it regards verse, and meet what is really the objection on other grounds. The "form" of Browning's work, by which readers are often offended, springs from and expresses its dramatic individualism, and its want of beauty—by which is often meant merely melody and repose—from its dramatic realism. The form and tone of the work ought to express the mood and mind of the person thinking or speaking for the time being, and so such work cannot have the harmony and ought not to have the uniformity of typical or epic work. And as

to the question of beauty and the frequent want
of it in Browning's work—a fact no good reader
would deny—that question goes much deeper
than any matter of forms or sounds only. It
turns, we said, on the poet's dramatic realism, and
that is, perhaps, the right way to meet the
objection. It rests on the poet's vision of life—
what he sees of life, and how truly he sees all
within his view. If he, as a dramatic poet and
thinker, hold that his work ought to give his
sincere impression, ought to agree with his perception of the world, then he will put only so
much beauty into his work as he sees life and the
world to warrant, or only so much as shall be
true from the successive standpoints chosen. But
that may seem to reduce art to a measured or
even prosaic reproduction of life. Yet it is not
so, for it is the world not of common minds or of
literal and simple fact, but the world as a poet of
large mind and generous imagination sees and
interprets it, that should be the "real-world" of
art. And the true question of realism is, whether
the poet who essays a dramatic expression of life
should make his work, in the aspect of it called
beauty, agree with his own total impression of
men and the world of experience, or should set
and shape it to some conventional and pleasing
standard of things; whether it should chime with
the laws and issues of the world as he sees them,
or should seek agreement with certain images and
preconceptions of art.

Browning, anyhow, has held by the former

principle, and it explains the matters as well as the æsthetic features of his work. The principle itself would by some be contested, though scarcely, we think, on a true judgment of what the principle is to a poet and thinker like Browning. For to him his view of art results from his view of the world. His " creed " as thinker and his governing conception as poet are the same— real idealism. No man holds more deeply, and no poet has given more forcible expression to a conviction of the higher issues of life—to the belief in the reality of a life and order more perfect and more beautiful than the actual world. But the way to it is through the realities of this world, not through dreams and fine sentiments, " vain opinions, false valuations, and imaginations, as one would." The light and beauty come as the facts of the world and the soul are seen truly, and transfigured on the ground and by the vision of that reasonable ideal which is the poet's truest dream and the thinker's surest result.

But so much being allowed as explanation of the form of this poetry, and of what some consider its want of beauty, it may then be urged that its difficulty and *obscurity* are neither justified nor removed. For so many readers complain of this obscurity that its reality must be frankly admitted—we mean, in the sense that there is something of exceptional difficulty in this poetry. We will even allow that there are parts more difficult than they need have been, and parts where the " darkness may be felt." And then we affirm that a great part of the alleged difficulty and obscurity arise from its mere merits, are natural to its subjects and its method. Let us, then, see how this can be shown, and, in giving reasons for the obscurity that is often felt, we may suggest to some a way of getting over and beyond its causes.

And first of the reasons I give for the obscurity of the poet is this—that his writing is often, perhaps usually, *immediate*, lying close to the facts as he sees them, and certainly to the matter in his mind. There often seems a vital transference of thought and of its motives and process in the mind supposed. The poetry is the frank and direct expression of the man thinking. Of Emerson's lectures it was said that they were not so much speech as thought made audible; and of Browning's dramatic poetry you might say that it is not so much verse as the thought and passion of the poet embodied, vitally conveyed. From the point of view of style, this is open to criticism; yet it not only results from, it conveys the dramatic energy of, the poet's mind. It is, therefore, most suitable to his method, and it gives a fine quality to his style

And this suggests the second reason to be given for Browning's obscurity — that is, the *method* and *quality* of his art. Nearly all his writing, we have seen, is from a dramatic stand point. Even his lyrics are so many dramatic utterances. The poet takes his stand inside the personality and experience of some person imaginary or historic, and he speaks for them or he makes them speak. Their character and circumstances are all assumed, and that without prelude or explanation. You are carried at once into the midst of these things and thoughts; you listen, you make the best of your way through them, and keep on until you know the " person " speaking, and his circumstances; and then, possibly, having grasped both, you read the poem again, and thus see the whole vividly, and most of all the " person " in the foreground. The matter takes time and patience, but you get your own out of it. Things are not plain all at once. But no one is to blame, and certainly not the poet; it belongs, in fact, to his method.

Then, what we may call his *complex use of his dramatic method* increases the difficulty. It is not, as he uses it, speech you have, nor is the scene outside. The " case " is not made clear as for some " third party," and the stage is really the soul, and what you have is the man's intimate utterance—thought very often. And very often you have not one person only on the stage, but another or others. It is not soliloquy you have; it is a kind of intense debate carried on with reference to several persons, or a kind of drama played through a single soul, where the necessity the poet is under to work in the whole situation and its details from the one point of view, and to adapt the utterance to the other " persons," must involve difficulty.

Nor is the point of view the *simple dramatic*, even allowing for the *interior standpoint*. It is not simply the " person " the poet gives you, animated and kept in spiritual action so that he may reveal himself through and in his utterance ; there is a modern thoughtfulness and curiosity, searching and explaining, rising from facts to their meaning, and from phenomena to their sources. The poems are not dramatic lyrics only ; they are dramatic studies also. This again is part of the complexity of conception and design in the poet's use of his method—his wish and aim to be " objective and subjective " too.

And this complexity of dramatic interest and expression may suggest another reason for his obscurity, and that is a reason it is not, perhaps, easy to get over and impossible to get rid of— that is, his swiftness of movement, his *energy* and *rapidity of thought*, his quick, restless perceptions and transitions, his swift and subtle qualifications, his strong grip and eager march of mind both among facts and thoughts. There is in Browning, indeed, that quality of energy and abundance ; that sense of a mind conscious of its own strength and movement, and rejoicing in it ; that fulness of flow both of matter and utterance, which Marlowe and Jonson, and above all Shakspeare, have. It is not easy to follow such writing, but it is a noble virtue, and the stimulus of it is excellent, and no poet of our time has given it in the same degree as the author of " The Ring and the Book,"

And when mental energy is named, that is only part of the matter. This poet is keen, alert, and ready with his *other powers*. His senses are quick and strong—eye and ear, sense of form and colour and beauty. He is active and observant, and of well-developed physical endowment. You find something of the external abundance of the great poets, in spite of themes and a method that hardly encourage this kind of wealth.

The complexity of dramatic interest and expression has been noted, but there are further points of that kind that add much to the interest and something to the difficulty of this poetry. The situations and moments of life and character chosen are pregnant and complex ; the persons presented are far from being simple, and you find them in moments of disturbance and debate when the passion and thought of years is brought to bear on some matter of the soul or the life. Such hours are those of intense action, congenial to the poet's mind, and best for his method of dramatic revelation ; but they are situations requiring energy on the reader's as on the poet's part.

And if the poet's choice of subjects and dramatic treatment of them means trouble, he adds to it by the *casuistic* and *speculative* activity which he often keeps up alongside the dramatic activity. It is not only that his dramatic poems are dramatic studies of spiritual quality and depth, nor only that they are studies of complex characters and situations, but the dramatic and argu-

mentative threads are often so worked together
that it is at times impossible to keep them clear,
or to know if the poet meant you to do so. And
to complicate matters further from the point of
view of art, and to add to the interest and depth
from that of thought, the poet contrives, or is
driven by interest of his own mind in the facts
and problems contained within the dramatic development, to suggest the largest aspects of
thought in its bearing on these matters of
human life—to suggest the uncertainty and incompleteness of art and of thought in dealing
with the complex drama, even of single souls, in
situations that involve their lives and their resources.

And the fact is, broadly, that Browning does
not and cannot use his dramatic power simply
as a poet or merely as a dramatist. He has
the power to present poetry dramatic and accurate in his kind of work. He is not, as some
think, a critic of life who uses poetry as the
medium of his criticism, or a thinker who uses
dramatic forms to state in the terms of life his
conclusions about life. He is a dramatist of true
power, and his poetry as such is vitally clear and
right. But behind and about all you have the
thinker. It is not necessary here to settle which
interest of the poet is the stronger, the poetic or
the speculative—and in some of the poems it is
impossible to settle it; but, without seeking to
determine that question for the poet's mind, it
is clear that he regards dramatic poetry as a

medium vital, and therefore most valuable, for presenting the problems of the soul and of life, and unless this be regarded in his work he must often bewilder.

Enough, however, of reasons arising from this side of the poetry. Many will deem that a reason more on the surface has much to answer for. We refer to the *style* of the poet. If that had been other and clearer, the business of reading had been easier. Browning's style is distinct and individual. Its merits and faults are mainly his own. His utterance is the energetic reflex of the man and his thought. As such it must be known ; and it is swift and abrupt like the thought, and condensed often as the thought is concentrated. Thought and fact are primary, and language must bend to the intense thinking. His elisions are often puzzling, his clauses numerous, his qualifications tiresome ; his similes, often happy, are strange at times ; and his metaphors sometimes run away with him, and become a thing apart and grotesque. There are parts that look as if they had been thrown off with a profuse energy and indifference to finish— parts that look like full and vigorous notes for work rather than the completed work. Beauty of expression seems of small account compared with distinct and forcible statement, and his own keenness and energy of mind have led to his thinking too little of other minds.

All that may be said of Browning's style, and yet this poet is really great in point of style,

original and powerful in this as in matter.
Casual, harsh, and capricious as he seems at
times, reckless and grotesque as he seems, he
is in his best work masterly and sufficient. He
is Shakespearean in fulness, rapidity, and mastery
of utterance. His style is, perhaps, the most
vital and natural of recent poets—the fit medium
and counterpart of his matter; with great simplicity often, great vivacity, with muscular quality
and grasp, and with nothing rhetorical or obtrusive
about it.

To compare Browning and Tennyson in the
matter of style, is to find a measure of their
merits and differences. Beauty, finish, musical
and emotional charm, care for every verse and
line and for the parts as parts, and care for
verse and phrase as things of beauty and pleasure
in themselves—these are Tennyson's qualities, not
Browning's; but in Browning power and mastery
of matter and word, tense grasp and alert speech,
force, animation, trenchant and decisive bearing
on the main purpose. There is manliness and
sincerity, an upright and masculine temper, even
in his speech, the pertinence and freedom of
animated and competent talk; and such style
fits his method, and lies close to his thoughts.

It is laid to his charge that he is never lyrical
and poetic, in the sense some have got to regard
as the whole of poetry. His tone and colour are
too low. Plain in word, and almost prosaic in
pitch, he offends some. But that is to miss his
standpoint and design. His style is framed t

his purpose; and in its qualities, and what some think its defects, it may be regarded as the reflex both of his mode of thought and his view of his whole subject. Its quality and tints are realistic. Its discords and grotesqueness of phrase and line belong to its dramatic humour, and give the key of the writer's thought. But the results are not art, it may be said. They are not classic, but Gothic art—a more natural and complete art, because more sufficient as an image of life. And our great dramatic thinker and poet sees so forcibly the quality of life, its completeness, its moral infinity; he sees how all character is manifold, intricate, never to be seized or expressed in its exact truth; he is set on the soul, and, as language can at its best but indicate the life of that, he is satisfied that his style should be the shadow and consequence of his "criticism" of life and of art's just relation to it.

As to *verse*, and his powers in that matter. In the opinion of some he has been indifferent here. But he is really capable of great metrical skill, as many poems show in all parts and periods of his work. So fine a judge as Mr. Watts speaks of such passages, "hundreds in which the music is quite new, quite his own, and entirely beautiful," though the critic thinks the poet often "led astray by his quest for new movements." His use of rhyme is a trying point to some, part of his humour often; but his blank verse is fluent and masterly, no doubt because it is the most suitable to his mode of art and his theme—the verse that is nearest to speech, as has been said.

It has now become clear that, on whatever side Browning's work is regarded, you can understand it only as you discern and allow for its dramatic quality and design. He is the modern poet of man, positive, comprehensive, and spiritual, and he has the largest qualification for the work of any recent English poet. The characteristics of his work, the way in which he touches and illustrates human life and man's nature, the body of thought and character through which it is done, the genius and personality that inspire and vitalise it, the outcome of it, and the impression made by the whole work as a view of the life of man,— these questions arise when we come to regard the work in its whole extent, and to estimate it with reference to its great subject.

Some of these matters we shall consider along with the groups of poems that illustrate them. It will be well here to mark certain *general principles* and features of the work and of the poet. And, first, looking at the poetry as *characterisation* of the lives of men, what wealth and variety of character it contains, through so many types, times, and races,—Greek, Eastern, Mediæval, Renaissance, Modern! And the freedom of moral scope is as great as the variety of type. It passes from Caliban to Aben Ezra. The readiness and versatility of mind this implies are only part of what it involves. The wide research and frank curiosity are matched by the

moral breadth and impartiality of nature. To
really present not the actions, but the minds and
feelings of so many "persons," to identify the
mind with them so far as to give the being and
body of their experience—this means a rare
width and freedom of spirit, a rare power to
enter into the thoughts of men. Nor is it intellectual comprehension only, large and subtle as
that is. There is free emotion. There is sympathy and frank regard, which throws itself into
the particular case for the time, making it real,
giving not only the process of thought, but the
play of passion and habit, so far as it belongs to
his dramatic art.

And this is part, of course, of that *vitality* and
energy which gives so strong a fascination to
Browning's dramatic work. The fascination that
vital energy has in every form is here in its
finest form as energy of will and spirit. He
seems alive at every point, at every moment, and
he animates every person of his drama and every
line of his work. And this not only with a keen,
alert intelligence, but with the touch of a well-
strung nature. Mr. Bagehot called attention to
the tenseness and alertness of Shakespeare's mind,
so that his plays have the excitement and activity
of the playhouse; Browning's work has a similar
quality and power.

And what courage, and frankness of judgment,
and interest! What health and naturalness of
speech and feeling! He is not afraid to give
men and women in the bold lines and simple

truth of their souls and lives. He understands
the passion and trial of men. He knows the
"joy of life, the mere living." He has a Shakespearean cordiality and humanity ; is open and
hearty towards man and life.

And, being the man and thinker we have
described, his characterisation is inclusive and
actual, not exclusive or abstract. He has an eye
for all significant facts, and is quick to catch
their meaning. As an artist, he knows the
worth of expressive detail ; as a dramatist, he
has a care for whatever throws light on his persons ; as a thinker, he is resolute to grasp the
whole problem in all its elements, and seeks no
vain simplicity, but the complex relations and
subtle balances of forces that belong to life and
fact.

These are some of the qualities of Browning's
characterisation, and out of them arise two questions. What is the principle of selection, what
the ground of interest, that has led the poet to
this gallery of men and women, so curious and
original ? It seems difficult to define his dramatic motive. Not beauty or pleasure or morality,
or any simple motive of poetic invention, will
account for these dramatic works. What, then,
is the point of attraction and of interest ? No
English poet of recent years has grasped so much
of the lives of men, has gone so far through the
field of man's history, or made such wide observation of its facts. Others have kept a narrow
range, and have offered familiar types ; this poet

has put before us, in the intimate passion and truth of their souls, men of exceptional and various characters. And his clue has been the human interest and significance of his themes. A wide and disinterested curiosity——nay, love and care for the things of human spirits——is one leading note of this poetry. At a time when a great general idea of science has given such interest and value to the simplest facts bearing on the history of life, and a new and grand unity to all research illustrating that history, Browning has felt a similar interest, has given something of the same unity and value to all facts bearing on the interior life and its laws.

But Browning's interest in the facts of human life, though wide and disinterested in the sense just stated, is not so universal or free as Shakespeare's. All kinds of characters and situations do not interest him. Many of Shakespeare's people would not answer his purpose. The stimulus of interest and expression in his poetry is not, as in the "objective drama," action or what bears on action, but the "soul," and what moves or reveals it. And so his critics have noted that the crises and situations that do this are of special interest to him——the times that throw the soul off its habits and on to its deeper forces, that make clear the drift and power of those forces; the energies that are usually quiet, but that take or make their hour by laws deeper than ethics or psychical science may grasp.

From this comes another point of his work——

that his *dramatis personæ* are such as afford these
crises and the forces that generate them or respond
to them.   As tragic situations belong to the
drama of action, and test and develop the will,
so tragical moments and decisions belong to the
inward drama, and test and develop the soul;
and the souls that give scope for these crises are
the deep and passionate people who have the
elements of disturbance in them.   From the first
it is these people who have interested him.   Even
lives that are wrecked by the conflict are his
element, for they unveil the human spirit—lives
in which there is a large composition and unstable
equilibrium of forces.

And then, looking at the drift of the above
criticism, and at the lists of " persons," we come
more fully upon a question touched before—
What is Browning's essential interest ?   Is it
poetic or scientific ? curiosity or human regards ?
Browning is human and cordial to the core, and
his poetry is so too.   But the question is one
raised by his poetry and method far more than
by Shakespeare's.   What is the " end " of all this
curiosity about, this description of, human life ?
What is its higher interest ?   " Man is of peren-
nial interest to man," and of deeper interest to
the dramatist than to any.   Is it, then, only the
animation and play of his puppets that he
regards; or does he watch the parts and the
play with an eye to the larger play of life itself
that he may find clues to the plan and issues of
that ?   Shakespeare, it has been thought, gave i

up, and threw his " book " away, and laid aside
his powers to return to the common duties with a
sense of its mystery and goodness, but nothing
more. Browning is of another age and the poet
of another drama, and, as was said above in
speaking of the complexity of his method, his
work involves the interest of the thinker as well
as the poet. His interest in the facts of the
play goes with an interest in the laws and
issues of the greater drama of life itself. Some
find much fault with the poet because this is so,
and some seek to " defend " him by maintaining
that he writes only and always as a dramatist.
But the defence is not valid, and there may
surely be an activity of the thinker without pre-
judice to that of the poet.

And this reference to the thinker and his survey
of his own drama from that standpoint reminds us
of one great characteristic of his poetry—we mean
the way in which you have over and through it
all the suggestion, and even the expression, of
the poet's personality, the free mind of the poet.
Browning is not, and for many reasons could
not be, as Shakespeare is thought to have been
in this. His mind and personality are impressed
upon his work, and conveyed through it to his
readers who can read. And after all talk about
the duty to hide and suppress personality in
poetic work, vital contact with a true and strong
poet is surely one of the most stimulating and
precious things poetry can give you. But will
not this interfere with the truth and balance of

the work? That will, of course, depend on how
it is done, and it must in no case be primary or
obtrusive; but the dramatic presentation may
surely be made, though you have about and
beyond that the mind of the poet: and what is
the dramatic element when most vital but some
part of the mind of the poet?

In any case, careful readers of Browning admit
that in most parts of his work, and these the most
animated and striking parts, you find the poet
himself suggested or expressed. We do not
mean his opinions, but something more and
deeper—*the man and his mind.* You feel a rich
and strong nature, a fresh and vigorous spirit;
you have stimulated energy of feeling, thought,
and will. This is why some find him "hard."
He is too active and aggressive for them. But it
is a reason why others read him in spite of objection to subjects and style. They feel in his work
an ardent and potent mind. They get from him
the impression of greatness. Even in poems they
do not care about as a whole, they get the impulse
of vital power; they feel the depths of thought
and passion; they get a sense of mastery, force
and reality.

And this though it may be said that the per
sonality of the poet is an *unknown quantity*, re
served, subtle, and elusive, " always self-asserting
yet never defined; probably as mysterious to th
poet as to his readers," as Mrs. Orr finely wrot
in the *Contemporary Review.* But this is no
because the poet is not present in his work, or i

withdrawn from his readers. It is because the man and his genius make a complex body of powers in very stable equilibrium. His nature is full, and it is well balanced—intellectual and passionate; idealistic, yet concrete and accurate; spiritual, but shrewd; a " seer " and a " mystic," but also a humorist and a " man of the world "; capable of intense meditation, and also of keen activity and enjoyment; resolute of will and compact of soul, yet tender and brotherly.

Nor is it possible to say how you get all this and more; and another good critic, touching this point, speaks of it as quite inexplicable, comparing our poet, in this matter of personal communication and influence through his work, with Cardinal Newman, a great part of whose influence has been of this kind. But communication of the living spirit, of " the incommunicable qualities and secrets of the soul," is only partly explicable in any striking case of it. Poetic work is more finely adapted than any work for this expression and suggestion; and poetry like Browning's, everywhere in touch with men and with life, must be more living than most, conveying much of the poet through themes and tone, through what is said and what is reserved.

The poet is there, anyhow, to qualify and animate the work, and to give in subtle ways intercourse with his nature. And it is seldom in literature or in life that you find such substance and strength, warmed with such passion and kindled by such fire. And this, which is part

of the power, is also part of the worth of this
poetry. Its masculine quality, its intellectual
force, its impartiality, its irony, yet spiritual
tenderness and depth, reflect the mind and the
poet.

And this poet's *sense of personality* is exception-
ally strong, and has been so ever since he made
himself known through literature. It is so in
" Pauline." And this is not merely an aspect of
his energy of will and force of brain ; it is not
always found with these : it is a principle of his
mind and of his genius, so intense that it seems
a central idea, and has given his dramatic work
its keen individualism. So marked and pervasive is this principle that some take it as the
chief ideal and quality of the work. All his " persons " have something of the intense personality
of the poet ; the greater figures among them have
it in a degree that makes them unique in modern
poetry. The depth and power with which they
realise themselves, with which they live and illustrate life, is extraordinary. Both the personality
of the poet and the principle of his art give his
poetry a keen animation, and render his persons
in the scope of passion and consciousness. And
this principle is in deep agreement with the poet's
spiritual ideas, since he has such ; as Mrs. Orr
sees, it is a central spiritual truth as well as a
principle of art. Every dramatic " argument," and
all the poet's thoughts turn upon it. Knowledge
and faith derive their quality and get their scope
from it. In other terms, the individualism of his

art rests on a strong sense of the individuality of thought, the unique import of self-consciousness, the spirituality of mind. Self-conscious mind is the chief fact known to us—is strictly the one fact known by us, and as it is for us the centre of the mystery of experience and its final fact, so it must be the master-key to its meaning, implying it may be an Eternal mind, source, and home of all minds. And if it be said that this intense consciousness and spiritual energy is so rare that Browning's art is untrue in this, as in its tense passion and strong speech, the objection is met by reminding the critic that the persons are chosen in those moments and situations when, if ever, they throw themselves into keen self-expression, and realise themselves to the full.

CHAPTER IV

PAULINE

"PAULINE" is dated October 1832. It was printed, scarcely published, in January 1833, without the poet's name. It was not reissued until 1868, and then the poet explained that it was reissued with "extreme repugnance, of necessity," because certain "misprints" were being put forth to gratify public curiosity in regard to this poem. It was then printed without change. But in the final edition of his works he "removed solecisms, mended the metre, and strengthened the phraseology" a little.

He speaks of the work as "boyish," as an "eyesore" to him, and as recording against him the faults of his youth. It was done when he was but twenty years. It is youthful and it has faults. But besides the interest and significance the poem has in relation to the poet's after work, it has in itself not a few points of interest, and in parts of it no small poetic merit, freshness, and beauty. One can well understand its interest for early discerning readers. One can see why Mill liked it, and why Rossetti loved it. Its literary sympathies, its spiritual temper, its climate of thought, its romantic beauties, and a certain soft musical quality explain its charm for Rossetti, its interest for Mill and others.

It is entitled " A Fragment of a Confession." The confession is of a life, an experience, and is made to Pauline, by a somewhat nebulous " hero," who had loved her, and returns after various vague and unsatisfactory experiences to her love, her soft sheltering breast. It is a confession made in the stress of a crisis, whose nature is even more obscure than the hero's career and character. He has gone through much, and suffered much, inwardly at least, and as result some revolution impends; but naturally, considering the theme and the youth of the poet, what the fruit of all was to be is left very much in the clouds.

The author spoke of it as " the only crab " remaining of a certain " shapely tree of life," which he dreamed to rear in what he calls his " fool's paradise " of youthful fancy and ambition. This refers to a scheme of dramatic studies of typical souls," which he projected in his comparative ignorance of life, though such a scheme shows the bias and hints, the range and energy of his mind even then. And " Pauline " is a study of one such " typical soul," filled in and presented as he could, at the time—a " typical soul," we say, not a " character "—and presented through its own narrative of the experiences and moral states by which it has been led to the crisis, which is the occasion of the " confession " to Pauline.

Regarded as a " type " the general features and

qualities of the lover of Pauline can be indicated, if not drawn, though the precise series of states and experiences through which he is described as passing is a more obscure affair. The author spoke of it as "a crude preliminary sketch" giving hints of the subject. This it surely does. The "speaker," we said, is the lover of Pauline, but he has been, he implies, faithless to her, and it may seem but little faithful to any one or anything, save a vague, expansive, and greedy "self." He is in fact the sort of spiritual egotist, so often found from the days of "La Nouvelle Héloïse" and "Werther" to those of "Don Juan." His guiding principle has been a devotion to a sort of "ideal self," conceived as a unit and apart; and of this "self," the main feature has been a craving for an ever fuller consciousness of life, emotional and intellectual. It is the filling of consciousness to the brim that has been his quest, not with vulgar pleasures, though even such pleasures are likely to count when such is the quest—not with vulgar pleasures, but with the pleasing and stimulating side of all higher things —with art and thought and humanistic admirations, with philanthropic and religious passion too as bringing the beat of a fuller pulse, and the throb of an ampler life. He would be all men nay all things, would enter into all experience and know the thrill of all life, in all its stages He has been restless, ambitious. He is profuse in his confessions of follies, excesses, shames even and one can see that though these are only hinted

as the young poet had no grasp of such things
then; and the "tale" as far as it gets is of emotions,
aims, ideas, not deeds at all, that these errors
were likely to come to such a mind in this world.
No one who sets out with such a principle, with
such an aim, can miss these among the conditions
of human life. To place as one's nearer and farther
aim the sentimental and conscious gratification of
self is to grasp at best a shifty and uncertain, at
worst a mischievous and disastrous, clue amid the
waves of passion and the ways of life.

And the reason why the young poet chose
such a "type" so early in his career, and for the
only one of his "monodramas" he ever worked
out, is surely thus implied above. It was because
the type drawn, the mood expressed, had been
often found, especially among cultivated and
poetic persons, since the rise of modern senti-
mentalism and self-consciousness. Rousseau is
the literary type of it, though he did not invent
it. Even Goethe had to work it off in "Werther,"
and it is part of the trouble of Faust. Byron has
much of it. And even Shelley brings airs of it,
not wholly cleared off by his generous ardours.
In fact, "Pauline" owes something of its theme
to "Alastor."

We have said that neither the stages, nor the
conclusion of the experience typified in "Pauline,"
are clearly given. The poet was too young to do
either. But there is perhaps more significance
than has been recognised in the fact that so soon
he drew the type, and saw its defects and dangers,

while seeing its value and virtue too. Your self-conscious cultism, your sensitive spiritual egotism, your quest of the Infinite through the life of the emotions, or through a life of personal gratifications, breaks down. The poet has intuition of this, though he cannot yet work it out. While he felt deeply that we not only may, but must, seek expansion, fulfilment, he saw thus early, if vaguely, that we are set henceforth to that quest of the Infinite which is the trouble and the greatness, in art and life, of the modern time. But how through the life of thought and action, of love and duty, this quest is to be approached, he does not here suggest, except so far forth as his poor " hero " confesses the error and defect of his past search, and indicates love and lowliness as a better way. It is, however, a problem that has been before the modern spirit for long years and in several forms, and to it we shall find the poet return again and again through his studies of the moral and mental life of his time. It is, in the next poems he made, more fully grasped—in " Paracelsus " and " Sordello." It is in the " Grammarian," and naturally in " Rabbi Ben Ezra " as a noble ethic.

There are other points of much interest in " Pauline," some of which have been touched before. Browning's early culture, his love of the Greek myths and poets, his idealism and admiration for Plato, his love of Shelley, his appreciation of Keats,—all these are in it; and besides these we find certain traits of his own mental character, and the fine romantic notes of his first poetic style.

As regards the first point, some of the most
striking lines of the poem, and remarkable for a
youth of twenty years, are from the poet's own
character.   They are the lines on pp. 14, 15 of
the final edition, beginning—

> I am made up of an intensest life,
> Of a most clear idea of consciousness
> Of self, distinct from all its qualities.

Then further on this other point—

> A mind like this must dissipate itself,
> But I have always had one lode-star; now,
> As I look back . . .
> A need, a trust, a yearning after God :
>
> .   .   .   .
>
> . . . I saw God everywhere.

—that is an intense individuality, a deep religious
passion, and a strong conviction that the passions
and problems of the mind must somehow find
their goal and their solution in a Supreme spirit.
At a later point, at a point just past the editor's
apology for the hero's excitement and obscurity,
on pp. 37, 38 he recurs to the same idea as his
clue, and has these touching lines—

> Can I forego the trust that He loves me ?
>
> .   .   .   .
>
> O thou pale form, so dimly seen deep-eyed !
>
> .   .   .   .
>
> Have I been keeping lonely watch with Thee
> In the damp night of weeping Olivet,
> Or dying with Thee on the lonely cross,
> Or witnessing Thine outburst from the tomb ?

The references to music in "Pauline" are also from the poet's own mind, p. 18; *cf.* 41—

> . . . . music (which is earnest of a heaven,
> Seeing we know emotion strange by it,
> Not else to be revealed).

And there are many fine touches of romantic fancy, not a few lines of lovely nature-poetry, and that thrill of fresh passion at the interest of life and the beauty of the world, which the very first critic of the poem, to his honour, felt in it.

> . . . violets opening from sleep like eyes.

> The morning swallows with their song-like words

> . . . whose renown springs up
> Like sunlight which will visit all the world.

> . . . two lonely things
> Created by some power whose reign is done,
> Having no part in God or His bright world.

Or these regarding Greece, as seen through Greek literature, p. 16—

> Yet, I say, never morn broke clear as those
> On the dim clustered isles in the blue sea.

Or the noble lines on Agamemnon, p. 26—

> . . . that king,
> Treading the purple calmly to his death,
> While round him, like the clouds of eve, all dusk
> The giant shades of fate, silently flitting,
> Pile the dim outline of the coming doom.

Or the lines on Andromeda, pp. 29, 30—

> . . . so beautiful
> With her fixed eyes, earnest and still.

CHAPTER V

PARACELSUS

" PARACELSUS " was Browning's first published work, for " Pauline," though printed, was scarcely published. And " Paracelsus " was published in 1835 when the poet was in his twenty-third year.

As very early work it has its interest—interest in regard to the poet—interest with regard to the time when it was done.

A poet's early work, whatever its essential value, has value with reference to the poet himself. His early interests, bias, ambitions, show in such work, the points at which he began in the freshness of his powers and early grasp of life.

" Paracelsus " has this interest plainly written upon it. The themes that drew and engaged our poet of two and twenty years, his early enthusiasm and affinities of thought, the questions his mind was busy with, the lives that interested him, his first quality in the study of man, and the art he then affected,—these are all plainly declared in Paracelsus."

And such work in given cases, in this case, has also interest with reference to the time during which was done. The silence of ten years had been

broken by only one new and significant poet.
Young Tennyson had done his first works when
Browning, still younger, came forth to take up and
extend the great traditions of English verse, as
they had been left by the group of romantic poets
whose early deaths left the blank in English verse
spoken of above. Both the classical, romantic, and
national strains and interests were obvious in
Tennyson from the first pretty strongly, and
a tendency to lyrical and dramatic-lyrical poems.
In Browning the romantic had clearly the upper
hand, and a strong human and ethical interest;
and his tendency was to the same dramatic standpoint and form.

"Paracelsus" then, just because it is early work,
has these points of interest; and, it must be added,
as early work, as youthful work, it has its faults,
its defects, plainly written in the structure and on
the face of the poem. We can be quite frank
about that without involving any disrespect to our
poet, or to the interest of his theme.

The poem has grave faults and defects of
structure, quality, and style. It is diffuse. The
dramatic situation and motives are by no means
clear. The characters or the types—for the figures
are rather types than persons—are by no means
distinct. The speeches are numerous and lengthy
—too many and too long, often. And there is a
times that "excess" of phrase and colour which
young romanticists mostly fall into.

Such faults are on the surface of "Paracelsus,"
and have made it easy for some to set it aside

and give reasons for doing so. Its merits are somewhat more involved, and ask tolerance, study, and sympathy with the theme of the poem, and the aim of the poet to ascertain them. But the merits are solid, and the poem has essential interest. There is a wonderful fluency and abundance of style. There is so much poetry and thought in it, and it leaves so many passages of fine poetry and noble thought in the memory, that one recurs to it with pleasure, even from the heights of the poet's stronger and fuller work.

You infer that we do not defend the scheme and build of the poem. We do not. As regards the scheme and build of "Paracelsus," one can hardly defend that. It is not drama, nor is it mono-drama—dramatic-lyric. It is a dramatic poem. Now, we are not going into the vexed question whether a poet may make poetic drama to be read; if it express his mind, and he can get it read, he probably will make it—that is, if its production vitally interests the poet, and the product his readers. But, if "drama" of any sort be made, we must have *personæ* vitally acting and reacting on each other, and together bringing the conclusion; and if the drama could never be "played," never be spoken, it must still be evolved under its conditions in and through its *dramatis personæ*.

Now we are probably pretty well agreed that Paracelsus" does not fulfil these conditions or meet these tests. We have said that the *personæ* are not persons. Aprile is a type, Michal is a type, even Festus. Paracelsus is vital and fairly

8

defined. But it is not merely a series of scenes rather than a drama, but the "persons" do not steadily act and react on each other to evolve the conclusions. Paracelsus alone "acts." It is true the others have some influence on him, largely passive, indirect; but the drama of his career in its power and its weakness springs chiefly from within. The development is the development of the mind and character, of the genius of Paracelsus; the others, even Festus, and Festus even in the last scene, are quite subsidiary to the play of his mind and will.

The poet himself was aware of the objections that might be made to his form. In a preface to the edition of 1835, which it is a pity he has not retained in its place, he explained that his design was to display, not the external things that led to the internal results, but so to display the internal results as to suggest the external factors, and even the incidents leading to them, his care being for the mind and for results there.

The æsthetic problem he is thinking of is thus made plain. Drama uses a more or less external machinery of actions, events, and persons to develop its story and present its characters. And this method has advantages and restrictions. Is there, then, a method and form of dramatic art that, while keeping external elements and factors in the background, shall be able to fill the foreground vividly with the characters in action, and at the same time give the story, the circumstances

the factors, so far as these are essential to understand the history and qualities of the soul of the
man in himself? The poet held there is. " Paracelsus," anyhow, is not such a form, though the
aim of the poet, and the quality of the poem in
certain respects, are dramatic, and keenly so.

But though Browning did not find his form he
found his theme and his field of work. He entered
the province he was to make his own. He took
up the study he was to prosecute to the end. In
a phrase of his own, " Paracelsus " is a " Study of
a Soul." It is the development of a life through
inward growth and debate, through outward experience, friendship, work. It elicits and presents
the crises and results, it implies and so far unfolds
the factors and incidents in the development of a
life; and it does this chiefly through the mind of
the man who lived it.

The interest of the soul in this sense may of
course be questioned. It may be matter of doubt
how far this way of inward research brings out
really and accurately the life of man. And men
are likely to be divided to the end of time on the
relative pertinences and interests of the worlds of
act and action, and the world of thought, emotion,
motive, character. Browning anyhow, as thinker
and poet, has always been clear on the point. He
has always affirmed the interest of the inner world,
and the value of the knowledge of it. And for
that view his poetry is the *apologia* — a long
and strenuous defence of the interest and value
of the life of man—of man in and for himself.

Many of us seem to think that conduct and the outward relations of our lives are the whole of life. It is held to be vain, morbid, even to concern one's self about anything further—to spend care on, to turn regard to the inward order or spirit. If the outward order and relations be right all will be right. And much can be said for that view and régime. The court being set among the ways of practical life, the judge being common sense, and the jury the men who seem to have fixed much attention on themselves of late—" the men in the street"—the case for an active and wholly outward life can be made to seem complete. Nay, even in the court of conscience, in certain schools of ethics at least, it is made to appear so.

But it is not so, and though our poet does not moralise about it, it is one of the outstanding " lessons" of his whole art that the inner order, the springs and play of life within, are of essential account. The centre and ground of the drama of life are there. You must find and know the man there to know him really; you must test matters by their results on the soul. Harmony with self and not with the out nature only is our obligation and our law.

Such words and Browning's conception may of course be taken narrowly, and in such a way as to miss the true sense. The very use of the word " soul" may seem to involve things that men are not agreed about, and that are outside the scope of literature as such. It is the word

Browning uses and prefers. But he uses it in its freer, its fuller sense, for the man within, in all his vital elements; and what is meant is, that the interior facts and laws are of first-rate interest in our study and towards our knowledge of man, as they are of capital value in culture and well-being.

The way in which Browning came to take this view, to choose this theme, to take this special field in the study of man, is an interesting question; and such a poem as this of " Paracelsus " coming then, and coming so early in the poet's career, and with the qualities it has, raises the question. We need only say here that this more inward note, developing towards what is sometimes called psychological subtlety and search, came in with the romantic revival in Germany and England. It is in Goethe and Schiller. It is in another way in Wordsworth. It is very much in Coleridge. It is in Shelley. It was not only a new sense of the interest of all human facts. It was a new and haunting sense of the depth of the life of man; as it is often put, it was a sense of the infinity of human passion and of human nature.

We shall touch on this aspect of the poem again. For the present we turn to the poem and its theme, and have to consider the relation of the design and form of the poem to its subject. What is this relation ? The poet claims that it is dramatic, historic, and that under the conditions of art chosen he has " presented " Paracelsus. In what way, then, are the man and his story

" presented " ?   The poem is no story or picture
of the life and deeds of Paracelsus, no scrupulous
reconstruction of facts, so far as they have come
down to us, whether it gives us the personality
or not.   Browning, indeed, says that the poem
might be put within the leaves of any good life
of Paracelsus as an interpretation of the man and
his aims.   And, in a sense, we may allow that
true.   Browning knew the facts and grasped fairly
the ideal aims of the life, but not closely or
exactly.   He fills the " story" with his own
mind, with his time, with the modern spirit.   And
so, it is a larger part of the truth to say that
the story of Paracelsus, as it has come down to
us, would not have suggested the inner story here
told to any one but Browning in the year 1835.
The poem is not, in other words, so much the
actual man as a poetic-spiritual interpretation of
his ideas and motives, seen from the poet's standpoint and through the poet's mind.   Not a true
story, then, do you say, but only an imagination ?
But are not the sincere creations of a poet's mind
truer than " true stories "—truer to the heart of
man ?

It follows, of course, that in reading " Paracelsus," though you are not kept close to the facts
you must know them in outline at least, and the
age of Paracelsus, to understand the aims and
ideas, the central figure, the scope of the poet in
his " study" of this soul, of this mind and this
life, and of life from this point of view.

Paracelsus was born in 1493, the year after th

discovery of America, and died in 1541, two
years before Copernicus. He won fame and
honour, also dubious reputation and dishonour,
as a physician and chemist. In both lines his
services and *ideas* were critical and valuable. He
felt deeply, and boldly proclaimed the absurdity
of the medical notions and practice of his time.
He led a revolt against authority and tradition,
appealed to experience broadly, and set himself
to seek facts. He sought, however crudely, to
put medicine on the ways of knowledge. He
brought physic into some relation to chemistry.
He had a right idea of the nature of diseases, and
insisted on the need to study them in their course
and growth. He introduced some valuable medi-
cines. In all such points he got sight at least of
a new era in medical art.

And the man was ambitious and original. His
desires outwent the desires of ordinary men, as
his ideas in important points surpassed the science
or the ignorance of his time. But he was not
scientific. He came too soon for that, and he
had not the temper for it. He came in the
transition time, when the dawn of scientific ideas
and method was beginning to touch the horizon
of the modern mind. He is a mystic, with a
leaning to magic as well as to observation, what
is called an occultist. It was a natural position
for " students of nature " in his time. But he had
such impatience, audacity, and vanity as to make
it specially dangerous for him.

And the age was transitional in other great

matters, and well fitted to bring out the strength
and weakness of such a man. It was the age of
Luther and Erasmus—of the Reformation and
the Renaissance ; the age of Columbus ; the age
when feudalism and scholasticism and Catholicism
had broken down in the social, mental, and moral
orders, and when the first great period of modern
life began. It was a time of much discontent
with the past, a time of expansive thought and
desire, and Paracelsus shared its spirit. In medicine he was something of a Luther, using something of Luther's methods—" burning their books,"
as Luther the papal bull, and, with fiery tongue,
denouncing their errors, that he might free the
bodies of men, as Luther thought to free their
souls. He provoked bitter opposition, of course.
Unfortunately, his aims and methods were not
pure and high. He was something of a quack as
well as a dreamer, and so laid himself open to
disaster.

The poem is an attempt to present vitally and
explain the course and aims of such a man, keeping closely by the circumstances of his life so far,
but construing the inner life more freely. The
man, the age, the failure, and the results of his
mind and his life, are all so construed as to
disclose their inner truth and their significant
relation to human experience.

The poem is presented in five scenes, marking
the crises in the course and trial of Paracelsus
and Paracelsus himself is made to express what
at those times passed through his mind—hi

"moods in their rise and progress." These
scenes are taken from his life, and turn on
events of his life. Along with him, a very few
other "persons" are brought in. They give
occasion for his speeches, and their lives and
tempers make his more distinct by contrast.
They also give an element of beauty and
interest to his career by "touches of nature"
and strains of human kindness. You are the
more disposed to take interest in and have
patience with Paracelsus in his singular and
solitary career when you see the kindness Festus
and Michal had for him. And their careers,
their gentle passions, and simple satisfied love,
their lives of an ordinary type, not only plant
you on the earth, but make more distinct the
so different life of the bold and restless
thinker.

In the first scene Paracelsus and his friends
are found in a quiet garden at Würzburg, in the
autumn of 1512. Paracelsus explains the passion and purpose of his life. He sees that new
knowledge is needed. He believes it can be won,
and he devotes his life to win it. His friends
plead against his scheme, and try to draw him
from his way of seeking his end; but the glowing
speech, the energy, and radiant impulse of Paracelsus overcome them. They fall in with his
hopes, and declare their faith in him and his
greatness. The large restless search of the
man's mind, his vague hopes and ambition, his
intellectual assurance and courage, his fateful

desire, which was in the Faust legend, which was in the Tannhäuser legend, urging and urging him on,—these grow stronger through the scene, until, in his closing words, they touch their climax.

The man has high aims and a scorn of common aims. His passion is to know, and no partial knowledge can ever seem to him enough. His desire is to know "the secret of the world, of man, of man's true purpose, path, and fate." But how reach such knowledge? for he is sure God impels him to seek and will guide him to gain it. Not by the common ways, or at the usual sources. Results have shown these vain. His way must be one apart—a way of genius and daring. But surely it is wise to use the past and its gains? No! The past is wrong, or mostly wrong. The cureless ills of life prove its failure, and impress the urgent need of a better art and a deeper knowledge. To serve man by winning that knowledge is his ambition; "to serve man," but apart, in a temper of proud isolation and conscious greatness. Here is one peril. Man needs the encircling love and help of his fellows even in great tasks. Humility and sympathy are needed for the soul and for the work; pride brings failure and disaster.

So his friends remind him; but his ambition and passion for knowledge fill his soul for the time, and he bears down their fears in a great speech, telling the sort and scope of knowledge he seeks. The true knowledge, light in its fulness, is within. It is near to all. Set the sou[

free from flesh and custom and ignorance, mis-
named knowledge, and it will be found. And it
has been found partly by those who have touched
its sacred "springs." He goes to gather it so.
This is pre-scientific mysticism and "divination"
of Nature's secrets. It is the occultist, not the
scientist. And here is another danger.

We next find Paracelsus, after an interval of
nine years, at Constantinople, in a conjurer's
house seeking, it seems, the help of magic to
master life, to knows his next steps and the
future. Both situation and mood tell what has
happened since he made his "plunge" to find the
pearl of "sacred knowledge." In eager passion
and vague effort he has wearied himself in vain,
and the dangers of his method, as of his mood,
have grown clear. The great secret is unreached,
and life is going. He must mend or end matters
and his search, if it be by help of the conjurer.
He is not the man he was. Inner ruin threatens,
he feels. And though he has given all for knowledge, even youth and life, he has not won it.
And, worst of all for him, he seems to be losing
the power and freshness of the mind itself. But
"God, who is the Master Mind," surely values
mind too much to let this happen to him.

At this point Aprile, a poet, who has also come
under shadows of failure to seek the conjurer's
help, is heard singing a song of those who have
failed and are "lost." Aprile comes in. He is
one of those who have failed, and his failure
becomes the means of a warning and a lesson to

Paracelsus, just when the shadow of failure has
fallen on his life and aims. Aprile has followed
a very different course, and used a widely different
method. Aprile has loved with eager and endless
passion all things in the world and the life of
man, has sought to grasp all things and give
them to men, that men might love him for the
new sense given them of the joy and beauty of
life. But he lost himself in the egoism of sensation and passion, and in the vague sense of
loveliness he knew not how to express. His life
and powers have thus been wasted. Love and joy
were right, but the artist must know as well as
love, must " make " and not only enjoy, must
submit to the limits and master the means of the
art through which he is to give men what he sees
and feels, and perpetuate among them his joy in
and love of things.

Paracelsus sees this as the life of Aprile is put
beside his own. He has ignored love and put
aside enjoyment, caring only for knowledge. Let
Aprile know and Paracelsus love, " love infinitely
and be loved," and their tasks may yet be done.
As to the poet, it cannot be. He is spent and
dies, seeing as he dies that the true poet is he
who, without thought of self, has power to create
and give his creations to men, not because of
enjoyment only, but from love, and not from love
of things and the world only, but from love of
men. In the lesson thus learned Paracelsus seems
to himself to have " attained," the lesson being to
use the knowledge he has won in love for men,

and not to postpone service or life at the bidding
of a vague ideal passion.

With this he makes a fresh start, and in the
third scene Paracelsus is at Bâle, in 1526. It is
the mid-point of his life. Famous now, and a
professor, he is using the knowledge gathered,
and seems to have got that opportunity of serving
science and his kind which is regarded as the
right sphere for such men. How does it seem to
Paracelsus? Is he satisfied? Is this success?
He pours forth his mockery and discontent to
Festus, who is proud of his "success." He feels
himself no better than a zany in a show, the chief
fool helped by other fools in a farce. Both knowledge and opportunity seem fragmentary and
trivial beside the mind's ideal and the soul's
passion, and those about him, with their ignorance,
prejudices, and vulgar aims, make things small
and hopeless; and "truth is far away as ever."

But it may be God's will men should not reach
the knowledge which Paracelsus desires, and, if so,
our duty is to give our best and do what we can,
since we cannot do what we would. It may be
so, but he cannot rest there. He cannot shut
himself within those limits. Neither his pride
nor his hunger for knowledge will let him, and,
besides, he is at war with his duties and circumstances. He has no faith in either, or in men, or
in himself in relation to his tasks and circumstances. He foresees failure, partly from faults of
his own, and more from faults of others. His
aims are the same as ever. He has the same

scorn of common aims. He cannot love and
enjoy and rest in the good of things, and wait
for the slow progress of the world. Life is sink-
ing into compromise, and the hypocrisy of custom
and contentment. He must maintain his search,
give a wider range to thought, destroy error, and
build up the true knowledge. Why not do this
through the press, then, where his qualities need
not involve their defects? The whole of his work
could not be done that way any more than
Luther's could have been in his sphere. The
"false gods" must be thrown down visibly, with
scorn and denunciation. So these two talk and
debate together.

They have talked the night out, and as the
dawn comes, Festus, puzzled and feeling that
this life is not likely to prove satisfactory to his
friend, speaks of another. Paracelsus is fretted
for a moment by the thought, for it seems to
make this life a "makeshift"; and then he reflects that for man a life that gives scope for
"love and hope and fear and faith" is after all
best, although he, acting as if man were mind
only, has ignored these essential qualities. Anyhow his way of life is once more breaking down.

In the fourth scene he is at Colmar, in 1528,
driven from Bâle. He has sent for Festus, and
tells him how the episode at Bâle went and ended.
The affair of Leichtenfels (the patient whom
Paracelsus cured, and who, refusing him his fees,
was backed by the authorities in doing so), was
only an incident of it, the deeper cause being

aversion to his aims and ideas. He is bitter and
unstrung. And what is his plan now? "To
know and enjoy at once," he says; and the words
seem wise, but not the mood, or the life he is
living. He has neither mastered life nor self, and
his pursuit of knowledge seems more a thing of
passion than of purpose; for even while he speaks
of toil to gain it, he says, "Mind is disease, and
natural health is ignorance." And his labours
are now desperate, and, though he will not admit
that his aims are mistaken, his life proves that
they are.

It is in this spirit that he sings the song of the
men who "clung to their first fault and withered
in their pride." Will he be like them, and cling
to his first scheme, having proved its mistake, or
must he change? He can't. He must keep on
in the hope that that way will bring him to his
end. And Festus thinks there must be for such
natures another law than for most men, and a
hope that will not fail. This he is the more encouraged to think, because, if Paracelsus has sinned,
he has also loved; and the scene ends with proof
of his love, for the heart of Paracelsus is touched
when he learns the death of his friend's wife, and
he forgets for the time his own troubles to comfort Festus.

The last scene is in the hospital at Salzburg,
thirteen years after. Paracelsus is dying, and
Festus watches beside him in love and prayer.
He is slowly returning to consciousness, and dreams
of Aprile. He has heard the poet, now full of

music, chanting soft melodies all night, and in the pardon of the poet he feels the promise and the grace of his own forgiveness. Wild words follow about his own life, and then, as he dreams of Michal and Aprile together, he seeks to keep by them and love. Then he longs for the old power, for full attainment and divine approval, only to see that this world is not for such things, and that, as it is not, there must be another. Then he wanders again, and when Festus steadies him on the present, he sums up his whole "attainment," the results and lessons of his life, impartially as a mere "spectator" might do, and with the breadth and seriousness of one standing on the verge of "the boundless life." He has sinned, and he has failed, but God's praise has not missed, and he gains the high end of life now in seeing God's will as to man's scope and duty. A searching and impetuous soul, he felt himself made for some great task. Though not free from doubt, he had that inner sense and hold of things which made "the secret of the world" his—which made him, in a way thought could not explore, aware of what God is, what men and life are. And he reviews the plan of life as he sees it, and man's place in it—the ascent of life up to man; the ascent of man through the higher minds towards God; the task of the greater spirits being to anticipate and help the spiritual progress of all. His task was of this order, and his design was man's service. Yet he failed in this service. Why? Because of his pride o power and knowledge, and because he did not understand the gradual divine order of the world, or the vital uses and necessities of that order; would have made an order of his own. He thus made his task monstrous and impossible, and brought himself to despair. He then learned the place and power of love in man's life, and sought to serve men,—but still apart from them, without sympathy, without self-denial. Driven again to despair by his failure at Bâle, he then came to see that he had a further and harder lesson to learn—a lesson without which such work as his could never be done: love in his heart had to be wise and pure to discern the dim beginnings of light in the minds, of love in the hearts of other men. He had to learn trust, tolerance, hope; to see that hate even may be a mask of love, and error a stage truth. He saw at length the vital unity of the great scheme which, by long evolution of many lives, accomplishes at length the one life.

Such was the career of Paracelsus, as the young poet, even then set to these high and serious themes, understood it in 1835, such the problem of the poem as he then presented it.

But now, let us ask, does the whole seem the study of a type and career no longer significant— an impossible quest by a wrong road? It is apt to look so. And yet it is not so, and without going into details, let us try, on a survey of the whole poem, to show that it is significant as study of mind, as criticism of life. The career and pro-

9

blem of " Paracelsus " has significance, and still
further it is so presented by the poet as to grip
the life of thoughtful men in every time, and
certainly so as to touch questions that have gone
through our century, and are not in the larger
life of the age resolved yet. Let us look at
those questions.

And first, What was the *career* of Paracelsus, the
quest and *problem* of his life? The type and career of
Paracelsus certainly, as here conceived, are good for
the poet's purpose. The type is that of a man of
genius,—intellectual, aggressive, self-confident, with
thirst for new knowledge, with sense of its value,
and gleams of ways to find it. When he starts
he does not know himself or the order of life
He has to measure himself against both to find
himself and life, to learn the nature and conditions
as well as the limits of man's power.

His quest at first has been defined as a ques
for the absolute through knowledge—or say, fo
self-fulfilment through knowledge, and the prouc
and masterful uses of knowledge for others—ther
he began. He finds that mere knowledge doe
not "fulfil" even the mind, and still less th
moral life of man—the "self" so fulfilled is but
fragment of man, and leaves his deeper desire an
higher function still to satisfy and achieve. H
learns that love, not of one or two, but of me
and of the world,—love, and service inspire
and guided by love,—must *use* knowledge to kee
it from being futile. He sets about the use
his knowledge, as teacher, as physician, but wit

out *the love that is moralised*, with the love that needs men because it feels itself a fragment, but without the love that is one with men. He fails again. In reaction he throws himself upon a life whose aim is described as knowledge and enjoyment at one and the same time. But the emphasis of that means really a life of *passion*, and for a shallower and poorer nature than that of Paracelsus that life turns quickly to failure. In his case it is but the bitterness of a reaction which others have helped to provoke. Perhaps for that reason it takes some time to work it out, but when it is wrought out we find him at length accepting the gradual divine order of the world, and the vital uses and demands of that order, as one great scheme of moral evolution, which is the fulfilment of all lives through the slow advancement of all up to the high consciousness of the highest lives. And so Paracelsus passes, pressing " God's lamp " to his breast, and sure that the splendour of that light will pierce the gloom that appears to gather about the close of such a life as his.

So much in survey of what seems to us the main problem of " Paracelsus." The question of the *method* of " Paracelsus " has interested some critics, and as it appears to be coming into a kind of vogue again it may be that a word on that side of the poem will be in place. What was the method of " Paracelsus " ? Occultism we call it,— but what is that ? A kind of mystical divination we have called it. So it is; but let us explain.

Roundly, it may be said, men seek knowledge within or without, or by some combination of both—by careful generalisation of the facts of the outward nature by study of the inner facts and principles, or by some combination of these two. Occultism is a special combination of the two. It seeks the secret of knowledge and of life by intuition of facts which flash on the qualified mind with a light from the centre—that is the theory. It assumes that the sensuous meanings of things are not their true meaning. The true meaning is hid. Only, it flashes out in particular facts, and as the system of the world and life are *one*, these facts give to those who catch their meaning their hints, clues to the else unknowable secret This is not science or philosophy, but a kind of imaginative guessing—a sort of personal equation of certain minds and Nature. It not only assumes that there is more in heaven and earth than is known to any philosophy or science, but that it is not of the sort to be known by these methods or by any modes or order of research, but only by a kind of " inspiration." It did not produce much in the case of Paracelsus. It never will produce much; so some of us think. But it is recurrent passion of human nature. There is mystical sense in most of us,—not all, perhaps,—a sense of a veil, and something behind it. Our disappointment with the sensuous show of thing our disappointment with knowledge even—our sense of its limits and of the vastness beyond it—our yearning towards a Reality that sha carry reason and desire to the height, and meet them there—these and like things and emotions in us lead to it. Spiritualism, theosophy, " psychical research," and other such phenomena express it. Browning was early interested in this side of the mind, and the facts belonging to it, and he seems early to have understood that, however little it may tell of nature, it tells much of human nature.

And this brings us to the next of the points suggested by the study of our poem as a whole, the early time when the poet found, and the way in which he kept right through, the romantic and idealist spirit. From the first, and through years and years of our century, dominated by a physical scientific temper and method, Browning stood for a fuller view of man,—let us say, he stood for man and human nature against a merely physical order, a mechanical nature. He was a man of *facts*, but the facts that interested him, and that seemed to him for ever significant, were the facts of human nature—the facts of thought and feeling, and of all the passion and all the endeavour of man. These facts seemed to him supreme in the world as we know it. And if it be our aim to understand that world, if we seek squarely to make out its meaning, we must keep these facts in their place, and read them to the heart of them. And though we may not set out to guess and construe the meaning of the outward nature, of he kosmos, by casual gleams and guesses, and a kind of inspired reaction of our minds on single and exceptional facts, we must hold by the principle, that the age-long aspiration and higher reason of man are a clue to the meaning and to the destiny of things—that unspeakable problem which Agnosticism tried to shut out, but which is coming back by queer ways on many who fancied they were done with it.

There is another question, at once old and new, which "Paracelsus" raises and illustrates; —the question raised by the contrast between Aprile and Paracelsus in their types of mind, in their ideas of life—knowledge the one, we say, and love the other. And some critics of Browning hold that Browning, more or less all through his work, and very definitely in the later period of it, esteemed *love* and condemned *knowledge* as an organ of interpretation with reference to the question we have just alluded to—the question of life's larger meaning. Browning, these critics hold, is agnostic as regards knowledge—trustful as regards love. He has little faith in philosophy, but much in the heart. The formulations of science will bring you little or nothing for " the life eternal," but the great emotions, the great sentiment of religion, is the breath and medium of that eternal life. So they read him.

What is to be said? This, we think, is what is to be said,—that such critics fall into the error of reading Browning's terms too narrowly, and measuring a poet by a philosophical standard. As regards "Paracelsus," for example, Aprile does not stand for mere feeling. The poet, the artist, cannot work through emotions only. In point of fact, no mind ever does. And though the stress may here seem to be, may be, on emotions, and though some have unwisely laid it there in expounding Browning, let us urge, from all we know of the poet, that that is not the whole truth in regard to him. There is no doubt a sort of thinking that is all head, as there is a sort of love that is all heart—if one may be paradoxical in order to get the meaning clear. But there is another sort—a heart within the head—a head within the heart—which, upon moral and practical questions, is the ground of wisdom. We take it, Browning recognised this. His love is the intuition of the larger life, of the right posture and temper upon the larger questions. And we cannot think he would have favoured that division of human powers, that split of human nature, which some favour in order, it may seem, to get the "oracle" to speak their own message. Only that which is *wise*, tested by experience and the total nature, can continue to satisfy—can be held for truth in life. Our highest knowledge of reality, if it do not come to us through—and into that we do not here enter —must be certified to us by the *whole mind* and the whole of life. In "Saul," in "The Epistle of Karshish," in the pope's speech in "The Ring and the Book," in part of "Ferishtah's Fancies," and finally in the poem called "Reverie" in "Asolando," our poet gave his conviction, his intuition as a poet and critic of life, on this great matter. It comes to what has just been said, though a fuller statement must be postponed.

Another leads us out upon a further question deeply implied in " Paracelsus," though a little in the background. I mean the question, Where, and what, is *satisfaction*? and how does a man reach that solution of the vital problem which gives him mastery, power, peace, reconciliation, and rest, a clue to living as to all else that presses on him out of the erewhile unknown infinite?

This question hangs over " Paracelsus " right through, and is, as was indicated at the opening of our study of " Paracelsus," the echo in poetry of the question with which our century began both in the spheres of art and thought; forced on life by the revolt from the old régime, forced on thinkers by the course of thought. It goes without saying, that the question really raised was not new. It was, indeed, the old question under new conditions and in new terms so far,—the question that haunted the spirit of man at the close of the classical age in Greece and Rome, at the opening of the Christian era. It is a question that came into modern life with the Renaissance. It is in the old Faust legend, and in Elizabethan literature in the drama of Marlowe and of Shakespeare. It revived with a new subtlety and breadth at the beginning of the century. Forced on thinkers by Hume, grappled by Kant in philosophy and by Goethe in his spheres of art and criticism; it is felt in Shelley and in Byron—the large desire, the restless search, the pain of discord with the world as it is, the longing for a surer and fuller knowledge, for a better world and a divine life. It is the question we are still working out, and in truth it has always to be freshly stated and resolved anew.

What is to be said? That man as man seeks and must seek the infinite—seeks and must seek "the life eternal." But how? Some through the life of feeling, of art or pleasure; some through the life of knowledge, through thought and the gains of science; and some through action, through power, through the life of affairs. And there are those who tell us that the infinite is not to be come at by man any way, though they see man impelled by thought, and by passion, and by will, to seek it. How, then, is it? We bring the full question of such lives as those of Paracelsus—of such dramas as "Hamlet" and "Faust"—of such poetry as that of Byron, and of Shelley even, to their most vital point in that question, and what is the answer? A fine writer recently gone from us, Walter Pater, spent much of his time over this very question, child of his time as he was. At first in the Renaissance essays he said, seek it in keen and vivid moments, in pure and lovely sensations. In *Marius* he gave that up, and set forth how ideas and ideals have more to do with it. And in *Gaston de Latour*, so lately published, he was back at the old question again, to affirm and illustrate how the great sentiment of religion must be met, and has the clue.

Now, what is to be said of the question thus raised? Two things, we take it, speaking from

our present standpoint, and within the scope of
"Paracelsus": (1) that no final intellectual solution is to be had or imposed; (2) that a moral
solution, reached through such discipline of life as
brings us at length into touch with life's facts, is
to be had and meets our need.

We say, no final intellectual solution of the vital
problem is to be had. This is why all solutions
are apt to seem only a compromise, in which you
are started on a high level and are left depressed
and disappointed at a lower one. The lesson of
life is that we must seek, and that rightly seeking
we find, a moral solution, and such solution meets
the vital and practical needs of life. As to the
relations between the two, that does not come in
here. But what is this solution as "presented"
here? Some "doctrine, simple, ancient, true"—
so true and old that it leaves us where men have
always stood; or some great idea which makes
"all things new," which has been the spiritual
desire of many of us? The answer is surely that
it is faith in the ideal, and faith in the fact, faith
in ideals of the reason and the conscience, and
faith in the practical life of man—in the social
life and common good of men. Love and service,
union with man in work, progress and eternal
hope,—on that line only men can find both scope
and rest—rest from the burden of insoluble
problems, and impulse for all labour and endurance.

And if it be said, on survey of the whole, that
this question is so essentially a *modern* question

that the poet is scarcely justified in carrying it into the Reformation era and the life of Paracelsus, this is matter of criticism. There is fair warrant for it, as we have seen. The intellectual excitement and vague aspiration of the story of Paracelsus and the legend of Faust belong to the same moods and the same period; and these have in many respects been repeated on a larger scale and with clearer consciousness in our era. This Goethe felt in selecting the Faust legend to depict through it the modern spirit, and so Browning probably felt in taking this theme. Intense individualism and restless aspiration belong to many of us more than to Paracelsus; and to this spirit, full of the passion for knowledge, and haunted by great questions, a moral solution of the problem of life has sometimes seemed an impertinence. It was all the solution Goethe had to give. It was the solution Comte offered from a different point of view. It is in a large sense the outcome of philosophy too. And though Browning has thought the question out more maturely in later work, it is the spirit of his thought that for the cardinal problem of life no other solution is possible.

CHAPTER VI

SORDELLO

"SORDELLO" was Browning's next work, and remained, until the publication of "The Ring and the Book," his most elaborate poem. Still more strongly than "Paracelsus," it marks the matters that were of interest to him in his early years of poetic work, his intellectual power and high purpose.

It is harder reading than "Paracelsus"; it even remains, with perhaps two exceptions, the most illegible, the least read, of all the poet's works. Most of his readers, and many of his critics, put it aside in impatience or despair. Some admit they have not read it, and don't mean to; others declare that they have tried and failed—and life, they think, is too valuable and too busy to be spent laboriously over the mysteries of the career of a dreamer who did nothing, and whose inward achievement seems a blank or a puzzle.

And the poem is hard reading for the best practised; nor is it, save in parts, pleasant for the most devoted. Now, why is this? Is it the weight of matter or the depth and subtlety of ideas in the poem? We cannot think so, and those

are not the reasons why some have broken down
with it. It appears to us that its ideas are
capable of such statement as should bring them
within range of readers of the poet's other works.
What, then, is it that makes the poem so great a
trial of patience, and even of wits? Is it the
theme, the structure, or the style? All three
have to do with the matter. As to the subject,
the poet said long after that it had roused but
little interest. The structure of the poem is
seldom satisfactory and often unsuitable; and
the style has many faults—undue condensation,
strange ellipses, abrupt transitions, long paren-
theses, an original and unpleasant use of inverted
commas, and many things brought in that add
to the substance, but not to the essential matter
of the poem, and that certainly do not conduce
to the clearness of the poem.

The poet thought of re-writing the poem (*vide*
Dedication to edition of 1863), and one fears that
is the only cure for its faults. But it was not
possible, of course. He might have made another
poem on the same theme; he could not remake
the "Sordello" of 1840. So all he did was to
put that analysis of the poem which you find in
the form of headlines to the pages—brief lines
that are often useful and often useless.

But for all its faults "Sordello" is well worth
study. It has fine thought and poetry to reward
its mastery. In every such poem there is part of
a poet's mind expressed that he does not again
express; and great matters both of life and art

are here. And so, without attempting exposition in full detail, it may be enough to explain the source and theme of the poem, its plan and course of thought, and the poetical and vital questions it throws light on.

"Sordello" is a study similar in theme to "Paracelsus," though different in method, and in the type and career chosen. In Paracelsus you have the student and thinker; in Sordello the type is poetic. He is more like Aprile than Paracelsus, though there are marked differences. Then, in "Sordello" the whole story of a poet's life and growth are told, and told through the mind and with commentary of the author himself. The structure of the poem results from this. In its form it is narrative; but the story is so told, and is so much broken by reflection and dramatic statement (brought in by help of inverted commas), that the form proves unfit for the matter, and is one of the chief causes of the difficulty of the poem.

Browning calls the attempt made in "Sordello" *quixotic*, and describes its design as a "*study of incidents in the development of a soul.*" And the poem is one of the first examples on a large scale of that kind of study. But "Sordello" has much matter that hardly comes within that design. The story of Sordello in its historical circumstances, the poetic function with its duties and perils, and the spiritual problems illustrated by the life and failure of Sordello, are the matter of the poem, and from elaboration of those three

lines of interest comes part of its difficulty. The
poet was thinking of his own art, and of a special
type of experience in relation to its higher tasks.
He was thinking of the poet in contrast with the
man of action, and in relation to the duties of the
world. The career of Sordello interested him,
because it gave scope for that theme, and led up
to still larger spiritual problems.

The *subject* was suggested in part by the special
position of the Mantuan poet Sordello in early
Italian literature. Sordello was a troubadour,
born in 1194, who wrote under Provençal influence and mainly in that dialect. He is the most
distinguished of Italian troubadours, and his service lay in what he did towards the rise of modern
literature in Italy; the help he gave in rousing
the Italian mind to, and preparing the Italian
language for, the expression of poetic thought.
Sismondi speaks of "the harmony and sensibility
of his verses," and also of the "pure and delicate
style" of some of his songs, which have been
collected. Yet his fame afterwards came less
from what he did as a poet than from what he
was said to have done as a knight. Sismondi
quotes him as the most striking instance of the
way in which the troubadour was invested with
chivalric glories, and became the hero of romantic
adventures.

But the *conception* and *theme* came rather out
of the "Purgatorio" than out of the history or
the legends about Sordello, for Dante's words
about him, and not his own verses or fame, have

kept his name alive. Dante treats him with respect. He recognises his place; he ascribes dignity and chivalry to him, composure and disdain—"the manner of the couchant lion." And in the cordial greetings of Virgil and Sordello we have the meeting, not merely of two Mantuan poets, but of the classical and modern literatures of Italy (*cf.* "Purgatorio," cantos vi., vii.).

Dante calls the poet "the good Sordello"; but he places him at the entrance of Purgatory alone, yet among those who are expiating failure, and far from the Paradise of God. And the Mantuan troubadour singing, in the best verse he could make, the praises of love is a graver and more serious figure in Dante than he seems in history. We are not aware that the facts of Sordello's career warrant the notion that he had the ideas and opportunity of Dante, and missed his chance through lack of power. But there is enough in the "Purgatorio" to suggest that the great poet who founded modern Italian literature condemned the poet who came only a few years before himself, for not having done more than he did, both for the language and the literature of his country.

Browning credits Sordello with a perception of tasks and ideas that were neither conceived nor undertaken before Dante, and his poem thus becomes a study of the failure of a poet who had seen these things, but had not the power to realise them through his art. And the poem takes a still wider scope; for he not only attributes to Sordello impulses and ideas that belong to Dante, but thoughts and emotions that are more modern, and so boldly makes his poem, with all its burden of Italian history, a study of poetic culture and the proper service of the poet, and of a high type of ambition.

The Sordello of our poem, then, is, in the process and matter of it, largely a creation of Browning, but it is presented against a background of Italian history, and amid the circumstances of the life of the actual poet. There are graphic pictures of the doings and condition of Italy in that thirteenth century, when Guelf and Ghibellin were struggling so cruelly with each other in its cities, and these pictures help us to understand the difficulties, as they excuse the failure, of Sordello. As Sismondi says, the age was one of brilliant chivalric virtues and atrocious crimes—an age of heroes and monsters, among whom the figure of Sordello seems strange and out of place.

But it is in the nature of the problem, as of the method, of the poem that these things bear on its leading interest only in a general way, and the poet takes these things freely. Sordello is said to have taken passionately the side of the pope; but Dante was Ghibellin, and saw in the empire the best security for right government in Italy and Europe. And Sordello, living in Lombardy, took the same side. There are other points at which the poem departs from the history. The Mantuan poet remained, as we have implied, merely troubadour, and did not, as Browning's Sordello, leave that stage behind him, moving on to the

10

ampler scope and higher aims of the later books of the poem.

But this is much as it ought to be, and readers suffer rather from the industry of the poet in working up "all the chronicles of that period of Italian history" than from his "inventions." The figure and story of the Italian Sordello are dim, and without such importance as to engage or repay attention now. The theme as Browning conceives it, and the career as he construes it, have that importance. This kind of romances, based on the suggestions rather than the facts of history, and attaching historic names to figures so different from the people who bore them, is open to criticism certainly, and "pure invention" would have advantages; but we must take what has stimulated a poet's mind, and regard the poetic and spiritual results as our proper gain. And so with "Sordello" we follow the outlines of the story only to make those results clear.

Sordello was born at Goïto, near Mantua, where his mother died immediately after his birth, and his early years were spent there in perfect seclusion. He was, in fact, retained at the castle of Goïto by Adelaide, wife of Eccelino da Romano, who, because she feared he might prove a rival to her own son if his birth and parentage were known, kept both a secret, and gave out that he was the child of an archer named Elcorte. At Goïto he was left almost wholly to his own thoughts and wanderings, and grew up a dreamer and a poet. The place was

fitted to nourish the dreamer, if not to develop
the poet. The gloomy castle and the lonely
woods, the great font with its marble figures,
the arras with its mysterious forms, all appeal to
his fancy. A slender youth, his calm brow and
restless lip make plain his temper——one framed
to receive delight at every sense; of rich and
refined sensibility, apt to invest all things with
the colour and life of his own nature, and
quickened by a mystic sense of joy and beauty
in the world. But there are two classes of minds
endowed with such sensibility. There are those
who, blending their lives with outer things, and
aware only of their beauty, depend on the external
charm of things. They have need to belong to
what they worship. And there are those who are
roused by outer things to a fuller self-consciousness, and who turn inwards the interest and the
homage others direct outwards. So lived Sordello, pleased with his life and with his active
fancy; the real world kept out, without task or
duty, alone, moral sense and social sympathy
dormant. But he awakes; he becomes aware
that his paradise is not complete. Judgment and
a sense of the need of others are born in him.
Has he learned pity, sympathy? or is it only
an egoistic craving for a crowd in whose eyes to
live his life and show his powers? Vanity, is it?
Anyhow, not finding a " world," he makes one——
giving his own life to each figure or name in it.
In this world, and no longer in the world of
flower and tree, he now lives. Boy as he is, he

cannot act and be those folks; he can only fancy
their deeds done—can only appropriate their
powers and be in imagination what they have
been in fact. And this he will do. He will
gather all their qualities into one and be spiritually that one, and so more than the best of
them. So he imagines himself a poet-emperor.
He is Apollo, in fact, with Daphne for lover.
Nor can he doubt that for such endowment as
his this must happen some day. But when?
All has been but dream so far. Yet his dreams
touch reality as one evening he sees Palma with
her golden tresses. All that he hears of her
fixes his fancy on her. But time fleets, and he
does not yet see when or how he can escape
from Goïto, and meet the lady of his visions or
the world of men.

That time comes, however. Adelaide is at
Mantua, and Sordello has his freedom. It is the
spring, and he wanders forth, ripe, as he thinks,
for life, dreaming most of Palma. He gets out of
the woods and comes to Mantua, and beyond hope
he finds Palma. She is there, holding a court of
love under the city's walls. A minstrel is singing
of Apollo. Sordello listens. The song of Eglamor is left incomplete; Sordello takes up the song
seizes and finishes the theme with fuller passion
and surer insight. He carries the crowd with him
wins the prize, and is chosen Palma's minstrel
This triumph, so new and strange on his first
contact with the world, and this act of Palma, sen
such surprise and delight through him that, coming

on the excitement of the song, he swooned. He was carried, still unconscious, by a troop of jongleurs back to the castle of Goïto, where he lived the whole over and over again, trying to understand it, and he sees how he surpassed Eglamor, and sees, as he thinks, the poet's relation to the people. It is the part of song, made in fine enjoyment of all it sings of, to set free the fancy of others—to rouse them to see and feel the good of things.

And what of Eglamor? He sees and accepts his defeat frankly. Sordello's is the fuller song, and as his own art has been everything to him, as he has loved it and identified himself with it—finding in it the purpose and the good of his life—so now that this is lost life is without use. He dies, and is brought by a company of those among whom he had been chief minstrel, to sleep among the pine woods. Eglamor is the *typical troubadour*, who loves art for its own sake, who is more aware of his song than of the things about which he sings, or of the soul whose passion song should express, and to whom, therefore, art becomes the whole of life and an end in itself.

Thus life has begun for Sordello—the very life for which he seems to have been waiting—and now he finds out a story of his birth, and the reasons why he is at Goïto. Apollo, as he thinks himself, he is only the child of Elcorte. What can such as he do? Dream himself " monarch of the world," but only through song? Be all, but only in consciousness and imagination? Still through song and its power he may do much of what he wishes. Only, what is it he wishes? Not the perfection and triumph of his song, but the triumph of the man through the song; self-assertion and the consideration he thinks his due. Through his work he would claim and win his place among the great men of the world, holding that the power to express and depict is the power to be and to do. But is it so, and will the world take him at this estimate, or even from this point of view?

He returns to Mantua with this ambition and with these thoughts, and very soon finds that, having looked to art for ends outside art, he must use and so degrade his art to obtain these ends. And having begun, he must go on as he has begun. He does so, and pleases so far. But why not himself enjoy this life, these passions, he expresses? He is tempted to do so, only he sees that to live the life of narrow and momentary joys would be to sink the poet to please the man. The poet must grasp the soul of joy, not simple joys— "each joy he must adjure even for love of it"; to lose himself in it is to lose the power to express it. But then comes the thought that these abstractions, these "essential" passions, are not men. He will try to give men the very stuff of life. He tries, and finds the language he has to use an obstruction. He works the language to his ends "welding words into the crude mass from the new speech round him," and then, having formed so far his medium, he seeks to present an action with its actors, real and alive. But language fashioned by thought will not answer to such vital expression as he seeks. Perception may be one and whole. Thought can only be partial, abstract, and speech is its instrument. It is "as hard to obtain a muse as to become Apollo," he concludes. Still, if he cannot reach his aim and satisfy his sense of things, let him satisfy the crowd of admirers in Mantua. He sings Montfort and his exploits, but only to find that Montfort counts for them all and the singer nothing. No one dreams that the singer could do what he sings. He turns on them with angry declaration that their praise is worthless. Thus, the man at strife with the poet, and the poet with his own ideal, all goes wrong with him. He is depressed and weakened by the double discord, and, out of harmony with himself, he gets more and more out of sympathy with his circumstances. Art and life become a compromise, which naturally he can neither accomplish nor accept. He discovers a want of readiness and tact, of the shallow plausibilities that are necessary to the business. He speaks too late, and much beyond the occasion, and is easily beaten by conventional wits and minds of merely practical scope. The result is that his just confidence is destroyed. He takes his opinion and style from others, and loses himself and his proper power, and grows contemptuous towards both his work and his audience. In this mood, of course, no one is pleased. Naddo—your conventional and altogether practical person—tells him why he is failing. Let him limit his aims and keep close to life. Let him use common sense and speak to the "healthy heart of man." These things he cannot do, at least not Naddo's way, and such criticism only makes matters worse. Having lost the right ground and light within, he is swayed by every one, and his uncertainty becomes hopeless.

With matters at their worst, he is set free by events. Adelaide dies, Eccelino retires; Salinguerra, the leading soldier of the Ghibellin party, is coming to Mantua in consequence. The minstrel must prepare a song in his honour. The minstrel tries, but cannot; the power of song seems dead. So he returns to Goïto to get out of it all, and from those places of his youth reviewing his Mantuan time, all seems a mistake and failure. Why had our troubadour, starting with that first success, failed thus? Was the will itself at fault? Possibly so. And yet he resolves he "will be king again," as he drops his poet's crown into the font. How?

The months go past at Goïto once more. The troubadour episode is left behind, and his reflections bring him to a new point. He sees that life has yet to start for him—real life and positive experience, and this with the years going and youth gone. Nature can change and recover; man has but one life. He has become aware of powers he ought to use, and through whose use he will gain not enjoyment only, but life. So far he has been renouncing life to live in his art His intense self-consciousness, seeking to assert,

and complete itself, has put actual things aside.
But his art has failed to achieve his end, and his
renunciation seems now only a path of despair.
How is he to escape the dilemma thus arising?
A way opens—not that of the minstrel, but quite
another. Palma sends for him, and he goes to
see her at Verona, in the autumn of 1224. Her
father, who has withdrawn from public life and
made peace with the party of the pope, has promised her to the Guelf Count Richard of San
Bonifacio. She has no mind to marry him, and
with the help of Salinguerra she means to put
it off, and even to set it aside. She tells Sordello
of her love for him, and hints what they may do
together, with the help of Salinguerra. For years
she has aspired for his sake, seeing in him that
"out-soul" who should help and complete her
own soul, and now her hopes may be made good,
and she explains that they are to meet the great
imperialist at Ferrara, and learn the rest from
him.

Browning now introduces a long *digression*,
having come to the crisis of Sordello's life. He
is at Venice, and tells how there the impulse
to set forth the story of Sordello came to him,
and defends the kind of poetry he has made
in the poem. The digression is of much interest.
It expresses ideas important in their bearing on
Browning's aims and work, and marks the relation
of the poem to these, but belongs less to the argument of "Sordello," and so may be here omitted.

In the Fourth Book we find account of the

sufferings of Italy from both parties, leading up
to a graphic picture of the man who has spent
all his life in action—the strong, decisive soldier,
Salinguerra.   He makes a complete contrast
every way to Sordello, physically and morally.
But, leaving his story, we must follow the
career of Sordello.   What is he to make of his
chance of a great practical life?—that is for
him the question now awaiting answer.   So far
his thoughts have been of himself, even when he
thought of art.   Now he comes to Ferrara to
make a grand discovery — to find a world of
men not made for ends he has hitherto imagined,
but requiring service and manifold help; and he
is anxious to help the masses of men.   But how
can he ?   He sees that Guelfs and Ghibellins are
equally selfish and injurious — that the people
suffer terribly from both.   Is there, then, a cause
distinct from both, and higher, purer, than either ;
a cause through which mankind may triumph ?
He is pondering this question by a dying watch-
fire, full of pain at what he has seen in Ferrara,
when a sentinel bids him sing of the Roman
Tribune Crescentius.   This gives his mind a fresh
impulse, a new idea.   He dreams a dream of a
New Rome—the Mother City, whose upbuilding
should bring new life and a just order to
mankind.

But can the good of man be realised in and
through this shining city after all?   Almost as
soon as he imagined it, great shadows of doubt
fell upon it.   Such work must take ages.   The

life of man, the social order, is a slow, manifold, and practically infinite evolution. One man, one age, can only add a little to such a task. We may imagine the whole; we can never see it in fact; and our only way to realise it is to do the task of the day. But all this may help, and the work of each lives in the life of all, and the work varies as the ages do. There are ages of power and ages of knowledge, and workers who help through knowledge and workers who help by strength. The new age and order must be built up spiritually; it must work through the Church and wisdom. The empire must help it, and as the best of what he can do he will persuade Salinguerra—the soldier who has spent his years in fighting the Guelfs—to turn Guelf! Only Sordello could dream such a thing. But he throws himself into it with his new zeal for mankind, and puts forth all his passion and all his eloquence in the effort to induce the Ghibellin soldier " assist the pope, fill the scope o' the Church, thus based on all, by all, for all." At first he stumbles and hesitates; but, roused at length to his best, he essays to prove the spiritual power of the poet even over the great men of action. The poet is the highest, most enlightened, most energetic spiritual nature. By affirming the higher being, the higher truth, he is royal, and rules. In virtue of this he stands for man, and lays the behests of mankind on those who have the practical power of the world at their command.

He fails, of course. But Salinguerra is moved.
He sees the love of Palma for Sordello. It is in
his power to make any one whom he shall choose
Prefect of Northern Italy under the emperor. He
throws the badge that elects to the office over
Sordello's neck, and thus makes for him a fresh
opportunity or a great temptation. He has
pleaded for the Guelfic cause; will he, after all,
for personal reasons, take the imperial side and
marry Palma? It is then that Palma tells the
story of Sordello's birth, and makes his decision
more difficult. He is the son of Salinguerra, not
of Elcorte. The soldier is both surprised and
delighted; Sordello is surprised and confused.
To give him time to grasp the situation, Palma
draws Salinguerra away, and Sordello is left alone,
with the badge about his neck, to make his final
choice. It is the day's close—his life's close too,
as it proves—and our poet, looking into the sunset, thinks the matter out. Many arguments urge
him to close with the offer for Palma's sake, for
his own, and many plausible arguments arise
in his mind of wider bearing; but in the end
after a severe struggle, he plucks the badge
from his neck and stamps it underfoot. Palma
and Salinguerra hear the stamp, and return, to
find the badge on the floor and Sordello dying
" A triumph lingered in his eyes," and his hear
still beat as Palma " pressed in one great kiss he
lips upon his breast," but the strain had killed him

Such is the story and such the close of Brown
ing's " Sordello "; but we can hardly leave th

matter here, since it will be said that certain
questions raised by the poem have not been
answered. It is more or less clear why Sordello
failed as a minstrel, but it is not so clear why he
failed in the second half of his career, or, it may
be said, whether he failed at all, since spiritual
attainment is success, though not a complete success, and the last act of Sordello's life shows
nobility and purity of nature of a rare kind.
True, he breaks down under the strain, showing
that neither in body nor in will was he strong
enough for the tasks imposed on him ; but his
will made at least the higher choice.

As Browning puts matters, Sordello came
within sight of high tasks, both literary and
moral. He had a high conception of art and
a noble idea of the public good. But he found
no way of achieving either. He did not make
poems expressing his thought ; he did not define
and fix his ideal in life, or among social forces.
But could he have done so ? Salinguerra yawns
immeasurably at the futility of the notion, so far
as politics go. The soldier is a very imperfect
judge, we know, but his practical instincts were
right here. Neither through the Guelfs nor the
Ghibellins could Sordello have realised his ideal.
What, then, could he have done ? What Dante
did, shall we say ? He could have done the day's
task to the measure of his power, he could have
given noble expression to his ideas through his
own art, and trusted the Power that rules all.

He did neither. Why did he fail ? This

question is answered in the poem, though Dean
Church has said in his essay on "Sordello" that
it is by no means clear to him what the answer
is.   At an early point in the poem it is indicated
that Sordello is an idealist, and one of those who,
for good or evil, can never rest in his art.   The
dangers arising to such are threefold—(1) To
think life and work small beside the ideal, and
so scarcely worth troubling about by comparison ;
(2) to attempt the impossible task of forcing the
ideal within the circumstances and tasks of life ;
(3) or regarding art as a means only in the
service of man, and of the spirit, to care less for
it than is due and necessary, and so either to
seek some other way of more immediate service,
or to bend art forcibly to the service of ideas.

Sordello suffered from these tendencies and
from the circumstances of his life.   His youth
was visionary, tending to develop an undue self-
consciousness.   When he failed and lapsed again
into dreamy isolation and discouragement, he was
delivered by events rather than by principles.
He did not know life or mankind then, nor had
he had that opportunity of learning the due
relation of his ideas to the affairs and possibilities of the world, and to the minds of men,
which is so important a part of the discipline of
every man who is to help and tell on his fellows
in any great way.   The defects of his first work
are its want of heart and sympathy, its want of
spiritual quality, and also a failure on the poet's
part to master the materials and principles of his

art. And he suffers loss of power by his failure.
Soul and will answer less readily than they ought
to, but he keeps, it may be, he has deepened, his
ideal purpose. He will not sing songs of merely
pleasant trifling; to serve and give truth as he
may, he declares to be his aim : and if he hesitates at first before Salinguerra, he rises at length
with fervour to real power and a very high view
of the poet's task. But he has spent himself in
reaching the vision; he has been dreamy, not
creative, kingly, and his life has disqualified him
for that highest kind of power—spiritual will.

It is, however, at the close, when he has to
decide on the offer of Salinguerra, that you find
the fullest statement of reasons for his failure,
and the largest review of his life. To condense
those is to give a very adequate answer to Dean
Church's question. He reviews his own life, and
what does he see ? He considers arguments, and
what does he think ? He has been sensitive,
many-sided ; he wanted unity, central passion,
great conviction, a great love, or a great aim—
power of some kind to lift and support his power.
For years he met with nothing of this kind ; so
others of less ability and poorer nature found a
task while he found none. And this sensibility
and dispersion is not all. He is an idealist,
impelled to seek the sum of all he admires and
loves in some perfect form. But the " best " such
spirits seek, passing beyond the good, never is
actual. Nature seems full of hints, of promises
even, of the wealth of it; yet it is never found.

Perhaps there is no such power or object. All is within, and man must be a law to his own sphere. Can, then, the necessary power be found within the human sphere? Can the service and love of men prove such? But that includes himself. And how serve men? Can he make clear the value and greatness of such service as rendered to " the people "? He cannot. Yet it is plain they need it. Only how little can be done! Let one proclaim his truth and do his part, and it will be years and years before it be accepted and used, and there is probably all the truth needed or likely to be used in the world at any given time. These are doubts.

But here seems a clear point—if it be hard to serve men to much purpose, you can at least keep from oppressing them, and show your sympathy and sincerity that way. This will do some good. But is that so certain? When he thinks it over in the full survey, it seems far from clear to him how much of the ill in man's lot can be removed, or even whether it ought to be. Good and ill seem so bound up with each other; the ill seems so often the basis and occasion of so much of the good. Take it away, and where were the occasion for much of what is most excellent in man's life—for help and pity? In fact, in regard to the large question, it does seem that if you could give men the whole, you would take away all use in the parts. So doubts give him pause again.

But just as the gain of the people by his refusal

seems doubtful, so his own gain by accepting
Palma and the office seems great. All that
men could gain by his sacrifice they will gain in
due time and by other means, while he loses all
by refusal. But if he lose, there is the life to
come, it may be said. There may be; but life
is now, and he craves life—the little stream
certain and near rather than the rocky fount on
far-off heights. Then he reflects that this cup
of life, that he makes so much of in the debate,
has been easily dashed aside many a time. Yes,
by those who had the faith or the hope that
mastered life. Let him find such power, and he
will renounce too, he thinks.

But much of the debate, so far forth, has, we
are to conclude, been on the surface. Sordello
now passes into a mood touching the deeper
thoughts of the past. He sinks through all
secondary states, and seems to get to the core
of principle and passion within—to lay hold of
the essential truth. He sees how all our notions,
even good and ill, may be but modes of time,
and how in other spheres things may prove
quite distinct. But a sense of this puts a man
out of time; and gives him a tendency to force
eternity upon time, the soul on the body. If
you look at matters of life from that point of
view, that seems the right course. And yet such
course neglects the conditions of this life, and
puts it, indeed, out of place; to insist on the
soul's absoluteness is to destroy the body and
miss life. So it had been with Sordello; his

11

spiritual vision had been won by the " flesh-half's
break-up," and had resulted in his showing himself inadequate for life.   The problem was to
have kept these in their due relations, and take
life on its proper conditions.   Yet how many
do that ?   Most men brutalise the soul—the
opposite mistake.   Who shall find power to solve
the problem and conciliate both elements of
man's life ?   Who shall find wisdom through
love to " see the great before and after, the
small now," and, seeing both, do the duty that
is at hand ?   Plainly, some power or principle
Sordello did not find is needed for this.   And
the poet, speaking for Sordello, says that what
is required is some power above man's nature
and sphere—some divine power, both infinite
and loving—revealed within man's sphere and
nature, and giving its transcendent yet clear and
practical sanction to duty.   Idealists like Sordello
need such a vision, such law as this, divine and
human, resting on the eternal, yet touching close
the tasks of life, and giving these a large relation
without loss of practical point and fitness.

To some it will seem on survey of this poem
that the whole problem is only the creation of
a poet's dreams.   No one, it may be thought,
ever made so " sorry a farce " of his life as this
Sordello.   So mad an idealist never went at
large.   Never, it may be, one so consistent and
complete, for circumstances leave few men free
for such consistency ; but the strife of principle
is very common, and perhaps very few earnest

minds have kept quite clear of compromise in the conflict.

Browning, we may judge, felt the strife in his own mind, and with regard to his work, and he had to adjust the relation of principles in both, as the growth of his art proves. "Paracelsus" and "Sordello" both speak of the ideality of Shelley and the so-called "metaphysical" bent of Browning's mind. His dramatic art was his "escape" from the dangers of his first poetry, while the double quality of his mind became clearer and better balanced as his genius matured.

Sordello anyhow, as Browning presents him, is your poetic idealist, dealing first with the things of art, and then called to deal with the things of life, and finding his ideal in the way of his handling either effectively. There are other difficulties in both spheres for Sordello. Circumstances in both obstruct. But a chief difficulty, when he grasps his thought fully, is his idealism of spirit and aim. Reason seeks truth, imagination beauty, the will right, and all the ideal. Yet the ideal—whether as truth, beauty, or right—is never to be come upon or expressed; and life as we know it could not go on if it were come on or expressed. Why is this? What is the principle of the matter? the reason of the Law?

In "Sordello" the answer to this special question is scarcely clear; it might well have been clearer. We shall, however, find the point come up again and again in Browning; and it is, perhaps, best to hand over from this early poem

the solution of it as it comes within his poetry.
Yet we may here suggest how, by force of his
perception of life, and by pressure of his own
thoughts, our poet was grappling a question upon
which the whole drift of Hegel's thought bore,
whether as interpretation of mind, of life, or of
religion ; and the solution of the problem offered
by him is found in his doctrine of the immanence
of God, the unity of the divine and human, and
the ideal significance of thought and duty, which
means, with reference to the chief problem of
" Sordello," that only as the thinker and worker
see the ideal as the law and meaning of the real
can thought or work be good.

The further question, raised by Sordello in his
hour of critical debate, whether it were good to
" realise the ideal," whether defect and evil are
conditions of good in man's life, must also be
reserved.   Thus early Browning saw the question
In " Reverie " he is still engaged with it, as an
idealist with a sacred trust in the conditions of
life and the laws of the world.

CHAPTER VII

BROWNING AS A DRAMATIST

BROWNING'S plays are, we fancy, little read, in part because they have been thrown into the shade by later work. But their place in his work, in the growth of his art, and in the expression of his genius, give them interest besides the interest they have in themselves. For, in a century that has produced very few dramas of true value, the author of Pippa and Colombe and Mildred Tresham, of Berthold and Valence, of Ogniben and Luria, has added distinctly and worthily to our stock of dramatic figures and conceptions.

Browning began with " Strafford " in 1837. It was given at Covent Garden on May 1, Macready and Miss Faucit taking leading parts, " with all the evidences of distinct success," but was of greater promise than achievement, as Forster felt in reviewing it. The character of Strafford is well conceived, though not effectively realised through the play, and as a whole it lacks the proper energy and interest of acting drama.

The next of the dramas was " Pippa Passes," 1841. It is not a play, but a series of

dramatic scenes bound by a lyrical thread, and
shaped to express a poetic idea. Browning, so
we are told, was walking one day in a wood
alone, winding his way among the trees, and the
thought struck him that in like manner, in the
great wood of this world, many lives seem to
wind their way among other lives, apparently
without contact or influence. A little reflection
convinced him that, in spite of appearances and
conventions, the fact is not so; and he devised
when the seed of his thought had grown, the
series of scenes presenting the "passing" of Pippa
to express his idea. That idea is the way in
which all lives, even lonely and lowly lives, have
a world of lives about them upon whom their
influence is greater than they know; and also
how we each judge partially, or it may be quite
wrongly, of the lives and happiness of others.
The design of "Pippa" was to present these
truths in dramatic form, and it has been done.

It is New Year's Day at Asolo, and Pippa, who
works in the silk mills of the place, is thinking, as
the day dawns, what she must do with her one
holiday. For one day she will be happy, if only
in dreams, with the happiness of the happiest four
in Asolo. She will be Ottima, lover of Sebald.
Yet no; that is a mad, bad love. Phene, then,
the Greek girl, who has come to be married to
Jules the sculptor. Yet again, no; that love is
new and uncertain. The love of the mother for
her child is deeper and surer; she will be the
gentle mother watching over her son. And the

she thinks there is a higher love still—" God's love." She will be the bishop who is to be at the house by the Duomo Sta. Maria that evening.

And yet it occurs to her, that even as Pippa she has God's love, and there is, perhaps, less need than seems to change places. For what says her hymn?—" All service ranks the same with God." So, with that idea in her mind, she goes forth to her holiday, to pass these people and see their happiness, and test the hymn's truth.

She passes them, and we see their lives in scenes of true dramatic power, made more expressive by their contrast with Pippa. First, Ottima and Sebald, who, to be free in their guilty love, have murdered the lady's husband in the night. Day breaks here, restless and "ablaze with eyes"; and, though they recall passionately past hours of pleasure, and resolve to bury all remorse in love, as he is in the act of crowning her his queen, more proudly for their sin, the words of Pippa's song fall on his ear—

> God's in His heaven ;
> All's right with the world ;

and conscience awakes. Sin is horrible, and the strong, just, divine order rules, calm and mighty. Sebald kills himself in his remorse, and Ottima shows the nobler side of passion in possible self-sacrifice.

In her dewy freshness of soul, Pippa goes next where Jules and Phene return from their marriage.

Through the talk of his fellow-students we learn
that the sculptor has been entrapped into marry-
ing a Greek girl who has acted as an artist's
model.   He finds it out.   What can he do?
Give her all he has and leave her?   But the girl
loves him, and has found life in her love.   As he
is anxiously deciding what to do, Pippa's song of
the queen whom the page pined to bless is heard,
raising the question, Why should we in love be
always page and never queen, getting rather than
giving?   Here, for instance, is a soul with need
of help, and to whom his mere touch has given
life.   He will take her and go to some isle of the
Greek sea, with silence all about it, and begin life
and art in a new spirit and with vital aims.

Next Pippa passes to the turret where Luigi
and his mother are in talk about his schemes as
one of the Carbonari.   His purpose is to slay the
Austrian tyrant, whose tyranny is cursing his
country.   The mother pleads against her son's
purpose, and tries to draw him from it.   She talks
especially of one whom he loves, to draw him to
the sweet domestic life still possible even under
Austrian tyranny.   He wavers, when the song of
Pippa, about the good king who lived in the morning of the world, by its contrast with Austrian
tyranny, rouses his patriotism.   He goes, seem-
ingly to fulfil his purpose, faithful anyhow to its
patriotic core, and so escapes the police, who were
on the watch for him.

Lastly, Pippa passes the house of a brother
of the bishop, lately dead.   There is talk there

between the bishop and a steward over the
bishop's family affairs.   Through this we learn
that Pippa is child of a brother of the bishop,
with claims to his wealth.   The steward plans
her ruin, that her wealth may go to others.   The
bishop listens and is tempted, when the song of
Pippa, with its note of faith and innocence, touches
the bishop's better nature, and reminds him how
God has care for such lives.   He revolts from the
scheme, and has Maffeo gagged and arrested.

It is evening now, and Pippa goes home, her
holiday spent, her songs and "fooling" done.
What is she now ?   The mill girl only, who, if
she touch these people at all, can only do it
through the silk she winds.   So it seems to her ;
and the day sets in cloudy gloom, the truth of
her hymn not clear to her.   Yet the poet has
made the truth clear.   Pippa has, in fact, touched
every one of those lives for good, and is happier
than they.

The next of the dramas was " King Victor and
King Charles," in 1842.   It depicts and interprets
a dramatic situation, rather than a dramatic action.
Victor II. of Sardinia, having ruled with energy for
fifty-four years, abdicated in 1730 in favour of his
son Charles, whom he had neglected and despised.
It was a surprise to all, to the son most of all.
What was the motive and object of it ?   That he
wished to declare a marriage he had privately
made, and spend his closing years quietly ?   or
that he had certain designs he thought he could
carry out best through his son, whom he expected

to control? The latter, Browning thinks, and i
working out the effects of the situation on th
characters of father and son is the interest of th
theme for him. The son, who had been though
weak and pliable, was, in fact, strong, and mean
to rule now that he was king. He rules well fo
a year, when his father, not finding himself able t
carry out his scheme, plots to recover the crowr
even by force. The plot is found out, and th
father is brought a prisoner before his sor
Charles, resolute so far, shrinks from so strang
a strife, and places the crown on his father's head
who dies from the excitement, and so cuts th
knot of a difficult situation.

" The Return of the Druses " (1843) was th
next of the plays. It is a romantic theme, tragica
and uncommon, with more " plot " than is usua
with Browning. Certain Druses, driven from thei
home, by the Turks in the fifteenth century, settl
on an island near Rhodes, under the Knights c
St. John. They are governed by a bad prefec
who kills their leaders. Only one boy, Djaba
son of an emir, escapes and goes to Europe. H
there gains help of a Breton noble, and of th
Venetians, in a scheme to free the Druses, an
returns to carry it out. At home he falls in lov
with Anael, who has vowed to give herself only t
her tribe's deliverer ; so the passion of love unite
with patriotism to urge him on. But how is i
to be done ? His people think God only can fre
them within the due time by means of the Hakeen
a divine manifestation. To rouse them, he claim

to be Hakeem, is able to satisfy his tribe of his claim, and for a time " believes " it himself. A day is fixed for deliverance, and they wait. But before it comes his " faith " wanes. What is he to do ? He tries to be true in the strange situation, but is forced on by circumstances and events. Anael, afraid of the love she feels for the man, wishes to prove herself worthy of the divine caliph ; while he, thinking her love depends on her delusion, is afraid to make known the fact. She slays the prefect, a deed he meant to do, and so forces the crisis. He tells her now the truth. She will not have it so, and when she believes him she holds by her love. Seeing this, he resolves to keep his secret. But on the discovery of the prefect's murder, Anael, in reaction, denounces Djabal. He admits the justice of her denunciation, but declares his utter love for her. She accepts her lover, and in strange excitement dies with the cry of Hakeem on her lips. The cry is taken up by the Druses, and before Djabal can confess, the Venetians come, and his task is practically accomplished. He puts on two friends the duty of leading his tribe home, then kills himself. So did these two, by their love and death, restore the Druses to their home ; so did they become " divine " to their tribe, and prove that " all great works in this world spring from the ruins of greater" plans and ideas : men " design Babels and build Babylons."

" A Blot in the 'Scutcheon " is a tragedy of

simpler and more human interest. It was given
at the Theatre Royal, Drury Lane, February 11,
1843. Miss Faucit played Guendolen, Mrs. Stir-
ling, Mildred, and Mr. Phelps, Lord Tresham.
The play was given again by Mr. Phelps at
Sadler's Wells, in 1848. It was not quite a
"success" either time. The public thought it
unpleasant or worse. Tragical it is, but surely
human and touching, as the poet gives it. The
leading figure is Lord Tresham, whose strength
and weakness meet in his pride and honour—
pride and a long line and a family name without
stain. And he finds, as he thinks, the family
'scutcheon hopelessly stained by a sister's weakness. He does not know how or by whom the
dishonour has fallen. He has one feeling—
wounded pride; and one thought — vengeance
on the man who has done the wrong. He is
too proud and too angry to take thought for
anything save his name, because it is his. So
he slays his sister's lover, and then finds how
partial and arrogant he has been. He has
murdered Lord Mertoun, on whose behalf he
had supposed himself acting—has killed the man
whom his sister passionately loved, and whom
he wished her to marry. His sister dies broken-
hearted. He poisons himself in his despair, and
hands on his name and home to those whom he
warns to beware his pride and avoid his haste.
Self-consideration, veiled by a passion of honour,
has been his motive, leading to worse wrong than
Mertoun's—to worse selfishness.

The figure of Mildred is tender, but too pitiful; and that of Mertoun boyish and touching. Guendolen has fine sense and womanly feeling. But the play leaves an impression of slightness in character, deficiency of action and vital detail. There is a lyrical pathos and beauty of tone and style in it. The sadness of the high-minded proud Lord Tresham, over a deed he sees unjustifiable and irreparable, is well given. When in his pride and wrath he had slain Mertoun he saw the narrowness of his judgment and view of life, and "thro' all the troubled surface a depth of purity immovable" in his sister's heart.

This drama raises a question in the criticism of art, and one that has been pressed by the poet's critics. Life is often pitiful, and we have to take it as it is, but these tragedies that sadden us are a mistake, it is said. And they are a mistake, unless they suggest those higher powers and fuller issues into which the sorrow passes, when nobly borne or expiated, unless they purify the heart and leave it more heroic. It is a world of many mistakes, in which the nobler hearts often make the mistakes, and in which sensible and ordinary folks escape the sorrows and get the good things of life; yet the world is made better and richer by the pains of these hearts, and they envy not "the common lot."

"Colombe's Birthday" was the next of the plays, and is in most respects the finest. Made in 1844, it was produced at the Haymarket in 1853; Miss Faucit, who took a special interest in

Browning's heroines, playing the part of Colombe, the most subtle and difficult of his women. The play is localised and dated but we know of no historic basis; nor is it, as here given, of any special age or place—whenever the heart, tempted to make a lower, is upheld to make the higher choice, there the essential action of the drama has taken place. The interest and development of the drama lie in the play of feeling and in the transformation or definition of character.

Colombe of Ravestein has been Duchess of Cleves and Juliers for a year. Her father contrived she should succeed, but by the Salic law, which rules the succession, she has no title to the duchy. It really belongs to her cousin Berthold, and he comes to claim his rights. He has sent a message to advise Colombe of his purpose, which is given the lady through an advocate who has come to plead the cause of Cleves. This advocate is the hero of the play. A total contrast to the courtiers, he brings the duchess the breath and power of the world where words are real, goodness true, and loyalty sincere and unselfish. He had seen her a year ago, and had been struck by the nobleness of the woman, while the duchess put her far above him. He now finds, as the duchy is lost, that the woman is nobler than he had imagined her.

Though Colombe had known of Berthold's claim, his message was a shock to her; in part for the loss of the duchy, but more because it made clear to her the hollowness of the basis on which

she had rested—the court and its vanities. She
will resign and give all to Prince Berthold. But
on reflection she cannot, for in Valence, the
advocate, she has one subject at least, and he has
made her aware of duties. She will try the
question on its merits,

And the prince comes—a large, practical man,
easy and confident, making his claim quietly, as
aware of its strength, and counting it a small
thing on his way to far greater. His maxim is,
that if there be little real difference between the
objects and satisfactions of men's lives, " mere
largeness" is something, and he holds that in this
world we must go by size, and settle about kind
in the next; a deliberate and principled worldli-
ness and unspiritual irony is his temper.

On the arrival of Berthold, it proves harder
than she had thought to leave her father's halls.
She appoints Valence to speak for her. He
declares how every true subject will stand by his
lady. Alone she may seem ; but in loneliness
men come to reality and power. The court and
its fictions gone, the duchess will fall back on the
people. The dominion that rests on force only
is a name, and the good will of her people no
force can take from her. Berthold, who goes by
the size and forms of things, is struck by the man
and his spirit. But he feels the justice of Valence,
and he puts the whole case in his hands. The
advocate knows it is a question of law, and will
decide and advise on that ground. He is to
consider the papers before the evening. As he

goes to do so, Colombe retains him to make him aware that she has grown to true clearness and power of spirit, and can accept justice. It has been to her a birthday for heart and soul, doing in her the work of years, and the power has been mainly his. So she helps him to his duty. But as she goes she makes clear a fact that may bias and perplex his decision. She loves him. In that matter there is more hope for him in her ceasing to be duchess; so he calls Cleves and its woes to help him to be true.

The matter is, indeed, easy. The claims of Berthold are clear. But now comes the hardest of all questions for him to settle. Berthold offers marriage to Colombe, not on the ground of love, but on every other honourable and convenient ground; and Valence presents the whole question on its merits. She is not duchess in law, but may be so in fact by accepting a man who is in many ways worthy of her—a man of power and purpose, so definite and so strong through his very limitations that he gathers "earth's whole good into his arms," and stands forth the type of earthly success. The lady avows she had looked for such a man as the advocate's generous words tell of to complete her life, but wonders if he loves. Valence says no. But how can he tell? He knows love's way, and the prince has not a tone of it. He knows through love; then, whom does Valence love? Colombe follows up the question, until she forces from him the confession of his love. And yet she puts it aside for a time

as if to test both. He appeals to her to prove
that love is best, and vindicate the pure and
simple nobleness of life. But for the moment she
feels as if his loyalty were less great. She will
see Berthold. The prince is advised to play the
lover and the man, but does not care enough for
the part to feign ; and when the lady asks, " You
love me then ? " he admits frankly it is not in his
heart or his plan. There is no need, he says, for
such fiction. He offers all that matters to sense
or to ambition. Before such cold alienation
from all rights of the heart she draws back, and
he puts the matter bluntly, as a choice between
taking the empire and giving up the duchy.

And then Valence is put to a last test, his
integrity proving equal to it. Melchior, a friend
of Berthold, assures him that the lady is only
kept from accepting the prince by an impression
that the services of Valence claim her hand.
Valence leaves her free to make her choice. This
decision Berthold deems heroic, and asks what
" reward " there must be for thus " yielding up
love's right." And Valence, in his noblest tone,
asks who thought of reward ? And yet only to
have known Colombe, and been helped by her to
all that is good, is the true reward. He now
gives her the requisition. She subscribes it, and
asks him what on her birthday, which is to be her
wedding day, he wishes from her. One thing
only he asks—that the wrongs of Cleves be set
right. Berthold grants this. And then Valence,
thinking Colombe has taken the prince, is about

12

to leave her, when she asks him to read what she has written on the prince's summons—"I take him; give up Juliers and the world. This is my birthday." Berthold, seeing now the full quality of the lady, knows that she was too fine for his ends. "Any garish plume will do to deck a barren helm"; this "costly flower" is for rarer uses. And he admires, though he does not envy, and could not imitate the choice.

This play, as a presentation of its theme, is beautiful and effective. Whether for acting drama the theme be really fit, is another question. The characters of Colombe, Valence, and Berthold are vital and vigorous, though it may be Berthold is rather a type than a person. He is the embodiment of secular ability and good sense; of the success resulting from indifference to every principle and feeling that does not help his ambition. He knows there is a thing called "heart," and he has heard of "spirit" and a "life beyond," but the first he regards as in the way of life's business and the other as not pertinent to it. Some one has spoken of Berthold as our poet's ideal. There are elements in Berthold the poet has strong sympathy with — efficient ability, realism, and sheer will; but his defects are so great, his range so narrow, that he cannot be regarded as ideal. He is the opposite of Sordello, and for many "uses" of life better than the "mad poet"; but the single and capable judgment, the heroic unselfishness, the steady regard for "general ends" of Valence, bring him nearer what may be called

an ideal. And the two are not so much contrasted
as compared. Valence does justice to Berthold,
and on his practical and intellectual sides admires
him. And he does so because he has all of his
virtue and much of his power, only qualified by
principles Berthold does not regard. The test of
Colombe is in her choice between these two—a
choice heightened by the fact that the duchy goes
with the one, and a simple life with the other.
She likes the energy and practical scope and
manly quality of Berthold. But she must have
heart as well as brain, self-denial as well as self-
reliance; and in her and her decision the drama
depicts a pure and generous womanly ideal. Life
should rest on reality, not on forms; on love and
humanity, not on gold and rank and name. She
might have found reasons for taking Berthold,
and only a conviction that the heart has its rights,
that go to the core, not only of the happiness
but of the rightness of life, would have led her to
choose Valence. People take such decisions at
their peril, but those who can maintain them
alone know the proper worth of life.

"Luria" (1846) was the next play, romantic
and tragical. Luria was a Moor in the service of
Florence, proud of and devoted to the Republic,
but distrusted by her as an alien. It is the eve
of a great battle between Pisa and Florence, and
it is feared at Florence that, if Luria wins, he
will use his victory for ends of his own. Braccio,
the organ of these suspicions, is with Luria,
collecting what is thought "evidence" for a trial

of Luria then going on, and to be completed on
his victory. They mean to use him, and then
destroy him. Tiburzio, the Pisan general, who
gets to know the scheme, comes to tell Luria of
it, and draw him away from Florence. But the
Moor will not hear of betrayal, will not open the
intercepted letters. It is a pain to him to lose
faith in Florence. He clings to it; joins battle,
and beats Pisa. Then he demands of Braccio the
facts, which the commissary has to admit. Urged
again to punish Florence at the head of the Pisan
army, he will not, though he does punish a city
unworthy of such souls in his own way. He
poisons himself, and dies just as news of his
entire acquittal is brought from the city. Luria
is a fine conception, a heroic figure, bringing "new
feeling fresh from God, teaching what life should
be, what faith is and loyalty and simpleness"; in
him the passion and depth of the East come into
contact with the thought and purpose of the West,
feeling the greatness of the West, baffled by its
duplicity, but keeping its own heroism and greatness of soul; in him is the despair of a great
heart that has loved the power and brilliance
and then learns the selfishness and baseness of
Renaissance Italy. But the play is poetic rather
than acting drama. Its long speeches and developments of passion rather than action, and the want
of other characters beside Luria, are against its
representation.

There remain two dramatic fragments of much
power and interest—" A Soul's Tragedy " (1846

and " In a Balcony " (1853). " A Soul's Tragedy "
is in two parts, one giving the poetry of dream
and promise; the other the prose of fact, as tested
by opportunity, in the life of one Chiappino.   He
is a confident and effusive man who would, in his
own opinion, quickly put the world right, if only
he had the chance.   The chance offers, and he
finds himself without purpose or principle—a
creature of plausibility and expediency and self-
interest.   He has denounced the rule of the
Provost of Faenza, and been sentenced to exile.
Luitolfo, a friend, a quieter but surer and better
man, has gone to get the sentence revised.   In
his absence Chiappino gives himself the airs of a
hero in talk with the lady his friend is going to
marry.   He loves this lady too, and grudges his
friend his better fortune.   While he is abusing
his friend, Luitolfo knocks.   Chiappino mocks
the fright in which he supposes him to have fled
from the Provost, but finds that the quiet friend,
failing in his suit, has struck the Provost, and
thinks he has killed him.   He flees, followed, as
he thinks, by a hostile crowd.   Chiappino helps
him to escape, and then goes out to find the
crowd friendly.   So he takes over the whole
benefit of his friend's act, and plays the part of
the hero of revolt.

In the second part we find the results of the
false start thus made, and of the man's want of
solidity and sincerity.   It is a month after, so
that things have had time to grow.   And here
the true hero of the piece comes on the stage—

Ogniben, the pope's legate. He comes just as
our hero of the revolt is giving "reasons" for
being in no hurry to realise his visions of a perfect state, or even common obligations. Now,
the legate is every way the man to detect his
conceit and expose his weakness, his want of
grasp and conviction. He is a typical Italian
ecclesiastic—human, humorous, with much knowledge of men and life, subtle and able, knowing
too well man's weakness and the irony of life.
His part is that of critic and humorist. His
convictions, if he has any, are well in reserve.
He finds these people with ideas and schemes
interesting and not dangerous. Their own weakness and the extreme difficulty of moving the
world keep them harmless. And his way with
them is to feign agreement, and carry their
notions on to conclusions that show their futility
and the shallowness of the minds in which they
arise. He has really a deep scepticism, and likes
to show, as matter of satire as well as argument
how the intellect can always be got to argue on
behalf of what men wish. In his opinion, one of
the best uses of that very fallible organ is to find
ways of making the best of things as they are
He does not think well of men's motives gener
ally, does not pretend much that way for himsel
and knows that self-interest, active in all, i
specially acute in leaders of revolts. He has see
twenty-three of these, and knows too much t
take them seriously. He easily shows the vanit
of Chiappino's fine words; exposes him to th

people as one who had been trading on another's deed ; and, with words of light mockery, dismisses him to profit by the fall his pride has had, and by his new experience of affairs of State.

The piece is not a play, but is forcibly dramatic. Ogniben is the most definite impersonation in the dramas. The interest is in the characters ; the development and catastrophe are in the soul, not in events, and the incidents are clearly invented to present this.

"In a Balcony" is a fine fragment, character-istic in its dramatic quality and in its bearing on life. It takes us into the heart of the situation, and presents the crises of the soul. Norbert loves Constance, and has served the queen that he may win her. His success may claim her now ; but the lady, knowing the queen, advises him to put his suit as if his love were, in fact, for the queen, and only took her kinswoman as a next and possible best. The queen, with womanly hunger for such love, takes the fiction for fact, and comes eagerly to grasp the life it seems to offer. She tells Constance all she means to do to take Norbert's love. Constance tells Norbert, and protests her entire love for him, but sees he has other objects. The queen finds them thus. Norbert declares his love in her presence. Con-stance, having decided, if that prove best, to give him up to the queen, tries to turn all his words away from herself and upon the queen. He counterworks this design, and in the end makes it clear that his love is for Constance. This discovery is painful to the queen, and the drama ends in gloom and peril, but in clear and certain love.

We have now before us Browning's whole dramatic work, and two questions arise, What is *the quality of the dramas* he made? Was drama his proper medium? His own decision and course appear to answer the latter question. He has made no plays, we may say, since 1846. It has been said that that is an accident—a serious one if the poet's genius were really for drama. Let us look, then, at our first question. Active development and expression are the sphere of drama, and characterisation must be through these. How do the above plays answer these tests? The themes the poet chooses, and his treatment of them both, we judge, show that his interest and sphere are not the older dramatic. There is a want of active development, of graphic and characteristic conversation, of outward interest and detail, and there is interest and matter of another kind. Their main and growing power and scope are such as do not fit the theatre. These dramas, as they are made, are inadequate to the dramatic interest and bias at work in them. In their power and their defects they show that for the poet's genius another form was necessary. There is dramatic power, but it is power trammelled, not expressed, by the forms and restrictions of drama. The poet's intellectual and spiritual interests in man's nature and life are, in fact, too strong for that free contemplation of action and active relations required in drama.

CHAPTER VIII

FIRST DRAMATIC LYRICS (1836–1846)

THE history of a poet's art has more than a technical interest, for the growth of his art is in degree the growth of his mind and of his subject. It indicates his grasp of his matter, of his own powers in relation to that, and the right means of expressing matter and mind. And as to the last point, mastery of matter and form in some sphere of art, genius is more subject to growth than is often thought to be the fact.

These early dramatic lyrics of Browning are an instance of that law of choice and growth to which genius is subject. When the first of these lyrics was made, the poet had not made sure of his method—had not found that form which he felt to be the best for the expression of his mind. By the time the last of these lyrics was made he had become sure of both. Between the two is a period of ten years. Part of the work of that time we have taken in the dramas. The poems now to be taken will help to fix better the value of the dramas, and will enable us to test in early and simple instances that form and method of dramatic work which the poet has used since

1846 as his most congenial and adequate form of expression.

The history of his work as it bears on this point makes clear, we have seen, the accuracy of what has just been stated. "Pauline" was mono-dramatic; "Paracelsus" was dramatic in spirit and design, but in a form more freely adapted, as the poet thought, than drama for the expression of the mind and passions in their vital action. The form did not answer his aim, but such was his aim. "Sordello" was narrative, discursive, but with dramatic interest and statement breaking through it.

In 1841–2 the poet made drama, and also in 1842 he put forth the "Dramatic Lyrics," explaining in a brief preface what they were—"lyrical in form," but "dramatic" in principle. The booklet had only sixteen pages. But it had such lyrics as the two "Madhouse Cells," "Queen Worship," "Italy and France," "Waring," "In a Gondola," etc. These poems were issued in 1842, but some of them had been composed as early as 1836.

The first poem of the kind made by the poet, and given in the little book, was "Porphyria's Lover." It was at first entitled "A Madhouse Cell." In 1863 it was put among the "Romances"; and in the edition of 1868 you will find it beside "Childe Roland," as akin in matter and principle. A strange poem, it may seem.

It is the lover of Porphyria who talks in an

intense dream. He is alone; a rainy night and a sullen wind outside; his one thought Porphyria. He sees her come in, and at once all is changed. She has come from a feast, through the rain and the wind, to sit with him. She puts his head on her shoulder, spreads over all her yellow hair, and tells her love. He sees the truth of her heart, the weakness of her will—she loves, but will never break through circumstance, and be his. But her true life is in her love, and to make this moment eternal were best for love and for the soul. To free her from earth is the only way to that, and so he strangles her with her yellow hair, and sees her pass without pain to the freedom and goodness of the after-life. And they sit the night through in a peace that seems God's approval of the deed.

But what a theme! And did it happen? It is a romance of overmastering passion. It took place only among the wild motions of a lover's brain. Dwelling on his love, and seeing no way of hope for love but this way, he affirms so passionately that love is all and death better than the vanity of false life that he *sees* this happen— sees death set love free and keep it pure.

But it is, then, it would seem, a study of madness, of monomania, and ought to have kept its title. Why remove the title? Because the man in whose brain it shaped itself so vividly might never have done it in fact. There is much mania that never gets beyond the brain, and there are moods trenching on madness that never cross the line.

Another poem published in 1836, and also called
"A Madhouse Cell" in 1842, was "Johannes
Agricola." It is a case of fanaticism, of religious
self-love, so complete as to be a kind of moral
insanity. Any strong passion or great idea may
in certain natures result in such mania, and the
madness is never pure and simple, because great
errors are usually the perversion of great truths.
John Agricola was a Predestinarian, so far gone
as to become Antinomian—so far, that is, as to
have set aside moral law. "Elect of God" from
eternity, he could do no ill, and nothing could do
him ill—that is, bring his soul into any danger.
Every act and detail of his life was part of God's
plan, for and through him. This plan and the
divine will are above all criticism of the reason,
and even of the conscience of man. The necessities of the divine nature are absolute—neither
moral nor immoral. Of this will the soul is the
special object; beyond all else the souls of the
elect are dear to God. It is impossible to assign
a reason for this divine regard; no virtue or goodness makes any difference. The only "reason"
is in the elective Will of God, and in God it is all
a necessity—the last mystery of the divine nature.
The divine need of certain souls to love is the
secret of "salvation," and the inscrutable ground
of all hope. "Elect," sin's worst poison leaves you
"safe"; non-elect, your best virtues turn to sin.
It is strange, it is very strange, but the last ecstasy
of faith in it comes from its mystery, and the
absolutely free grace of God thus involved.

But again you ask, Why depict such a mind? The passion of belief makes the meditation lyrical, as the man in his exultation thrusts aside the whole physical universe to get to God—God and the love of God "all in all" to him. This is his interest, that he realises so madly a curious and profound idea of the human soul—the soul in God, and God in the soul, as all that has finally any value or meaning.

The place given the poem in the latest edition of the poet's works must mean that he attaches real psychological interest to it. He puts it among "Men and Women," and beside the "Epistle of Karshish." The problem there is the effect it would have on human conduct were one to die and be brought back again to life. The balance of life, it is inferred, would be so lost, its centres so shifted, that life would be no longer practicable. And in this poem, what is it? The idea of God and of the Divine will may be so held as to destroy all will and all morality, and reduce life to a meaningless necessity. And yet this "God-hunger," this passion of the soul, which in coarse natures has such ugly results, has refined higher natures to an unearthly beauty, and in both the instinct has a deep meaning. Agricola and St. Agnes are far apart, but St. Agnes's dream of the "Heavenly Bridegroom," and the "Sabbaths of Eternity," and Agricola's idea of "God's breast," as "his own abode," are the same cry for a God of the soul whom physical splendours hide rather than reveal.

The next of the early lyrics, done also in 1836, is of different quality. It is a lyric of sentiment, perhaps the only lyric of the kind in Browning. It is that called "Lines"—"Still ailing, Wind?" And the poet laid hold of it to criticise, and reject it years later when he wrote "James Lee's Wife." Its weakness is the "pathetic fallacy," the assumption that nature is caught up in our moods. It is a natural weakness, and the voice of the wind not merely touches, but seems to echo and share our grief at times. But this is not Browning's note, nor could he ever have given the magic or the force of poets to whom it is natural.

The "Cavalier Tunes" are also lyrics of the dramatic kind—spirited songs imagined for certain cavaliers; and what might be called "Ballads," such as "Count Gismond," and an "Incident of the French Camp," were among these lyrics. In them you have a story told dramatically. In the ballad, lyrical and dramatic elements are in this way often present, and the life of the narrative is gained by the effort of the imagination to see and put all from some dramatic standpoint. Rossetti's work has the most brilliant modern examples of this, but Browning too gives the ballad-form and quality.

"In a Gondola" is a series of these lyrics, a love song in the form of a dialogue lyrically conducted between the lovers, and giving vividly their feelings, the situation, and the story. Their love is secret, their meetings stolen, at risk of the lover's life; but danger and death only heighten their passion and as they glide through Venice in the gondola, the life of the city seems the dream, their life the reality. He is found and stabbed as they part, but cares not; for, having lived, he can afford to die.

Placed next is " Waring," also of 1842. It is a " romance," suggested by fact. A friend of the poet, a man lovable and of much promise, rich in feeling, but proud and shy, wanting self-confidence, has suddenly left London and gone to " the far end of the world." And the poem depicts the man, expresses all the surprise and regret, the thoughts and hopes, that came into the poet's mind because of the departure of Waring. He wishes him back if only to tell him his esteem, while he is aware of his defects. He knew and loved good work and true praise, and should have put himself frankly forth in a world that goes, and must go, by what a man has done rather than by what it is in him to do. But there is power and hope of most things in Waring, given scope and stimulus; and the second part of the poem sets these forth, on occasion of meeting some one who has caught a glimpse of Waring in the east.

In many of the " Lyrics " of the " Bells and Pomegranates " series there is thus a keen dramatic quality. But the finest, the most " dramatic " in this poet's quality of drama, were the poems now called " My Last Duchess," and " The Bishop orders his Tomb." In these the mind and art of the new poet were distinctly and decisively declared—his field, his quality, his power.

For dramatic point and animation, indeed few

of Browning's poems surpass that named then
"Italy," and since named "My Last Duchess."
Its humour, its rapid delineation and suggestion
of the speaker's own character, and also of
his wife's, show well the poet's power and the
capability of this form of dramatic expression. The speaker is the duke. He is showing a portrait of his last duchess to one with
whom he is arranging for another. The dead
lady has become one of his art treasures, kept for
himself; and as they look at it he supposes a
question as to the depth and passion of her
glance. There was her offence. Her quick,
impulsive nature, easily roused and pleased,
offended his proud, cold nature. The glow was
in place when given to him, but when given to
everyone and everything as freely as to him and
his "nine-hundred-years-old name," it hurt him.
It was not a thing to speak of, nor to be put up
with. In his proud, hard way he took means to
stop it. He stopped it, and it killed the lady
Is he sorry? Was it overdone? Not in the least.
He will exact just the same devotion and reserve
of the next that he did of the last duchess. She
is dead, but she is there, and his in her beauty
still. He is satisfied with that, and goes on to the
question of the dowry and the next duchess, and
his other works of art, as if all had one use only
—to be his and please him.

Later, and better even, among these early
lyrics is "The Bishop's Tomb at St. Praxed's.
It was published in *Hood's Magazine* in 1845

and republished among the "Romances and Lyrics" in that year, and now put with the poet's Renaissance studies.

The scene is the deathbed of a Roman bishop of the sixteenth century. It is the bishop who speaks. He is dying, and has accepted the fact so completely that he sees himself dead and buried, and lying through the years on his tomb in St. Praxed's Church. His one thought now is to arrange for, and, if he can, make all sure and clear about, a tomb such as shall fit his value and his taste, and he has called his sons round his bed to talk to them at large of this matter. He describes the tomb and his whole wish regarding it, so that his life and soul are disclosed. He has had, by his confession, his share of life's pleasures ; he means to have his share of death's honours, since life, unhappily, cannot go on. Both may be "vanity," but both are the world's way and good to man.

With his sons about him, he recalls their "mother" and his gay life many years ago. Sorry, is he? Not at all. It was good while it lasted. It is past and gone, and vain regrets are a bad kind of folly. And the woman is dead, and now it is his turn for that which comes to all. Looking back, he wonders what man's life is, and what death may be which ends it. He doesn't know and scarcely cares, yet often as he lies in the long still night all seems a dream, and he hardly knows whether he is dead or alive. But it will be death soon

13

for him, and so about his tomb. He has bee
done out of the best place in the church, b
he will have the best tomb—one that will mo
the envy of his rival even in the grave. H
has worked out the design for it, and enjoy
the triumph of it as much as if it already stoo
in St. Praxed's. The tomb is to be of jaspe
the slab antique black basalt, the columns peac
blossom marble, the frieze bronze, and a ball
lapis-lazuli between the knees of the effigy. An
whence came this precious ball? He stole
from a burning church, and hid it for this ver
use. But will his sons give it him, or steal
from him, as he from the church? He has fear
but he bribes them with all he can offer, an
goes on to finish the frieze, with its Pans an
Nymphs, and Christ and Moses. And he
exigent as to the epitaph. It must be pu
Latin, Cicero's every word; not Gandolph's ba
Latin.

Such is his plan. Will the sons carry it out
They get tired of his talk, and, he fears, wi
take his property and give him a beggar's tom
He begs them, more than he would for his sou
not to do so, and tries to hope as he dwells o
his plan, until he hears the Mass, and feels th
incense, and tells how often in the night h
seems to turn to a piece of sculpture as he lie
on his bed. But now he is tired, and wanders
and ends by admitting that his scheme has n
chance of being carried out. His first impulse i
to punish his sons, but he does not. He send

hem away kindly, tolerantly, with sense, perhaps, f retribution in their selfishness.

That the poem has fine dramatic points and ue characterisation is thus clear. And there e still points of exegesis it may be well to lance at as bearing on the bishop and his ge—for he is a type of his age.

1. The bishop has a few serious phrases, but o serious beliefs. His survey of life, his concern with death, both prove it. "The world's dream," he says, though for him it has been nd is still the only reality. Yet there is ncerity in his phrase. It looks and feels so o him now because it is remote, its pleasures one, only memories left, no inward gains. So hen he speaks of his life as "brief and evil," e reminds us of what Martial said — that though many of us have too much, none of s ever have enough." Life had been "good," ut it had gone too fast. There is wrong in ie fact that it should go at all, and death is ie last wrong to those for whom the flight of ie years is never a process of gain, but always f loss.

2. And how little difference death makes to im! It is not great and solemn to the bishop. Ie is the same man. The rivalries, the care or artistic show, and all the vanity and worldness of the man you find beyond death and n the tomb. And that is the fact of life. o the frivolous, death is trivial. For what does ie bishop think of?—Of "what is beyond."

And what is beyond death for him?—The grav
and nothing more; and so the grand questic
is about a satisfactory tomb.

3. And how curious the passion of which tl
bishop is so full—that passion for monument
and all our care for what may happen to ou
names after we have passed away! Is it ration
or is it the vainest of man's illusions? our sel
respect carried beyond death, or only a wis
to keep a kind of place and value in the wor
when we have no place more in it? Two thing
seem clear about it in the bishop's case—tha
it is a sensuous rather than a spiritual wis
and that the bishop does not think of hims
as dead. He is in the church still, not in tl
grave, but on the tomb. That effigy becom
the man; he feels through it and lives in it.

4. And what of the bishop's religion? H
has had a Church and a ritual, and he has car
for them, but hardly a creed, and not a fait
"The blessed mutter of the Mass," "the perfun
of the incense," "the aery dome of the church
—these are the notes of it. It is the religic
of a sceptical and sensuous age. The "ange
live" in the dome. There is no heaven for hir
His thoughts get no higher than the materi
suggestions of ritual and art.

5. And his care for art is the bishop's stro
point, as it was the strong point of his ag
He is the epitome of the Renaissance in th
and in his style of art. His frieze, with
mixture of mythologies, and his good Latin ar

ad morals express this. And Browning has
liking for that age and its men and a secure
astery of its types and secrets. This mastery
orings in part from sympathy. He likes the
ensuous energy and frankness, the vigour and
njoyment and audacity, the care for art, the
earning, and all the picturesqueness and force
f the men and their lives, while aware, too,
f their terrible faults.

6. And so, as forcibly as Ruskin, he suggests
ae ways in which the temper and character of
ae Renaissance told on its art. This bishop,
orldly, selfish, and sensual, would invent such
rt, and carry into the Church all the vanity of
is heart and his life. His art, indeed, is as
reat an offence to his faith as his life itself.

But, leaving the bishop, let us recur to the
uestion of art we began with. Such poems
aake clear the principle of the work the poet
rst made in these dramatic lyrics. Drama
ould have put the bishop before you through
ction and speech. Here he is put by speech
nly. That is the sole action of the piece, and
et it leaves on you a clear sense of the man
nd the scene. How is so distinctly dramatic
result gained without the usual dramatic
aeans?—By the energy of speech, which is
aought—intense and immediate self-expression.
he character is in action, and the poet's medium
ives that action vividly and directly.

CHAPTER IX

POEMS OF LIFE AND DUTY, AND BROWNING'S CRITICISM OF LIFE

HAVING studied the rise of Browning's art, an
the ideas and aims of his earlier works, we propos
now to take his work more at large, and to con
sider certain groups of poems with regard to the
substance rather than their form.

And, first, we take a group dealing with certai
problems and parts of life, on the ground tha
they throw light from this poet's mind on ques
tions of duty and spiritual culture. To do this, w
know, is likely to please some and offend other
—to please unduly those who care for literatur
only as it has ethical value; to offend those wh
think it should have no such value or bearin
All cordial readers of Browning are thought t
belong to the first class, and Browning is the
prophet. But, though this is true of some of th
poet's readers, it is not true of the poet, nor is
a possible view of literature. Browning's poetr
in spite of its inward problems and spiritua
quality, is as just and profound in its idea
literature as in its ideal of life, and both ar
necessary to wise and great writing.

But the question now touched has been much discussed, and of all recent poets Browning is thought to raise it. Let us consider it so far as to make clear our point of view. Literature, some think, should be ethically neutral, simply human, its use consisting in its interest and its beauty only. But what, we must ask, is meant by "simply human"? Morality is a very human interest, and may surely occupy the place in literature it has in life. Truth, too, is an interest of man as well as beauty. And if beauty be art's vision of truth and sense of man's pleasure in it, there must be regard for truth, and not for beauty simply. While all literature of power has sprung from a passion and care for human life that laughs to scorn the exclusion of any of its interests, its "voice has been to the sons of men," its thoughts about the life of man, and the modern mind is only more explicit and deliberate in the matter, more spiritual and universal.

But, granting the principle, and allowing some relations to be normal, the question may be thought to have been shifted, not solved, because we have still to define the right relation. Is it, for instance, that held by some earnest people who think literature nothing if not "moral"? But morality, and still more life, includes much these good people do not include in their conception, and their view is even narrower on its literary than on its ethical side. How, then, shall we indicate the right relation? A phrase put forth by a critic, whose phrases are

often happy and light-giving, has been taken as
fairly answering the question. He described the
relation of literature to life as "criticism of life,"
and declared the higher value of literature to
depend essentially on its worth in this respect.
By some it has been thought that this is really
a Puritanic view of letters, and that Mr. Arnold
only stated that personal bias and inner thought
which he has shown in all his later writings when
he put forth that view. As he had said, besides,
that "conduct is three parts of life," and as
literature must to that extent be concerned with
"conduct," the matter seemed very serious. Mr.
Arnold's care for literature and mastery of it was so
true that we should not much fear the effects of his
"Hebraism"; but his phrase is not large enough,
and may be put to perverse uses. Shall we say,
then, that literature is the expression and interpretation of life, wise, large, and free, and that
according to the power, breadth, and truth with
which it grasps and states man's experience will
be its value to men?

And how is this done? In what ways does
literature help men to interpretation of life? Not
in any way of "criticism" in the narrower sense,
let us be clear. The proper concern of art is
with life, and not with notions about it. It must
present life itself in such ways that men shall see
it as they could not by their own insight. It
must put some significant part of life so that its
significance may be felt. That is art's first and
proper business. But that is only representation?

Let us not mistake. Neither in science nor in
art is the pure objective possible or intelligible.
In other words, art is not life, but life as seen
through the mind and experience of the artist.
The ethical value of a writer will therefore depend on the power and reach of the man, on his
scope and sanity of nature; not only on his point
of view and the value of his distinctive ideas, but
on the power and passion he has put into his
work; not on his wisdom only, but on his vital
power as a whole.

If this be our standpoint, and these our principles, how do matters stand as regards the value
and characteristics of Browning's work as interpretation of life ? How does he help his readers ?
After what has been above said of the poet's
qualities, it will be seen that in all the ways just
named he helps them. The man himself is a
moral power of great worth and energy. He has
breadth, variety, and strength of nature ; great
force, not so much of single qualities as of many
qualities acting well together. He rouses you to
the reality and to the interest of life; to the
valour and force of man's will and mind. He
braces you by the vigour and clearness of his own
temper and bearing, both by the firmness of his
hold on things and by his manliness. His frank
acceptance and straightforward enjoyment are in
the nature of a witness to the worth and health
of things, with many uses in the poet's own
time.

And in the matter of moral truth and moral

impressions, the personality of a writer has much to do with his influence. No man can ever convey explicitly the whole reason of any of his deeper convictions, still less of that most complex conviction which we call his "view of life." And it is the humanity of a writer, the "open secret" of his sense of things as a whole and his own relation to them, that moves and helps us beyond all he directly conveys. Browning has much of this kind of power and value.

It often happens that characters of much breadth lose something of power. It seems as if here the breadth and the power proved themselves together, and found means of conveying themselves through the work. There is power at every point, and yet, except on certain great principles, no emphasis.

So this poet has essential moral truth, essential spiritual power, yet great freedom and naturalness; a large independence of rules and opinions and yet a strong hold of those principles which alone get to the heart of duty and right. He has, as moralist and as poet, the instinct and sympathy of life; a care for what is alive or makes for life.

And it is, we think, in this vital power, not only of the poet, but of his poetry in its whole principle and scope, that great part of his ethical value consists. His poetry is almost wholly dramatic, free and varied representation of the facts of life and of the minds of men; and by this he liberates our humanity, teaching lessons

of intelligence and sympathy—nay, giving power
for these by setting us free from personal limitations, and making us aware of that larger world
of passion and experience which, though it lie
beyond our bounds, is a most real part of life.

As part also of the dramatic aspect of his work
and its moral bearing through that, we must
understand that "criticism" of life which is conveyed by the very principle of his characterisation.
At the basis of his dramatic method will be found
certain ideas of high import in this reference, that
the soul is individual; that it has supreme worth
in the scheme of life; that the value of experience
is in the culture of the "soul"; that, as the worth
and result of life are found finally within, none
need miss life's good; that the experience of each
is so far adequate to the well-being of each; that
as experience develops the spirituality of the soul,
life gains depth and scope.

But here we touch distinctive ideas, or "views,"
of life as found in this poet; only, let us be clear
that even as to these the poet is not a "moralist"
simply. He does not select a world out of the
world by coming to it with a set of notions it
is to illustrate. As Mr. John Morley finely said,
speaking of Emerson: "All great minds see all
things; the only difference lies in the order in
which they choose to place them." This order,
and the estimate it implies, is great part of their
criticism of life. It both reflects and determines
leading ideas. And Browning, though he has
looked at the world's order and each man's good

constantly from the dramatic point of view, has his order, and so leading ideas. These I now put, through a study of the chief poems containing them.

I will begin with the poem called " The Boy and the Angel." The poet calls it a " dramatic romance." It may seem rather a " legend " wrought as an allegory. It has the dramatic form of many of the ballads. It is an invention of the poet's imagination, giving quaint and fit form to truths that were dear and beautiful to him. Its inspiration is thus akin to that of many legends of religious faith that sprang up in the Middle Ages, blossoms as they were of deep feeling and simple faith, quaintly shaped to the utterance of sweet and noble ideals. In theme, spirit, and moral this poem is simple, devout in the right sense, cordial, and quaintly wise. The story may be thus told : A boy in a monastery followed his trade, doing his work well, by the work and in the pauses of it " praising God." And Blaise, the monk, was pleased, and told the lad that his " praise " reached God as surely as the pope's at the great Easter festival at Rome. But the boy was not content ; he longed to " praise God " (*i.e.* to please himself) in some " great way "—the pope's in St. Peter's. And he got his wish, with Gabriel's help. He became a priest, and rose to be pope. But, as he had been carried out of his proper sphere by the mistaken kindness of the angel, the boy's place was empty, his work now undone. So the angel took his place. But the

work and praise of the angel were not the boy's,
and could not replace the boy's. In time the
angel saw this, and took means to put matters
again in their natural order. He went to Rome, and
found Theocrite there as pope, preparing for the
great Easter service, proud of his place and of his
realised ambition. Gabriel made known to him
the great yet simple plan of life as he now saw it.
He is out of his place. In his place only can he
fulfil his proper tasks and God's will. Another
may fill the pope's place; none can fill his. In
the angel's words Theocrite first saw the divine
way of duty and peace. He went back to his
craft, and grew old at home. A new pope dwelt
in St. Peter's; and when Theocrite died, craftsman
and pope went together to God.

The legend is thus fitly made of the times
when men were learning the good, the social, and
religious worth of honest and useful work. In
classical society labour was slavish. In the feudal
age it was menial. The monastic rule, and the
temper of the best monastic minds, helped to add
to Western culture a principle greatly needed by
helping to make work as such honourable among
men and dear to God. And that idea had its
battle to fight against many discontents and
ambitions. To Theocrite the simple task and
daily round seemed poor. Piety, as he thought,
and pride much more, said that it were better to
do something " greater " for God. And he reached
the highest point of the monkish ambition, only
to find that, as wandering desires mistakenly

helped had carried him from his own tasks and place, his life had ceased to bring its due praise to God. The old way was not better only, but the only good way. The lowly task was best heeded and most valued by God, counting well in His great plan—a thought to reprove vain desires and sweeten simple lives.

And so through the legend Browning suggests, with a mystic glow and depth such as he likes, ideas to which, in the spirit of them, he attaches great value—the worth of each soul and of all sincere work to God; the personal quality of all real work; the duty of each to keep his own place, to respect his own worth, and to rest satisfied with his own tasks. In their proper place, and at their own tasks, men are spiritually equal; God is " praised," and the order of the universe is served by the least as truly as by the greatest. " Greater " and " less " are words of no essential meaning in the matter. The only really great thing is the whole divine order. All value depends on helping that, and all can help it. All lives rest on a divine order, enter into a " scheme " that none of us comprehends, but that all further by simple discharge of duty. All work is consecrated and made right by its due relation to that. If we move from our place, we mar the music of God's order. If we keep our place, the highest value our work can have comes from its being our duty.

In the first of " Pippa's Songs " you have the same idea, and it is the keynote of the drama— " All service ranks the same with God." All of

s, least and greatest, somehow serve Him, and
His will equalises all events and souls. We are
ll near to Him whose presence fills the world
nd all our lives. This is a dramatic principle
nd a vital truth for the poet; no "sentiment,"
s it often seems, but a law holding all lives.

In "The Statue and the Bust" you will find
hat seems a very distinct, but is a perfectly
ongruous, idea of duty. In the poems we have
ist taken, the idea is that the simple duties and
ircumstances of life are enough for happiness
nd for the soul. Here the doctrine appears to
e, that it may be a duty to break through cir-
umstances in order to reach a fuller life. Let
s see how it is. It is another legend or
omance. It arose in this way. In one of
he squares of Florence is a statue of Duke
erdinand I. The statue is so placed that the
uke seems to be looking towards the palace of
he Riccardi as he rides away, that palace stand-
ng at the corner of one of the streets running
to the square. And this posture of the statue
ppears to have given rise to a legend. The
gure looks fixedly at one of the windows of the
iccardi palace, and so fancy read design in the
osture and meaning in the look. The story got
oroad that the duke had loved one of the ladies
f the house of Riccardi; that her husband,
nowing it, shut her in his palace, so that, if they
w each other, it could only be from a window
oking into the square. The duke, in love for
e lady and scorn of her husband, had himself

put where he might seem to wait and catch h[...]
every appearance.

That is the tradition; but our poet, no doub[...]
regarding the whole thing as an invention, too[...]
it his own way. To make it a better vehicle f[...]
the truth of human hearts he saw in it, he adde[...]
to and gave it fuller meaning. The bust is hi[...]
and the reality the love had for a time. Th[...]
lady, newly married, but with heart quite fre[...]
sees the duke ride past. The duke sees th[...]
lady at the window. They love, and life begi[...]
for both. At a feast the same night they me[...]
and the duke found means to make known h[...]
love to the lady. But the husband heard, o[...]
anyhow, knew, and determined to keep the wi[...]
a prisoner within his palace. The wife seeme[...]
to submit, inwardly resolved to flee in disguis[...]
which she always found reasons not to do, unt[...]
as the years passed, the love passed too, remai[...]
ing only as a dream. The duke also had h[...]
plans, which he, too, found reasons for delayin[...]
through months into years. They could see eac[...]
other—she from the window, he from the squar[...]
To that they were faithful, with that satisfie[...]
And then, when they marked the flight of year[...]
and the change of passion itself to the memory [...]
a dream, they knew the thing past hope and vai[...]
yet wished to commemorate it. And so they h[...]
on the device of the statue and the bust, awar[...]
now that their lives in the matter had been n[...]
more vital—an "idleness which had only aspire[...]
to strive" and dreamed of being. Yet it please[...]

of it. It is your thoroughness, your sincerity, your power. And this answers the other and highly important question,—What is the use of life? The use of life is to live; not the game nor the game's gains externally, but the full, free play, the honest and even intense development of the life itself, in all its powers and all its good.

The "Grammarian's Funeral" is another poem in which we have characteristic moral ideas. It is a romance of the later Renaissance, invented by the poet for the character and ideas of which he has made it the picture and the symbol.

A body of scholars is carrying the grammarian to his grave, and the leader of the band tells the story of the dead scholar's life as they carry him. The man whose life has just closed had devoted himself soul and body to classical learning. He was a man very capable of other things, both in literature and in life. He had the face and throat of Apollo, and for a time his days had been spent, if not in pleasure, at least lightly. But it dawned on him that life was going, and nothing done, so he set himself to grapple the substance of things. The way to that, then, was the scholar's tasks. So he turned to "those who knew man best—the bard and the sage," and won learning, but wore himself out. Friends suggest that it is "time to live." But no; he will live when he has mastered all learning. He will then be able to live a full and really wise life. What good living until he can do that? But time and health are both

failing fast; it will soon be too late. That cannot be. With so much to know, and to use when
known, man must have time for it all somewhere.
So back to his books, and to harder toil. Disease
comes of the tireless toil, and friends beg him now
to rest. But he cannot. His passion is keener
than ever. He meets death at his work, the
hunger and hope of the perfect science strong
still, the fact of it far off.

That is the story. Why tell it? What do such
lives imply? What is their bearing on man's
nature and scope? In an evident sense such
lives are most incomplete. They miss " living '
in many respects, and win only a little part of
the full life of man. But these lives are noble, if
partial. Their object may be narrow, but their
spirit is great. They do not miss life as the duke
and the lady did. They throw themselves with
ardour and reality into their part of life.

But this is not enough. To narrow life to a
pursuit of " grammar," however keenly we seek it
is to make the loss of life almost too sad, if the
scholar have only this life, is it not? We can see
gains in, and still more by means of, such lives
Their concentration has its gains, and the scholar
has his own joy, and they help to build up
knowledge and the life of the race. But that
does not satisfy us in thinking out the problem
of such lives. And these lives themselves seem
to involve more and fuller life. They seem so
strong in their instinct, so deliberate in the
choice. Their passion and their idea of know

ledge seem to gain scope and ardour as their
physical powers fail. Their plans ignore death
and time, and assume eternity, as if they had an
assurance of things other men cannot see. They
appear to throw themselves on God, as if in the
faith that He will not make their noblest parts a
mockery. And their idea of culture—the idea of
perfect mastery of anything, even of " grammar "
—is a counsel of perfection, a master passion of
the mind ; part of that sublime ideal, which, at all
points of man's labour, has made the present and
the accomplished seem so small a part of the
possible and the necessary. The narrow tasks,
the brief years, the small results, the large
passion, all look out into the Infinite of man's
life, and so surely of man's hope. These lives
are no caprice ; they follow a law. That inward
obligation which throws them on their tasks is
part of a rational order. It must be because the
mind of man has its issues elsewhere that it
impels men to such devotion and denial.

There are lives of another kind, sharply contrasted against these lives of the scholar and the
thinker—lives of limited and practical scope, or
lives set upon mere earthly ends. They reach
their ends and have their rewards, while the
other lives, just because of their larger scope,
appear to fail in reaching even that they were
set upon. Can it be that because of their
success," because the system of things seems so
far in their favour that the lives are to be
preferred ? The higher lives certainly help man

more, and there seems that in the best minds which draws them to such devotion and idealism. And it is better to have your ideal and to follow it with pure passion than to live a life which reaches contentment and secures success just because its scope is narrow and its aims poor. The soul lives only as its tasks have that scope and depth; and while the lives that look to the present may end because "they have had their reward," the higher lives are of good augury and promise, and carry us onward in hope as generous as the principle on which they have gone.

The "Grammarian," with its type and its ideas, has other bearings pertinent to our life at the present time. The specialisation of work and life has grown, with the growth of knowledge and of the world, every year more narrow and intense. After a certain point in life most men have to throw themselves very much on one line and one task, and they soon find how little of all that was ideally possible to them can be actually reached by them. It is obvious that for knowledge, and for the arts, this is good and even necessary. But it is surely a mistake to persuade ourselves that it is all right, and that there is no loss attaching to it, either as regards the work or the worker. The work itself suffers, and grows much more dull and mechanical, and the worker suffers far more. What is the remedy, and where must we look for compensation? Is it that the spirit and thoroughness are the great thing; the mastery of the man's powers given by duty, and even by

sacrifice? and is the sense of the ideal made
more solid for us by the difficulty of doing anything really well? This at least is certain, that
intense specialisation makes it more necessary to
keep the sense of the ideal alive by thoroughness
and zeal, and that only as we put that quality
into duty can we keep hold on the powers and
hopes that make us men.

And we shall find that the whole question of
the relation of circumstances to man's life and
growth has been deeply grasped by the poet.
In the poem on a group of children by Woolner,
called "Deaf and Dumb," he has put a thought
often present to his mind in his studies of human
life. The children in the group were deaf and
dumb, and, looking at them as the artist had
made them, the poet saw finely suggested the
solution of a question life often raises. The eyes
of the children spoke, and their faces listened as
if the loss of the power of speech and the sense
of hearing had roused all the other senses to finer
life and fuller power. So it is, he thinks, with
the limitations and hindrances of life. It is the
prism reveals the hidden glory of the light by
stopping and breaking it up. So obstruction and
loss act in the life, and on the soul of man. They
bring out a quality and power that would in
other circumstances have remained unknown.

Parts of "James Lee's Wife," which we shall
refer to here simply in this connection, deal more
at large with the same things in experience, with
some things that touch all our hearts through

all our lives, though it may be never in the form
in which they arose to the wife of James Lee.
The theme of the section called "Under the
Cliff" is that "old woe of the world"—the
constancy of change, the inconstancy of all
besides. "Nothing endures"; nothing we gaze
upon in nature, and nothing we love, but is ever
being taken from us by this law. No perfect
moment, whether of dawn or of childhood, whether
of twilight or of love, but fades and gives place
to some other moment and something else. Yet
this, it may be said, is only a sentiment and an
appearance. To human nature it is, however, a
fact, and no one with much hold on life, or any
deep care for it, but has felt the pain of it,
making the past sad and strange. But things
change only to give place to something better.
It may be, but even the something better is
another thing, and what our hearts crave is
something above change. What is the function
of this law, then, in our lives, and why are we
subject to it at every point, in spite of the heart?
It exhilarates the soul and keeps it alive and in
motion; it enriches experience; it enforces progress. Let us rise to it, and move with it, and
gather all the wealth of life as God fashions it.
The law of change, like all else in the order of
life, has this for its end and result—the in-
vigoration and growth of man.

"By the Drawing Board," section viii. of the
same poem, puts the problem of our losses and of
the defects of life in fuller outlook. From our

present standpoint we may regard it as a parable
got from the relations of art and life. Which for
the artist is the more profitable field of study—
life, or the works of art in some of their most
perfect forms? Life, certainly. Life is not
abstractly perfect or beautiful. It does not answer
our wishes, or meet our æsthetic demands. It is
not, as we find it, ideal. In our hopes we plan
such a life, and then find the facts go against us.
What then? Life is best. We need its lessons
and discipline, and only so can we ever reach a
true art. The great artists have not worked in
dreamland, but in the world of life. They have
spent years in mastering that, not for its interest
only, but because they saw there the one way to
a right art. And in life it must be the same.
Experience and self-denial, mastery, not avoidance
or dreaming, are the method of that most difficult
art, the art of living. And we cannot make life
beautiful our abstract way, because the matter
and scheme of it are so much larger than our
thought of or wishes about it.

The imperfection and disappointment, and also
the stimulus and strange satisfaction, of life are
most forcibly expressed in "The Last Ride
Together." The speaker of this poem has loved
wholly one who has not returned his love. He
accepts his fate, and only asks the lady for one
ride more together, in which they may still seem
lovers. She grants his wish, and as they ride for
the last time together he surveys life and the
experience of men through the mood and from

the standpoint of the situation. He gives himself
to love once more, and thinks this perfect moment
better than the risks of life. And if he has not
won, how uncertain life's gains mostly are! How
few really win, and how barren is most " success "
—statesman's, warrior's, poet's ! Who knows what
" success " is really?—and does not the " Infinite "
beyond every partial deed and attainment make
all attainments seem poor, and all results inadequate to the demands of life? Perhaps it
were best, could it be, to eternise such a moment
as this ; and since that cannot be, since he knows
this must end, he concludes that the scope of life
is restricted as compared with the demands of
love, and with the possibilities of the soul under
the stimulus of any great passion.

But this is not a question only of things that
hinder and opportunities that fail. That is part
of it, certainly. But it has another side and a
better meaning; and that meaning we find in a
poem, puzzling to many readers—that named
" Two in the Campagna."

This poem is in the main a love-poem, but it
deals through that with a wider theme, and with
a larger aspect of life—with an experience that
relates to life as a whole.

Its general position is this: that the satisfactions of life are really inadequate to the heart;
that life's amplest experience leaves man still
unsatisfied. Man is mastered by a yearning after
what is perfect, and life in its finest passions and
purest unions remains partial.

Two lovers are together in the Campagna. It is May, and the silence and the passion of the season, the breadth and peace of the wide spaces open everywhere to the vast sky—these, as they touch the yearning of love itself, rouse the still deeper desire at life's heart. It is the man who speaks. " I touched a thought now has tantalised me many times." In this situation, and with his present mood, he may seize and resolve it at last. And for a moment he fancies he has the clue, though it be light and delicate as a gossamer thread, and he follows it a little way, only to find it lost again.

And so it ever is. We seem, now and again, to find some " secret " of peace and of satisfaction. It is in conscience and duty, in knowledge, in love, or it is in the soul itself and some highest truth of that; but as we close upon it and test it, we find its sufficiency gone, and we are left again to that experience of—

> Infinite passion and the pain
> Of finite hearts that yearn.

Explain it how you will, such is the experience of man. Change hurls him from point to point of life, so that he has no rest in outward things. And of the soul itself it is a law to reach always on past its best things. It is kept from repose by its own nature. We yearn for perfect trust and oneness. We touch the heart, the truth, and then stand away. How is it?

> Where does the fault lie? What the core
> O' the wound, since wound must be?

There is no account of the matter so good as this.
It is because we find within both the finite and
the Infinite, the human and the divine; limited
power, yet indefinite desire; a passion that clings
to the parts, and yet is haunted and held by its
sense of the whole.   It is the pain and mystery
of the ideal that it impels us to realise itself, and
yet reserves us always for itself.   It is in all good
things.   It gives those things their worth, and
yet we never find it.   It is within, and yet far off,
as it seems, for ever.

"Two in the Campagna" thus deals through
love with man's quest of the Infinite.   And in
dealing with that quality of our nature it touches
other points—(1) that even the best and closest
affections do not fill the scope of the heart; (2)
that at the core of us all is that mystery of
personality which makes affection possible, and
yet in the last resort shuts us off from each other,
and reserves us for the Infinite,—

> I would you were all to me.

But the mind, the heart, will not close and rest
thus, it seems—

> I yearn upward, touch you close,
> Then stand away.

And so the poem indicates how deep in the moral
structure of man, and at the core of passionate
love even, are found reserve and yearning, the
sense of an Infinite haunting and eluding us, of
a Universal claiming yet escaping us.

This is the romantic, spiritual note, felt one way in Goethe, and in another way in Byron, and heard so often in our century, and in this poet. Has our poet through his intuition of feeling read it well? or only, as it has been read in too many cases, negatively, with stress on the limits,— as it is in Carlyle, as it is in Goethe? The point is in " Sordello," it is in " Fifine," it is in other places, and at times the stress is on the limits, but Browning's drift on the matter is positive. Feeling, thought, spirit are Infinite.

But next, in illustration of the moral spirit and ideal in this poetry, let us take a group of poems that deal with the force and majesty of man's sense of right. And first, with those that deal with it as it bears on work and action, on the true motive of the patriot and the artist. There we find the moral idea affirmed as a final law— right is right, whatever happen. " The Patriot " puts this simply. But a year ago he was the hero of the hour, acclaimed of all; to-day he is brought forth to die, and the only reason is that though he has added a year's service to his former service, those he has served have changed. What then? He is satisfied; for his reward rests with God, who is not put out by these events, and his will is kept pure by being thrown on what is high, eternal, and made to depend on that alone. For him it is best so.

At the same height is " Echetlos " (" Dramatic Idyls "). It is a Greek myth. The legend was of one who fought at Marathon and did noble

service in the great battle and then vanished, and
did not leave a name or a trace whereby to follow
him, or to commemorate him. The Greeks were
very curious to find his name, and pressed the oracle
for a name, and the answer was, Let them give
him only a name symbolical of the deed he did.
Let him be known simply as " the Wielder of the
Ploughshare," his weapon in the battle ; for " the
great deed ne'er grows small. Not so, alas ! the
great name "—as the Greeks knew only too well.

The closing lyric in " Ferishtah's Fancies "
finely, and you may think boldly, carried the
same principle to the highest level, both as a law
of work and a principle of faith. The poet is
there speaking of the motive and aim of his own
work. He has not taken his law from the world,
nor worked for its praise, and so the utmost he
looks for at its hand is justice. If the work be
good work, let it be taken for its worth. The
worker has had his reward in the power to do and
in the work done. With God, and for the soul,
the highest law is loyalty to the mind's ideal, and
the proper " reward " is fruit in the soul itself of
duty thus done.

" Instans Tyrannus " is a romance made to suggest the strange authority of conscience in natures
where you would not expect it. A king had a
subject who puzzled and rebuked him by his
mere temper, and whom he therefore hated and
persecuted every way, in order to drive him to do
something that would excuse the king in destroying him. The man, in his patient, simple good-

ness, bore even the worst, until at length, in embittered hatred, the king resolved to be rid of him right or wrong—utterly wrong, he knew it. And just as he was in the act of destroying him, the man, meek hitherto, rose erect and threw himself on God. An arm seemed to shoot across the sky, sheltering the innocent and threatening the wrongdoer. The king stood confronted, as from divine heavens, by his sense of guilt, and by the majesty of retributive law. The poet held that just such power hides among the forces of human nature and of the world.

The story of "Halbert and Hob" ("Dramatic Idyls," i.) puts this question of conscience in a striking way, both as a moral and dramatic question. A father and son were together alone one Christmas night, and they quarrelled. The son with brutal strength dragged his father towards the door, with the design of throwing him violently forth into the stormy night. They were both strong rough men, and yet the father was like a child in the hands of his son. The son was struck by this, and the father told how, years ago, he had in his passion done the same by his father, and that he felt that punishment had come on him now for it. The son was struck calm before this new power, which awoke also in himself, and stopped; and father and son went back to their places by the fire. The father was dead by the morning, and the son an idiot. A similar story is found in Aristotle, *Ethics*, but not as Browning tells it, and not with his point at all.

Aristotle quotes it as the case of a man who excused himself for beating his father, on the ground that such outbursts of anger had run in his family for a long time. For Browning the law and issues of the case are deeper, and very different. It is no case of the "naturalness of anger." It is the case of one who, recognising retributive law at work with him, bows before it, with a new sense of right and wrong, and by doing so touches the same sense powerfully in another. The point is, that even in rude and violent natures there is a slumbering but strong sense of right. "Is there a reason in nature for these hard hearts?" Lear had asked; and Browning replies, that whether there be or not, a "reason out of nature" seems necessary "to turn them soft"—a power above the common, and yet within the true nature, divine and human.

To conclude our study of the poems of this class, I will take four that *consider life as a whole*.

And first of these and most notable of this whole class of poems is "Rabbi Ben Ezra." In it you have a large and mature expression of the poet's thoughts about man's life. Ideas found in other poems are here brought together and presented in fuller and more connected statement, and the thoughts are more here, and the dramatic design less, than in other studies. The ideas have indeed a dramatic fitness to the imaginary speaker; but the ideas are more to the poet than usual, and it is, I think, right to find in the

poem, not "his philosophy of life," but certain
principles of that philosophy to which he attaches
a personal and large value.

It is a study of life from the point of view of
Hebrew thought. Aben Ezra was a Jewish
scholar and theologian of the Middle Ages. He
lived from 1092 to 1187. He was born at
Toledo, and made himself famous among the
thinkers of his people and faith. He lived, as
the dates show, to a good old age—ninety-five
years; and, as he believed in a future life, the
dramatic meditation here assigned him may fit
very well with the thoughts of his later years.

The poem is a survey of life from a point
beyond its maturity. The rabbi is looking over
the past and into the future, and is weighing the
gains of experience and the whole meaning of
life. He looks at the facts and the changes and
the drift of the years to find what it means and
to what it tends, and he concludes that life must
be an education of the soul. It seems to him
that, whether he look back or forward, the only
real and lasting use he can see in experience is
to mature the soul. The growth and power of
the soul is the proper test of the results of life.
By that standard you must try all attainment and
success. You are on the right way, you succeed,
as you gain spiritual power. If this be so, then
the best part of life is that in which experience
and culture have given you knowledge and mastery
of your own nature. The best part, then, is not
youth nor middle life, but mellow age. When

15

this is seen, and the scope of life is ascertained by this test, it is found that what men often count the whole of life must be but a part of life; that our life here is one of experiment and development, not of accomplishment. Its higher test is not what a man does, but the power he unfolds, what he is on the way to be. The inward aim, the entire thought and aspiration, of the man —it is these that measure the man's worth and the proper fruit of his life. The "divine judgment" is an inward judgment, and looks less to the work than to the spiritual quality and character of the man. It is this great principle that explains the process of life—the pain, failure, and loss that human lives so often contain. They result from the soul's scope, are a means of keeping it from resting on anything done or reached in this life, and urge it on to its proper fulfilment.

These are the general ideas; but now mark the course of thought a little more closely—a matter you will not find clear all at once.

The rabbi starts with the idea that the best of life is to come. The common idea is that man's years up to his prime are his best; but that is to make life dependent wholly on the body. And yet even in youth it may be seen that man is spiritual; for youth shows its discontent with the actual, and overleaps all satisfactions. As the life of the body is then at its best, that could not happen if the sense-life were the man. If man were "animal," sensuous, then present selfish ends and gains would satisfy. These do not prove enough, and the reason of this is, that man shares the divine nature, and must give, not get only. Now, whatever throws us on this true nature, be it discontent, failure, pain, is good for us; and the finest use of " the body " is to " project the soul on its lone way."

But though this be the chief use and guiding principle of life, man should not be ungrateful for any good, and the proper rule of life is not ascetic. The world is good and beautiful, and so is the body in its due place. Do not let us put soul and body against each other, or regard things in that spirit. Let them rather combine in one service, and realise the full good of the Maker's plan. Only the end must ever be the soul's advancement. The man must come out of it more plainly a " god, though in the germ." The proper gain of life is wisdom and spiritual manhood. And youth, with its discontent and conflict, being past, a man must test his experience so far, and make clear to himself what he has gained. This can only be done, in fact, when youth is gone. Youth was uncertain—in it was a war of minds and experiences; but in manhood we see and know. Experience and the soul bring matters to the test; the right and good are discerned; and, the noise and dispute having ceased, the meaning of the past and the way we are on grow clear to us. And what is the meaning and function of the past? Discipline, growth of faculty, inward knowledge, craftsmanship, and a fine use of all tools given us.

The world looks to and rewards work only. And
from the world's point of view that may be right ;
but it is a " crude," outside view. The true view
makes note not so much of what has been done,
but of all a man's instincts and purposes ; all the
things that could not be done, that could not
even be expressed ; all that went to make the
man. A man's worth to God is his true worth,
and God finds a man's worth in " the man's
amount," as he is in himself, and not merely in
what he has been able to do.

It is thus the rabbi finds his final clue to life
and its process. The Hebrew idea of the potter
and his wheel gives him that image of life which
makes it all clear. It is just that shaping of the
pitcher on the wheel that explains it, that is what
it all comes to. Life and its changes are the wheel
on which man is being shaped to divine uses.
We think at times that all things, within us and
without, change and pass away with the flight of
years. It is not so. That is the illusion of the
sense-life. The fact is that all that has told on
or entered into the soul, lasts and is. God and
the soul endure, and all circumstance is but
machinery shaping the soul as God wills.

The rest of the poem, in which the rabbi applies
this image to the whole scope and full interpretation
of life, belongs to the question of immortality, and
is dealt with under that section of these studies.

The next poems of this group we take are the
two called " Pisgah Sights " (" Pacchiarotto," p.
75–82). In the first of these the speaker looks

back on life from a point at which he can see the whole like a globe lying beneath, and he states, as the sum of wisdom gathered thus——a lesson of unity and reconcilement; large acceptance, not because all the questions raised are clear, but because he sees how " good and evil, joy and sorrow " work together, and need each other in the world as we know it.

In the second of the " Pisgah Sights," the closing thought of the first is taken up. We reach these large views only from some remote height at life's close, and when we can make no use of them. This is sad, thinks the speaker, and he describes how he would have lived had he known life as he now knows it. Cheerful acceptance, but also indifference, would be our mood could we see all; contentment, so far gone as to be inert submission, would be the temper of life. The man of complete experience would regard a great part of the things men strive for as trivial, and all situations as equal. It is, in fact, the situation of Lazarus. Does the poet, then, mean that a really large and wise view of life would take all interest and energy out of it? He does not believe in that kind of wisdom. If life be only a game of no great essential value, play it well for the soul's sake. That is the end. And our best wisdom is of the kind which gives light and power for that. You cannot reach any absolute truth about life; you cannot see all, nor would it be well if you could. Use well, therefore, your best working view," and the rabbi's idea that spiritual development is the proper good of life gives the principle and even the substance of such a view.

Such are the poems dealing more or less directly with the "criticism of life." It must not, however, be supposed that these are the only poems of Browning dealing with such interpretation. So far is that from being the fact, that it may in truth be said that the whole of Browning's work, from "Pauline" to "Asolando," is a criticism of life and of the nature of man. And special groups of his poems are more closely so, the love poems, for example, and the art poems. Such poems as "Old Pictures at Florence," and such a poem as "Evelyn Hope" are clearly so, for the main criticism of the former rests on a certain view of the mind and life of man; and the love passion of the latter, and of other love poems of Browning, implies a profound criticism of the meaning of man and the destiny of life. In the view of these poems the soul is capable of an infinite expansion, which is guaranteed and reached through love. Our destiny is to grow through love into the life of all things. Love is thus the central principle of life—the power that holds the universe together — the clue to all meanings—the condition of all knowledge.

And this is why the clue given so simply in the little poem called "The Guardian Angel," is the clue to so many solutions in Browning. The point is thus put in the poem—

O world, as God has made it! All is beauty:
And knowing this, is love, and love is duty.

Beauty, love, duty, in life truly seen and well understood are all one, and the core of all meanings and all claims is still love for ever.

The poet goes with his wife to see Guercino's picture of the guardian angel at Fano by the Adriatic. He gazes on the figure of " the dear great angel " sheltering and guarding the child, until the idea of the picture fills his mind. It then seems to him that the picture is an image of life as it might be were men true, trustful, simple. We largely make our world what it is by our lack of truth, trustfulness, simplicity; and duty is hard and strange for us, because we are unloving. Let us get back to the " world as God has made it," to a world of duties resting on love, and we shall find it beautiful. For as love springs when beauty is felt, so duty is joy when love is its ground. It is an old and a simple philosophy. It is not, however, the temper or the consciousness of childhood. It is rather, like all real simplicity and right trustfulness, the ripening fruit of just feeling and fine insight.

Our study of this group of poems has made it clear that Browning is what is called an optimist. He is vigorously and generously so. He believes and looks for a " best." It is a big hope, and it were interesting to look into its grounds in Browning's work. But it involves larger considerations than belong to ethics or the moral interpretation of life, and must not be entered on here. But before we close this part of our studies, studies presenting or suggesting the

poet's view of life, we take three poems that
involve the optimistic temper and outlook which
are so characteristic of him.

The poem called " At the ' Mermaid ' " is in the
main a defence of poets and poetry against the
prejudices and misjudgments of common opinion.
People think that with the writings of these poets
in their hands they know all about them. Yet
they do not know the poets as they think. That
is the drift. But there is one passage of this
poem that is more general. It is that in which
Browning scornfully rejects " Byronism," as a
poetic temper and creed. He will not carry
" the pageant of a bleeding heart " anyway, or wail
a wail of woe at all. He has found life good and
he will say so bluntly—

> I find earth not grey but rosy,
>   Heaven not grim, but fair of hue.
> Do I stoop ? I pluck a posy.
> Do I stand and stare ? All's blue.

—a sarcastic retort on Byronism, and on the
" decadents."

The poem called " Apparent Failure," which
deals with a grim subject, yet gives, after the
harsh details of a visit to the Morgue, a note of
bracing cheerfulness even in face of such facts as
it is a comment on. The purpose of the Morgue
by the Seine in Paris is well known. In it they
lay out the unhappy ones who have been taken
from the river dead, the many suicides of the gay
city. The poet goes there one day and finds
three bodies laid out for recognition.

"Poor men God made, and all for that." He
cannot think so. He glances at them as they lie,
in tragic stillness. He finds one a mere youth,
and one an old man, the other in lusty manhood,
—all of them gone this quick way to death.
Does he see there the tale of those lives ended?
Were they given manhood and a "life-rent of
God's world" only for that? He cannot believe
it; and in face of such fates he declares his hope
that no lives will be thus cast away, but that a
sun will one day "pierce the thickest cloud" this
"earth has ever stretched" over human disaster
and despair. Sentimental, some will say. But
that is never his quality, and the hopefulness of
such a passage, facing the worst and blackest facts
of life, rests squarely on his whole view of things.
He would have rejected an optimism "resting on
mere feeling." Unless hope rest on fundamental
intuitions, on great principles and the law of
things, "on the nature and on the unity of God
and man," it is of little power and less value.
Browning had no sort of respect for "lies," however pleasant. His dramatic quality in the apprehension and presentment of life, and his build of
mind, secure a close care for fact. In his own
way as poet he grapples the question of the vital
grounds of such a creed, again and again, at a
score of points. We find him at it in "The Ring
and the Book," in "Ferishtah's Fancies," in the
"Parleyings," in certain poems of "Asolando."
Only here, and as a capital test of the robust
quality and broad grounds of our poet's optimistic

faith, let us dwell for a little on a quaint and
difficult poem, with one of those grotesque names
he liked so well and used so often——the poem
called " Jochanan Hakkadosh," with a legend as
queer as the title, and drawn from one of the
poet's favourite sources of "fact and fancy," the
" Talmud." The legend of the old rabbi repeats
in another way, and with fuller scope, the parable
of " Pisgah Sights." The rabbi is dying in his
eightieth year, with mind sound and clear. His
disciples come to hear the sum of all his wisdom,
and he gives them his last message in words of
discouragement. We have power when without
wisdom, and wisdom when the power is gone, and
so a great part of life is wasted. But they refuse
to take that as the old rabbi's last oracle. They
must gather riper wisdom than that from him.
A way to do so is found, for they contrive to
keep him a year longer by getting him one
quarter of a year out of each of four typical lives
——lover, warrior, poet, statesman——that he may
distil wisdom's soul out of all experience. The
rabbi takes up the lives offered him, and from
his point of view, and with his consciousness, lives
through them. But it is vain, this game of a
double self, and a life seen through ere it is lived.
It is a natural fancy that, if we could only start
wise, we should then make the best of life and
be happy. How is it with the rabbi? The
experiment ends in disappointment. Why?
Because ignorance and illusion are necessary to
life, and to forestall experience is to prevent, not

enjoyment only, but wisdom too. Life is a process whose results can only be reached on the lines of natural growth, and to force results is to arrest and destroy, not to help experience. And so his disciples, who had looked for a science of man's life, are sad. But this is not the end. Fear of persecution scatters his scholars, and when they return three months later, they find the rabbi still alive. And when, becoming aware of their presence, he opens his eyes on them once more, that which no lengthening of the earthly life could accomplish has been, it seems, accomplished—light and joy look out from the old master's soul. He had got the child-heart, and won the seer's vision. He has somehow reached a standpoint from which life is so seen that cordial acceptance and profound reconciliation are possible. He has, in fact, been kept on earth three days after the spirit has reached the "other life," and so he sees life from a point outside and above the earthly experience. He thus sees the law and the results of all, and is "absurdly happy." But what is it he sees from this strange new standpoint? What is the knowledge that explains and harmonises all? That life's method of "encountering opposites" works out a divine good, in which "every dream's assured of soberest fulfilment." It is, in the nature of the case, impossible to do more than hint what might be seen from such a standpoint; but the main matter is in the suggestion thus made, that for the higher criticism of life such a

point of sight is necessary, and that the principle
is clear, though the process is perplexing. Every
view we can frame is but a relative truth, and our
largest view of life must be partial until from
some point above life we grasp the principle and
see the drift of the whole. Only as we plant ourselves on the high ideals of the Spirit and trust
them can we get the "vision" that will inspire
and steady us. And to this in degree the poet
as seer helps us. From the high point he can
reach he assures us of the best. The issue will
justify the cost. All we do not and cannot know
confirms and surpasses the best of all we know.
And if the stress appear to be on ignorance, it is
not really so, for such confidence as this rests at
length, not only on the higher and purer trust, but
on the larger vision.

Life is thus, in our poet's view, a winepress,
from which, by the free mingling of *all* its elements, there comes in the end so strong a wine
that it may be drunk by those only whose brains
can bear ecstasies. And this is the poet's *optimism*,
not one of evasion, or illusion, nor any "dream
of good" to be won by impossible changes, but a
robust and free acceptance of the order of the
world and the condition of life as a divine way
to the soul's ideal. Things work for "good,"
but we must abide the full process, and await
the true issue We are on the way to that good,
as we live with energy and purpose; with hearty
care for life and the soul, for a full experience,
and a free development. We must not fear.

All good comes to those who persist and believe ; comes not in spite of but through experience, and what are called the *limits* of life; and is the " slow fruit of an enhancing toil," strengthened by love—a love which endures and trusts and doubts —a trust that falters, but holds on and does not fail.

That life is then a somewhat austere discipline Browning sees, and he accepts the situation heartily, though not ascetically. He accepts the situation not as punishment, nor as destiny, and not to repress nature, but for its results. He sees that will and heart and character in men are braced and ripened, and that strenuous joys of life and duty come out of it for those who live and keep on living. We are, it may be, " hurled from change to change," and never allowed to rest long anywhere, but the régime is good for those who accept the law and catch the drift of it, and he held its promise infinite for the true and the brave.

CHAPTER X

RELIGIOUS POEMS: SAUL, CHRISTMAS EVE, THE SUN

PASSING from poems that interpret life, I turn to a group that may be called religious, not that they are the poet's only or chief religious poems in the larger sense, but that they deal more explicitly with religious ideas than is usual even in Browning. The poems differ much from each other in certain respects. The emotional key and musical quality of " Saul " is very distinct from the argumentative spirit and style of " Christmas Eve," or the didactic aim of " The Sun." But in all of them the ideas as such stand out, and they complement each other the better for their differences.

Their dates are widely apart: " Saul," 1845 ; " Christmas Eve," 1850 ; and " The Sun " (" Ferishtah's Fancies "), 1885. Standing thus forty years apart, they show well the depth and stability of the poet's interest in their themes. He has always been and he remains deeply interested in these matters. Through his career as a poet, the greater facts and ideas of religion have found in him a student. Other poets besides in our age have been drawn to these questions, but no one has so well expressed the inner spirit and worth of religion or the essential greatness of its ideas.

The mere mention of religious poetry is apt, we are aware, to prove an offence to lovers of art; it has so often, in all but its highest examples, been a poetry of special emotions and narrow ideas; it has so rarely had value as literature. Yet only in so far as these and similar poems in Browning have the general truth and broad interest of literature do I present them for study. And it seems to me that these poems, in their method as in their matter, have that quality. I judge them to be a proof of the depth of modern poetry, and an instance of the modern spirit as regards the whole subject of religion.

Religion in history is a great body of facts, throwing light not merely on the institutions, but on the very life of man. And religion in the present is not merely a tradition from the past, but a part of living experience. It has sprung, it springs out of the nature and relations of man as something strictly natural. In that sense these facts of religion belong to and bear upon all who have to do with man or human life.

And Browning has explored the facts in that sense and with that aim. He is in deep agreement with the great modern view of religion—of religion as part of the vital study of man. He has sought out these facts in his own mind, and the facts of other minds and lives, for their proper

interest and large significance as regards the nature
of man. Religion interests him little as a body
of opinion; more as a faith, though rather in a
way of suggestion than of definition; but most of
all as a revelation of man, and as a clue to man's
thought and passion, and only through these to
what may be known or guessed of the cosmic
order. With a wide, if not impartial and really
comprehensive interest in the facts of man's nature,
he has shown a special interest in the bearing and
import of the emotions and beliefs we call religious.
He has appreciated and shown the unique place
and power of religion among the facts of the
mind, among the factors of life. He has, as a
poet freely interested in man, exhibited the natural
energy, the inner power and reality of religion.

But it is as a dramatic poet. Let this be distinctly said and clearly seen, for two reasons.
However true theology may be, and however
valuable " edification " from their own standpoints and within their own spheres, these are
not the poets, and with these the poet meddles
only to muddle, to lose his way and his value.
Looking at facts and ideas within the province of
religion, his part is to see them in their place, to
catch them in their action, to interpret and render
their living value. If the modern mind, looking
at the facts of religious history, regards them as it
regards other facts in their order, and seeks to
explain them in relation to man and experience,
and man with due regard to them, the poet must
carry the process and principle to a further stage

and a higher power. He must present them "alive and at work" if we may say so—present them as they play their parts in the souls of men, or as they reveal the passion and play of the natures of men at high points and in great moments.

We have said that Browning approaches these matters as a dramatic poet, but many think that he does not handle them as a poet, with lucidity and beauty. This class of his works has certainly given more trouble than pleasure to some of his readers. Poems like "Christmas Eve" and "Easter Day," "A Death in the Desert," and others, seem to them more of the nature of religious discussions than of poetry. They are, they think, too subtle, and carry too much thought. They deal with philosophic, not poetic aspects of their themes, and illustrate the bent of the author rather than those parts of his themes that are of best interest, while some of the themes seem unsuitable. Fair objections lie against some of them, let us admit, and some of us will not care for this kind of verse whether Dryden or Pope, whether Tennyson or Browning write it; and Browning is certainly the "greatest sinner" in the matter of intellectual elaboration. But it is not true to say that in these poems, or anywhere, he stimulates and engages the brain while he leaves the heart untouched. And it may fairly be said that poems that on sufficient acquaintance deeply interest many minds, not only for their matter, and not only for their dramatic energy, but for a quality of poetic conception and expres-

16

sion in them, have " justified " an honourable, and in
certain cases a high place in their class; the inability
of many readers to grapple them, and the distaste
of others, being accepted as in part resulting from
faults of excess and defect that characterise some
of these poems.

The further questions raised by some of the
poems of this group, whether a poet does well for his
art and wisely for himself in treating such matters
as those taken in " Christmas Eve " and " A Death
in the Desert," must turn on the vital interest of
their themes, and on the quality of the treatment.
Drawn by his own interest, and that of his time,
the poet chooses them. If they have the interest
he assigns them, and he is able to grasp and
present the human truth of the themes thus
chosen, then he has made good his choice. So
far as he leaves them in any sphere of partial
interests he fails, as he does if he chooses themes
that have only such interest. How far this is the
case with certain of the poems at present before
us, and with certain parts of them, may remain
matter of difference as between different readers.
But broadly we repeat, with regard to these poems,
that the poet's ground is human nature, and his
scope the cordial exposition of that. It is in this
way, as a dramatist of spiritual passion and faith
in man, that Browning has sought to present the
facts and ideas found in these poems. And the
interest and power of some of his studies of the
kind are so great, his statement of certain religious
ideas in their relation to the soul and to life is

forcible, that he may be counted in the class of
those who, by sheer vigour and vitality of conception, have given independent and original witness
to the human truth of religion.

The larger relations of this poetry to spiritual
religion will be considered under another group of
the poems. For the present we take only the
ideas presented in the poems now chosen. And
first let us take "Saul." This poem is one of the
early dramatic lyrics. It belongs to the "Bells
and Pomegranates" series in its first form. Its
date is 1845. In that form it only went as far
as section ix. When reissued in "Men and
Women," in 1855, it was much enlarged, and,
from our present standpoint, had got a new purpose. The poet had in the interval added its
great sections (x.–xix.). The subject had clearly
attracted him, and he threw all his power of certain
kinds into its development—his power of passion,
of music, of mystical thought and hope. In its
kind it is one of his finest poems—one of the
finest proofs of his poetic power, of his swiftness
and sustained energy of feeling and of verse;
while, in the matter of it, it has several aspects
of deep and permanent human interest.

Let us follow the development of the poem, and
make clear as to its scheme. Saul, Israel's chosen
king and special hope, is mad, driven so by his
own wild and wilful passions. Those about him
are impotent to control or help him. David is
sent for as one likely to bring help. He comes
with music and song, and even more, with his

humanity and faith, to try what may be done for the mad king. He tries all kinds of song and all earthly appeals, and is only very partially success-ful. When impelled to save, he is driven by his very helplessness and yearning out upon God—on "the Christ in God"—and finds at length in that (when the whole feeling and resource of his nature has been roused) the saving help and vital power he was seeking. The divine love and pity, the essential humanity of Deity, are our last ground of hope for such cases, and if, in a life such as ours and with men as they are, that be not a necessary truth, it is surely a beneficent and reasonable faith.

The poem is a dramatic lyric. It gives an account of the whole situation from a single point of view. David is the speaker, and tells all that happened as he saw and felt it. And, most fitly, the whole is high-strung. It was a task to put his whole nature to the test and bring out all his passion, and Browning makes you feel it so, not only in the resource of the poet, but in the strain of the man. So it is highly lyrical. In other words, Browning seeks the heart of the situation, by taking his place within its chief actor, and relating all thence. The poem is spoken by David after the events are past, but only just past, when the whole effort and experience are still fresh, vivid, and strange. He has left Saul, and returned to the pastures and the flocks; and the day follow-ing he shapes the whole thing into song, seeing i now in its course and from his higher standpoint And, as he gathers the story into song, alone, with his sheep only round him, it seems to him dream-like and yet most real, because most deeply impressed on his soul.

The dramatic circumstances are simple, yet need to be clearly grasped. Having gone from bad to worse, Saul now seems a ruin, melancholy mad. In his high place, and with his special responsibility as divine minister, he has taken his own way, not God's, and the wrong has eaten into his soul—banished him, with his risks and his burdens, from God. His nature has become morose, has lost its balance. In the language of the old time, he is " troubled by an evil spirit sent from God." For three long days in the mid-tent's deep silence he has been alone, nor given sign to tell whether he be still alive, or how the dark strife goes. But David has come, and Abner greets him out of his deep anxiety with hope. David, with his gifts, may help or even heal the king, and bring the long sad strife to a close. His very coming seems to bring freshness and health with it. The radiant youth, " God's dew on his gracious gold hair," and the lilies from the pastures tied about his harp, both speak of a region quite different from this region of arid desert and anxious minds. By such sweetness even the scorched soul of the king may be refreshed. David kneels to God, and then makes his way into the tent. Having come to the inner tent, and seeing only its darkness, he speaks to the king, who had sent for him; but the king is lost to speech. But in the blackness of the tent he sees at length the giant shadow of the king, then a single sunbeam falling on it through the tent-roof; sees the king, drear, stark, speechless, blind. He takes his harp, and, stripping it of its lilies, he plays the tune used at the sheep-folding, and then other tunes such as touch and please the creatures of the pasture lands—the *simple songs* that win all living creatures with the mere sense of the good of life in its simplest states. Then the glad song of the reapers, their wine song, with its joy of men and their fellowship in labour and the good of life, he struck from his harp. And again other music, mournful or glad —the gentle lament for the dead, and the happy song of love and marriage; then the great march of the union of men for help and defence.

But none of these touched the king; neither the elemental pleasures nor the general emotions of man's common life have any response in his nature, or any power to recall him from his gloom and isolation. He remains still far apart. So David tries the deeper *strain of worship*, the sacred chant of the Levites as they go to the altar of God. And this does reach him. It goes to the root of his woe and his loss—not with healing yet, but only with pain. It recalls him to the reason of his lonely sorrow, his shadowed faith, his lost fellowship. It brings his misery to life. He shudders so that the tent shakes under the pain of the strong man. But that was all. The body hung erect in its pain. He had been reached, but remained far off still.

So the singer tries again, and he sings this time

the jubilant *song of man's life*, in its pleasures, in its tasks, in its ties and affections and memories—all that makes life good, whether to the senses or to the heart; the song of all this man's life had brought him, and had once been to him. It was a song meant to set his life in its true light, and to carry the wholesome sense of it far into the king's heart—into the very midst of his oblivion and gloom. Full of sadness and remorse as he is, how much life has given in the past! what uses it has had, and good and honour too, lifting Saul's name out of sorrow and above shame! Let him now recall these things. Even his wrongs cannot obliterate them, and his remorse ought not to keep them out of his view. What gifts had been given him! All gifts, given singly to most, combined on his head, and high deeds and fame of heroes.

And here, in the first instance, the poet stopped, either unable then to carry it farther, or not feeling the need to do so. It has been said that he then meant us to suppose that Saul was freed—that that song of the good and kindness of the earthly life was enough to restore him. It does not so appear in the light of the fuller song. He had been touched, roused out of torpor and death—that was all. Death was past. Life had not come; aware of life, he had yet no care for it, no real concern in its affairs. He was released and stood now on its brink. His eyes and face wore the look of pallid autumn sunsets, out of which the life of the year seems gone, and all the glow and activity only a memory.

What more can be done to give life? What
appeal can enliven and sustain? The whole good
of life poured into song had only awoke him from
death. He let the singer praise it, and he heard;
but for his part life was gone, and he would die.
So the mind of the poet seeks intensely for further,
greater truth; for higher, fuller stimulus. And
from the *sense-life*, with its good, he rises to the
life and good that are *moral*. He sings of man's
higher work and influence, the long fame of those
who have done great things. He sings the dignity
and honour of man, and all the fruits of kingly
will and works as they live on through genera-
tions.

At this the king was more deeply touched, more
fully roused. He had stood lifeless before; he now
sank and sat, and the singer by his vast knees.
Resuming the kingly motions, he lifted his hand
and placed it softly and gravely, but not listlessly
—rather now in "mild, settled will"—on the
singer's brow, bending back his head "in kind
power" and looking into his face "intent to
peruse it."

As the great eyes of the king looked at him,
the heart of the singer was filled with even fuller
love and fuller desire to bless, and there was much
still to do, to give. So the passion of help sprang
higher as he looked into the sad face, and knew it
Saul.

But how help? What is there beyond what has
been sung—the good of life, and noble memory
and long influence after death? Can there be

more? He feels that that does not restore and fill the broken heart, and he would do all, give all, that would heal and restore.

And so in this mood, with this " divine desire," he is carried beyond harp and song, into *the vision and message of the prophet*. This vision and message fill sections xvii. and xviii. How is this reached? He has put all that this life can yield of good and power even to the great ones, and it falls short. It leaves the heart still yearning amid the misery of such lives as this of Saul for a fuller hope, and therefore an ampler power. Can it be? He looks at the world, and he sees evidence of vast, possibly infinite, power. " God is seen God " at every point, and all is goodness and perfection ; but all is law. And yet love rises above the whole order, and would give and bless and heal for ever and infinitely. And this longing of endless pity and help is surely the best thing, the most god-like in man. If God be God, then it must be in God, this great pity and love—and highest in Him. The very greatness of God's gifts, the very build of man's heart, seem to require this—the very ideal of the " good God." Surpassing at every point, in every power, the Creator must surpass in this too. He must will to save, and, willing, He must have power to do what is highest. There is, therefore, a Life to repair and complete these broken lives, and a God who is Power and Law, but also Love for ever helpful. Surely it must be so. Man is indeed of little power, soon spent ; and yet it is not what a man does

or can that tests him, but what he "would do."
And greatest of all he would do is the act of saving
another, even through sacrifice and suffering. So
it must be with God.

> Would I suffer for him that I love?   So wouldst Thou—so
>   wilt Thou !
> So shall crown Thee the topmost, ineffablest, uttermost
>   crown—
> And Thy love fill infinitude wholly, nor leave up nor down
> One spot for the creature to stand in !
>
> .   .   .   .
>
> As Thy Love is discovered almighty, almighty be proved
> Thy power, that exists with and for it, of being Beloved !
> He who did most, shall bear most ; the strongest shall stand
>   the most weak.
> 'Tis the weakness in strength, that I cry for ! my flesh, that
>   I seek
> In the Godhead ! I seek and I find it. O Saul, it shall be
> A Face like my face that receives thee ; a Man like to me,
> Thou shalt love and be loved by, for ever : a Hand like this
>   hand
> Shalt throw open the gates of new life to thee ! *See the*
>   *Christ stand !*

As the poet-prophet made his way home in the
night, his soul full of this highest truth, whereby
as it seemed to him all the pain and sin of human
life might be healed, the intensity of his motion
his ecstasy of hope, gave all nature and the whole
of life a new meaning. The universe seemed
aware, seemed in sympathy. His hope had
become an "open secret." All the hosts of life
seemed to press about him, and the stars beat
with emotion, until the tumult and the rapture
were quenched in quiet and rest.

With the dawn, the trouble and sorrow and

wrong seemed to have withered from the earth,
in the opening light of a final era of hope.   The
birth of day and the grey of the hills had a new
tenderness, a new promise.   The breath of the
morning air seemed a thrill of fresh joy, and all
the creatures knew the truth.

And what, you ask, is the *general value* of such
a poem ?—(1) It is a study of " a mind diseased,"
and the means by which it may be restored—by
music and song and human sympathy, and by
the influence of a generous and healthy nature.
(2) It is a study of character in one of those crises
that call forth all its resources.   David, face to face
with the mad king, gloomy as the blackness of the
mid-tent itself, is a striking picture of courage and
tenderness.   He tries one means, and then another,
and, unsatisfied with partial success, he rises by
sheer magnanimity of nature to that hope and faith
in which a full success is assured.   Two kingly
natures, Saul and David ; but David the greater,
the richer, more spiritual.   (3) It is, too, a study
of the inmost *spirit of the Psalms*—of the relation
of the faith of these to the story of the passionate
and heroic king to whom so many of them were
ascribed : " Like as a father pitieth his child, even
so the Eternal pitieth " ; " The mercy of the
Eternal is from everlasting to everlasting."   (4) It
is a subtle and powerful exposition of the *central
problem* of Christianity, and the great faith by
which that problem is solved.   The relation of this
faith to the moral necessities of life, and to what
is best and deepest in the heart, is forcibly and

greatly shown. It is the sorrow and sin of the world that raise its deepest problem, and force us on to the highest question; and whenever a strong nature is face to face with such facts as this of Saul's deterioration and madness, these questions are raised. The question is raised by love and care for the individual soul even more than by thought. The idea of self-sacrificing love as the only one adequate to the facts of life, and as essential to the ideal of divine excellence, was never so finely expressed or so vitally " argued." The revelation of the Supreme Humanity of Deity and the commanding power and grace of this conception of God, are most forcibly presented. The splendour and tenderness of the Christian faith and what may be called the moral argument for it are here at their best. (5) And this new and fuller thought of God seems to shed light, not only on human life, but on the whole life of the world. All things have part in it. It gives the secret of the life of all; it is the mystery of that " pen knowledge " and hidden law which waited to b " revealed " in the upward strife of Nature.

But obviously there are two *objections* to such a poem. It is not historic. David could not have reached these ideas, and certainly not in the form they have here. This train of thought is modern and Christian. That is true. The dramatic lyric as Browning used it, allows, or at least uses, that freedom, and the reader gains by it, since the ideas are amplified by the imagination and passion of the poet, while they keep a real fitness in regard to the speaker and his circumstances. The large and tender heart of the royal psalmist, as imagined in Hebrew history and poetry, would have responded to such sentiments, though there is no reason to ascribe them to him, except in so far as the Messianic strain in certain psalms gives a basis for it.

And in the judgment of some the matter is not poetic — it is theological in these closing sections, and they would have liked " Saul " better without them. The poem, in point of form and passion, in flow and charm of verse, is one of the poet's best, and that seems to argue that the matter has been transmuted. And so it has been. The ideas are presented as part of the passion and insight of the singer. It is the very soul of the singer become faith and song. Nor is the tone of the poem didactic—it is dramatic narrative. The ideas are given as they grow out of the circumstances and spirit of the speaker.

" Christmas Eve " belongs to the early years of Browning's married life and to the discussion that had then begun to occupy the serious mind of Europe. Historical and other criticism, particularly in Germany, had raised the question of the trustworthiness of the early records of Christianity, and the still deeper question of their true meaning, and the historic relations of the Founder of the Christian Church and faith to that faith and Church. The sensitive interest of his wife in the questions thus opened, and in the deeper

question of the essential grounds of Christian belief.
told on the poet's own interest in the matter, and
led him thus early, 1849–50, to take the theme.

The poem may indeed be described as a study
of the central theme of "Saul" from a different
standpoint, through a different *persona*, and in a
very different atmosphere. That is a moral presentment of its theme set in circumstances of life
—this is largely intellectual. That was concerned
with "the Christian Idea" in relation to the needs
of human life—this with the story and personality
in which the divine Idea has been centralised.
The one is a sort of prophecy and intuition of the
truth, and so of the fact; the other a criticism of
the Christian statement of the truth, of the historic
"evidences" for the faith of Christian men—that
the great truth became fact in the life, spirit
and teaching of Jesus. The one is a lyric, the
other largely an argument in visionary dramatic
form. It is, we may say, a *vision of Christ*; of
the great figure and idea of Christianity, as seen
by a modern mind amid the division, debate, and
the doubt of the present century. And the
question has become, on the eve of the day
consecrated to the memory of the Christ, what
is to be thought of and believed about Him and
His religion. The Christian religion has become
so various and contradictory in its sects, and the
history of Christ has become so uncertain, that
the question now is, whether any of these sects
express the true idea—whether the divine idea
found historic expression in Christ, or whether the

idea has fashioned the character and the legend. To the speaker's inner thought the great faith clearly remains—the figure and spirit of Christ remain the highest authority and law ; but that inner faith has much difficulty to keep any relation to " the Churches of Christ," and even to hold its own clearly against modern criticism.

The poem is a kind of *dramatic romance*—an imaginary narrative, presenting the sections of the debate in scenes of a kind of dream. The speaker, who is clearly not the poet, relates what passed through his mind one Christmas Eve as if it had happened externally. He is in a chapel on the edge of a common—a poor place, with wretched service and vulgar worshippers. Driven in by the night's storm, he would worship and listen for an hour with the others to that gospel of the Christ who came as Saviour centuries ago. But what he sees and hears is very trying, and soon drives him well within his own thoughts and fancies, raising within his mind, by the quaint worship and gospel of these people, the question whether indeed any form of Christianity be pertinent or credible any more. He fancies himself, in disgust of this particular form, quickly out of the little chapel again into the stormy night, with nature alone for temple and teacher ; and the contrast between the narrow chapel and the spacious night seems a fit symbol of the difference between their creeds. Here at least God seems real, near, and great. And as his heart is expanded with the sense of that, a great and rare thing happens.

He sees a double lunar rainbow in mystic splendour arch the heavens, and on its summit a figure
which seemed the Spirit of the glory. It took its
place beside him, and he knew the divine Master
"with His human air." But he saw only the
back and the vesture of the Master, and the
Master seemed to be leaving him. Was this,
then, because he had left the poor chapel with
proud thoughts? He clings to the garment's
hem, and explains that he only left in the search
for a purer and truer worship, and for a truth
that should more fitly express the divine Spirit.
The Face then turned upon him fully, and he
was lifted in the folds of the vast vesture and
carried to St. Peter's at Rome, that he might see
another manner of worship and another form of
Christian belief. He sees the great church and
its crowds of worshippers waiting with rapture
the change of "the elements" into the flesh and
blood of the Lord—one form of that mystery by
which religion has seemed to break up earth and
time, and let in on man the new day of a divine
and endless life. He did not enter the church,
but the Master did. And why? Some part,
then, of His truth and life were here, in spite of
all the error and superstition. So said reason,
and remained still outside, afraid to risk a nearer
approach. But the heart spoke. Above all the
error there was and is love—the greatest thing;
the love that gave Christianity its first power, in
the might of which it conquered "the antique
sovereign intellect," and made a new world, and

in time a new art—though always more or less "blind." Feeling that, he went into the church.

And that is well so far, but he would seek the whole; not faith and love only, but intellect and knowledge too. So they leave St. Peter's; and he is carried again in the folds of the Master's garment to the hall of a German professor, who is lecturing on the origin of Christianity, on what he calls the Christ-myth—trying to show how much fact there really is for it to rest upon—that is, how little. He is left outside with the hem of Christ's garment, but Christ enters; only he sees the professor and his audience, so different from St. Peter's, and he hears the Christmas Eve discourse—hears the professor argue that Christ was a "right true Man," who taught much wisdom and retains high value, though little understood by any who have been His followers. He did not enter the lecture-hall, "the exhausted air-bell of the critic,"—nor did the Master ask him. He bade adieu to the professor, having had enough, and began thinking this theory over. Stripped of all superstitions, and all accretions, is this what it really comes to? But, he then reflects, if Christ be only a man, able, wise, and good, and there be no more "God in Christ," does not the whole of Christian faith and worship fall to the ground? Neither intellect nor goodness can give a man any supreme right over men, and the highest powers of these leave him only a man. The teacher who should master the entire system of nature, and make known all its secrets, would still be a teacher, not a creator. The creator's part is far other and higher than this—to impress the truth of his own will and nature upon mind and heart, and to furnish motive and power to obey that truth, not to observe and teach only. Now, the " God in Christ " does this —gives power and motive to men by His life and death ; and His own claim is to do this—not by belief of men in His wisdom, but by faith of men in Himself as the Lord of life. If you believe this, and feel the divine love to be so shown, you gain a new and tremendous truth.

So he argues against the professor. Yet Christ is Himself inside the lecture-room. There must, then, be truth inside, since He stays there. What is it? He puts it thus. The proper conclusion of the argument was surely, " Throw away your faith, now proved mistaken." But our professor does not so ; he says, " Keep your faith, venerate the myth, adore the Man." There must, then, be love even here, and a sense of the divinity. Nor is this all. There is intellect and learning, and much regard for that kind of truth. Such doctrine as this can never be enough for life, it is true ; but there is power beyond the reasonings and theories of men in their hearts and aims, if honestly set and in the order of life.

In this way he draws a lesson of genial tolerance—really of indifference to every form of belief a mood that gives up search and care for truth, and, seeing that no belief can be perfect, regards them all as very much alike—a lazy benevolence without real conviction, and so without the powers of life. On this the storm broke out afresh, and the divine figure and vesture seemed to leave him alone again. Something must be wrong. He sees how it is in the flash of the fear that fell on him as he saw the garment receding. This mild in-differentism is worse than the poorest belief. The great matter is not to see the defect of this and the other belief, but to find what is true and good for one's self—not by any means the whole truth, but as much certainly as we can honestly come by, and heartily live in. Belief and life are individual, of the soul. Take sincerely your own way of life ; you cannot know more really, except by putting things to that test.

With this he was safe again in the garment's folds, and aware again of the little chapel and its service, not of the wandering world of rain. Had he been out of it? Had he been asleep and dreaming, or only day-dreaming? He hardly knew. Only this had passed vividly through his mind, and had been *real* to him. And what has he learned with reference to present circumstances ? Not to despise the bald service and the poor talk, but to see in the one a helpful worship, and in the other a divine message—living water, though with a strong taste of earthy matter. The very sim-plicity seems best as casting sensuous and worldly aids behind, and letting " God's all in all Serene show with the thinnest human veil between." And the poor congregation, offensive before, now seem to witness to the justice of his conclusion by the fact that, being as they are, they are helped and bettered by their faith.

But what is the speaker's conclusion? the intuition in which he rests after his quest? There seems to be a difficulty here, judging by differences among readers of the poem. It has been said that the point of "Christmas Eve" is to affirm the utility, and even the necessity, for undeveloped minds, of definite and historic forms, of what offers itself as tangible and certain. It has been so certainly, and it seems likely to remain so, nor are the minds for whom it is so "undeveloped." But is not the thought of "Christmas Eve" rather this, that any sincere form of Christianity, morally used, is a way of life, and far better than the finest form of intellectual superiority or indifference; and that, therefore, all sincere forms of Christianity are Christian, and have vital relations to the truth and spirit of its Founder: a conclusion that settles nothing as between St. Peter's and the little dingy chapel, and not much as between the German professor and the common belief. That is so. It does not decide between them. Only it gives these principles of wider use—that some great faith as to God and man seems necessary, and that not only must such "faith" be brought to the test of life, but that the root of every real faith is vital. It is a matter of life, and all of it that has sound meaning springs from divine dealings with each, and from the daily experience wisely read, and by no means from historical or other criticism, or so-called "evidences."

If it be said that the poet need scarcely have
written so many verses to set this forth, since it is
by no means new, however true, the answer must
be, that under stress of the new criticism, and also
from the quality of the old belief, this truth was
being forgotten. Many were disturbed because
they feared, and some because they thought, to see
the fate of a great religion settled by a narrow
criticism. Browning recalled them to the truth and
ground of religion, so far forth.

That the "argument" is developed from a
point of view, and through a type with which the
poet has only a partial sympathy comes, we think,
from the circumstances and mood to which it
addressed itself. We shall find the fuller mind
of the poet in poems such as "A Death in the
Desert," and "Epilogue."

But why the *style*, some ask, the tone of
banter, the grotesque rhymes? Is the speaker
half in earnest? Or is it the mood he is thrown
into by the chapel and service—all the quaint-
ness, etc., of it; and, as he never really leaves it,
does he keep this pitch as in tune with it? The
style is dramatic, and fits the mood of the speaker,
and it varies finely, as in the description of the
rainbows and St. Peter's. At bottom the speaker
is earnest, as he implies in his appeal to Christ
at the close, though his earnestness is mainly
practical; not the search for truth in its highest
sense, so much as the care for what is sincere and
real in the higher life of men, and a desire to
follow experience as indeed divine guidance.

The sections of "Christmas Eve" that criticise
the Gottingen professor set aside his "doctrine of
Christ," and return to the doctrine of His divinity.
These sections are valid against the professor, but
also touch the deeper question raised by "Saul,"
the need to conceive the Deity as revealed in
terms of human life and love.   In "The Sun"
("Ferishtah's Fancies," p. 33) this question is
considered in its more general form as the question how, for all moral and religious purposes, we
are to think of the Ultimate Power, whether in
terms of nature or of human nature; and its conclusion is that, though we never can reach the
"nature of Deity," which is by us "inconceivable,"
our idea must contain "man's everyday conception of himself," since our instinct of worship,
our gratitude, for us both natural and good, are
meaningless if we may not do so, and there would
be moral loss both ways.   And the mystery of man's
own nature is witness in its degree to the credibility
of the divine mystery.   Man's "dust, instinct with
fire unknowable" makes the higher mystery con-
ceivable.   What we reach on such a matter is a
moral conception, not an exact truth; and, though
we are certainly unable to "make square to a
finite eye the circle of infinity"—though we cannot adjust our knowledge of the scheme of nature,
or our abstract idea of divine glory and perfection,
with such a doctrine, we must hold modestly by
this way of thinking, and firmly by this truth.

Browning has come many times, in the course
of his work, full upon this question of the *validity*

and *character* of man's thought of God. It is a question that has been more openly and completely raised by the thought of our age than by that of any previous age. It has passed out of the sphere of abstract discussion, and has become a great spiritual and even practical question. It belongs, for this reason, to the scope of a poet to whom nothing is alien that enters into man's life, and the way in which a poet and thinker with Browning's qualifications sees this question as it bears on man is a matter of much interest even in the consideration of the question itself.

As to the way in which Browning has regarded the question, one might insist, were it fairly or strictly to the point, that his statement is philosophically inadequate. He yields too much to agnosticism. It was the spirit of his time. It has also been in a sense the spirit of thoughtful and imaginative men in all times, since the psalmists and prophets of Israel and the higher classical thought. But Browning, and all earnest men really stand on the deeper ground, though they may not recognise it. What we mean is, that they stand on the reality of knowledge, on the validity of reason and conscience with reference to the nature of God. In the terms of Browning's allegory in "Ferishtah's Fancies," your earthly fire, though small, is akin to the heavenly sun, and gives assurance of, and acquaintance with it. Notions of quantity or extent, our little and the divine great, are quite misleading, since it is really a question of quality and principle. The question is only, Is it knowledge? Does it interpret? If it does, then we are in the universe of thought to which all reality belongs, and not shut out in darkness.

But Browning's way of thought and his speech are poetic, his scope moral. Yet within his scope, and through his speech, he has given well certain main points of the life of his time, and its higher thoughts in regard to the things with which we are now concerned. I would note these points as shown in the poems above taken. The reality of some Supreme Power, the validity of some great Ideal, seems to be assumed. The question of the worth of man's thoughts about such a matter is frankly met. But the matter is regarded, not so much as a question of knowledge, but as a question of life. It may be that in the former sense the question is too large, but, brought to the test of man's history and life, the ground is clear. And if any faith be valid, if any thought be reasonable, then no better thought is possible than such as is provided by the higher terms of man's own nature; and we not only may, but ought to, regard the instincts of man's heart, and the higher uses of man's life, as leading parts of the problem.

As bearing on these ideas, let us here refer to three passages—one in " Sordello " (pp. 206, 207), in which the poet gives obscurely the solution of part of the problem of that poem. Sordello, he tells us, had two great wants—the need of some Power far above his life, and so out of " rivalry "

with it, and the need of some "representative" of
that Power within his own sphere—

> Who, being for authority the same,
> Communication different, should claim
> A course, the first chose, but this last revealed—
> This Human clear, as that Divine concealed.

Is this representative found in Reason and Conscience and the service of mankind, or in some
"revelation" of the divine? The answer is not
clear, but the passage implies the need of faith
in some transcendent and present Power, whose
excellence is the meaning of all good, the ground
of all duty, and the inspiration of all love.

A striking passage in the "Epistle of Karshish"
is more definite. The Arab physician, after de-
scribing the "case" and the character of Lazarus,
goes on to speak of things Lazarus had said to
him, and of one thing especially: he had said that
the Man who had "cured" him (or, as Lazarus
believed, brought him back to life) was "God,
Creator and Sustainer of the world, who came
and dwelt on it in flesh" for thirty years or more.
He is ashamed even to have reported such a
notion, and goes off in haste to other things.
But he returns to it, next time as giving a new,
tender, and sublime idea of God—the idea of a
gentle humanity behind all the power. Strange
and incredible, yet how winning!

Such passages mark the poet's interest in that
idea of Incarnation which is so much to Christian
faith—it may be they show his sense of its value
and his grasp of its ground. In "Saul" and

in "Christmas Eve" he presents the same great
idea; in the first as a noble power in human life
and the soul of man; in the second as in some
sense a just interpretation of the Christ of Christian history. But his most explicit words on the
matter are to found in "The Sun." That poem
starts upon the aversion of some devout minds
from the very idea of an incarnation, as degrading
the greatness and profaning the mystery of God.
But Ferishtah argues that the ground of it seems
to be involved in any "working idea" of God,
and hints that if some "great fact" were credibly
found, belief in it might be rational, as to many it
would be useful.

In "Ixion" ("Jocoseria," 1883) we come on
man's need of God, and the sources of his belief
in another way. It depicts forcibly that moral
necessity which impels man to seek the highest as
God. By his pain, and the terrible injustice he
felt it to be, Ixion is driven within sight of a
truth that makes his pain a consolation and a
triumph. He rises beyond "the gods" to God;
beyond Zeus to the Perfection he feels must be
far above such as Zeus. The gods of fear, fancy,
and caprice give place to a God of conscience
and man realises his own dignity in realising that
supreme Law of Right, which must be one with
"the true God."

CHAPTER XI

BROWNING'S POETRY AND THE IDEAL OF RELIGION—LEADING SPIRITUAL IDEAS

OUR last group of poems was described as poetic studies of religious ideas. Even in these poems one can discern a quality of sympathy and conviction. In the present group we shall find this quality more distinctly, as it seems to us.

They raise, therefore, more fully the question of the relation of this poetry to religion, and the question of the spiritual ideas that are found in it. Of the first question we must say something now, the second at a later point. It seems hard to get the relation of poetry to spiritual religion clearly grasped. And as to the second question, readers either hold most of the ideas found in the poems as the poet's own thoughts, or they hold that he has never expressed any of his own beliefs at all.

In trying to make clear the poet's standpoint and relation in the matter, let us recur to part of what has been said before. Even yet, though less than in the past, religion is too much regarded as something peculiar and speculative—something not alive, if not made by theologians and

churches. And as in these senses it has los
interest and value for many of us, it is apt to b
assumed that there is nothing in it now to warran
a good poet in troubling us about it. And thi
is so, unless there be a religion of the free min
and the free spirit—a religion that was befor
"Articles" and Churches, and that will be afte
all of these yet organised are no more. But
religion, as the poet deals with it, be a matte
human and vital, the case is altered. Since the
things belong to man they belong to art, and a
distinctly within the province of the poet, on th
broad ground of life and fact.

To give art the range, depth, and sincerity
life was very much the meaning of the romant
movement of the early part of this century, ar
one result of the movement was to restore art
its right relation to religion. And this result w
as just on its historical and moral sides as
has been good on its æsthetic. The relations
poetry and religion are ancient and profoun
The great drama of Greece is but one instan
of a general law. Arising in religion, it remain
a religious service, and was animated by religio
ideas. And we find other literatures powerfu
affected or fashioned by these ideas. Man's fi
wonder, curiosity, and joy were religious. I
sense of law in human life, his sense of good a
evil, had reference to divine powers. And
proportion to the greatness and beauty of th
ideas has been the power and worth of the art.

But it may be said that this was a par

association and a temporary law, true and fit in
the past, but no longer so. The law of progress
disengages life and art from a visionary and puts
them on a true basis. It "secularises" both. In
freeing science from effete systems of thought, and
giving widest scope to reason and inquiry, this
law has done vast good. But is it rightly read?
And what is its true bearing on the higher
thought and art? Does it mean the "secularisa-
tion" of man? Many speak as if it did.
But that may not be. Man's mind and passion
cannot be secularised. It is awkward, no doubt,
and cuts off the completeness of certain generalisations; but it is true. Man's thought and emotion,
man's wonder and awe, keep their old depth.
The ancient sense is only larger and more
explicit. And Browning's art seems to me to
interpret justly the romantic spirit in its relation
to religion, as well as the new temper of mind in
its relation to matters of belief.

The poet's critics may help us to make clear
his true position in this matter. Some find fault
with him because his ideas are indefinite and
mystical; others because they are too definite.
The first because they seek special forms of
religious ideas; the second because they have no
care for spiritual ideas at all. The breadth of the
poet is seen in his respecting his own principle,
and giving you large "criticism" with true
spiritual conviction and a clear hold of great
ideas, a free study of types and convictions with
a grasp of the deeper thought and the larger life

—that universal sphere whence these particula
ideas take their meaning and draw their powe
Indeed, the sense and result of this larger though
is so constant that the poet baffles many, an
reminds them of his own Sordello, who lost valu
for, and even hold of, all " secondary states " an
partial forms in a sense of the spirit and trut
that he felt to lie within and yet beyond them.

And here is the ground from which to ascertai
the bearings of the poet's work on religious idea
A poet who is a thinker may tell in this matte
in four ways—(1) By the force and truth wit
which he states certain ideas; (2) by the way i
which his representation of man makes the greate
religious ideas, which are the only valuable one
credible; (3) by the insight with which he pre
sents religious ideas in their bearing on life an
duty, or by the way in which his " criticism "
life brings out the worth of religious ideas in th
relation; (4) or he may show the relation of ma
to his beliefs, and make men aware of that wor
of passion and thought behind all opinion.

And Browning has, we think, told on the inte
pretation of religion in all these ways, though n
in all equally. The number of spiritual ideas
his poetry is not perhaps great, but the power ar
freshness with which they are stated are grea
and so are the ideas themselves. And he has p
strikingly the bearing of certain ideas on the co
duct of life. But his highest influence has be
exerted at other points. He has so present
man in himself, and in relation to great principl

of the spirit, that he has made religion seem
greater, therefore truer, to many minds. He has
so exhibited the bearings of belief on character,
and on the higher work of man, that the vital
value of belief has been surer. He has shown the
human substance and depth of the great ideas.
He has forcibly exemplified the subtlety and
individuality of all our higher thought, and has
thus given a finer sacredness and purer depth to
all sincere faith. And his dramatic interpretation
of all belief, if it imply its relative value, implies
also its vital quality, so making it in every case a
witness to those "unseen" things that are within
us all, and on the basis of which alone we can be
understood.

But this last point needs fuller explanation.
Browning's religious poems are dramatic studies.
He applies the modern dramatic spirit, and his
method as a dramatic thinker, to the study and
statement of religious ideas. Now, that is to use
a principle and a method in the criticism of religious ideas that would have been impossible to
art, because unattained by philosophy until the
present century. And what does this mean as
regards religion? It means disinterested study,
a free recognition of facts, a free interest in ideas,
a free interpretation of both, and of man as expressed through them from the point of view of
the spirit. This may seem a large claim, and we
are speaking of principles rather than achieve-
ments—of a method, not of its application in
every case. It means a Shakespearean breadth

and steadiness of design and view in the expression
of man's " soul," with a Hegelian power of illustrating the spiritual quality of religious beliefs ; or, to
put it in another and it may be simpler way, it is
the free criticism of the modern spirit, with a free
yet sure hold on the elements and ideas and life
of religion.

And this will guide us in a study of what we
may call the double strain of Browning's poetry,
the dramatic and the vital. The dramatist, we
have said, may suffer a double wrong. All he
says may be taken as his own ; that is a " vulgar
error." Nothing he says may be deemed from
his own mind ; that is an easy criticism. We
cannot hold it of Browning's work. As to the
poems now before us, for example. Some of
them are clearly invented for the ideas of which
they become the dramatic statement. In others
we find that recurrence of and insistence on certain
ideas, which always let us into part of a writer's
mind, while about all the work you have an
atmosphere of sympathy, and, involved in it, a
basis of thought which surely come of the poet's
own insight and faith.

And first of this group let us take " A Death
in the Desert." This poem was published in
1864. It is among the religious poems what
" Rabbi Ben Ezra " is among the life poems. I
gives the poet's great principles in the interpreta
tion of religion, as the other poem does of hi
interpretation of life. It is a dramatic romance
clothing a serious study of modern thought in

dramatic circumstance and personality, and so making the expression of the whole lifelike, while keeping sincere the statement of thought.

The story of the poem is legendary, but the character and ideas of St. John are involved in the poem. The deaths of the apostles are mostly wrapt in obscurity, and legends soon began to arise about them. In that element of myth and wonder the poet found a medium fit for his purpose. How and where St. John died was soon forgotten; whether he was dead became matter of doubt. By some he was expected to linger "until the Lord came." The poet gives a simple story of St. John's last hours, fitting both the legend and his design. The situation is impressive and touching, fit for a message that is really from "another world," and for future ages.

But its study is even more of that early age of Christian belief itself and of *problems* then first raised. It is the close of the great first age of Christianity, when its apostolic tradition was fading, and a new state of things was coming in its place. St. John was the last of the first age. According to the traditions Browning follows, he saw the century out, and survived all others of the early band. He saw the new time and the new spirit. It is reflected in his letters. The Gospel inspired by him is addressed to it, as his testimony that might remain and speak, when he had passed away. And this is why the poet chose him as the *persona* of his dramatic argument, spoken to an age that seemed to require

18

another St. John to state the great Christian argument afresh. And he chose him, too, because he loves the tender profundity, the deep simplicity and ardour, of the apostle of love.

And what was the new time, with its new conditions? It was an age of speculation and criticism, coming after an age of testimony and faith. The Christian tradition, the doctrine of apostles, had come into contact with Alexandrian and Oriental thought. The simple message, with its great story and great ideas, must now enter into and hold its own against the modes and systems of man's reason. So long as personal testimony and teaching lasted, Christian faith and doctrine seemed a simple matter, and authority was clear. But even before the close of the first Christian age man's mind had begun its inevitable play upon the Christian tradition and the Christian ideas. It was making its first attempt to understand it, to put it in real relation to the mind and to experience. This was of course done crudely, and even childishly, and through many mistakes and with strange mixtures. The age of the "heretics" had, in fact, come. It was a necessary step in the growth of the Christian faith, the way to the only faith that could live and keep a living place in the world. But it was not seen in that light. It was looked on at first as merely evil.

The inner meaning and law of the great process that then began; the part it plays, and must play, in the life of man; the service it perform

for all ideas that are really spiritual;—this is the
main theme of the poem on the death of St. John.
Not, you may think, a poetical subject, but anyhow a subject no serious mind in our age has
been able to avoid, and according to the wisdom
of the answer given to it must be the worth of
one's religion, or at least of one's theology, in the
time that is to come.   For it is the question that
rose at the close of the first age, come up again
most explicitly and completely, Whether the
Christian story and ideas can make good their
place in the world of thought? and that other
question, What is the reason of all the investigation and all the uncertainty of the modern
mind, and why should the serious faith of men
be always liable to such debate? and, Is the
essence of faith really subject to it?   The poet has
a solution of the problem as manly as it is wise
and spiritual.   And in this poem, poetic in matter
and fit in style, he has given his fullest expression to that solution.

The poem opens with account of its own origin.
It is said to have been found in a manuscript of
Pamphylax of Antioch, who was with St. John
when he died.   Its owner and editor had it from
Xanthus, his wife's uncle, who was also with St.
John.   The manuscript has been sacredly kept,
and is now more precious because all who were
with the apostle are gone, as its present owner
soon will be.

The "manuscript" begins with the circumstances
of the death as told by one present.   In a time of

persecution, and in his extreme age, St. John fled from Ephesus in the care of certain disciples, who have brought him for security to a deep cave in the desert. They have been hiding there for sixty days. St. John is dying, and they wait the event with sacred sorrow. He is in a kind of trance, but they hope he will come back long enough at least for some final message. That they may lose nothing of all that happens, they have brought him from the inner cave to a place where they may see his face. There are dim signs of life and thought, and they use means to bring him to consciousness. Their best means only bring smiles, as of one asleep, until a boy in their company thinks of better means than wine. He reads from the Gospel the great words, so much to the point now, " I am the Resurrection and the Life." These words reach and restore him. He sits up, and in the cave amid the stillness of the desert he speaks his last words to them, or rather to the world and the ages to come.

At first all seems a dream to him—the past real and near ; the present, even his body, far off. But the soul is clear and complete, though kept by a mere thread to the worn-out brain, and with just enough hold on the senses for him to know the " sons " near him, and to know that his companions of the sacred days are all gone. Alone left of all who knew the Lord, it must be for some divine purpose, and that must be to give more love and truth to men. Very soon none

will be left who can say, " I saw." To say just
this, and tell what he " saw," has been his task
since the Lord left the world. This has been the
burden and use of his writings as of his life—to
tell men the way of life, and " urge them, for
love's sake and in love's strength, to believe," and
so get into the way of life. And as he spoke
men believed simply, for he could speak directly
of the great days when truth's sea was at the full,
and the Word of Life was with men. But those
simple days passed. The story grew older, the
time farther off; men had many questions to ask
about it. And so he told the story more fully,
and more to the point of men's new thoughts, and
at length wrote, or had written, the story he had
told so many times. And still men believed in
the main.

In the midst of this labour he fell sick, and
seeing death near, and thinking of what should be
when the last of all who knew the Lord had gone,
he could only trust his truth to God's care for
man's good. But, waking out of sleep, he passed
into a prophetic trance, in which he saw the days
to come, and knew the minds of men, the way in
which the Gospel would be regarded and the
questions that would be put about it. Men will
ask, Was it John really? and did he say he saw
all this that is put in his name? and can we
believe him? Foreseeing all this, his soul was
filled with desire to meet these questions, and so
help these men of the distant future to the
truth.

Yet how can he help them? The light is so near and full to him—nearer now that the body is worn thin and lets the light through at every point. He wrote of the divine life and light, " It was—I saw "; now he would say, " It is—I see." It is the meaning of all the world to him —love ever at work in the world, conquering the wrong, healing the pain, and using even sin and death to reach the good, and fulfil the glory of life. He *sees* this, having seen the divine life; but those far-off men cannot see as he sees. How, then, are they to see the great truth? Even in his Gospel it will seem only a tale of what *was*, long ago. And yet, if they gaze with love on the life and death these facts make known, the world of meaning and light that is in them for all will grow clear.

And this is the end for all, however reached. The meaning of life and its use lie in the chance it gives of learning the secret of that divine life with its gospel of love, and, having gained that truth, sum and soul of all, to keep it, despite all that seems against it—to keep it, and live in it, and grow like it.

This is the end, he says, and may, so put seem simple; but it is not so, for the soul does not learn as the senses do. Physical experiences and truths, once reached, are clear and final. Spiritual truths, because they are spiritual and must enter into the life of men and interpret life, are not of that kind or capable of that proof. They must be grasped by the soul and proved through life. And this is good. The life and progress of the body are brief, those of the spirit endless. The truth it has to grasp is infinite, and so must be its progress towards it. Time's whole purpose is to prove the soul. The soul's proof lies in its growth in truth. If truth were clear, the soul's prowess were impossible. As it is, there is scope, for the search can never cease. Each age has to work out the great questions for itself. Nor is this an accident, still less an evil. It is a great law, and a great good. To have it otherwise were to evade life's proof, and so miss the very life of the soul.

And this explains even St. John's experience. Those who *saw* the Lord would, it may be thought, hold fast the truth. But they did not. They took time to grow into it. On their first trial they did not know it, and forsook their Lord. Yet later, in the martyr age, how very clear and brave all were! He sees now that even in that age faith was passing from the stage of simple trust in "the tradition of the elders," into an effort to understand the truth. As soon as that attempt began the "heretics" arose. He put forth his Gospel to meet the needs of that time. And now that he sees an age of deeper investigation and profounder thought, he would meet that need too—would meet, if he might, the whole thought of man, that nothing may keep men from the divine truth.

And he listens to catch the argument of that

later age, and he hears it. Your story comes
from a time long past. Such stories we have
proved to be mixed with error, and your
"wonders" are a trouble to us, not a proof
at all. Your doctrine is good, and this life is
very good, but as it comes to us it may be
only one of those myths man's imagination loves
to invent and likes to believe in. And what
you teach of God is good and commends itself
to the mind, but we cannot know that the fact
is so. Man has always made God in his own
image, rising from lower to higher ideas—to
will, reason, and love; but these are man's, and,
for aught we can prove, they may be man's
only. Your faith is but the last and purest
phase of an ancient and fallacious mode of
thought—highest in its ideas but *true*? How
can we ever know that?

Having stated the whole thought of the after-
time, he meets it frankly. He goes back on
his idea of spiritual progress. Man exists to
grow, *lives* only by growth of the soul. The
conditions of faith change with the conditions
of life. Miracle is first, and may serve then.
But once the truth has been planted in the
world miracles pass. Truth must then be proved
otherwise, and miracles may seem difficulties,
not evidences, to man's new thought of the
world. God will not overbear man's thought.
Enforced belief can never be living faith, and
the argument of faith must ever be morally
fit, vitally cogent.

And what is the *grand test* of divine truth? Its power to explain life, the nature of man, and the system of God. And this it does. The acknowledgment of God in Christ has this final evidence — that it solves man's greatest questions. Finding this so, ought men to fall into that worst of doubts, and doubt life itself, or waste life's brief space in searching about the roots of what commends itself to the soul, and has become power and light within? No! In itself it seems deeply true. Can it matter so much how it arose? To use such a method is to make a loss even of gain, and out of life to fall back into death. To argue, for instance, since all is might, what need of will, while will is the one source of power really known to man, is to fall back on a lower idea from sheer want of faith in the higher, which is to turn round on man's progress. And so to argue that love is so human that it cannot be divine, and that the legend of divine love has been made by hearts impelled by their own deepest life to think that way of God, is to reject the Christ through very need, and in mere worship, of Him.

But now suppose it said that the story as we have it cannot be true, and that thus it involves in doubt the great idea it has made historic. How is this met? By criticism of the records, such as may separate exactly the facts from the legend? No; but by appeal to the method and the ends of man's life. Uncertainty and error are parts of everything human, and on

every line progress is slowly made by throwing
these out in the growth of knowledge. Our
idea of God has been subject to this law. When
man asked, What is God? he became aware of
himself and of his place as man. Man's progress
since has led him to esteem will, wisdom, and
love as highest and best. It were strange if
we must conclude that, being all they are to us,
they exist in man only, and so think of God
as simply power and law. That were to lose
by gain, and fall back on a lower idea.

Then, if it be said that as men we really
cannot know what God is, he answers—That
is so, only let us admit this law of our knowledge as a whole, and accept its consequences.
Let us admit our partial ignorance and accept
progress as our true quality in the sphere of the
highest truths, even more than in other spheres.
Let us see that by the nature of knowledge,
as by the law of life, an absolute "revelation"
is impossible, though men have vainly wished
and affirmed it. Spiritual knowledge has no
such finality and certainty, and ought not to
have, and if we affect that for it we arrest our
progress, and miss both knowledge and the
harmony and fulness of life.

Having delivered his "burthen," St. John
died. They buried him in the evening, and
then parted.

This is St. John's message, as Browning read
it, holding, it may seem, as little relation to
any historical teaching of St. John as " Saul

to David, and as little possible for the apostle as that for the psalmist. In what sense, then, is such a poem *dramatic*? Does anything but confusion result from calling it so, or putting such essentially *modern thought* under the mask of the apostle? The poet arranges for the difficulty, if he does not avoid the objection, by making the whole a result of prophetic trance; not St. John, but the mind and spirit of the apostle as developed by—shall we say?—or as related to and arguing upon very recent thought and criticism, subsequent to Tübingen criticism and scientific philosophy. And so, from Browning's point of view, the question is, Whether the *spirit and ideas* of the poem are in any real relation to the *principles* of St. John—to his great ideas, as we know them through his writings. We judge distinctly that they are. That being allowed, you may inquire what is gained by such imaginative utterances—for, on any ground, imaginative they are. The poem is, we take it, the best answer to that. Its circumstances add to its force and interest, the poet's mind is stimulated by speaking thus, and his whole argument—for argument it is—is more fully developed through the medium chosen. For him it is a natural form. The matter shapes and vitalises itself most readily and fully in that way.

But, weighing the matter of the argument, let us ask, not whether it be historic, but how far it is valid. So far as St. John is concerned, he would necessarily be so full of the matter,

of the ideas and facts of the "wonderful life,"
that he could never get far enough away from
them to put them in line for proof. The poet
appreciates that point, and expresses it forcibly.
But does it not prevent the value, and narrow
the scope, of the argument? You may, of course,
look at that either from the dramatic or the
didactic point of view; and in the case of a
poem like this it is perhaps not easy to say
which has the leading place. Most readers
would say that the leading impulse of the poem
was interest in the ideas, not in the dramatic
situation or in the dramatic relations; and, if
so, that would settle its leading quality.

And what are those ideas, and are they valid,
or only valid from St. John's point of view?
The poem would be justified if the last point
only were true. (1) The spiritual and vital
nature of all the higher knowledge and of all
real belief about the highest matters. (2) The
spiritual nature by consequence of all progress
in such things. (3) The necessity of doubt as
implied in experience, involved by discipline
and essential to real knowledge. (4) The relations of spiritual convictions to the body of
man's other convictions involves progress in the
apprehension and in the application of spiritual
ideas. (5) The true progress in such matters
is one of evolution, not revolution, involving a
truer apprehension of vital principles, not a denial
of them; it does not, for example, follow because
man has seen that his nature and thought are

no measure of the world, that they have no relation or value with regard to its interpretation. (6) Spiritual ideals and vital powers are a far greater thing than any critical or historical inquiries. Inquiries as to the origin of these ideas are all very well in place. Their existence and worth, the light and energy they give, their service in life and for its interpretation, are the greater things. (7) The only, or, at least, the only serviceable and practical "revelation," the only true faith, is to be found through the spirit of man and the best attainable knowledge of man. (8) Man, in the fulness and freedom of his nature, is the end of life. Knowledge is not the end. And one great test of belief is what serves man and life best.

The view of religion that is presented, rather obscurely, we fear, in the poems placed as an "Epilogue" to "Dramatis Personæ," is in fine agreement with the points which have been developed through the preceding poems.

There are three poems, and in each religion is presented from a different standpoint and in a different idea of it. In the first David speaks for the Judaic religion and conception of God, the religion of sensuous symbols and localised manifestations. The "dwelling-place" of Jehovah was the temple at Jerusalem. There the Lord filled His house, bending porch and bowing pillar by His presence, and making it holy with His visible glory. And there, though forms and ideas were crude, was the joy of worship, the strong sense of a divine greatness and mercy.

In the second Renan speaks. What a way the world has travelled between the Hebrew psalmist and hero, and our superfine, critical French man of letters and sentiment! Here we find religion historical and sensuous, destroyed apparently by reason and criticism, "all gone across the dark." A star shone out of the wide heavens, and came with its light to men; a face, a form mild and great, grew upon the reverence of men. The Deity seemed knowable and human. But it is so no more. That simple faith is now incredible. The legend takes its place with all other legends, sweet but untrue. The facts were far otherwise. We are alone; only the infinite vault and the unknowable universe! Watchers of the twilight, we look up to find the void. We turn to earth only to find, to our dismay, that man is the highest known. Oh, the pity of the discovery! But truth is truth, though man may shrink from the sceptre and curse the crown.

But there is another and purer conception of religion and Deity, another and truer relation of man to God. This the third speaker represents and though he speaks of himself very modestly, as "witless alike of will and way divine," he has a very clear view and sense of this big question. His we may term a religion at once *natural and spiritual*, and this religion is confirmed, if not given, by life itself. God does not hold the Judaic, specialised relation to men or to a tribe

Nor does His presence depend on any interpretation of history. It is not a matter of the past. It
is a living and universal fact. The ground and
centre of it is the personality and experience of
each man. For each life is a real centre of things.
The universe for the time works towards and is for
that. The fable of the rock about which all the
waters played for a time is the fact of man's life.
Such is the play and function of Nature about
man during man's life. It is the fact, so far clear
and solid, that the play of the universe unfolds or
confirms this intense self-consciousness. What it
means, whither it leads, what it ends in, we may
not know ; but so far it is. Through that the
universe becomes a grand temple, Nature a great
ritual, experience a divine culture, life a high
service, and the Deity a living relation and presence for all.

This idea of personality, its central importance
in ethics and in art, and its mystery, is one of the
leading ideas of Browning's poetry. It is the
basis of his art we have seen. It is the centre of
his philosophy, and the key to his religion. Life
derives its meaning from it, all thought is condi-
tioned by it, and it may be that the clue to the
future and all its developments lies in it.

The poem called " Fears and Scruples " well
illustrates the spirit and humanity of Browning's
thoughts about these matters. It is put in a kind
of parable, and is a simpler and more familiar
statement of thoughts about man's faith in God.
Can we know that the invisible God is, or what

he is ? Can we make the grounds of our belief
honestly clear to others ? There are two friends,
one greater than the other. They have never
met, and the only evidences of the existence and
character of the greater friend are letters which
bear out his high character as far as they go.
The humble friend is full of hope that some day
they will meet and his trust have its reward. But
the great friend does not come, and makes no
clearer declarations of himself. Acquaintances
whisper doubts about his very existence. And
some one suggests that perhaps the unknown
friend keeps at a distance to put the other's trust
to the test. It may be so, yet to friendship's
heart it seems sad and strange. And then the
poem breaks forth. What if the friend be God,
and these be our relations to Him ? The bearing
is obvious. The little poem touches simply a
frequent thought of the poet, the spiritual uses of
uncertainty. It also, we think, suggests a criticism
of the ready and easy reasons some good people
have for the often obscure relations between God
and man, and how human analogies hardly explain
these or give their *rationale*.

And, in considering Browning's criticism of
religious belief, a due place should be assigned
to the *pope's speech or meditation* in " The
Ring and the Book "—to that part of it which
contains what may be called his " confession
of faith." It is again dramatic, but for obvious
reasons it touches the inner mind of the poet, as
it states not the public but the frank, private

thought of the pope, who is, it may be said, a man after the poet's own heart. And the occasion is one fit for it. The pope has spent a long day in considering the case of Count Guido. He has decided that the man is guilty and ought to die. And now, in the late evening of the day and of his own life, he reviews the story and the merits of the actors in it. He reviews, too, his own judgment, and the very grounds of it—those great principles which make it right for him to punish with death the murderer of Pompilia. His tone is grave, modest, and sincere. He is clear as to the story. Life is difficult and man liable to error. Yet use and experience give a man faculty and right to judge of the things of human life. But how of the sphere above man's life, upon our knowledge of which depends so much of the value of our conclusions in this narrow sphere? The pope feels strange doubts forced on him by this story, and by the life of his own time. Shall he face that doubt and dare to ask of the light in light's own sphere? He allows that his light is little, but he holds that it is from the sun and he must go by it. Still, life to the end is trial, and here he will try his faith. And he begins with his idea of God. Man's knowledge of God is like the eye's vision of the immensity of heaven—a vision of scattered points. God is measureless; man's mind an atom within the Infinite. Yet God is appreciable by each creature in its own degree, since a true love of God, which must for each be the end of life, is impossible without

19

knowledge. Why things are as they are, and each of us in his place for God, we know not; the choice is God's. And the universe, which gives some true knowledge of God, does not give an idea man can regard as complete. It shows power and intelligence in full measure, but not goodness in like degree, and not love. But there is a tale of God in the life of Jesus which makes the idea complete.) That story the pope finds credible in itself, and necessary to his ideal of God. The story as such may not represent the full and proportioned truth of the divine nature, but only a truth relative to man's life on earth, and so far to man's heart; but it is the quality of all our knowledge to be relative to our nature and our needs, and so that it be really true any way, he is not exigent in regard to it. For here is its grand use : with its story of love unlimited in self-sacrifice, it both completes the idea of God and interprets the world and man's life in it. "The dread machinery of sin and sorrow" can then be understood as giving man scope to learn the perfection of God, and become creative, on his own part, through self-sacrifice. And the very difficulties of the great story agree with life's whole quality as " probation " or discipline, and with that necessity of progress and growth of spirit which are the very life of man's life.

But there is a difficulty which he feels strongly It is not that men take the present and forget the future, and even reject the great truth. Men mus be free to do that. The real difficulty is tha

those who profess to believe it live as meanly as
worldlings. Take the archbishop who thrust Pompilia back to her brutal husband, or the friar who
had not the courage to help her, or the nuns who
lied about her to secure her property. Can such
deeds be the proper fruit of " God's death for
man "? Are such effects proportioned to so great
a cause? But perhaps the fault is in the nature
of man? No; love and faith have sprung up pro-
fusely in the past, and they spring to-day out of
natural powers in men. The impulses of chivalry
and love do more than faith does. Then he notes
sarcastically with what energy his priests spend
themselves on mere trifles of ritual or dogma.
And he asks, almost in terror, Is this all that was
to be; only this, seventeen centuries after the
advent of the Christ of God, and as whole result
of the divine power then shown in the world?
Can this we see be " salvation," that " immeasur-
able change " we surely had the right to look for
when the Maker of the world came to save it?
This question is forced upon him by the state of
things about him, and yet he leaves it feeling sure
that God is, and that even this must be consistent
with His goodness—that goodness being to the
pope a first, and last, and necessary truth. He
partly sees how it may be. The very weakness
of a faith may be the most beautiful power in
it, making it a test of moral will and spiritual
truth in men, and a finer incentive to humanity
and self-sacrifice than its triumph could be.

Then the question takes a new form. There is

a world of men quite outside our Christian world, and many of the men of that world have lived better than your Christians are doing.   Euripides, for instance, who taught so steadily, four hundred years before St. Paul, that virtue is the rule of life, waiving "rewards and loving for love's sake" only.   How answer Euripides as to the higher truth of the Christian faith?   Frankly thus: that faith has been partly lost in its own dogmatism and security.   It was better at the dawn.   It will be better again when the unspiritual certainty of "the ages of faith" has been destroyed.   Its ignoble confidence makes it worldly, and heroism impossible.   But this "torpor of assurance" will be shaken from their faith.   The age of rationalism is at hand, when their dogmas will be broken up; and then faith, which has got to be "faith in the report," may become once more "faith in the thing," in the living God, when men are constrained to

> Correct the portrait by the living face,
> Man's God by God's God in the mind of man.

There are dangers in this process, as he sees by men's lives already.   The faith of many will fail and impulse will have too much power, leading to good in some, to evil in others; but faith, and the power of God in man's life, will gain in the end.

The argument here is dramatic, fit in its general sense and spirit to the aged pope, though he must have pretty well advanced into the age of reason to have seen things as they are here put.   An

in spite of the fact that the pope speaks at the
close of the seventeenth century, and St. John
at the close of the first, they show many resemblances of idea and spirit. In those resemblances we come upon part of the mind of
the poet. We thus come back on a question raised before. Browning has hardly ever
spoken in his own person. And when an argument is dramatic, even when the standpoint and
line of it may be of the poet's own " invention,"
as in the case of some of the poems above, you
can never take the argument as expressing the
whole mind of the poet. At the same time,
you cannot doubt that you have part, and an
important part, of the poet's mind expressed in
such poems—great ideas or principles that interpret man's spirit as he sees it. And these ideas
may be got at, with all due allowance for the
dramatic method of the work, through the ideas
that recur, and through that medium of thought
which the dramatic studies involve; and the
continual use of the dramatic method is itself a
clue to the poet's conception of the problems of
human life and to his criticism of " faith."

The subject is one of great interest. We are
aware of the difficulty of it. It would take a
chapter to itself, and require a careful citation and
comparison of poems throughout. But we have
taken so many of the poems on which the study
must proceed that it may be allowed us to sum
up briefly. It is the more necessary to do this
because, as was said, there is a want of clearness

about the point itself.   Many have taken a line of
purely dramatic exposition, and others have treated
our poet as Shakespeare has been treated—taking
all serious opinions in his writings as if they were
his own.

We can, of course, do no more than state some of
those *vital ideas* that are to be found in or inferred
from his work, and that go to *indicate* his body of
thought as it bears on what we call religion.   And
in doing this we shall not attempt an exact arrangement of them, but be content with suggestion as
both most fitting for the matter and for the space
we can give to it, and congenial also to the poet's
own mode in putting forth his ideas.

Upon the great questions it may be thought
that a man's standpoint and balance of qualities
are almost his whole secret; and so it is, but
many of us will still need his help to see the
consequences of his greatest ideas.   In Browning
certainly, his personality stands in very distinct
relation to his leading ideas, spiritual and moral
The key to his position is found in his spiritual
passion and intellectual strength, his broad and
disinterested contemplation of the world as it is
and his ardent and generous sense of that higher
world revealed in, and necessary to, man's heart
and mind.   Shelley's sense of the ideal and
Hegel's idea of "spirit" seem present in Browning's sense and grasp of "the soul." The religious
interest and power of his poetry spring from this
in combination with robust realistic humour and
acceptance of life, and life's method.

As to the first aspect of his mind in this relation. He sees in men, he knows in himself, he recognises in the arts men have made to express their minds, a large passion that no art and no work of man has sufficed to express fully. Religion has interest for him in so far as it conciliates and interprets this "sense of the infinite," this large desire, as much of the intellect as of the emotions. It interests him because of the way in which it explains the depth he feels in man and the world. With Carlyle, he knows not only that a man's faith, "fit to be called such," is the deepest and truest thing within, and that it reaches out to and grasps the highest without, but that only as a man has such faith has he a way of understanding himself and life. And so, in a sense for him, religion, "fit to be called such," is its own evidence. Its greatness is its evidence; it is only true as it is great. The ideal must be true if only it be ideal and keep spiritual. And the Christian religion is true to him, not because he is concerned with the doctrines that have grown up about it, but because he accepts the spirit and ideal of Christ. In his temper and scope he is Christian. No poet has so finely, with such sympathy and power, interpreted the Christian ideas, their greatness, their humanity, their spiritual depth. No one has better seen what they have done in the life and thought of the past. No one more frankly affirms their essential promise. For him, as for Hegel, the Christian religion is true because it is the

religion that has most profoundly read the spirit
of man, and presented the purest spiritual ideal,
both for duty and for hope. And so, as we read
him, this poet is religious and Christian, not
because he accepts any single statement of the
greatest truths, but because he would keep for life
and the soul a free way to the Highest; because he
would keep the freedom and depth of man's mind
as religion indicates and promotes these—would
keep for the spirit of man its full power and scope.

These words may seem vague, as words are
apt to be, about an aspect and function of
religion that has not been much recognised in
this country; but, in agreement with his genius
and quality of thought, Browning has aspects and
truths more obvious. We said that no one had
better understood the *humanity* of the Christian
ideas; and that is true, whether we regard his
"doctrine" of God, or the way in which he has
grasped the problem of the world and the facts
and needs of men's hearts. As a dramatist and
thinker he has the clearest and steadiest perception of the conditions of life and the facts of the
world. He takes men and the world as they
stand for us all. No vain idealism hides from
him the state of things. He refuses bluntly to
disguise or evade the real problem by any partial
solution of it. His world is the world of all
experience.

And what light has he to throw on the problem
of problems there, the wrong and pain, and all the
evil and sorrow of the world? The answer of St

Paul and St. John mainly, though not in their terms nor quite on their grounds—divine love working out human good through a law of sacrifice as well as retribution. And something very like the great Hegelian idea of the nature and function of evil and pain you will find. Good and evil, truth and error, if not complementary and necessary in the great scheme, certainly work together towards some result not to be reached in its fulness, so far as we can see, without both factors. That is a difficulty for most who either think or feel deeply. Some of us seek escape in a kindly optimism that reflects our own pity rather than the world's order, and in some way or other many of us hide the facts or forget them. Poets like Browning, and thinkers such as Hegel, meet the facts in full, state the problem in its integrity, and seek a principle great enough to give a clue to the world - process, that by moralising may rationalise it.

Nor are they afraid of the principle in which, as they suggest, the solution may be found. In the case of Browning it runs all through his work and thought. What has been called "the unity of opposites" is both a poetic and a moral principle with him. His form of art and his criticism of life both go upon it, and the casuistic and tantalising quality of his thought, as many find, results from it. It is part of his real-idealism. Through it he seeks that "unity of things with each other, and with the spirit of man," which art and thought both aim at.

Matter-of-fact and critical, more aware of all the world and life present and suggest than concerned with theories of them, he is not, so far as we can see, careful to have a " big theory " of his own. For him " all things end in mystery," and the scheme of things is unimaginable. We regard the above ideas as part of his thought and as in his works, but he leaves the impression of holding all but the largest principles lightly. His dramatic expression means this, and reflects it so strongly that some have regarded the poet as agnostic, to use the term that sprang up appropriately in his time. At earlier points of these studies it has been indicated that he is not so, though partly from his strong sense of the " littleness of reasonings and the greatness of things," and partly from his sympathy with the more serious and modest spirit of his age, he stresses the limits of science, and thus gives to his position an apparently negative quality that does not really belong to it. His position is fairly described in his own strange phrase as " ignorance confirmed by knowledge "—knowledge gained from the life of thought and within the little circle of experience, but trusted with reference to that " circle of infinity " which cannot conceivably contradict the great and simple principles of our minds and hearts. This, it seems to us, is Browning's position on one of the great controversies of his time, a faith, felt to fit the folds of the heart and the fields of life, yet tempered and qualified by wise doubts, and by a sense of all that lies beyond knowable possibly but unknown. And this we may say is a kind of Christian Agnosticism which not a few of the strongest minds of Christendom have held. It confesses ignorance while modestly claiming knowledge, and its faith is chastened by doubts of the adequacy of any "symbol" yet devised or statement yet made. And ignorance and faith are cordially qualified by a sense of all that life and the soul suggest. The faith is thus the faith of one who believes in God and the soul, though caring little about and not looking for any ordered and finished scheme of doctrine as to either, while sincerely affirming as to both the substance of the Christian ideas.

Browning is then, we have said, very conscious of the limits of man's knowledge, and possibly stresses these limits on certain points too often and too much, but he quite understands, and never in fact forgets, that these are not the limits of man. Man, as well as the universe, is "greater than we know," and man's own thought, his intuition of himself and of things, is greater than his science can state. The facts and powers of man's nature are our largest suggestion of the law and truth of things. And these must neither be ignored nor explained away, because our "theory of the world" for the time being cannot interpret them, cannot be squared with them, cannot even find room for them, it may seem.

Such, then, as we read this poetry, and the mind expressed through it, was this poet's relation to the ideal and mystery of religion, at the points where the consciousness of his time was so acute. The test of the power and breadth of minds is found in their ability to transcend while they interpret the spirit and larger convictions of their age, to give the truth and worth of these and yet stand away from their limits, and never to fall into the fallacy of their finality, but to keep clear consciousness of horizons beyond the passions and thought of the time. The sense of mystery has been emphatic in religion as in science, in our day, and will be for years to come. Browning has it strongly, but holds firmly by the significance of religion not as aspiration and awe only, but as inspiration and light too.

Religion thus becomes the cordial and serious endeavour of man through intellect, emotion, and will, towards all that is highest, in the full belief that such effort not only is the law of man's nature, and a means of all good to man, but "reveals" the Highest in and to man, and unites him with the Highest in vital fellowship and realisation.

CHAPTER XII

POEMS ON IMMORTALITY

THE difficult and fascinating question of man's immortality has had a marked and continuous interest for the mind of the present century. The literature of the subject—from Wordsworth's "Ode" in 1805, through Tennyson's "In Memoriam" to Browning's "La Saisiaz" and Meredith's "A Faith on Trial"—is not only abundant but earnest and beautiful.

And even more remarkable than the number and value of these poems is their spirit, their quality of argument, their broad approach to the subject, their sympathetic yet free consideration of the question on its merits and as a part of life.

In Wordsworth's great "Ode" the old question is presented in a new way. The ideality of mind, and so the spirituality of man, is inferred from the glow, the energy, the independence of mind in the early days of life.

"In Memoriam" is a great human record and argument from love and life, from man's affections and powers, to a spiritual destiny for man, far from confident, yet wistfully, earnestly trustful. And George Meredith's fine poem after his wife's

death is an argument from love and nature against
death. He goes forth in the spring morning, and
there flashes on him, self-absorbed in his sorrow,
the vision of a cherry-tree in bloom. And he
springs to the mystic conviction that loss and
sorrow are not final, that life is more and greater
than death in a world where that outburst of
beauty seems the law after all.

And Browning's poems of the group we are
now to consider are capital instances of this
interest, and fine examples of this spirit, this new
approach to the old theme. No poetry of our
time, indeed, has touched the whole question so
often, or treated it as a whole with such power,
freshness, and freedom, as a question raised by
man's nature, and by many facts of his life in this
world. You will find it in his work, from
"Pauline" and "Paracelsus" to "Ferishtah" and
"Asolando"; and whether love or life, work or
art, be the poet's theme, he is aware of and often
leads up to its bearing on this matter.

The poet's approach to, and interest in, this
theme are then cordial and deep. But it will be
well, before examining the poems in which directly
or indirectly he treats the theme, to make still
clearer his standpoint and aim, and our purpose in
the study of this group of poems, and of certain
poems related to them. We do not wish here to
treat the philosophy or the theology of human
immortality. We do not propose to handle these
poems as a plea or as a polemic on the grave and
great theme that is central to some of them, and

important in others we shall deal with. We must, of course, touch points both of the philosophy and the theology of the question. And we do not disguise the strong interest the points of argument and interpretation have in relation to the value of the old hope for the life and heart of man. But our main purpose is apart from any formal doctrine or dogmatic position as to a "future life." Our object is to make a free study of those parts and ideas of this poetry which bear on the question in its larger and essential meaning. The words often used to state the question, and the issues raised, are apt to carry meanings poorer than this poet's thoughts and narrower than his aim. The old words, "Immortality" and "Future Life," do not well or sufficiently express it. It is a question essentially of man's spiritual quality and scope. It is a question rather of the range, growth, and fulfilment of life, and of the high and precious aims of men, than of continued existence or of deathlessness. It is study of literature and matter of humanity that concern us first and most —the substance, outlook, and ideas of this poetry as they bear upon a true and sufficient conception of the life of man.

Now, what are the *grounds* and what is the *scope* of the poet's interest in this question that has had so much interest for him? It will make that question and the significance of Browning's work upon it clearer if we recall certain principles of art. And first, art, like philosophy, must be deeply human. Made by and for man, it must find its centre and deeper ground in man's mind and experience. It must interpret life and the world from man's point of view. A purely objective art, we have said, is as impossible as a purely physical philosophy. Thought and imagination must work from the same standpoint, with the same scope, in this regard. In other words, the higher problem of art is the problem of thought as stated by Hegel —to reconcile " nature " and " spirit," to interpret both spiritually, and let us say humanly.

Humanity and spirituality, then, we require in the art and in the thought that shall express our sense of things, our thought of ourselves. More than ever we are aware of an outer and an inner world. At the dawn of modern culture, and in revolt from a partial and crude inwardness, men sought the outward scope and joy, and this has been emphasised by the growth of the world and of knowledge ever since. But a simple outwardness, though possible as a reaction at the Renaissance, and though it has seemed, for reasons indicated, possible to many since, is not really possible to the modern spirit. The growth of thought, as well as the " Christian consciousness," stand in the way of that. Whether we can, as some think, reach a truer ideal and a fuller interpretation of life or not, it is certain we can only now do so as we front the whole nature of man. Our ideal and interpretation must satisfy all man has become.

And Browning's art stands the test of such principles. The mere fact that he has dealt with the question at present before us as he has done proves that he has the required scope. More fully than any poet of our time, he has presented this question as a true part of his study of man, and it is there we come on the ground of his interest in it. It is part of his vital dramatic work. His interest is in all the facts of thought or passion, of belief or desire, that belong to the matter in the first place. Then, not resting on the facts, and certainly not in any opinions about them, both as poet and thinker he seeks out what they may really tell of man's nature.

It is because he has taken man for his theme and man's soul for his field that he deals with these beliefs and desires. He comes to them as dramatist and also as dramatic thinker, that through them he may know man, and that he may, if possible, throw light on that greatest of all questions—*the meaning and scope of the soul* itself.

But just what, you may very well ask, is meant by the phrase "a dramatic thinker"? and what is that problem exactly which you say offers itself to Browning as such a thinker? Let me answer both questions so necessary in the study of this poet, and not least in connection with the theme now before us for frank and full consideration. By a "dramatic thinker," then, we mean one who not only seizes the facts concretely, and in their place in life, but one who so grasping them is urged on by his interest in them, and by his way of regarding them, to the question of what they really tell of the nature and power of man. He

20

sees the facts of passion and thought, of desire
and belief, in their place and at their play in the
field of life—in the world of man, and he does
not take them merely by themselves, but also in
relation to the man, and to the hidden whole of
his life—or, as we put it, to the meaning and
scope of the soul—" the man as God sees him."

That is the largest and most significant aspect
of the question in Browning's poetry as we read it,
and it is perhaps the deepest question present in
his poetry as a whole. The whole of his work tends
to that question. Its depth and suggestiveness
spring from his grasp of that question, from his
sense of its large meaning, from his power of
placing his facts against it as a background, or
in relation to it as a clue to what men think and
seek and are. His studies of character, his studies
of passion, his studies of art, as well as his studies
of belief show this—" Sordello," " Luria," " Easter
Day," show it; his studies of life in the " Grammarian " and " Rabbi Ben Ezra," and his studies
of art in " Abt Vogler." Thus the beliefs and
large wishes of men, so trivial to some wise people,
have immense interest for him—as human facts
and products, and so as revelations of the soul.

And it is at this point, and in relation to this
question, that we see more fully the reason for
that profound interest in Christian ideas of which
we spoke. He finds there the deepest and highest
idea of man. Christianity has been the creator
of the spirit. The Christian faith and the Christian
centuries have developed the greatest of spiritual

promises and ideas—emotions and ideas that have deepened and enriched the consciousness of man, so as to have penetrated all art and all thought with its own quality. And Browning has realised that divine spirit—that great idea—as perhaps no poet has done since Dante. His work rests upon it. And what is the meaning of this? Does it mean that, like Dante, the poet accepts this idea as a definite and final solution of the mystery of the soul? So far as his poetry is concerned, we would not put it so, though we take it he would say it has put man on the eternal way—has thrown open for him the divine scope of his life. And the grand use of the idea in his art and in his dramatic study of man is the way in which it reads for him the meaning and explains the powers of human nature. The facts and problems of the soul and of life are lightened by such a principle; and if the moral facts of the world do not actually warrant such a faith, these facts are not only more tolerable, they are far more intelligible on such a basis. The human problem is more thinkable.

And man's development has made this faith not less, but in some great sense even more necessary. Christianity not only planted in the general heart the idea of "eternal life," but an idea of man and an ideal of life which made that great idea of "eternal life" credible. And the growth of man's spirit and thought has only given it fuller meaning. The things men desire and their conception of the universe are very different from what they were, but the passion and scope of the modern mind are really greater and more exigent than ever, as "Hamlet" and "Faust," as Goethe no less than Carlyle, shows. And Browning, as our dramatist of the soul, presenting its facts and seeking for some symbol of its secret, has thrown this out, has expressed this greatly——finding in Christian ideas the best and most sufficient principle of interpretation of life and the heart.

Turning to the poems to find what the poet has to give on his theme, you will find two kinds of poems bearing upon it——those in which it is touched only, and those in which it is the chief or only subject. We can but glance at the first class, though some of them throw much light on our theme.

"Pauline" depicts a "soul" with something of the large longing of Shelley, "Sun Treader" of that poem, and the strange inadequacy they are apt to give their lives. This man has missed his way, missed the love he needs and knows, and yet, ending by confession of and surrender to love, he ends "happy, free from doubt, or touch of fear," because, as we read him, he takes love's way to be life's way, and he can trust love for ever.

In "Paracelsus" we have a rich and capable mind to a great extent wasted, as regards this life. He has wandered, and searched, and dared, and sinned. He learns wisdom, as too many have done, when the time and power to use it are gone. Can that, then, be "attainment"——to see the light of life, and fade into a darkness on which nor sunlight nor starlight will ever break? No!

The gains of life, which are its end and use, are not scattered on barren fields of death. They surely belong to the soul, and live with it, and the soul's grasp of and care for them, finest and firmest at the last, is its pledge of " life to come."

The close of " Paracelsus " thus means, from our present point of view, that the ideal passions of the soul, the size of its problems, the long and splendid evolution of life, the drift of its discipline, the still expanding grasp of man, learning through error, winning through defeat, the eternal quest and promise at the heart of life—all of these assure Paracelsus that the good passionately sought by such minds as his will somewhere be found. And so he clasps God's lamp of hope to his breast as he sinks into the darkness, sure that some day he will " emerge."

The bearing of " Sordello " is the same. The poet's career is a " failure," and yet the light in his dying eyes is of " triumph." True, in his narrow way, to the soul, he found at length its freedom and hope. Much of the point of " Sordello " is this, and most pertinent to our present theme, that it is the whole that satisfies us—not time, but eternity. The spirit's quality is " absolute." The partial circumstances and opportunities of life satisfy us only as we break beyond them into the infinite of the soul. That is the meaning behind all conscience—the scope behind all duty. He only lives truly, even here, who learns to break a way into the spiritual. We spend, indeed, much of this life in learning and achieving that. Surely we do not learn it only to lose all use for it so soon as death makes appear.

Thus we get both in " Paracelsus " and in " Sordello " a strong sense of the way in which, in certain lives, at least, the problems of conscience and culture run out beyond this life, by the depth and character they give life, and by other facts which carry us beyond it,—not to explain the situations in which men very often find themselves, but the nature they find within them—the powers life unfolds but does not fulfil, the ideals that are grasped and left quite unrealised.

" Saul," we have seen in our study of that poem, is full of these ideas : (1) that there are natures that only an Infinite Power can rouse, only the wealth of an infinite good, conditions that only such power and good can reach and recover ; (2) that what rouses man to the height and power of his nature is likely to be true and a measure of reality. And the bearing of these principles, if they may be accepted on our present theme, is direct and close. They are an argument for the higher hope where hope seems hardest.

The " argument," again, of the " Grammarian's Funeral " on our theme is patent. His passion for knowledge is no " fad " of his merely. It is of the mind's ideal—it is of the very build of mind, so to speak, and the willingness, nay, the vital impulse driving the scholar, to " sacrifice " so much of life in the high service of that ideal, surely infers a kosmos, an ordered system of life, that will find use for

and give scope to such souls as this of the scholar.
And there is other matter, there are other points
bearing on our topic in the " Grammarian." The
poet boldly infers that those who trust the larger
scope, the far ideal, and do not clutch at the
moment's gains, are the nobler. They do the
higher service,—they enrich with wider aims and
nobler works the life of humanity, and the world
knows what it knows and is where it is largely
through them. And the question presses, are
they to be sacrificed to build up the good and
achieve the work of humanity? But that is not
all. He implies that they are in themselves, and
not merely in their uses, the nobler. They live
best, most wisely, who live so. They catch the
divine way and fit the large manner of the world.
They catch the aims and think the thoughts of
God—they guide the way of all progress. Are
they, for that reason, to " fall out," and miss " the
land they saw afar off"? or is it enough to have
seen it? The " Grammarian's " passion for knowledge is from the mind's own ideal, and tells better
than earthly opportunity the soul's orbit.

Browning's " Love Poems," such a poem, for
example, as " Evelyn Hope," and the depth and
quality of the passion, and what we may call its
vital function, as our poet reads it,—all this has
bearing on our present theme. For what is the
use of love?—to develop the soul. And what is
the deeper idea and spiritual ground of these
poems for the poet—the idea, so puzzling to some,
so startling to others,—the idea that the soul's

inmost passion means and requires not one life, but, it may be, a series of lives rising through much and long experience to a full glad life at length ; or, say, rising through all experience ever nearer that ideal in which is life's fulfilment —that ideal to which love is the best clue, and of whose realisation it is the assurance, since, born of the deepest and holding of the best in us, it is part of the order through which we live.

Then " Abt Vogler," interpreting the scope of music, reads the scope of the soul. It is partly the note of " Saul." " Thy power can fill the heart, thy power expands." " There shall never be one lost good." " On earth the broken arcs; in the heaven a perfect round." " All we have willed, or hoped, or dreamed of good shall exist." All high passions and aims are a " music sent up to God," which He hears, which we shall hear in full by and by. And the failures of the sincere and the true are never final, but " a triumph's evidence for the fulness of the days " to be in God's time. The passion of noble souls, the aspiration of the infinite within the finite—of the divine in human hearts, is the evidence of its divinity and the promise of its fulfilment. For life's system is set to a great music—with a sweep and a harmony which we cannot catch now, but will catch some time.

" Old Pictures in Florence," as ethical criticism, rests, as we shall find, on the Christian and spiritual idea of life. Even more in life than in art, limited perfection passes—is doomed by its very "perfection" to fade and pass. Spirit is in the nature of it ideal,—the ideal is never realised, but only approached. It thus asks "for ever," and opens for the natures that *need it* really the spaces of eternity. And this is an æsthetic because it was and is a moral truth.

The *absolute ethics* of our poet in such idyls as "Pheidippides," in such poems as "Hervé Riel," declaring that goodness and right are their own sufficing reward, implying that he who does the right and loves the good, even though he suffer, and even though he die for doing so, "does very well for himself,"—in Whitman's phrase, may seem to dispense with immortality. But does it? Supposing we put it thus, and say that the "reward" of such lives is not only the consciousness of doing, but the fuller power to do, right, it will then stand as in the promise of the Gospels, will it not? Your reward is in "heaven" and with God, in the love and vision of the perfect right and good, in the "heaven" of a purely perfected nature and will.

And that, indeed, is the point of the "Patriot," —with bearing thus on our present theme,—men have not rewarded the true patriot. He is safer so, for the soul is then left freer, purer, for the divine and essential reward—the reward of a life that fulfils life to its height, and fills it with the fruits of its own high principles.

"Apparent Failure" also touches our theme, and throws light upon it from the heart. It declares, we have seen, our poet's faith that there

is not, that there cannot be, any absolute failure.
What God loved once and made, and blessed,
cannot be wholly cursed! That were to say
that there "the system" somehow fails—
love, reason, power exhausted in vain — the
whole broken down at that point in that case?
No, he says—

> My own hope is, a sun will pierce
> The thickest cloud earth ever stretcht;
> That after Last returns the First,
> Though a wide compass round be fetched.

That clearly will take more lives than this, and
to that hope for such cases the poet pledges his
heart!

When we come to the poems in which our
theme is more expressly found, we have two
groups to be considered. First, three poems in
which it is part of the matter or design of the
poem; then two in which it is the main purport
and almost sole matter. In the first group are
"Cleon," "Rabbi Ben Ezra," and the "Epistle of
Karshish"; in the second, "Easter Day," and
"La Saisiaz."

There is other matter in "Cleon." It is a
dramatic study of later Greek life and thought,
expressive in that respect, with style and feeling
finely adapted to its theme; but the point it leads
up to is the contrast between the attainment of
Greek culture and the promise and power of
Christianity on the ground of the spirit. The
results of Greek life are shown, its love of wisdom

and beauty, its care for art, its love of pleasure, its ideal of earthly success and satisfaction, its final decay and despair.

The form of the poem is that of a letter from Cleon, poet, artist, and thinker, to Protus, the king. Protus had sent the poet princely gifts, and a letter asking him how he faced death, which drew on for both. Protus thought that Cleon, having works to leave behind him, must meet the close better than he could. What thinks Cleon ? He will tell his thought and feeling fully. And what is it ? A sense of discouragement, non-fulfilment, and fear of death. And how is this for the man who gathers up and perfects in himself the powers and results of Greek culture ? He gives the king the reason of it. He has made the works Protus has heard of, and is master of the arts. He can do both more and less than the men of the earlier days. He has greater variety; they had greater force. And it is clear that both work and life were more to them than they are to Cleon. And what is the secret of the evil ? It is found, he says, in self-consciousness and man's power of reflection. For thus man not only became aware of himself and of the joy he had, but of a world of capability for joy that he could not gratify. With the birth of self-conscious thought the desire of man grew indefinitely, while the power of enjoyment was reduced by this very growth. The soul became the life, and yet without the power to find satisfaction. The animal life was limited, and so perfect in its way. The soul, freed from those limits, becomes painfully aware of its own limited powers.

> Life's inadequate to joy:
> A man can use but a man's joy, while he sees God's.
> We see the wider but to sigh the more;
> Most progress is most failure.

He agrees with the king. But the king would say, Surely there is joy in making these works and leaving them to men, and living in them after death ? Not so, writes Cleon. That after-life of the worker in his work and through his influence is a shadowy thing. The man is gone, though the work remains. And, in truth, the poet is worse and suffers more than other men; for, with larger power and keener desire, he often gets less of life than they, and he is more aware of its limits and defects.

It is so horrible that from a sheer sense of need he almost dares imagine there must be another life, where this infinite passion and the pain of unsatisfied hearts should give place to satisfaction and a due balance of desire and capability. And he takes the image of the butterfly as a possible suggestion of what may be. But no; since it has not been revealed it is not possible, for were it so Zeus must have told us. In this case all that can be done is to make the most of life while it lasts—to " live long and die happy," glad for what has been. And he ends with a sneer at Paul, regarding whom Protus had made inquiry. He knows nothing of him except that he is a barbarian Jew, and not at all likely to have the grand secret of that other life, of which Protus above all things wanted to know.

That is all Cleon can see of it. It is the "joy-hunger," the sense of contradiction between the larger desire and the limited life of man, that urges him to a surmise, not to a hope, of an after-life. Greek, is it, though not of the best Greek thought, and selfish—issue of a philosophy whose worst charge against life was that it did not give "joy" enough. It is Greek thought, not of the era when life was great, but of the decadence. It reflects the weariness and discouragement of pagan life on the edge of the Christian era—part of those moods to which Christianity appealed with its "sanguine sunrise" of faith and hope.

But is there not something deeper in the argument than the tone and phrases of Cleon grasp? When the "joy-hunger" becomes a hunger, not of the senses, but of the *man*, not a cry for pleasure, but a cry for the just fulfilment of the soul, it has then gained a higher and fuller value.

We take next part of a poem already taken in part on another theme, though not then in its last section. The first part is a survey of life; its last section, of life's close and sequel. In it you find another type of thought and another ideal of life, and the bearing of these on a question of a further life to develop the uses of this is very forcibly presented. We refer to " Rabbi Ben Ezra," where are set forth the rabbi's views and hopes in regard to the life after death. Cleon is *Greek*; Ben Ezra is *Hebrew*. To Cleon life should mean

fulfilment of man's thirst for joy and beauty. To
Ben Ezra life is discipline—a divine education, a
training and unfolding of the man for divine uses.
Progress of the soul in insight and in power; the
amount and worth of the man himself,—that is
the test, as it is the end, of life. Life must not
be judged even by the work done, by external
and tangible results; but by the more essential
and real results that develop and make will and
wisdom. All external things, both deeds and
circumstances, change and pass. The living man
abides, and the function of all circumstance, and
even of all duty, seems to be to fashion and
mature the soul. To Ben Ezra life does not seem
adequate to fulfil the soul's purposes. We only
learn how and what to do, and find ourselves on
the verge with faculty matured, wisdom and skill
gained. Can it be, then, that death steps in just
to undo and waste all that? Can it be that,
having fashioned the cup on the wheel with pains
and success, the potter will but break it? To the
thought of Ben Ezra that is incredible. All experience seems to declare that life works to a
certain end—that end, both to reason and conscience, implies a goal and uses beyond—and
upon that life he throws himself with confident
hope. "Not down, but up" you must look—
that must be the soul's path. Higher uses for
which this life has surely prepared. And he sees
the feast, and the Master's joy in the cup He has
fashioned and will use. Done with earth's wheel,
what he seeks now is the closer, finer touch of

God, and that sphere of highest uses which must be the complement and explanation of earthly experience.

This is a higher strain—that hunger and thirst of the soul after righteousness which we have been told is blessed. Blessed! how? why? Because, whatever may happen, it is the highest thing? the best for man here and everywhere? Or blessed also because it shall be filled and satisfied—because the order of life is finally in its favour?

The force of the special argument of Ben Ezra will, of course, depend on the strenuousness and vigour of the moral nature—on the freshness and zeal of the soul, so to speak; but if the order of things be moral, the argument is good.

In the next poem, we take, the matter is approached from quite another point of view. In "Cleon" we see the futility of longing based on the lower view of life. Cleon did not dare to hope. And yet at that very time there were hearts quick and large with this very hope. It is matter of history that Christianity gave an immense impulse to the idea and faith of a life beyond life and after death. This new and vivid faith is illustrated in certain Gospel stories—stories of men raised from the dead. The story of Lazarus as given in the Gospel of St. John is the most detailed and striking of these. Browning had read and dwelt on that story, was fascinated and interested, as thinker and poet, in certain aspects of it, and his impressions are recorded in the "Epistle of Karshish." Like "Cleon," it is a dramatic study, as well as a study of our present theme; we take it only in the latter sense. Karshish is an Arab physician, who has come into Palestine to gather facts bearing on his researches and pursuits. He writes an account of what he gathers to Abib, his master in the medical art. He has in his wanderings come to Bethany and found Lazarus, and he gives an account of this strange case. This man says he was *dead*—dead four days; was brought back to life by a certain Nazarene, a physician of course, and he has since lived for many years in the most perfect health. Dead he could not have been, of course. It was a long trance—a case of epilepsy—so complete that it has led to a "mania." Still, that physician must have had strange powers to heal so completely. And the man really looks and lives as if he had been dead—had seen some great life beyond the bourne of death, and had come back with its ineffaceable impression upon him. He is dreamy, withdrawn, fantastical, with hidden fountains of light and passion within, and strangest ways of taking common things. Of course, the whole case is only a curious case of madness, and Karshish apologises for making so much of it, and turns from it to certain trivial discoveries of a professional sort, as much more important for his master. Still he is fascinated—is uncertain as to the adequacy of his explanation; and that Nazarene who wrought the cure must have been himself an uncommon man and a great physician, not only working cures like this, but speaking strange things—strange new things about God and the divine love.

And we must admit that the case would have been strangely interesting, if Lazarus could have been met nearly forty years after the event recorded by St. John. But it is not the historical case the poet is set upon; that merely puts his mind in motion on his problem, and gives him a setting for it.

And the problem is this. If a man should die, and rise again and return to the uses and limits of earth for years, what would be the effect of it on the man and on his life? It would destroy his moral balance and his interest in life; it would incapacitate him for action, for judgments really fit and practical. Most events and things would seem so little, and he would so far have lost that sense of proportion among things, that wise action would be impossible. The things of the soul itself would alone seem important. Tell a man, who had gone through such an experience and reached the conviction it would give him, that his child was dying, and your words would not move him; but let him see the least signs of evil in the child, and he would be strangely moved. He must, in fact, live with so strong and vivid a sense of the unseen universe and the final relation of things to that, that he would judge and act, not with reference to the sphere he was living in, but with reference to the invisible—a mode of action that could only perplex his conduct with reference to earthly duty. His impulses and

principles belong to the unseen, his tasks and
actions to the seen.   And his submission to the
divine will has a quality of awe and prostration.
He does not even care to proclaim his faith
learned from the Nazarene, in spite of the strange
importance it has for him, for he has seen how
truth *must* prevail.   And yet he is not cold or
apathetic ; on the contrary, he is kind and loving
—cares very gently even for the birds and the
flowers.   And he is indignant at the folly and sin
of men, as if he saw its madness from some
height far above our common life.

The leading idea here is an idea most characteristic of Browning, and to which he recurs, perhaps,
more frequently than any other ; and the aspect
of it that is found in this poem is nowhere put
so clearly.   A man who had come back from the
dead would be out of place in life.   The mistake
of Sordello would be a necessity for one in the
position of Lazarus.   For a wise and proportioned
conduct of this life, we must not be too conscious
of the spirit and its ideals.   For the moral conduct of this life, we must not be too sure of a
life beyond.   Certainty about a life to come, and
" sight " of that life, would put most things in
this life out of place, and render duty impossible.
The position in which we actually find ourselves is
as necessary to the uses and conduct of life, as it
is to the moral quality and activity of faith.   There
is here a truth many of us cover over by a host of
unreal words affecting a certainty about that " unseen world " such as we cannot honestly have,

such as would not be good for us if we were in earnest about things. Let as understand the conditions and limits of life; let us be sincere and wise. Let us live and judge by the best stand- ard of earthly duty, and not affect impossible elevations. But this, you may think, is the principle of Blougram, and agrees with his worldly realism. It is to avoid the mistake of Sordello, and the Grammarian, and Lazarus, but only by keeping too firm a hold of this life, and letting the next take thought for the things of itself. But that were to make the positions alternative and choose the lower. And that is not Browning's sugges- tion, nor is it the temper and bearing of his thought. We must live with a due regard for both sides of life—for the ideal and universal, as for the real and temporal, for the seen as for the unseen; keeping well in view the sphere of duty as of divine rela- tions and truths, and modestly testing all principles and truths through that wise service through which only they can be realised or even known by us.

We now come to the first of the poems in which our present theme is the one theme, "Easter Day." It belongs to the middle period of Browning's work, the time that followed "Men and Women," the early married years in Florence. It has poetic qualities of the earlier, and intellectual qualities of the later, work. It is dramatically conceived, and often vivid in conception and statement, and yet so subtle and elaborate is it that for many readers it is difficult, or impossible.

As in the companion poem, "Christmas Eve,"

the choice of theme and strain of thought were
no doubt influenced by his wife's devout and
ardent yet liberal Christianity, and by the discussions then going on among scholars as to the
facts of Christian history. The poem ought therefore to be read on some reference to the " Leben
Jesu " of Strauss, and beside those poems of Arnold
and Clough that touch the same questions.

The question of the historical evidences for the
resurrection of Jesus, of the grounds and value of
Christian belief in that event, had been fully
opened, and was bewildering many minds nour-
ished in the Christian tradition. The debate had
indeed, in many minds (*cf.* Clough and Arnold,
in loc.), gone so far as to have set aside those parts
of the Christian story.

It is characteristic of Browning's approach to
and treatment of such questions that he only
glances at the above question, grave as it seemed
to many thoughtful minds just then. That is not
the question the Christian Easter-tide raises in
his mind. His question is not of history and
difficulties as to facts long ago. It is a question
of life, and difficulties as to the standard and
conduct of that.

The poem is in fact, as its title implies, a study,
in a certain way, of that idea and hope of which
Easter is the symbol and the festival. Untroubled
by the doubts, and not greatly concerned as to
the evidences above referred to, the poet is profoundly interested in the Christian idea and hope
in its relation to life and the soul. He saw there

a theme congenial to his kind of dramatic research, or, as it may seem here, of psychological drama. Thus, in an atmosphere troubled by the problem of satisfactory evidence for a unique and moment-ous event, the poet set himself to test within the soul the inner worth and true meaning of the idea of life involved in Christian belief. In other words, his test of the credibility of human immortality is not the proof of any physical event, but its fit-ness for the life, its value for the soul of man. Immortality is credible, and an after-life natural, if the principles and passions of the mind make it possible to require it, if a " divine life " be the right and good life always. So in " Easter Day " the soul is set in action, and it is dramatically shown how the spirituality and greatness of the mind and heart appear to affirm and require the scope of such a faith; or, if the dramatic point of view be more rigidly regarded, the vital process of the Christian ideal is presented within this particular soul. The difficulty and greatness of the ideal are most forcibly shown, and the fact that, how-ever difficult of application in life, it is the only ideal that satisfies certain souls, and is involved in all their desires and thoughts.

In harmony with this, the poem opens with the moral question, the depth of which it is to show, " *How hard it is to be a Christian.*" And from that point a dramatic argument starts as between two minds—one representing reason and worldli-ness; the other, faith and spiritual earnestness. And it is the believer who in this case feels the difficulty, because the difficulty is not a difficulty about Christian writings or beliefs, but the vital one of being really a Christian. The difficulty, in fact, is not intellectual; it is moral—the difficulty of realising the idea honestly in life. And if it be said that this is a matter of course, since every task and purpose has a degree of difficulty, if you apply yourself earnestly to its full accomplishment, he replies that there is something special in this—something that makes it harder than is the case with other aims. It is higher and greater, shall we say, and for that reason harder? It is great and high, but that is not really the heart and ground of its difficulty. Perhaps it is, then, that God fixed it so—made it harder than other duties? That is a mere "perhaps," and explains nothing; only the fact is clear, whatever its cause—the duty is hard, and its hardness increases as you go on, and become more fully aware, not simply of the greatness of the duty and of its relation to life, but of its proper grounds; its want of that absoluteness which so many suppose it to have. But this looks like putting the matter the wrong way. The difficulty, surely, is to really believe; only believe, and you can do what else you are required to do. Let a man be sure that it is God's will about him he should be a Christian, and that this command is enforced by an eternity of joy or pain, and he will have motive enough for obedience, will he not? This looks a plain issue and a simple case. But the case is not, and cannot be, like that. It is true enough, from one

point of view, that "could we joint this flexile,
finite life once tight into the fixed and infinite
life," it were easy to spurn the earthly life ; only
the essential choice cannot be made so. Your
choice must be made on grounds proper and vital
to the question—must be morally pure and free, so
to say. A choice made on such cogent reasons
would leave the will non-moral, the heart unspiritual, and would destroy the discipline and the
worth of life.

And anyhow you cannot do that. We have not
this positive knowledge and certainty. We have
only faith and moral evidence, and, seeing that so
much of life goes by that kind of evidence, and so
many things take their value from it, cannot we
take the will of God and our higher obligations
on the same grounds? This seems fair. But
surely, though this kind of "faith" may be fit for
man's ways and affairs, it can hardly be the
method of God. He should go by more exact
laws. But this, again, is only a guess in the dark,
and is even wide of the facts. For look at the
world, in which you have the works and method
of God, and what do you see there? Everything
so plain and certain? Can you build your conclusions into so perfect an order? Or are the
greatest points there too often obscure? They
are. And what then? Here our man of plain
sense and commonplace faith is not very sure of
his ground. A scientific faith is "absurd," he
allows, for it would defeat faith's end ; but we
must, he thinks, at least have a rational, that is a

clear, *probability*. On the strength of that he could
do all that is required.   Men often, on very slight
motives, practically " renounce the world."   One
man devotes his life to completing his list of
Coleoptera, and another surrenders all objects in
life besides, that he may have for his own " a
grignon with the regent's crest."

Probability will do, then; and all that is required
is to renounce the world in the sense you imply?
In that case the matter seems to have become
easy.   If you wish to be a Christian you can find
" evidences " of the kind you desire, no doubt—
evidences to confirm what you wish.   You look
for the " external " sort, and find, say, a mummy
scrap proving Moses really lived, or you explain
the story of Jonah and the whale ; or you seek
the " internal" sort, and find the human heart
made exactly for the creed you incline to.   Only
what then ?   How does this help you to the
Christian temper and ideal ?   You believe, what
is called belief, but has your belief given you any
new moral power ?   Are you less worldly for it ?
Can you now in heart and will give up the world ?
You might, perhaps, if the crude, impulsive way
of asceticism were the way to do it ; if it could
be done once for all, and under some excitement.
But you won't do that ; you will find arguments
ready for an easier way.   You will make it a piety
to enjoy the good things, and go on in the old
way of the world, only with gratitude to God for
His gifts.

But can that be all ? and how, if it be, are we

to understand the tremendous facts of Christianity as they are usually understood and "received"? Did all that is said to have happened, happen only to give a reason for so much temperance and restraint as should make pleasure safer in the end —life continuing on the same level, and seeking at heart the same ends? Can that be a reasonable view of the great history—a result proportioned to it? It cannot be. And, besides, there are certain words that put other commands very plainly on "Christians." You will now say, "Take the safe side and deny yourself. It has been done so often that it can't be very hard, and there seems reason to do it." "Yes," says faith, in all this, seeming to turn upon shallow and commonplace religion, that finds these precepts of renunciation easy because none of its words are real, and none of its precepts are realised—"yes, it is very well to say that; but how if, after all, death be the end, and we throw life away upon a vain hope? It is easy to give up if the gain be clear or your faith strong, but how different when neither is the fact! Your friend of the Coleoptera gave up—his way of giving up; but he had his beetles, and for him that seemed much. How if I should renounce, and still renounce, and then have only death—the shadow?"

And what is the true reply to that, both frank and brave? This only—that the gain cannot be *proved*; but, whatever happen, we have "saved the soul" by choosing the higher part, as such, and on its own grounds. Now, to make such a choice must be hard, and the difficulty does not lie in belief, but in the *ideal quality and obligation* of the Christian life.

Thus we have returned upon the point at which our argument began, and now the friend who would like to make a middling " best of both worlds " is made uneasy by such thoughts, though he does not see how to meet them, and he complains. What is the good of making the matter so hard ? Why not leave him his " hopes " and his easy view of life ? " Because," answers the earnest man, " ' blind ' hopes may be false and are hurtful. They may spice the meal of life, but disguise the fact and issues of it and hide its bitter close." But no faith with any depth or truth in it can consent to be used that way, and no man with any sincerity could be put off on that issue. And then, to make clear that he means all he says, and has felt in his own mind its full force, he relates an experience and crisis of his own life, so vivid that it seemed a thing outside him—an experience in which the depth and nature of life's choice were disclosed to him with startling power.

And it is here you find the dramatic situation of the poem. Two friends are together on Easter Eve. One of them is in the habit of watching through the Easter night, pondering the meaning of its story and hope; and he does this because of a strange and solemn thing that happened to him just three years ago. He was crossing the common that night, thinking of the

Easter-tide and its meaning, and he asked himself gravely the question as to what that story meant for him, what its faith really was to him; whether, in simple, inward truth, it was anything at all. This kind of directness and honesty, he says, had in other things always been his habit; even as a child he would know the fact, for good or ill. And as he examined himself, common sense, which looks to the outsides and customs, and has but a low ideal, encouraged him to take a flattering view of the case. He made progress on the whole, and he believed in the main. Of course his progress was not rapid, and with his knowledge there were many things he couldn't be sure about. But he'll reach the port, some day, and that is enough. But he insisted against the Voice, is it enough, this kind of Christianity, that at the most means so little? and, with his habit of seeking out the facts, he wishes it were clear. It will be clear some day. Some final Easter morn, perhaps, will bring in the great judgment in which he affects to believe, and prove that this shallow dream has been folly and loss, never life at all. This is said or thought in a half-mocking way, but the word "loss," with its note of threatening, provokes him, and, with the remark that such talk is rather for children than for men, he throws back his head in mood to give up the matter.

But the "debate" was only beginning. As he threw back his head with a light laugh, the sky seemed suddenly to become one blaze of fire, night was gone and all the earth lit up, and the end of

the world seemed to have come, and that great
judgment, that a minute ago had seemed so far
away as not to concern him. The sense of this
burned all darkness from his soul too. Here was
the clear light he had affected to seek, disclosing
the inmost fact. He saw his choice; he knew
himself; he felt and understood his essential
worldliness. He had reasons for his choice, and
was very ready with them. The world was so
good, so fair, so near. He could not, in so short
a life, give it up—at least, not wholly. That was
too hard; and he was going to give up some day,
and the command was not so plain or so exacting.
Surely at worst this cannot be so great a sin, or
merit a hell as its punishment.

Then the sky was ablaze again, and he heard
a Voice that said, "Life is done, and thou art
judged"; after that, all looked as it had used to
look. He could not make it out. The world
gone, yet here; judgment past, and eternity
begun, and yet all things as in other days. It
must be a horrid dream. He tried to shake it
off, and was regaining quiet, when the Voice spoke
again beside him, and he saw now a Figure that
seemed the Angel of the Judgment—sombre and
vast, and its tone one of profound decision and
stern pity. He fell at its feet, and heard the
Voice declare the state of the case and the nature
of judgment. It declared the intense individuality
of judgment, and how judgment consists in the
revelation of the soul to itself, and in giving
the fruits of its own choice. Judgment strips

away the shows and vain impressions of life ;
God and the soul are the inner facts of a man's
life, alone. The test of man in the mortal life
arose from its mixed character. They chose well
who chose the spirit, because they knew it the
higher. While they who used the spirit only to
put a starry heaven far over earth, to give life zest
and finish, were earthly, not spiritual. So he did.
He chose the world ; he has the world. It is his
to glut his sense upon it.

This was his punishment. He did not feel it
so at first. He was glad to have the world and
all its treasures. But the austere Voice was
scornful. So soon and so easily satisfied ! The
world you take for so much is but one rose out
of the summer's wealth of God's infinity, thrown
you out of the heaven from which you have shut
yourself by its choice. You have the world
indeed, but you are shut up to it and within it
by the conditions of your choice, and it must be
now unvisited by any gleams or depths of the
spirit you despised.

Yet all the world ! He thinks there is enough
there for man—enough in its beauty and wisdom
and good. But the Voice again. The world is
indeed all, and more than you know; but the
whole of it is only a little part of God's fulness.
All the beauty of this world is but the promise
of the infinite beauty and good that are God.
They who choose this world take the part and
miss the Whole. And the world has no substance or meaning as you take it. And now

we see the spirit is not and cannot for men be shut out. And this is how it is seen.

That thought of meaning and beauty beyond the shows of sense touched the springs of the spirit within. His trust was gone from mere natural things. But there was art, where beauty takes meaning from the mind and passion of man. He will take art, and that will give joy and permanence to nature and to man—that is only the beginning of new departures. The deeper thought has only started, and it sinks deeper still, and searches farther. He will take Greek sculpture and Italy's painting. These will satisfy.

But the deeper thought awoke again—that far searching of the soul of which the Voice is the organ has begun and proceeds. The Voice spoke. Take art; but art itself is the finest witness to a beauty greater than art ever expressed. Art seizes moments. The Whole is felt, imagined, but never grasped. The very spirit of art is an effort towards an ideal never reached. His best works disappoint the artist himself. And he is greater than his work. His mind is unexhausted, and in good part unexpressed through his work. Such spirits are our amplest evidence of the things that remain beyond. Here they have enough only for one stage. By use and mastery, and by the soul itself, they reach on to the glory of that fuller revelation—when, the world being broken up, eternity shall let in upon them the divine fulness. And so Art, being what it is, seeking what it seeks, involves the soul.

There is still thought and science left—the finer sense of things. He will take mind and all its knowledge. That will break his bonds and give meaning and reality to his world yet. So he thinks. But even as he spoke he had a sense of illusion in it, now that the end has come and earth is all. Science needs a goal, and the pursuit of knowledge is great part of its pleasure; and besides, intelligence, as much as art, implies the unseen Whole. The quest of truth carries us to a "world of spirit," and its ideal is meaningless if that world have no reality. The best minds, in their best hours, have a sense of "gleams" that come from a sun, and "sting with hunger for the fuller light"—centre and source of all light.

With a kind of despair he now chooses love. But even in doing so he feels that love has lost its substance if earth be all. Men and women are but masks, passing phases and moments of no man knows what, and life a show, if there be no soul in them. And how does the Voice beside him take this final choice? It reminds him severely how late his choice of love is; how he had missed the meaning of the world's good— the love of God in it—and had ignored the highest revelation of love—the love of God in Christ—as an incredible story, or a tale of man's fancy. Nor does he know yet that love, above all, must be divine and spiritual.

His devices are now spent, and earth has failed him. The soul has tested itself upon its choice, and has proved its vanity. To have all the world and be shut within it, to be enclosed within time and matter, is despair and death for the soul. Better far the old life, with its sorrows and hindrances. Best of all the old life, with its trials and duties and spiritual horizons. So he throws himself on God's mercy, and prays to have the "old life again, if only he may go on and on, hoping some eve to reach the better land."

The prayer was granted, and the poem closes with some hints of how it all happened—a vision the speaker had, or a dream that passed through his mind, as he thought over these things intensely that night three years ago. It was a *new birth* for him, anyhow, and the truth then found remains a spring of higher life to him every way.

And what is that truth? The close of the poem suggests the speaker's gratitude for a life that tests the soul and keeps it from becoming earthly, and he speaks as if his own temper and ideal were somewhat timid and narrow. But the poem itself suggests other and broader truths some of them very forcibly. The essential spirituality of all the higher things in the life and world of man seems to involve "another life." Man's use and enjoyment of this world depend on its not being final. Once shut a man within this world and he would discover that the limitation was fatal to his proper life here; while man's art and science, his poetry and philosophy, stretch inward and upward to a perfection and a truth that experience does not contain and yet suggests.

Man has, in fact, become aware of *the spiritual infinite*. To restrict him within the limits of a worldly choice or an earthly hope is to embark on a career doomed to failure and futility. It is no more possible to rest in the lower choice now that the higher has been revealed. To prefer the higher as such, to guide life in the spirit and by the law of such preference, is not only duty but well-being. It is no exterior command only; it is a law of life.

But the poem and its train of thought may be looked at from another point of sight. Many people would like another life to follow this who do not see or care what that means as to man's nature, and who have no care for what it means in regard to duty. They think of " going on," without seeing that the power to go on must rest on *greatness*, and must imply a higher idea of life altogether than many use. Only as man has powers fitted for eternity can he expect eternal life, and if he have the powers of an endless life, his ideal of life now must be of the spirit. Looking at the matter from this point of view, we may put it thus : that the divine and the infinite belong to man, not as they are revealed *to* him, but as they are revealed *in* him ; and only as they are revealed within him can man hope for or truly desire the spiritual future of the Christian faith. And from this standpoint may we not describe his poem as an experiment of the soul on its own highest beliefs to ascertain the inner principle on which they must rest to be true, and to see how

22

they stand in relation to the life of man in this world—to the working ideal of this life?

And how does this bear on the question with which we found the poem open? That question we found to be, not one about belief and the evidences of the " resurrection "—the question that would have been certain to arise in many minds at such a time—but the question as to the Christian ideal and its practicability in such a life as man's. Where is its difficulty? In its quality, as in its greatness, and in the "mixed quality" of man's present life. And how is that question solved in the poem? The speaker takes a high tone, and has a fine scorn for compromise; but he appears, as we said, to fall himself into a narrow idea of matters at the close. His own "trial" lies towards worldliness, and he *hopes* yet to "escape" with care. But that is not Browning's idea; and though it has been the temper of many, it is not an ideal. Renunciation is the method of that; but renunciation is not our highest word, though it may often be our wisest rule in given cases. It is certainly not Browning's temper or ideal, and so far as it is the proper result of Christian ideas, and particularly of the Christian doctrine of a future and purely spiritual life, he would differ from it. In this aspect " Easter Day " may be regarded as a study of a type that he has only a partial sympathy with—a sympathy with the earnestness and the spirituality and the resolve to take the higher side, but not with the notion that one

must watch for very life to "escape" the world.
His own idea is more nearly expressed in the
words of the Voice than in the closing words of
the poem—

> A world of spirit as of sense
> Was plain to him, yet not too plain,
> Which he could traverse, not remain
> A guest in.

But this and other points in the general theme
we shall find in "La Saisiaz." This poem has
unique interest in its class, and among the poet's
works even. It is one of a small number of
personal poems, and its subject is taken directly
at a later point of the poet's life. It belongs to
1877, and was written because of an event that
touched the poet deeply in September of that
year. The poet, his sister, and a friend, Miss
Smith of Liverpool, the "A. E. S." of the dedication, had gone for an autumn holiday to La
Saisiaz, a quiet little place on the mountains near
Geneva. They were there in August and September, and Browning greatly enjoyed his visit
until the shadow fell that gave birth to this poem.
He wrote at the time, "How lovely is this place,
and what wonderful views on every side, Geneva
lying under us, with its lake and plain bounded
by the Jura, and our own Salève near us—the
peace and stillness so delightful. And here I sit
reading and reading Euripides." And then after
the bright weeks Miss Smith died very suddenly.
Browning was very susceptible to strong personal impressions from events like this. And

thus the sad event, touching him so closely,
started again the old question, old as life, yet
new on every fresh occasion that impresses the
facts of life, and discloses the pathos and strange-
ness of death, while the questioning spirit of
the old master of life, whom he had been reading,
possibly gave tone to his thoughts.

The poem opens with account of the place, and
circumstances which gave rise to it. The mountain scenery, the pleasures of climbing, the society,
the talk of the evening, and then the sudden
shadow that fell with the morning. Looking
for his friend by appointment, he found her dead,
" captured in death's cold for ever." They buried
her in a place protected by Salève, where not
even the village sports encroached upon the
silence, and there she has slept through two days.
The poet is leaving next day, finding the place
painful; but before leaving he has climbed Salève
again, as they meant doing together. As he
looks on the hills alone, and thinks of the quiet
graveyard and the strange distance now between
him and his friend, the question springs up, Where
is that friend? To that question he would dare
seek a true answer. They had talked of that
question of " the soul and a future life," only a
week ago, with a mild, remote interest. What
point the question has now, for this is now its
form! Did that friend, so dear and true, end
and pass away when she died, a tribute only to
the flowers and the moss, her very memory to
fade with the friends who knew her, and every

trace of her earnest spirit to be as if she had never been? and this all the comfort, that others live and reach the fuller life, though we and all who shared life with us are dead and gone? The heart rebels against such a doctrine; but what of that. The question is, What is the fact? What may, in the full light of knowledge, be justly held and honestly believed about it?

So he proceeds to the question in that spirit. He sees these facts—the conscious mind and the universe exist, the soul and God. How and whence they are, he does not know. That they are, he knows. He finds himself in a stream whose source and end are equally hid from him. He *is*, then; will he continue? He tries the usual arguments in answer—God's goodness, uses of the belief, human hopes. But with our experience the matter is not made clear that way. He falls back on our ignorance and the narrowness of our experience, a point and moment in an endless series. We are, but what we are is unknown to us. We know what pains or pleases us—so much and no more. But this can only give you private judgment? That is all. " Knowledge stands on my experience; all outside is surmise" only. This ground clear, he states his judgment. He cannot understand this world as a final divine scheme; as a place where man is in process of training through good and ill, through pain and grief, it is more intelligible. But does it serve this end so plainly? He sees death. Then he sees, too, that death has its uses in life;

it gives zest to life, and that through pain men
learn sympathy, and that good and ill work
together for man's development; but the process, as this world is made, cannot be right,
" If the harsh throes of the prelude die not off
into the swell of that perfect piece they sting me
to become a-strain for." We are, it seems, led
up to an expectation life does not meet. And
further, with so much sorrow and wrong in the
world, the question is forced upon him, Was
this the only way open? If it be of *necessity*,
he will try to bear it; but if it be of Divine
Will, from a Cause all-good, wise, and powerful,
then he would wish to see far better the reason
and good of it to make it square with such an
idea of God. In fact, with the world as it is,
and man's life in it, and man's mind, he can only
" acquiesce " if there be another life, and the " soul
may carry high through death her cup unspilled,"
all life's gains for further use and fuller life. This
is his judgment. But he does not hope to prove
that it is the solution of life's riddles, and a consolation for all the sorrows of men. He has no
wish to play the prophet's or the critic's part;
only, with the thousand failures of life in view,
he finds experience tolerable on that hypothesis.

And then the thought of his friend recurs, and
the cry of the heart against death—the longing
for renewal of friendship. But this is sentiment,
he says, and all his argument so far may seem
" surmise prepared to mutter hope, but also fear."
He would keep strictly by the facts. So he tests

the question another way—by the very law and *first principles of man's soul and conscience*. He has been looking at it in the light of the moral inadequacy of life, and in the light of man's faith in God ; he will now test the belief in an after-life by its fitness for man's conscience and for the conduct of this life. Upon this solid ground he argues the question out as between fancy and reason, the soul standing arbiter between the two to judge of the whole case. We condense and arrange the debate between the two thus. You say there is another life, likely, by a law of progress we see even in this world, to be a better ; then why prolong this one ? What good does it serve to go on with this twilight, if we may pass into the day ? We do so, it is said, by a divine order which we break through at our peril—hell for those who break, and heaven for those who keep, the great command. But even if that command make us wait, it cannot make us live ; and if we *know* that life is yonder, not here, we cannot really throw ourselves with zeal into this temporary life. But may we not do so if this brief life take infinite value from its relation to that greater life, if it prepare for that life, and if that life be fixed by the decisions and conduct of this life ? That is not clear, for if we are sure of this, and thus have overpowering reason for the higher choice, does not our choice cease to be free, and our conduct lose its value ? Once fix your dogma in man's nature, and do you not abolish moral good and ill, and make this life a calculation of

gain and loss only ? Life, then, would have no
use for the soul, but only for the body ? This
cannot be, of course, not with man's nature and the
scheme of things as we know it. And so we are
thrown back on this side also upon uncertainty.
We cannot think the thing out in its full scope,
and reach intellectual assurance. All we can
reach is a probability that fits in with experience
and the heart. But that seems precisely what we
need. By the conditions of life, as by the nature
of morality, life's ends would be frustrated by
certainty ; they are served by hope.

This is the argument, put modestly and kept
deliberately in a low key, as if with a sense of
the greatness of the question, and the limited
value of all merely personal judgment on a
matter that involves the very constitution and
issue of life. But what, you may ask, is the
result—the judgment of the soul, calm and large ?
To the consideration of the great question you
may think nothing is here added. In a sense we
admit that. Nothing material is added to the
" argument for a future life," except in this way—
that you have the deliberate judgment of a highly
competent thinker, and one who has long considered the life and soul of man, that the best
solution of the riddle of most men's lives may be
found in the faith of another life. This is the
poet's deliberate judgment on a broad survey of
the moral facts of life. Its personal quality he
admits. Its interest and value on this ground his
readers will recognise. But this is not the main

bearing of the meditation recorded in the poem.
Its main points and most original " criticism " are
these—the bearing of the faith in another life on
the conduct of this life; the reason for our uncertainty in regard to the question. The first
point has been dealt with before, but never more
directly. So far as the doctrine of a life to come
damages or interferes with the effective conduct
of this life, it is hurtful, and must be somewhere
mistaken. The second question is the question
of this poem, and very pertinent to the theme
and to present hopes and fears regarding it. If
there be another life, why is not the question
made so clear that we need have no doubt about
it and may " use the fact " in this life? The
question, says the poet in effect, is just in that
state in which it ought to be for the spiritual good
of man. He lives his life better so.

And this connects " La Saisiaz " with a " Death
in the Desert," which in its own class has something of the personal quality of this poem, apply-
ing to the religious question as a whole the test
here applied to the question of a " future life."
It is greatly to the advantage of man's spiritual
life—that is, of man's best life in this world—
that these questions should have the quality, the
uncertainty, they have; and the " end " of life is
not science, but spiritual fulness and power. And
this, let us say, is again an interpretation of the
facts of life, and the order of the world; no vain
attempt to get away from them in the direction
of rationalism or dogmatism of any sort.

Of other and later poems that touch this question of "Immortality" we should wish to say something.

"The Ring and the Book" is in its general scope one of those large tragic statements of life, which suggests the sad and strange inadequacy of many lives, and some of the best, to fulfil the spirit of life that is in them.

"Pompilia," for example. Can you call the painful history of Pompilia "life," even if you grant the development of soul through tragic experiences and fatal circumstances?

And in regard to Guido, was not the pope human as well as Christian when he suggested, in regard to him, that the very use of death might be to flash in upon him the vision of a truth and duty he had not yet seen—to thrill him with the birth of a life he had not yet known? And our poet finely suggests the *possibility* of that when, after all his "lies" in regard to Pompilia, he makes the villain appeal for help, mercy, *to her*, last and nearest of all—as if to hint that deeper than his villainy was his sense of the purity and goodness of the woman who had been his wife. Strip off the lies and give this sense a chance, and there is hope for the man, and a future !

The Epilogue to "Dramatis Personæ," with its fine suggestion of a spiritual religion — a religion that does not wait for any future state to find God and grasp life—suggests, by that very conception, the depth and spirituality of life, and thus its range and possibilities.

" Fifine " rests broadly on this principle. The soul is trained, unfolded by the frank love of all things lovely ; the law of its experience is vital—a law of continual change and advance.

And in the " Bean-stripe " section of " Ferishtah's Fancies," Browning is found weighing up the interest and worth of " impersonal immortality," and arguing from the heart against it. If it be the best we can have, to put it bluntly, we must e'en make the best we can of it ; but to say that it solves our problems and fills our lives is contrary to the fact. It is much less than the broad principles and high passions of our minds seem set towards.

The argument of " Reverie " involves the hope, for surely it were strange and tragic if " Power " " should come full in play," and the brave hearts that desired it, and worked for it, be dust ?

And the Epilogue to " Asolando," and so to all this work, looks onward with courage and unending hope.

And now we can hardly conclude our study of the subject without looking back and asking, What is the sum of the poet's thoughts about it ? What has he added to the " criticism " of belief in this matter ? By the method of his art, as by the temper and breadth of his statement, he has put the question on its proper basis, and given it its true scope. He has taken the matter in a large way, implying the slight and uncertain value of single arguments, the cumulative force of the whole case. It is no question of evidences

and logic. It is a question of man and life; a
question of man's true nature and power; and
a question, not simply of the inadequacy and
unsatisfactoriness of life, but of life's drift and
" promise." And so he has dwelt on the energy
and reach of man, on the spirituality of thought
and passion, on the infinite and the eternal within
man ; for the argument depends on what man is
capable of and worth. And he is very frank
about the unsatisfactoriness of life as we see it,
whether tested by conscience or judgment; its
inadequacy to man's affections, aims, and powers.
The world is intelligible and tolerable, though
with difficulties then, if there be a " life beyond."
And the order and method of life seem rational
on that basis ; its experience and discipline seem
then to have a purpose. But the " heart " and
personal claims' perplex the question. It is not
what men wish, but what they are fit for, that
must count. Man's continued power to serve the
ends of the universe must be the ground of hope.
That is the principle and the test of the true
immortality. The endurance of whatever is essential, of the true and the divine, is assured—the
completion of the value, the solution of the problems, and the realisation of the ideals of the
spirit. Does that imply personality in the after-
life ?—that is the question eagerly pressed. We
do not know. Our poet has nowhere given or
distinctly implied an answer. He wisely leaves
it ; though the whole principle of his art conveys
that impression of the value of personality that you

may well hold his drift to be on the side of that idea, not as a matter of sentiment, but of science.

Then he has other ideas that may seem more practical. No one has so forcibly put the folly of " losing " this life in any way in the name of another. It is life that matters, not existence. Life here and everywhere belongs to those who live. The great question is not about a " future life," but about realising the true idea of this life, and so leading up with energy to the life that may be when this no longer serves. The poet's own energy and freshness are such that he has, far more than most, inward sense of the soul, as Goethe described it, as " an essence that works on from eternity to eternity." And as this sense of power gives him assurance, so it gives him his conception, of a " life to come." It is not a " heaven," a stage of finality and fulfilment. It is the life of the soul, rising and expanding through what may be an "infinite series" of lives, "unhasting, yet unresting," because it serves no "taskmaster," but in love and power fulfils the very spirit of life.

And here the poet approves his grasp of that principle of which we said he is so true an interpreter—the great Christian idea—the idea of spiritual ascent and evolution as the chief law of life. That is the meaning of this life. It is the ground and law of all life to come. If that principle hold good of man, life to come is possible and desirable; if it hold good, life and duty here and hereafter are great—are, in truth, spiritually infinite and of eternal value.

CHAPTER XIII

PSYCHOLOGICAL AND CASUISTIC STUDIES: CALIBAN AND BISHOP BLOUGRAM

"POETRY," said Wordsworth, "is the image of man and nature." And there is nothing clearer in regard to it than this—that in poetry you will find man's thought of man most fully spoken. These poems on "Caliban" and his theology, and on "Bishop Blougram," and his defence of his position as a Roman Catholic bishop in the nineteenth century, are a most pertinent and forcible instance of this law. In their curious interest and picturesque research, their original characterisation, and casuistic power and subtlety, they give a striking "image" of man as man is seen in our time. The poet who made them was making a new thing in poetry, but he was acting on the impulse and following the interest proper to the poet as sincerely as Shakespeare when he made his plays, and presented in that way his "image" of man in the age of Elizabeth.

We are of course quite aware that many who find "Hamlet" and "Lear" great and true "images" of man and of human life, find "Caliban" and "Blougram" and "Sludge" harsh and tiresome, and are little inclined to count them poetic "images" of man. They would prefer in fact to assign them to another branch of literature, and exclude them from poetry. The defects of Browning's qualities show more in such poems, we frankly allow. His argumentative and casuistic turn, his bent to over - elaboration and to carrying on several trains of thought together, his tendency to give a too intellectual quality to his treatment of certain themes are more or less felt in them, though the group we have just named must not be roughly put together in respect of these features. In "Sludge" the poet gives freest scope to certain objectionable qualities. In "Blougram," though the study is subtle and elaborate, the vigour is great, and the coherence and pertinence clear for those who will take trouble. While "Caliban" is so fresh and original, so well conceived and presented, that in spite of a certain subtlety inevitable to the conception, and the "philosophic" quality of certain parts, it gives little trouble once its situation and purpose are grasped. On the whole, then, we judge that if these poems be taken broadly on their merits, certain allowances being made, it will be seen that Browning acted as truly from the poetic mind as Shakespeare in his choice of themes, though with a less pure and sure instinct in his treatment of such themes as those we are now dealing with, even that being to some extent accounted for by the differences of atmosphere and point of view. Shakespeare's dramas were not merely a form of art for which the age gave

occasion, and in which it took pleasure; they
were the fit expression of its thought of human
life. We have already seen that nothing is more
striking in recent literature than the scope and
quality of its interest in man, and this interest is
other than the Elizabethan. And Browning's
poetry, it was stated, must be judged in relation
to that, and not in relation to the older thought.
But there are certain points of the modern interest
reflected in such poems as these that remain to be
noted.

The interest in man, which was at first social
and religious, and has in truth remained so, became larger and more varied with the growth of
knowledge and the rise of other interests. The
extension of science, especially in the departments
of man's own history, gave it new material and
ideas, and a wider range. It was no longer
ethical or spiritual only. It included, more or
less, all the facts and questions of man's life; and
our researches into the earliest accessible history
of man gave it a field of fascinating interest
and great extent. We are not, of course, now
speaking of poetry, but of other literature; only
both conception and matter have told on poetry,
and markedly on Browning's work.

And there is another question related to these
researches, and even more distinctive of recent
years and ideas, also reflected in the poems now
before us—we mean the interest now taken in the
study of early forms of belief, and in the sources
and formation of opinion generally. The natural

history of belief, all the forces that enter into and fix or shape belief in interesting cases, is matter of much curiosity to us in our present mood.

Human history we now see to be an evolution of ideas as really as of customs and institutions stretching back to the beginnings of experience, and forward through phases none can foresee. It is seen that the beliefs of men are very largely fashioned by environment, race, culture, and personal qualities. Belief, in fact, is a vital far more than a logical problem. Variation and development, so far endless and practically infinite— variation and development by selection of the fittest among ideas as among organisms—that, with whatever qualifications, is the modern formula for the growth of beliefs.

Now, clearly this process may rouse two sorts of interest—one scientific, the other dramatic ; the first in the beliefs themselves, their process and value ; the second in their vital bearings, the ways in which they illustrate the man thinking. Browning's is the latter interest, and it is a curious proof of his intellectual and dramatic energy that he has given such subtle and powerful statement to a special dramatic problem, which you will not find illustrated in any other poet. And in this, also, the poet, in subject and conception, is in sincere relation to his age.

And these poems, related as they both are to the researches and ideas just described, show diversity of power and reach in the studies they represent. Caliban, the study of a crude and

23

simple nature, a primitive mind, if mind it may be
called, that worked in that curious brain; Blougram,
a complex and cultivated, a powerful and modern
mind; yet both dealing with the same problem, both
studies of the sources and process of the higher beliefs—of man's conclusion from his experience as
to the system amid which he finds himself, and
the quality of the law that rules all things.

These poems belong to different dates in the
order of our poet's works: "Blougram's Apology"
is of the Florence time and the "Men and
Women" series, that is, as to composition, before
1855. It thus belongs to the period that his least
partial critics regard as his "best." "Caliban"
came in the "Dramatis Personæ" volume, and
thus falls as to composition before 1864, that is,
after Mrs. Browning's death and the return to
London. With other poems in that first volume,
after he had lost his wife's fellowship and criticism,
it is thought to show an increasing intellectuality.

The latter poem, it goes without saying, is
from those parts of the "Tempest" which present
that strange creature in the world of Shakespeare's
latest art, with Ariel and Prospero; Blougram
and Gigadibs are of a different age and a very
different world. It was surmised at the time
that Blougram was a "study" of the busy and brilliant Romanist divine who became Cardinal Wiseman; and it has been said that that prelate took
it to himself, in an article on the "Apology" put
out in the *Rambler* in Jan. 1856. The matter
seems uncertain and is of no great importance.

The position and writings of Wiseman were then a matter of interest. But in the case of " dramatic study " such as this, the poet is not dealing with a particular case, but rather with a typical case, generalised and interpreted through the resources of his own mind. It is well to see that.

We shall begin with " Caliban " as the simpler study, and see how he puts his experience together into a kind of " natural theology." It was a bold and characteristic thing of Browning to try his art and prove his genius by such a study. Perhaps to him only would the problem have occurred in this way, and no one else could have given it such congruous, subtle, and forcibly dramatic statement.

It is indicative of the range of Shakespeare's curiosity, as of his power, that he should have imagined, and in his last play should have embodied, so strange a conception as Caliban. It was natural that a poet of our time should see and work out certain questions only hinted by Shakespeare. The differences in interest and scope between the poets and the ages, and their resemblances too, are fairly measured in their conception and by their handling of the theme.

In Shakespeare's days men's thoughts about man had been much extended, and their curiosity greatly stimulated. Many causes led to this, and among them the discoveries and tales of travellers, who had visited those new and strange parts of the world then becoming known. These discoveries made it very clear that the past as

hitherto known, whether of English or classical
life, did not exhaust the forms of life or of thought,
and indeed were no measure of the ruder past, or
even of the present as found in little-known parts
of the world. And it was most natural that
Shakespeare, among the thousand forms of men
fashioned in his world-wide mind, should seek to
conceive the lowest and simplest type that had
existed with human properties.

And if in the age of Shakespeare these facts
regarding the dim and barbarous past of human
life were first becoming known, and an image
being formed of the variety of the human world,
in our time such facts have first been extensively
collected and scientifically studied, and their bearing on the history of belief and culture rightly
seen. The simplest elements of the mind, the
crudest ideas of primitive culture, have been
explored. And so Browning, started by the suggestion of Shakespeare, and working in the spirit
and with the ideas of modern science, seeks to
thread his way through the quaint problems of
Caliban's theology.

Shakespeare made Caliban in the maturity of his
genius, and placed him in one of his finest dramas
and the conception is, in fact, one of the most
original and delicate in Shakespeare. Trembling
on the dangerous edge of crude animalism and
even brutality, instinctive, yet with intelligence
made all of self-interest and the "struggle for
existence," without gratitude, affection, or morality
and yet with a kind of religion, he was a critical

task even for our greatest poet; and his success in the impersonation, both in its consistency with itself and its fitness to the world of Caliban, is wonderful.

And Browning has shown his dramatic power by grasping Shakespeare's image as a whole, in its subtlety and its crudity, in its picturesque and in its moral interest. Shakespeare only hinted at the latter. He saw the concrete "image" in its place among the thousand figures of his world of man, and only glanced at Caliban's "theory of experience." But it is the moral interest and the mind of Caliban that occupy the modern poet. A rapid analysis will show the method of the poem and its course of thought.

The opening lines give the creature and the situation. They are the words of Caliban, though, owing to his peculiar use of the pronouns, they do not seem to be his. It is the noon of a summer day, and he is lazily sprawling in the mire of his cave—a most apparent animal. But as he looks over the sea, crossed by sunbeams, through which at times a great fish leaps, he has thoughts, and he will talk them out to himself now, because there are times when it is not safe to do so—winter, with its cold and storms. He ought to be at his task; but Prospero is asleep now, and he loves to cheat him.

He has his thoughts, and, strange as it may seem, they are of theology. It had not then been imagined that the world could go of itself. So he has his deity, invented on a basis of experience. This deity is Setebos—name and idea got from his mother; for the "origins" lie behind Caliban even. And this Setebos is a moon-god, the moon having struck certain tribes more than the sun. And his god, "dwelling in the cold o' the moon," is a maker, if not a creator. He has made the sun and "this isle" (Caliban knows nothing of the earth), but not the stars. Why not? Because these seem to lie beyond the clouds and the lower heavens in a sphere of their own. And what was his motive in making these?—for some reason he must have had. He was "ill at ease"; could not get away from the moon, and yet was not happy there. That an uncomfortable deity must have made this uncomfortable world, is Caliban's view. But how did it help or please him to make Caliban's world and Caliban? It is all argued by analogy and from experience. Caliban is a matter-of-fact and logical person, and, granting his premises, you would find it hard to upset his conclusions, in the mind of Caliban. He is self-consistent, and, with other theologians too, self-consistency has been the leading test of truth.

And what is his theory, then, about the making of such a world as he finds? Spite partly, and sport partly, must have been its motive and design, seeing that both qualities are in it. It might have served Setebos better to have made a "second self"; but as he could not do that, he had to take the next best. Caliban, you see, understands blindly those "necessities of thought" which hold us to the final theses of the Paleyan theology.

And here comes an original view of another

matter. He has to explain his own power and
weakness in such odd combination. Man can do
many things nature does not, and so cannot;
Caliban can do more than Setebos, and yet all the
time is in his power completely. How is this?
It pleases him to have creatures he can admire,
and mock too? There is more sport that way.
Thus is explained man's freedom and power, and
the fatal limits of both. This must be, he argues;
for if he could make anything living, he would
keep his mastery over it by the most purely
arbitrary acts of power. And to him arbitrariness
is the quality of power and the proof of greatness.
He has the love of mastery and the caprice of the
savage. He cannot give a reason even to himself
for many things he does. He sees little reason or
order in things about him. To such a mind all the
most striking things that happen take place at the
caprice of some imaginary power; and the deity of
the savage, reflecting the heart of the savage and
his image of nature, is masterful and capricious.
It is within his " right," and he uses that right as
he likes, mostly in mere self-assertion.

But, though sure to take his own way and keep
man in his place, the deity is not bad in the main.
He is fairly good, as life is. And if Caliban has
his limits imposed by Setebos, perhaps Setebos is
limited too. And he is clearly; for, if not, why
should he remain " ill at ease " in the moon? So
Caliban asks; and to other thinkers besides it has
seemed that a " free and omnipotent Deity " does
not account for the world as we know it; if God

might do all things, surely many things ought to
be other than they are?

How, then, account for the limitation? What
hinders Setebos? Here again Caliban chimes
with others who have thought much on experience. He is a dualist, but of a novel kind. He
suspects a power over Setebos, whom he calls the
Quiet, as both hidden and impassive—a power
only guessed by the defect and limitation of
Setebos and his world. His mother was a dualist
of another sort. She held that the Quiet had
made all, and that Setebos vexed the world out
of devilry. But he cannot see that. The limitation of experience and the unhappiness of the
world must reflect the maker's own state; for a
deity that could do all things, being neither happy
nor unhappy, could have had no motive for making
such a world as that known to Caliban. Impassive bliss crossed by devilry does not explain
things, he thinks.

But things may change. The Quiet may "look
up" and make things awkward. So far it has
only troubled Setebos. He, seeing the happiness
of the Quiet, was set on to make this "bauble
world," with no object really, and possibly he will
"knock it all down again." Why not? Caliban
would do so. He has, in fact, no idea of end or
purpose. The world is neither rational nor
ethical to him. Casual and shallow from first
to last, you may think, and yet his speculations
have a quaint resemblance to more dignified
theories that we have heard of. His crude,

frank talk should give pause to some who essay lightly the great question of motives and ends in regard to creation and its scheme, and not least to those who, in the name of science, offer a view of things very like that of Caliban. His question of "ends" is, in truth, not merely insoluble; it is unimaginable, in his terms and by his method.

But though good mostly, Setebos is not always so, and might grow dangerous. How please him, then? You cannot know. He keeps the secret, and is not to be pleased except as he wills. For, again, going by himself, and by the random and often violent courses nature seems to take, he thinks you are likely to anger the deity by the assumption that what has pleased him once should do so again. It is all caprice, and you must take your chance. Not a cheerful outlook? It is the fact, however, and the only way out of it, should it grow intolerable, is death. That will make an end of it, he is sure, though his mother thought not. Meantime, humour the deity, do not seem too happy, keep your thoughts to yourself mostly, and the Quiet may conquer, or Setebos doze.

So Caliban accounts for experience. Ingenious, you must allow, and Calibanesque. Caliban's god is a magnified and very natural Caliban, only rougher and in some points worse. This deity knows nothing of law. Somehow things go on when he does not meddle, but caprice is his law. And he is not moral. He neither loves nor hates his creatures; he made them for his own pleasure; he keeps them under his power, and they must mind they pay him the tribute of fear and the compliment of envy.

But what is it the poet has thus put before us? A fancy sketch or a true study? There are two ways in which a poet might present the subject. He might master all the facts that throw light on the workings of the primitive mind and construe these, or, by use of his own imagination mainly, recover its elements and process.

Has the poet done either? We think not. He has rather taken Shakespeare's Caliban, and in the light of modern principles has made his image of Caliban's world on the basis of Shakespeare's conception. Caliban does not represent the simplest stages of human thought. In the " Tempest," and as Shakespeare made him, he could not. And this poem, though it throws much light on the method and ideas of early religion, is not strictly a picture of it.

Are we to take it, then, in any sense as a study of the genesis and construction of theology? It has this aspect and interest, certainly. The habits and assumptions of the theological mode of thought, when put forth with the crudity and courage of Caliban, may seem a satire, not a description. And some have used the poem as a polemic against theology, and regard it as a dramatic study of the evolution of ideas, that in more refined forms have as little value as those of the poem, because they have the same basis and use the same method.

Caliban's theology has two sources—his reading

of the world, and his own nature and habits. Now, that theology began in such sources and with very crude ideas is matter of history. Shall we, then, say it can never lose the baseness of its origin ? But all knowledge had a like origin. The origin of ideas is not the chief or final test of their worth. The value of experience and any theory of it must depend on the universal elements it has, and its use of them ; and the growth of culture in these things has largely consisted in a fuller and better apprehension of such elements of the mind.

Caliban's theology affirms that the deity is like Caliban. When a theology arises which affirms that the best of man's mind is but the far-off image and hint of the Supreme, the case is altered. And no merely historical study of the origins of theology can settle the question of the right of its highest ideas to stand as in some true sense a vision of the Invisible Reality.

Turning to " Bishop Blougram." What an interval of life and thought between the two ! Yet there are deep instincts in common. Caliban has no doubts, and talks his theology as the most natural of theories. Setebos is very real to him in the moon's cold sphere. Blougram is full of doubts, and of a sense of possible revolution in the whole mode of thought ; but the instinct and idea of the savage are in the Catholic bishop too, and in fact hold him out of nature's depths.

The poem is an able and elaborate argument, in which the bishop measures his mind and creed against those of Gigadibs. It leaves a strong sense of mental vigour and courage, but even more of personal force. It has two contrasted characters as well as contrasted views of life, and it is dramatic, not only in the relation of its swift and forcible casuistry to the two "persons" of the poem, but in its "study" of the process of conviction itself.

The bishop is not setting forth his theology as Caliban was, nor is belief the chief thing with him. It is his position in and his theory of life rather that he justifies against the criticism and theory of Gigadibs. Our bishop is not a theologian. He is a strong realist, a man of the world, masterly and shrewd, who values life highly, and all its good—the strength of whose "position" lies very much in the hold that his creed and conduct have given him on the good of the world.

As the poem opens we see the men and the situation—the hearty, kindly, worldly, overbearing bishop ; and the literary man, who is enjoying the bishop's good things, and is proud of being his guest. The bishop talks. He knows Gigadibs has a kind of scorn for him as a bishop—regards him from the point of view of a superior. For Gigadibs knows, or thinks he knows, that the bishop does not believe the dogmas and superstitions of his Church, and he looks on the bishop's position and way of life as very dubious, if not contemptible, for a man of honour and ability.

The bishop, on his part, does not mind the contempt of Gigadibs, the literary man. He knows that Gigadibs would rather be Goethe (ideal man of letters), or Bonaparte (ideal of ambition), or even Count D'Orsay (a clever man of fashion), than Blougram at his height. For he thinks the bishop plays a false part, and to be pope and not believe seems " eerie," even to Gigadibs. " It is best to be one's self."

The plain and true life of Gigadibs is really better than the best of the bishop's, then, is it? his ideal, sincere life than Blougram's real, which can never be true? No, the bishop will not allow that. Abstract ideals are not his aim at all, but very *realisable ideals*. The all he leaves for Gigadibs, content to be much. The one remains a fancy; the other may be made a fact. We cannot any of us do what we would—plant solid and detailed any of our fine schemes. We can only make the best of what we find, and wisdom lies in accepting things as they are, and making the most of them. We must go by life's laws and conditions, not by abstract plans—very good it may be, but quite beside the mark. For the world is the world, and can never be turned into a fool's paradise. If you must idealise, why, then, idealise the real world; that may be worth doing, and will have solid advantages.

For what is our situation? A simile may make that clear. We are all crossing the world's ocean in the ship of life, and have only a very limited space allowed us. Into that space we cannot put all we might wish for comfort or for higher uses. What then? Rebel against the

limits and throw all overboard because you cannot take all, or choose and take what you can?
Men of sense take what the space permits, and
let the rest go. If you fling all away, because
your large ideas cannot be carried out, you only
make yourself absurd and your voyage miserable.

And so it is in the outfit of beliefs. How
stands that? You can't believe fixedly and
wholly. Very likely not. No more can I,
perhaps. What then? Throw all over and
hold by nothing? Suppose we do, in what
situation shall we then be — in what precise
state of mind? Shall we then have reached a
life clear, sure, and simple? Not at all. We
have got a life of doubt mixed with belief, in
place of a life of belief crossed by doubts.
Fixed belief or unbelief are equally impossible
to men; certainty is out of reach. The grand
problem is for all of us insoluble in that sense.
" I believe," and doubts spring up, soon and
often. You deny, and doubts are flashed on
your mind by whatever touches the deeper springs
of passion or of thought. Nor is this done by
us; it is done within us by powers and instincts
" old and new as Nature's self."

The " grand perhaps," then, may be a truth.
There may be a God, and He may, being good,
have made Himself known to man. The Christian religion may be the way to and the truth
about Him. Many things in the heart respond
to it; it touches hopes and fears at the quick
of our natures.

But if it may be so, it is far enough from being clear. Admitted ; yet that may be in the nature of the case. It may arise from our position, or it may be a test of faith, even. Anyhow, what we have reached is, that neither faith nor unfaith can be simple or supreme powers in life or in the heart of man.

Let us allow them equal powers, and, left to a man's choice, are the man of faith and the unbelieving man equal in life? By no means. In this matter, again, a man's choice ought to be according to the conditions of life and its limits. Belief, then, enables a man to live in and work with the world as it is. Doubt does not give that practical advantage. Idealism and suspense set you dreaming of a world that ought to be, perhaps, but is not, while you leave the world that is to those who take it as it comes.

And if belief be so plainly best on this solid ground, what is the best way and kind of belief? The belief that is decisive and thorough, since that is practically the most powerful, and, indeed, among the forces of the world the only serviceable belief. On every ground of character and utility, if you choose to "believe," do so decisively.

This being granted, from the point of view of the actual world and real life there could be but one faith for Blougram, one way of declaring the probability of "the grand perhaps," and that is Christianity in its Catholic form—the creed and Church of Hildebrand, equally as a strong organised religion, as an ecclesiastical system, and as a social power. That system and creed effect for him, and for his whole way of life, just what he wants ; through it, in fact, his ideal of life is made real enough, and placed solidly in the world for him to enjoy. It has given him a way of life, power among his fellows, and most things as he likes to have them.

Such is his confession, frank and to the point. And now he supposes Gigadibs, obliged to admit the practical value and force of the argument, to object that both as argument and as conduct the apology takes low ground, and surely implies an ignoble nature.

" Well," says the bishop, " I take what is, myself included. I am Blougram, not another. I did not make myself, and I cannot remake myself; all that is in my power is to make the best of what God has made me."

This is one line of reply. But he has another. He does not allow to Gigadibs that the question about character and tastes is so clear as he thinks it. Not merely the foolish, whom Gigadibs despises, but wise men whom he respects would side with the bishop, and at last leave the question open. For how is it with these clever men ? They like such cases as this of Blougram. Not the plain and simple cases, but the dubious and difficult cases, interest them. They prove their own ingenuity over them, and see more in them than they contain. A para

dox is dear to them, and impossible combinations.
Besides, the age is favourable for such cases.   Its
very conditions make them possible, pardonable,
and interesting.

Still, though these clever men of the world
tolerate, or, it may be, admire, the bishop, who
unites sense and learning and faith, Gigadibs is
disposed all the same to scorn.   Well, then,
whom does our writing man, "clever to a fault,"
admire?   Let us see, for it is life and embodied
ideals that put things to the proof.   Is it Napoleon?   But for your unbeliever this case of
Napoleon won't do.   Napoleon must have been
a strong believer in fate or himself, and must
have been very sure there was no moral government in the universe and no divine judgment.
His career is unintelligible otherwise, or else he
was mad.

But a man of letters would rather be Shakespeare.   Blougram knows he cannot be the "divine
poet."   And yet, if only he might have the
power, the full consciousness, the self-delight, of
Shakespeare, these would be life.   And if the poet
said, "In face of my works and self-consciousness
your world is nothing," he could not gainsay that.
But does the poet say that?   Does Shakespeare
act on that view of the values of things?   His
life shows he did not, and proves that he was
the very man to understand the difference between having and imagining.   So we find him
leave the towers and gorgeous palaces" of his
poetry, "to build the trimmest house in Stratford

24

town." He "saves money, spends it, and knows the worth of things." So the bishop concludes that the poet and himself, wanting the same things really, he having more of "the things," has the best of it, so far as this world goes. But only get belief, *enthusiasm*, and the whole case is changed. Sincere conviction—fire and life within—Luther's great faith and life say, and his argument breaks down. Only you cannot have such conviction, and the bishop's course is the best remaining.

But Gigadibs will say, "If you can't be Luther, why not Strauss, in the changed times; that were at least sincere?" The bishop replies, "There's no fulness of life, no gain that way. It's all cold and hopeless. Luther had his 'heaven in his heart'; Strauss has not even thanks for his work, and, worst of all, he may be wrong."

Now he supposes Gigadibs to take him on new ground, and here, too, is ready for him. He hears Gigadibs say, "Such faith as this without ardour or conviction, can't serve or give men the power they need. A whole faith or none is our choice."

"Not so fast," says Blougram. Your talk is vain and abstract. You don't know man or life. We have already seen that in some sense faith lies very deep. Allow its use or need, and you soon get it. For when you sink deeper than all arguments, you find that faith is a vital force and necessity of the soul, which doubt itself only

tests and witnesses to. And this faith, which is
a vital function, is the very thing we want. We
need not "evidences" and "conclusions," but the
soul's claim and attraction for what is divine,
its choice on hidden grounds of will and passion.
And here it approves itself. Criticise as long
and as far as you may, its divine power and grace
win and hold men still.

Then as to talk of "whole faith," of absolute
belief in God. It is impossible in the nature
of experience. That were to "see God," which
no man ever did or can, nor was it meant we
should. Men think creation was to "reveal
God"; to "hide Him," it seems as matter of
fact. And all that hides God, all evil and defect,
is part of our discipline. In the "full light" we
could not live; it would burn us up. Experience
case-hardens us that we may live as men. The
balance between the forces of faith and unfaith
in our nature are the very element and means
of life for man.

But there was absolute faith once in "that
dear Middle Age noodles praise." And what
was it worth? he asks. Very little for life.
He has a contempt for the ignorance as for the
morals of that time. It is not absolute faith
that is good for men. It is when the fight
begins in a man, when he has moral choice to
make, that life begins for him, the soul wakes
and grows. Certainty destroys that. Incomplete faith is its very condition.

And so the bishop exults in "difficulties." He

scorns those raised by modern knowledge. There
is a real pleasure in accepting faith in face of
them—the sum of all being that, though he has
great doubt, he has greater faith, and that is the
proper condition of the soul. But it may be said
that, though you may exult in difficulties, you
surely need not put delusions and lies on faith.
And he replies that the whole of faith is needed
for the masses of men, and that if you once begin
cutting away there is no end to that. " Set eye
or heart or brain to that, and they all get drunk
alike." Best leave it, for the modern fancy for
religion as science is a mistake. Its use and force
in life are its working value.

Then the argument takes fresh ground. His
critic may say, " Your view of life, and even of
truth, is poor and worldly." And Blougram meets
this with a bold and blunt defence. What is life
for? Not to miss or throw away, but to live and
use, surely. This is the body's time; the soul's
comes after. There is a vain idealism which,
being always just ahead of and superior to its
actual state, misses life, and by that plan will
miss reality for ever. He turns from that with
contempt, and an emphatic preference of his own
way.

Gigadibs may next urge, " Your argument
makes no account of truth, and yet, ' special
pleading' apart, truth is true, and can take care
of itself and the world in ways we cannot see.
Let us be true, then, and, if we doubt, say so."

Blougram does not meet this quite frankly

" Act your doubt, then," he says, " and make the most of your views of things. You don't; and why not? Because you defer to instinct and the ' blind forces ' of life. I do, and my instinct says that to do or be aught, I must have a God, and to me my instincts are God's will, and so I live and you don't."

To this Gigadibs may reply that his wish is to know what is true, and to live honestly and fairly among his fellows. And Blougram cannot meet that. He cannot trust the world and man so. The man who can do it is beyond him. But he sneers at it as a view of the life of Gigadibs, and browbeats him because he knows that the life he likes is the sort Gigadibs esteems too. And his " belief" on that ground has this advantage—it has given him what the other's doubts have not. So he takes his stand on his success, and scornfully patronises his critic.

And this is the key to the argument and the situation. He has met Gigadibs, the dealer in words and views, the idle critic. He has not really proved his case or justified his life. He hints at a deeper argument in reserve; but, as Gigadibs never asked it, we do not get it, and may doubt, not of the bishop's ability to give it, but of his own interest in it.

And is the poem, then, merely a piece of strong special pleading, with nothing better in it? Does the bishop, who has sense of the depth of religion and of the quality of life, advance nothing of that argument he hints at in case of need? There are points of this argument, though not just as he uses them. (1) His frank admission of the uncertainty of belief, taken on intellectual grounds, though he puts his admission to a very ecclesiastical use. (2) The bearing of moral considerations and the conditions of life on the problems of belief, though here again he makes a strange use of the rule, and gets an "emotion of conviction," equivalent to certainty, by a process that will not bear scrutiny. (3) The inevitable and universal quality of faith. It is no matter of reasoning. It is part of the action of the soul. The bishop uses that to give him a basis for a very complex affirmation—makes it cover and affirm the Catholic creed, in fact; but, though it is far simpler than that, it is a fact, and a fact that is much ignored. (4) He glances, too, at the spiritual uses of ignorance and uncertainty, a theme our poet is fond of; and though the bishop only uses it to justify his worldly acceptance of a formal creed, it has wider and purer uses.

Blougram, in fact, turns the edge of Gigadibs whole argument by admitting his positions to show that they bear in his own direction, and no in favour of his critic's scepticism, for those who understand life. And this gives us another poin —the bishop's realism in religion and in life There lies his strength both ways. The criticisn of religion is endless. The business of life i urgent and close. Take the life next you an use it, and do not, like a fool, merely criticise an lose it. The value of beliefs is to be tested b their use in life. Life's problem being how to get the most out of life, tested by the standard of good sense and judicious acceptance of the world as it is, and not in the least how to reach a "superior" or even a true view of things at large, the value of "beliefs" and general theories of things must be tested by the way they place one for and help one to this broad result. That is your most solid certainty, and your leading interest as things are, and as men mostly are.

And Blougram is indeed the *prophet of compromise*, and he makes, against all such as Gigadibs, an impregnable argument in its defence. Admit his ideal of what is good, and you must allow his success and good sense in reaching it. But deny that, declare your conviction that there is something higher and better even for this life, and his argument falls to the ground, though he will possibly think poorly of you. And yet he admits in the case of Luther, as in the case of Shakespeare, that there is a heaven of the heart and of the mind—an enthusiasm of the spirit that, if you can reach and maintain it, puts his lower, outward success on one side. A high and strenuous realisation of what is best, and a care for what is true—set your life to these, and find your joy in them, and the bishop's comfortable realism becomes, by the bishop's own tests, and on his own grounds, a very poor affair.

CHAPTER XIV

PSYCHOLOGICAL AND CASUISTIC STUDIES;
MR. SLUDGE, THE MEDIUM

OF certain lines of Wordsworth's poetry Coleridge said that, had he found them in the Sahara Desert, he would have known whose they were. This might certainly be said of " Sludge, the Medium." Browning only would have taken the subject and made the study of it that is here; and its fertility, subtlety, zest of argument, and spiritual research, its caustic humour too, and mastery of the twists and turns of self-interest, as that plausible spirit guides the ways of opinion, and shapes beliefs to its own dearest ends, make the study of " Sludge " one of his most characteristic poems, with strong points of interest, in spite of those faults of excess above referred to.

The poem came in the series of " Dramatis Personæ " (1864), but it turns on events and interests of the later years of the poet's life in Florence, and things in which his wife was much interested. About 1852 the phenomena known as " spiritualistic manifestations " began to attract the attention of the curious and the credulous. The movement began in the United States, and

made a great stir there. Rumours of it reached
the Brownings in Italy, and then some of the
" mediums " came to Paris and to Florence. The
thing was exciting, with its sensuous and eccentric
" proofs" of an " unseen " and spiritual world.
Mrs. Browning, it is clear from the letters so
recently edited by Mr. F. G. Kenyon, believed
that the movement had in part the significance it
claimed. Believing intensely that there was a
spiritual world, and holding that there might be
communications from it, even of this " spirit-
rapping" and " table-turning" kind, her attitude
was one of sympathy, with a note of wistful
desire that the thing might be found valid on
the main point. She was impressed by the apparent " evidences," and rejected hostile attempts
to explain these away. Browning, on the other
hand, was impatient of the whole thing, regarding
their " manifestations " as trivial, morbid, or even
dishonest dealing with grave matters. Mrs.
Browning speaks of the " facts," meaning facts
pertinent to her chief interest in it, and tending to
" prove " the existence of " presences " and " intelli-
gences " apart from the operators ; her husband sus-
pected nervous sensibilities and excitements, but saw
in the movement, and particularly in certain cases
of it, psychological phenomena of much interest.

And so in the same series in which he gave
his readers " Caliban " he gave them " Sludge, the
Medium." The minds of Sludge and Caliban are
not far apart, and their theologies, natural in both
cases, have common principles, though Caliban

is slow and primitive, and Sludge, under stress of
this age, is alert, ingenious, and sophisticated.
We may prefer the savage as the more wholesome, but Sludge has more that touches our own
lives and thoughts.

But the choice of Sludge as a dramatic subject
may ask a word of explanation. In many ways
a "survival" from the age of Caliban, he may
seem too far behind our age for serious study.
In point of fact the study was suggested, not only
by the general phenomena above referred to, but
by Sludge's actual existence, so to speak, among
the *dramatis personæ* of an age of science. The
model of Sludge was no doubt the notorious D. D.
Home, the medium, who came across from the
United States to startle and amuse certain of the
citizens of Paris and London by his feats of
mediumship, and by more questionable feats. He
is referred to sarcastically in "Prince Hohenstiel,"
etc., because the Emperor Napoleon III. was one
of his patrons. On his visit to Florence he was
taken up by certain friends of the Brownings, but
fell under suspicion even of his supporters. Mrs.
Browning speaks of him ("Letters," vol. ii. 226)
as a "weak and vain young man, exposed to
the flatteries of unwise coteries." But in another
letter she writes of his having turned an English
lady from "infidel opinions," as a fact of interest, speaks of his "morals and his manners"
as "wonderfully improved," and "hopes to hear
of more wonders." The career of Home did not
at all justify these hopes of Mrs. Browning. The

trick described in the poem was done by him at the house of an American patron.

Here, then, was ancient superstition come to life again in the midst of an age boasting its reason and proud of its science—primeval cravings ready to follow crude excitements on old tracks, and to use the very facts of science to help it in its quaint search, on its blind path. Faraday and others argued that the things done in the mystical séances, and called intercourse with "spirits" and "another world," were capable of physical explanations, and suggested such. Mrs. Browning speaks of Faraday's explanation (*vide Athenæum*, July 2, 1853) as ignoring "the essential phenomena," giving as such a "fact," and one that quite disposed of Faraday's theory of unconscious pressure, "the moving of tables untouched by a finger" ("Letters," ii. 122). Elsewhere she says that when Faraday was invited "to go and see Mr. Home, to see a heavy table lifted without the touch of a finger," he said "he had no time" (ii. 247). In another place she speaks with mild scorn of "the eminent men of science, and other intelligent men" who are satisfied with a "scientific," that is a physical, explanation, and keeps recurring to what she calls "the facts," and the testimony of those who have "seen" the "wonders" done. She exemplifies well the difficulty in such matters to keep the "facts" clear of theory, to understand how "facts" may be honestly testified to, yet misconstrued and misreported.

Now, Browning could not help being interested
in the questions thus raised, but he took the
matter on another side of it. Supposing all the
phenomena explained, you have still to explain
the minds that can indulge these cravings, and
hold these beliefs. It was, perhaps, no great
matter what they did, or did not do; but the
process of thought and passion in their souls,
what they really thought, and how their thoughts
hung together with their experience,——these were
things of great interest. And the interest was
by no means confined to those people and their
doings ; for as these stood related to old things
of human history, so did they to principles of
human nature. It is a wrong view of such cases
that takes them as merely absurd, as having
nothing to do with minds that have been freed
from vulgar errors, and as arising wholly from
special fallacies. We are far from the time when
knowledge shall be so complete as to leave no
room for things of this sort. It may be that we
can never reach that time, and science itself seems
to leave us at points where those instincts and
surmises have play, that have haunted the soul
from the dawn of thought. The mystery of the
unknown remains for us all. And not only have
we all our part in the long history that has made
our "image of nature," but subtle affinities hold
us to the ancient passions and conceptions still.

Mr. Sludge tells his own story, and makes his
own defence. The poem is a speech spoken to
his patron, and meant to persuade him of the

medium's good faith.   It is a critical moment in
the career of Sludge that gives us his apology.
It may be he has not considered matters in full
before, and he is not doing so now for the sake
of the subject.   He has been cheating, which is
not new; but what is new, and what makes his
defence real, is that his patron has found him out.
Mr. Hiram H. Horsfall has proved that certain
raps, which Sludge said were "communications"
from the patron's mother, were made by Sludge's
toes.   The occasion made the trick worse, and
Mr. Horsfall is so angry that he means to expose
and ruin Sludge.   It is in face of this danger that
Sludge puts forth all his powers of plausibility
and persuasion, not to save his character, but to
keep hold on his means of living—one of those
situations that bring to a focus the history and
mind of the speaker.   He confesses, excuses,
attacks, explains, and defends; begins by seeming
admission that most of the medium business is
delusion, and ends by arguing that its essential
part is a great truth.

In our study of the poem it will be best to
follow the dramatic order, which is vital, not
logical; but it may make the points and bearings
of the argument clearer if we see what kind of
person Sludge was, and the life that had led him
to his calling, and so fix the type to which spiritualistic ideas and practices are most congenial.

Sludge was an American.   Many conditions of
life in the States have favoured these growths—
the stimulus, the fermentation of old and new, of

ignorance and progress, of primitive passions and modern ideas, and freedom unchecked by European traditions. His early life was one of hardship and poverty. He got little education or training of any kind—its most active part, in fact, being got in the streets, in that mean struggle for existence which sharpens the wits certainly, but hardens and narrows the nature. He could read, though his spelling, even when "inspired," was bad, and his reading only fed a superstitious fancy. All he knew was picked up at random, on the impulses of crude curiosity. He had heard of science, but knew nothing of it, and cared less. His whole experience had given him no standard of truth, except his own impressions, ingenuities, and wishes. He had read the Bible, and its miracles pleased him well. A world so framed and managed was just his notion of things. He liked the crude mystery, the pure caprice, and individualism of the older ways of thought.

And this is the key to Sludge. He is clever, but crude as Caliban; active and observant, but shallow. He has no curiosity of the mind, and does not understand knowledge. He has no sense of the relations or of the proportions of things. To him, as to Caliban, the bearings of things are all arbitrary. His private opinion seems to be that the world is quite unintelligible as a matter of reason. Omniscience might know things on all their sides, in all their purposes; science cannot. But, as was said, he has no care for that side of matters. All he hopes to know, or cares about, is that side and those bearings of things that touch his own life and interests

And that note is the man to the heart of him. He has the shrewdest eye for the " main chance." He is keen to see and quick to use all points that make to the advantage of Sludge. And that " eye " which others keep for human affairs he carried into nature. In fact, a narrow and intense egoism is his basis at all points. His nature is not small only, and poor, but trivial and mean. He has no soul, though much faith in spirits; and his spiritualism and notions of the unseen have been mainly used to help him to what he cares for in this life. The whole value and pertinence of things is to serve him. He might not say that the universe is a contrivance in the interest of Sludge, and an impertinence if it do not provide him with a good life here and a better hereafter; but he does hold, as a result of egoism and ignorance together, that that is the only aspect of it he can understand. Agricola put the universe aside to get to God, because the soul of Agricola was more to Agricola and to God than all besides. Sludge is no Calvinist, and " election " is not his way; but his ruling principle is the same—for Sludge as for Agricola, the higher ideas only serve to intensify selfishness.

With such crudity of moral and mental conditions he has taken certain ideas into his mind— the idea of spirits, of an unseen universe, and of special divine guidance. As he holds and applies them, his ideas are almost on the level of Animism, and you can hardly decide whether they have taken hold of him or whether he has laid hold of them to use them for his own ends. He tells us they are out of the Bible, and that he takes them as he finds them there. Most who profess to believe the Bible hold, that though the things there set forth happened long ago, they don't now; not that the principles have changed, only the mode. He holds by both as still good. There are spirits; there is an invisible and divine order. These things have not gone dumb and dead. The world is still in touch with the power and purpose of God. And his "experience" confirms his belief; not clearly, of course, but clearly enough for a man who likes ingenuity and jugglery on its own account, and who has private reasons for believing. It is a theory of things which fits his mind, and, still better, his way of life and his wishes.

So Sludge believes his Bible, confirmed by his experience. That arbitrary and often trivial supernatural, which used to hold the foreground in primitive religion, he has brought back to its old place. All acts and events of this life have their source in that, and must be explained by reference to it. And he has given a great extension to the primitive conception of things. That found God in what was rare and great. He has learned science, and knows that nothing can be really explained, and that little things are "nearer God" than great things. So he finds hints from God everywhere, and in the least things.

But as these hints are occult and arbitrary, how are they to be read, and the obscure relations of things to one's own fate made out?   Here, again, Sludge falls back on a primitive mode of thought. In the days when things had no rational meaning or natural order, when all seemed casual, when things had meaning only as they bore on the fortunes of men, and all came directly from some inscrutable divine power—the only way to find their meaning was to call in divine help, and this was done by divination.   And so with Sludge. If there be no order of reason in things, the right way to track them is by chance (which is somehow divine), by a mere trick, it may be.   And so he uses the old tricks, and tricks that make the ancient ones look wise.   Here, in truth, is the *reductio ad absurdum* of his entire mode of thought.   His devices expose the triviality of his ideas.   Life, law, and the whole system of God are made infinitely small in the name of a religion without morality or wisdom, and in which God is only the highest point and chief factor of unreason and self-interest.

And Sludge finds a society with uses and encouragements for him and his notions; without faith, but with much crude curiosity about spirits and the unseen world.   He easily feigns, or actually believes, that he has powers of intercourse with that world, and becomes a " medium."   He finds patrons, develops his art and his courage, and grows famous.   But his success, and the need there is for such things to grow and keep

25

their novelty, have led him too far; he has
cheated his credulous patron, and been found out.
Mr. Horsfall is so angry that he almost chokes
the medium; but Sludge, having got him to
listen, shows more ability than he had ever shown
before in an exposition of his ideas and a defence
of his career.

He allows, to begin with, that he was wrong,
but thinks his patron's "sainted mother" wishes
her son to let him off, and coolly begs the whole
question of his powers as a medium by proposing
to ask her. He will even quit America if only he
may start elsewhere with money enough. When
he sees his patron relent, he helps himself to a
seat and the good things on the table, and,
feeling happier after that, opens his defence in
earnest.

And his first defence is an attack on those who
blame him. It was they who made the things
they complain of possible. With their shallow
curiosity, credulity, and love of excitement they
induced it all. Were a lad to pretend he had got
money by supernatural means, they'd quickly call
him a thief; but if he only claim to have dealing
with spirits, that is different. Men have a concei
that there is an "unseen world," and that some
how and sometimes it touches this world. The
do not quite believe, and they do not disbeliev
such things. The question is left open with
balance on the side of belief, because of the storie
good men have told or credited. Thus the yout
finds his audience when he comes with his tal

He stumbles and blunders at first, but that proves his honesty, and they find excuses, because they are in league with the "delusion." With their glib phrase that there is more in heaven and earth than any of us know; with their notion not only of mystery beyond life, but of a mystery always at hand that is really the medium's own vulgar mystery, they give him scope enough. He soon sees all this, plays his game more steadily, and gives them what they wish. And once having taken him up, he becomes part of their *amour propre*, and a kind of distinction for them.

Thus the "lies" began; and yet, so far, it was not lies, but a kind of poetry of belief—a case of that "over-belief" which is really necessary to give belief its proper power over men's minds. For most men all facts and ideas readily lose that glow which is their life. This is why poets have such use for mankind; they bring the fire and fancy that make things live. And this is just what the medium does for his facts and ideas; he gives life to men's ideas of a spiritual world, and intercourse with it.

That this power is dangerous he admits, for the medium is pushed on by those about him. There is sure to be some "cool head" who hints, or says, that the thing is a delusion. But they do not believe him, nor do they criticise coolly, for now they have a personal interest in it, and object to be proved fools. Having failed to persuade, those who doubt keep quiet for the sake of the company and the wine, and take the

" spirits " as part of the price to be paid for these.
And so again the story grows, helped, as every
legend is, by the fancy and belief of those who
receive it, until it gets far past its author's design.
Nor is anyone to blame—not the medium, certainly, who is forced on by the wishes of his
friends.　In fact, the process is natural, and to
have stopped it the medium must have had such
courage and honour as few men ever show in such
cases, especially when self-interest is all on the
side of letting things take their course.　Success
had brought him a pleasant life, and he could not
sacrifice that, he admits.　What he did was far
easier, and also more natural.　He added to the
fiction what he saw to be wanted.　It was
dangerous to have got into the middle of such a
stream, but exciting too, and he rose to the
situation, and soon had all the spirits in free
communication.　The thing had got beyond his
powers, he felt.　The spirits made queer mistakes
and talked poor stuff.　Bacon could not spell his
own name, and did not know his birthplace; and
Beethoven made music no better than a Shaker's
hymn.　But that, too, is in the nature of the case;
it is because they have to speak through Sludge.

With the growth of the fiction doubts again
arise, and these doubts help him, for his patrons
argue that the doubts keep the thing from being
better; and if the doubter persist, the rights of
hospitality are invoked, or the doubter is quashed
by the argument that one man cannot be right
against a dozen.　So he triumphs, with help of

those who have now even stronger reasons of their own for backing him.

But this help and success have their cost. He gets to a point where he would be glad to pause, but he cannot. The sensation must grow, and his art with it; and of that art he explains a little. A mother full of longing for a dead child comes and asks his help, her heart so strongly on his side that she easily takes his fiction. But he must know something of her child to make it speak to her, and one who lays himself out to gather that kind of knowledge easily learns many things that come so pat as to surprise those who do not know this art of miscellaneous observation.

Then he goes further, and becomes more cynical in regard to his audience. He declares that, the conceit of the thing having once got to "the proper depth in the rotten of man's nature," it is really "impossible to cheat—that is, to be found out." And how is this?—Because they take the cheating as part of the very nature of the medium, as such. It belongs to his qualities, and proves nothing as regards the essential question. He is angry as he thinks of their contempt, and the injury he has suffered through it, ceases for a moment to be a sneak, and exults in the fact that he has cheated these people more than they guess. But he professes comfort in the service he has done what he calls religion. He has laid the atheist on his back, for, as sceptics (*i.e.* all who deny Sludge's religion) are liars, his "lie" was just the thing for them. Books and arguments are nothing — never prove what they mean to prove ; and for knaves, anyhow, his is the better way.

So some help Sludge for what they think Sludge's help to religion — help him without much care as to the truth of his spiritualism, for he has seen in men " a real love of a lie " ; of pleasant delusions, and what makes for their wishes or their conceits. And the fools are ready for him, and the incredulous and conceited—" men emasculated and cold," who take it for its novelty and trifle with it ; and your man of letters, who likes a subject, and will write on anything that pays ; and the fribbles who want something to prove their wits on over dinner,—all these have been his patrons, and he is glad to have " done " them all. They well deserved it.

But now the argument goes deeper. He chuckles again over his tricks and his art, but maintains that there was something in it all, and to prove this he gives the history of his own beliefs, above spoken of. We all believe in a spirit-world, to which have gone our fathers and the infinite hosts of mankind. That world must be deeply concerned in this world, is surely within reach, with the will to help, and the power. If they may help, how do they ? A long tradition shows how. The Bible, even, has its stories of spirits. Here, then, is the method, and it holds still. Then there have always been men of special powers in this matter—" seers of the spiritual." From his childhood he has been

one of these seers; never did rest in natural causes,
that cold and dull scheme of things. As were his
fancies about the " godsends " of his boyhood, so
are his notions about the things of life still. He
is still the one reality inside the " show," and reads
all from his own point of view.

The talk of many goes, or professes to go, on
the view that this visible rests on an invisible
order. They speak of Providence, but refer their
principle to rare events and great things only.
Yet, if their principle be true, it must be true of
all events. He takes and uses it so; he finds
signs and hints everywhere. You object that this
degrades the doctrine. That is your pride, and
is besides quite illogical. Or you say the Almighty
cannot be giving hints to Sludge at all points of
His work. But Sludge to himself is so important
that he sees nothing absurd in it. The general
notion in regard to the matter is in truth radically
wrong, and the root of the error is the cold and
remote idea of religion which most people hold.
Their religion, on the side of it of most interest to
him, seems a dead creed about a power and an
order distant from and unrelated to the world in
which we all live. To Sludge, on the other hand,
religion is " all or nothing "; " no mere smile of
contentment " or " sigh of aspiration " towards an
order one dare not believe in, but " life of life and
self of self." It is the key to all meanings; it is
the meaning of all things.

And if you say that Sludge's application of the
idea proves it absurd, he will allow much error,

and hold still that there's " something in it." Man is a blunderer, and life many ways obscure, but those who take all means and use all chances are most likely to solve fairly the one great problem of getting as much as posssble out of it all. That is the grand advantage of his idea and method— they enable him to make the utmost of the world ; to take yourself for chief of things, and be ever on the watch so that you miss nothing, is a good rule in such a world as this.

So much for the rule, but what of the idea it rests on ? You think it absurd that the Infinite should stoop to such care for Sludge, and in such ways. But Sludge finds no difficulty there. He takes easily " the great and terrible Name." He has never known awe or humility, has never felt the Divine Greatness, or that conception of the order of things which it involves. And so he is complacently ready to show that the divine infinity lends itself to the littleness of Sludge's creed. It is the very quality of the divine greatness that nothing is too small for it—since nothing can be without it. Then the infinitely great, after all, is made up of the infinitely little,—Sludge's thoughts run on *size*, of course. He even retorts on his critic that the less things are, you are so much the nearer to the Ultimate—" behind the atom comes the very God "—the only God Sludge conceives, one that hides in things and works in ways congenial to Sludge's notions and tastes.

He next presses Christianity and the Christian spirit into the service of his defence. The Christian idea of God and God's relation to men are in favour of his idea. The filial relation is the true relation of men to God, as nature shows by the intimacy and beneficence of her cares. And, being His children, we ought to take life in that spirit. He takes his life so, and is " guided " even in trifles ; he does not object to the word, for to a mind like his all is trivial, nothing trifling. If it be " heir," he means to live as " heir," and have the benefit of it, now and for this life.

He admits that many facts in our lives do not fit his theory clearly ; but what is more significant is that there are facts in all lives that do—facts not capable of a natural explanation. Such facts are usually put aside or reserved, or they are dubiously referred to. For Sludge they are leading facts, and fix the meaning of things. Most cannot see life so. He who does has his gains.

With such a " faith in use " the medium has advantages. But he has drawbacks, as his present circumstances remind him, and as he admits with something of appeal to his patron's pity. Physically he is a poor creature, sensitive and something of a coward, with too lively a fancy and too greedy for fame. These have been his temptations, and in part explain his conduct ; but his " gains " balance his defects, and he is content. He quickly leaves the defects therefore to rise to a bolder flight over his success. Mr. Horsfall is angry at his cheating, and he has confessed to " tricks." But he now inclines to regard his whole course as right, and himself as innocent of cheating. He allows that, had he seen whither his course was taking him, he might have drawn back afraid. But now, with results in view, the truth won, the insight proved, he does not feel so. The " lie " has given life to truth that had been dead without its help. And he holds this true in regard to all belief. In one sense he believes nothing, but in another sense he is ready to believe that " every cheat's inspired, and every lie quick with a germ of truth."

But if there be truth, and a true way to show it, why cheat ? Because, he says, " there's a strange, secret, sweet self-sacrifice in any desecration of the soul to a worthy end." Not that it is meant to go on in the false way. " After the minute's lie and the end's gain," the intention is to keep to the truth, only there is so much against that. And this lying for the truth's sake is the clue to much in careers like his.

Now he returns, with broader view, on an argument suggested before. His kind of " *lying* " is the sort of thing all men do. They all " cheat," —that is, feign and fancy. There is no other way to live in a world of " cheats "—in a world that itself is a " cheat," and where hardly any realise the life they seek. If men were to " take truth as truth is found," and the world just as it is, life were worth nothing. You must " force and mend it," or you will miss the good there is in it. Many do, and have " the life to come." But why not both ? And why not have " the life to come " brighten up this life ? That is what Sludge does,

and by the very means the poets use—" lying."
They get thanks ; why not Sludge, who does
more than they can, by his " influx of life " from
the world beyond, to take off the dulness and
discontent of the present life ?

But now Mr. Horsfall is tired, or vexed at what
he thinks special pleading, remote from the question of fact, and he brings the matter forcibly to
a close. He cheated. No casuistry affects that,
and he dismisses Sludge with a decisive contempt
that does not go into distinctions, yet not un-
generously. And Sludge, as soon as he is alone,
throws over the sneak and the casuist, shows all
his malice, is sorry he hasn't made a better bargain,
even by telling more lies, but takes comfort from
the thought that there are many more fools in the
world ready to help him, and that his " business "
is safe yet—with mankind as ally.

Such is the study of " Sludge, the Medium," our
poet's fullest dramatic study before " The Ring
and the Book." The poem is fertile in points of
dramatic and intellectual interest.

1. How is such a story to be read ? Is it
Sludge that speaks, or is it Browning ? Is this
the best case that could be made for the medium
by the subtlest argumentative mind English poetry
has had in our century ? We have before said
that it is a condition of all poetic drama that the
poet's mind should animate and unfold the minds
of his *dramatis personæ*. It is in the nature of art
such as Browning's that there should be a higher
degree of this in his work ; and what you fairly

may require is, that the growth should be dramatically fit. Sludge would never have made this apology. You may think he would not have understood it if made on his behalf. And yet it is made *within his mind ;* it presents his passions and his image of the world, and it carries out his principles. And so the poem is not a mere study in casuistry, what may be thought or said from Sludge's standpoint and for Sludge, but a study of things and laws in the soul of Sludge.

And what of the ideal development under such conditions and in such work ? Is it truth, or what is it ? The question is of much importance with regard to more than Browning's work. We should say that what is thus given is moral truth—truth of general human nature as the poet grasps and construes it. " Invention " in such work is not the devising of what never was nor ever will be, but the finding of what is at work within given types, and possible to the heart of man.

2. And the dramatic interest goes with another —the humour of the poet. This is seen in the details and externals of the man, but is most of all felt in the conception and breadth of treatment, the type and the justice done to it. The strange play of truth and error, of doubt and belief, of reality and delusion, of audacity and cowardice, of cleverness and crudity, of lying so deep as to have become self-deception and sheer inability to say how much is false and how much true, whether in soul or conduct ;—all this is frankly given, and thoroughly characteristic.

3. And if there be humour in the subtle and free appreciation of the type, there is fuller humour in the large and subtle suggestion through it of a world-wide comedy in which we are all engaged, and in which the serious opinions and aims of men bear no small part. This man is a sneak, a liar, and an egotist, you say, with hardly enough sound matter in him to keep him alive; and yet the poet not only brings him within the sphere of dramatic but of moral interest. When you have seen his picture of the soul, to which these things were possible, you not only see how this man came to be, but are startled by points of sympathy with men and opinions around you, with principles and temptations in your own soul. You see how much of the lying of Sludge grows out of social unrealities and follies; you see what opening there is for Sludgeism among the passions and opinions of men, their lazy or tired deferences, and conventions.

4. And this brings us to the chief points raised by Sludge and his apology—the bearing of the poem on spiritualism and on religious belief generally. As to the first point. Those who now study the question of " spirits " and mediums would say the poem makes too much of arguments and too little of pathology. Such cases are less a question of perverse and narrow inferences than of physical conditions involving certain powers and psychical conditions that involve certain beliefs and illusions. And the poet touches that side of the matter in his account of Sludge. The grounds on which he has chiefly taken it are perhaps of wider

bearing and greater interest. And what is his
bearing on spiritualism and the theory of spirits ?
Sludge seems to make his case for some kind of
intercourse with the " world of spirits " very plausible, on what may be called orthodox grounds of
belief. Grant him the common theory, the usual
beliefs, and how are you to close the door on such
developments as this of " spiritism " and Sludgeism ? He says you can only do so by letting the
beliefs lie dead in the mind. And Dr. Johnson,
we know, was somewhat of that opinion. What
has been gained since Johnson's time to alter the
matter ? That the climate of opinion and standard
of belief about such things has so changed as to
put such follies not merely out of fashion, but out
of court ? Or shall we say that Sludge answers
himself, and that follies like his are a disproof of
his theories ? Both are true and to the point.
And let us add, we are in no position to argue
such a question in the abstract. Even if ordinary
ideas be more or less granted, the question is one
of experience, not of inference from any general
beliefs. " Ghosts " may or may not be a possible
part of the universe. Whether they be an actual
part of this world is a question of fact and evidence. Just so, says Sludge ; and look at the
" body of evidence," the universal tradition. Or,
as Johnson said, there are more stories to confirm
the belief than to support anything else men have
held. But all or most of the stories appear to be
capable of other explanations, and for how few of
them, after all, is there any proper "evidence." It is

no doubt, in the nature of the case that this should be so. And, as with Mrs. Browning and spiritualism, when so many " facts " are witnessed to by so many people, the general opinion is likely to keep the question open, and to hold that there is more in it than has yet been explained. The learned Society for Psychical Research argues so much, and doubtless there is more in " ghosts " and " spiritism " than has yet been explained by any science. Only to bring the whole body of honest phenomena within the realm of physical and psychical causes, and so within a natural order, would seem to Sludge, and to others besides, worse usage than to leave them alone in their antique mystery. To Mrs. Browning and to Dr. Johnson the belief that there was something mystical, and possibly inexplicable, in the matter, seemed bound up with their belief in an " unseen universe " and " another life." And that has been always part of the power of such views.

5. But the bearing of the poem on the quality and method of religious beliefs generally is more to us. Is Sludge in any sense a study and warning on that matter? Have men, in the interest of their own beliefs, often shown as little regard for truth and as great powers of casuistry as Sludge develops? Without doubt it has often been so. The sphere of religious emotion is peculiarly open to illusions of self-love. Neither Blougram nor Sludge have any passion for truth, or so much as a decent care for it. There is no

chapter in the history of human errors larger or more curious than that dealing with the vagaries and perversions of religious belief; self-will and imagination shaping together not what is, but what is desired, have there had a wonderful scope, and the "souls" of men have been all too fertile of delusions made in what they took to be their own "higher interests."

6. And the success, as well as the argument, of Sludge may seem to go even deeper, and leave nothing of truth in human life at all. This man plays his game until all seems "lies" in his sense, and life itself a "lie" that needs illusion to make it satisfactory. It is an extreme case, but in less degree and in other ways the thing often happens; and the law of the matter appears to be, that the man who is not true has no faith in truth, and that those who set themselves the mean task of making their beliefs serve their wishes and answer to ends of their own, lose in time the very sense of truth, lose, too, the life and support of conviction. For beyond his exposure of Sludge, and all that is shallow in his selfish casuistry, the poet suggests not only the lies that ape truth, but the truth that is great above and behind all lies, and the need for a finer care for truth in these things where it is so very easy to find what one wishes to see.

7. And Sludge carries warning in another way. He is a fanatic. For him "religion is all or nothing." He would place and define certain instincts and ideas, and, thrusting aside all natural

knowledge, would dominate life by dogmas and inferences from them. He would do this in a paltry spirit and for low ends. Others have done it in a great spirit and for noble ends, but it is a mere "passion of the brain," and a pernicious fallacy in both cases. For not only is it impossible for the mind of man to frame or apply a view of things of such scope and authority, but a sphere and system that are in place and divine are set aside. And those who say with Sludge that religion is the whole of life are apt to make self-will and self-concern the soul of religion.

8. Then a word on a great question that runs through the poem—that of the "supernatural," and the bearing of the poem on it. Minds like those of Sludge degrade all they touch, and the notion of an "unseen order," after Sludge has handled it, may seem no better than a poor superstition. To Sludge, law is nothing, and God, as will, not reason, is the only thinkable explanation of things; and to him the visible rests on an invisible which is the real universe. But plainly, Sludge's theory of things is something shallow, is certainly in no way deeply considered. Are we left to the inference that the theory itself has no deeper value than this may imply? Or does the poet leave us with the impression that in the case of Sludge, and of the general mind, this view springs from fundamental principles and relations of mind that are true parts of human nature, and valid towards an interpretation of things? And does he, from the way in which this is put forth

26

as a study of mind in an age when a purely natural explanation is offered, imply that no science can abolish, and that only religion can purify and ennoble, the "instincts" that haunt the "confines of experience?" In the light of other works, there is no doubt that this is so. The facts of the world, and, above all, the facts of thought and of the moral nature of man, imply and require such an order. And as a student of that nature the poet appears to suggest dramatically that superstition or religion will govern the feelings, beliefs, and conduct of men in their relations to the Invisible and the Unknown—to the spheres that lie beyond death and beyond knowledge.

To sum up, then, on the questions thus raised, and which such dramatic studies do raise, however little some of us may like to have them presented in poetry. Caliban, Blougram, and Sludge all raise in different ways the question of the value of man's thoughts, or of the intuition of human mind, on the final matters of belief—Caliban, to explain the facts of his experience, and to fit himself the better for the world in which he finds himself; Blougram, to present in an age of science and criticism his "apology" for the type of religion he adopts, and for his part in life; Sludge to justify his spiritualism and his conduct as medium, dishonestly haunting the bourne of life. And when Caliban, Sludge, and Blougram expound our ideas and aspirations as to those great matters, they may seem only forms of self-deception—the data got from instinct, the argument guided by interest, the conclusions unchecked by verification. It may seem so. As we said in regard to Sludge's notion of a " Supernatural" Religion, it may seem no more than a crude theory, a primitive fear and faith, an illusion of the soul. It is not so. Caliban and Sludge are in their kind witnesses to the sincerity and depth of faith, and Blougram to the depth and humanity of religion as such, whatever we may think of his " apology," or his form of it. And so, speaking more generally, we may say that in his " criticism" of belief our poet has given ample analysis of its psychological elements and striking illustration of the quality and extent of these elements in belief. But the large impression left by his method and by his work of this kind is, that though much of the form, and possibly even part of the content, of faith may prove to be psychological in the narrow sense, something belonging to particular minds, or sets of minds only, yet the substance of faith is universal. And if he implies that none can " turn the whole of faith to rational thought," he holds that faith is as truly " life and light" of reason as of the " soul." While it always seemed to him, mystic as his wife called him, and as in part he was, that the deeper things of thought and art are the truer for this, that they never quite explain, because they can never exhaust, the facts of experience, or the powers and realities of man's spirit, with which they yet have real contact and profoundly significant communion.

CHAPTER XV

POEMS ON ART: PAINTERS AND PAINTING.

CARE for art and sensibility to its impression is one of the features of our time. It has united itself with some of our best things and aims, and it reads for us qualities and motives of our lives and of our books. It is part of our better culture —of our quickened sense of beauty, our new care for the good of the world, our escape from the too-much fact of so many lives, our quest for something gone from knowledge, as some have thought, and others feared, yet needed by the soul. In some points a new Renaissance has happened in our century, and this care for art is one of those points.

Our poetry, since Keats, who "loved the principle of beauty in all things," has been deeply qualified by this care, and in poetry few have shown such sympathy and power in this matter as Browning. This may seem strange, since the poet's own work is not eminent for beauty of form or colour. Yet his interest and power here are as true a part of his genius as of his relation to his time. He has been called the *artists' poet*. He is, in a larger sense, the *poet of art*. The artistic type and qualities are dear to him. He is a

cordial interpreter of the passion and aims of the
artist, and still more of the general passion and ideas
of art. He might, one fancies, have been a painter.

It is not easy to trace the sources of this
interest beyond the poet's own mind; but some
points are clear in regard to it. His early care
for Keats, and his lifelong care for Greek poetry,
have cultivated his sympathy. His residence in
Italy, the climate and home of art and artists, has
told on it, as many poems prove. And in him,
as in the rest of us, it is part of the modern spirit,
part of our keen interest in the past, and in whatever preserves for us its life, part, too, of our
romantic feeling for the beauty of the world, and
man's life in it.

But Browning's power and interest in this
matter are a most characteristic part of his own
mind, and throw light on the body and spirit of
his work. His vivid senses, and care for the
forms of things; his love of definite expression,
and sense of the soul made visible in and through
fit forms; his quest of the ideal through mastery
of the real; his feeling that the real world can be
seen only in that purer other light of the imagination, of which art is the sovereign expression,—
his love of art tells of these things in his mind.

It is part of his character too, and throws light
on his ethics. The method and spirit of the
artist are good in themselves. The artistic way
of taking things, through love and enjoyment,
seems to him to gain more of the truth of things
than mere science can ever gain. The life and

good of things is more than knowledge. And he has a cordial sense of that goodness and beauty of things, which is the soul and basis of art.

And there is another aspect of this poet's interest in and delineation of art that seems often missed. He is essentially a dramatic poet, and his great interest is the soul, and even his art-interest has this relation and scope. There are two ways in which art and art-work may be regarded—one we may call the æsthetic, the other the spiritual. One is concerned with the works and the pleasure they give, simply as art, or with analysis of the work and the pleasure; the other with the light thrown on the artists themselves, and the light cast on man and man's mind by the ideas and scope of art—by the impulse in which art arises, and by its aims. Now, Browning's interest not merely touches the latter, but often takes it as chief matter. His interest in art for its own sake serves his keen dramatic interest, his interest in man and in the soul.

The relation of art to character, the dramatic and moral interest of artistic work and ideas, is familiar now. Not so clearly seen is its relation to the soul, and yet an important aspect of Browning's poetry on art is neglected if this relation be not considered. He will here lead you to ask, What does art mean? Nor will he let you rest on the notion that it means pleasure only, and delight in "the shows of things." He believes that heartily. But he will carry you beyond that to a sphere of emotions and ideas, interpretation of

which he finds in, and himself seeks through, art
—ideas and emotions that are not imitative and
sensuous, but of man's own heart and mind.   The
soul of every true artist has sought, through the
medium of art, to convey its intuition and aspiration.   The higher principles and aims of art are
spiritual ideas.   And art, through these aims and
ideas, is as true an interpreter of the passion and
thought of man as philosophy or religion.

Coming to the poems, we shall find the poet's
interest in art proved by their number and variety
as well as by their value.   As a poet interpreting
art, he has dealt with painting and sculpture,
with poetry and music, and with power, sympathy,
and insight in each case.

Of these art-poems we take first a group dealing with *Italian painting and painters*—studies of
artists and types of art, or of art in a more critical
way.   We begin with " Old Pictures in Florence."
The poet is the speaker, and it gives us part of
his mind, but freely, humorously, and in relation to
the circumstances and thoughts of the time, and
its style is meant to give its lyric-dramatic quality.

On a March morning, with the spring begun,
the poet is gazing through the clear air on Florence.   He sees the fair city, but most of all the
Campanile of Giotto.   It startles him by bringing
up Giotto, who has lately seemed to trick him
over a picture of his own, that the poet has been
hunting for and missed—" a precious little thing
that Buonarotti eyed like a lover."   And Giotto
brings up the early masters and the spring-birth

of Italian art. The poet has been studying those
masters for months, and the dead painters have
become part of the city's life to him. He has
seen them in the churches, standing by their
pictures, and felt their pain as they saw those
works dropping away. Yet why should they,
who are safe in heaven, trouble? Because their
work is yet to do. The work of the great
masters is done and safe; but the great masters
have surely put out these early masters, and
taken away their value? They will not think so
who know the place and worth of these masters,
the value of their impulse and idea.

And what was that *impulse* and *idea*? It was
they who carried art forward from the point
where Greek art had stopped, and indeed failed.
Greek art had given the life and meaning of man,
so far as the beauty and power of perfect forms,
animated by clear and active minds, could give
man. Men saw that serene perfection of
Olympian gods, but knew they could never reach
it. It put before them a godlike humanity—
admirable grace, dignity, strength; but its only
lesson was submission to man's limits, not aspiration or effort towards a serene beauty that was
felt to be beyond man's reach. Thus soul through
body, and bodily perfection, as man's ideal, meant
an ideal both limited and unattainable, and
brought man's progress to an end. But the end
of progress is death in life for man. How, then,
was progress to start again with new life for man?
The new birth of hope and effort came when,

looking inward, man found the ideal of the soul
and of a spiritual humanity. It was then seen
that the Greek ideal is inadequate as well as
impossible. In the soul was felt the power and
promise of what is "eternal." The nature that
has this principle and vision cannot reach the
serene and bounded perfection of antique art and
its ideals. But for that very reason it will pass
beyond them, and see them abolished. The new
ideal requires and promises "eternity." The
sense of imperfection and inadequacy that belongs to life now is the result of the greater
ideal, and the evidence of the larger attainment.
What has come to perfection dies. We cannot
find the perfect form, because thought and passion
have grown too great for such absolute expression.

It is from this point of view that he regards
and values the *early masters*. Imperfect and
crude as they are in so many ways, they went
beyond Greek art because they were aware of the
spirit, because they first sought to represent man
in the light of that, and by that to give the
spiritual ideal. They "failed," but they took this
great step, and their aim and truth started art on
its new and greater course, and are yet to be
realised. So he reads the history of art.

Then after this flight he feels, as he leans on
his villa gate this warm spring morning, as if the
great ideal were too much for him. To go on
and on and never stop—an evolution of life
through an endless series of lives, always progressive—is that the idea that has come into the

world as the revelation of the spirit—as the law
of man's work and hope? It tires one to think
of it, and for the moment he leans to the notion
that some time we shall stop and rest, though he
has above suggested that we can only rest by
not stopping.

There is in this, of course, a turn of Browning's
humour, congenially used at points like these.
And such touches give us not merely the quality
of the poet—they give us his "criticism" of
certain matters. He checks his idealism by
frank recognition of the other side of human
nature. He is broadly aware of that other side,
and is so frank as to its existence, and the conditions of life attaching to it, that some of his
critics allege that his own intuition of the ideal
was apt to fail him. Yet the facts are so, and in
this as in other poems his humorous recognition
of both sides really leaves you with sense of
the higher unity in which the facts may be
harmonised.

With this fancy, anyhow, he ends his "philosophy," and goes back to the early painters, whom
he banters for not showing a wiser care for their
pictures, by guiding them into the hands of those
who know their worth—himself, for instance, who
would be pleased with a Gaddi or a Pollajuolo,
and does not expect one of the greater names.
In his banter he gives a list of these masters, with
critical notes of their works, and gets back to Giotto.
Then he turns to Florence, and the bell-tower of
Giotto, and longs for the days when, in a free Italy,

art may revive, and the Campanile be finished—
"completing Florence as Florence Italy."

Then come two *poems dealing with artists*,
dramatic studies, and also studies of artistic types
and styles, one in the second, and the other in
the third and great period of Italian painting.
The first of these, "Fra Lippo Lippi," put in
"Men and Women" (1855), belongs to the early
married years in Florence. The study was suggested by Vasari, though it departs from his
story at certain points. Filippo Lippi, born at
Florence in 1412, was left an orphan when two
years cld. He fell to the care of an aunt, and
led a hard life until, at the age of eight, he was
placed with the Carmelite fathers in the Carmine
monastery in Florence. Here he soon showed a
quick eye and a turn for drawing, but no taste
for learning. His use for his books was to cover
them with sketches of what he had seen in the
streets. The prior saw his bent, and thought it
best to use his talent. He set him to learn art.
The chapel of the Carmine had been painted by
Massaccio, and Lippi went there daily to study.
He learned and used for a time the manner of
that painter. He soon grew famous, broke away
from the convent about 1432, and had his travels
and adventures. On his return to Florence he
painted the "Coronation of the Virgin" for the
nuns of Sant' Ambrogio. They got him the
patronage of Cosimo de Medici, and for Cosimo's
wife he painted a Nativity, with a figure of St.
ohn Baptist. Lippi had a frank love of the

world and its pleasures, and a warm, impulsive
nature. The story that is the basis of the poem
shows this. Once, when the painter was busy
with a work for Cosimo, and was confined to his
palace, that the work might be done as soon as
possible, the painter got so tired of his confine-
ment that he made ropes of his bed-clothes, let
himself down into the city, and took his pleasure
there for some days. And the story agrees with
Lippi's life as we know it. In his life, more than
his work, he broke quite away from monkish rule.
He loved a novice of one of the convents, and
took her from the nuns; and their son was
Filippino Lippi, the painter. He had a facile
and affluent hand, and Vasari says the beauty of
his work atoned for the failings of his life. He
died at Spoleto in 1469.

In many points the poet has dramatised Vasari,
giving life and character to the old painter and
his idea of art. Lippi is out on his escapade
from Cosimo's palace, and has been caught by
the city guard on his way back, and is telling
why he is abroad in the spring night. In
doing this he tells the story of his life and his
aims as a painter. The key to all is set by the
situation and temper of the artist. His free
joyous energy, his humour, his cordial nature and
love of the common life of man, are in every line
He had been shut up for three weeks at his work
when, leaning out of the window one night into
the fresh warm air, he heard a sound of happy
voices and a rush of merry feet, and was off afte

them. But a "monk!" they will say. So he
tells them how he got into the convent, and his
life there. He laughs at the ascetic rule, but he
says there is one kind of renunciation he uses.
He has not the passion for gold so many are
learning in Florence; his passion is for the
beauty and good and joy of man's life. He
had always loved it, and in his early work had
drawn it frankly. The prior forbade him, and
ordered him back to Giotto's manner and religious
themes. He felt that art must soon break away
from that tradition and take to freer study; but
he kept the old way, and now it keeps to him.
It has been bad for his art and his life. Others
are coming who will depict life freely, and that is
art's proper business; not to tell pious stories or
"preach" to men, but to give men the joy and
beauty of the world as God has made it. He is
scornful about the uses piety makes of art—one
of his own pictures having been scratched to the
bricks; and then fearing he has gone too far, he
promises to make amends by painting the picture
for St. Ambrogio's, showing his humour and
sensuousness in his account of it; and at this
point, as he sees the soft grey of the spring dawn,
he knows it is time to be off.

The poem is, we said, a study of *character*—
vivid in that way—and a study of *art*; of the
motives and influence of the Renaissance as it
told on painting. Lippi belongs to the second
movement of Italian art, and the new desires and
ideas of that period are forcibly shown in him.

Lippi's work does not show so clearly as his words
the new motives and aims, but his life and art
together bear them out. He makes apology for
the want of truth and freedom in his work, and in
any case there was this conflict of ideas at the
turning-point. The ascetic temper and ideal had
become, in the growth of art and culture, too
narrow, and while art's themes remained religious,
its spirit and treatment were freer.

And so, if " Old Pictures " describes the central
idea of the early art, " Fra Lippo " embodies the
impulse that arose with the Renaissance. The
first gave only so much of " body " as should
show the spiritual idea ; the second took to the
study of life with growing zeal and care. The
first did not know, and was afraid of, " the world
and the flesh " ; the second began to grasp and
depict the value and significance of both. To the
first the world was a dream or a temptation ; to
the second, its beauty and good, its " divine
meaning," began to grow clear. There was a
new sense of form, of the meaning of beauty, and
of the function of art to express " soul " through
true and fair forms ; to rouse men to—

> The beauty and the wonder and the power ;
> The shapes of things, their colours, lights, and shades,
> Changes, surprises . . .

and give them sense, through free presentatio
of its mere joy and beauty, that " God mad
it all."

" Andrea del Sarto " is, again, a *dramatic stud*
—a study, also, of a type and of certain principle

in art. It was suggested by a picture of the
painter, with Vasari's story as a comment on it.

Andrea del Sarto was of the third and great
period. He was born in Florence about 1488,
and died in 1530. Vasari says his father was
a tailor, and hence his name, " tailor's Andrew."
Like others of that age with gifts for art, he began
as a goldsmith's apprentice. He did not care for
goldsmith's work, as Cellini did, but soon showed
talent for drawing. Having studied under one of
the painters of his time, he pretty soon won fame.
Vasari gives a list of early works of the painter
that were famous. He was set in 1509 to adorn
the church of the Annunziata, and some of his
best work is there. While at this work he married,
in 1512, Lucrezia del Fede, who was his fate in
more ways than one. His fame reaching France,
he was invited to the French Court by Francis I.,
and was generously encouraged there. He was,
however, drawn back to Florence by his wife.
When leaving France he promised to return, and
got money to buy pictures for the king. He
spent the money for his own uses, and remained
in Italy. Vasari speaks very plainly of the evil
influence over the painter of his beautiful wife;
and, though he has much praise for his many
works, he speaks also of their defects. His
design and workmanship, his colour and finish,
were so good that he was called " Andrew the
faultless." He wanted inward power, fervour,
and elevation of mind. His technical skill was
so great that with invention he might have stood

beside the great masters. There is a story that Agnolo said that, had his tasks been greater, he might have rivalled Rafael; but fire and power were both lacking.

The poem was suggested by a picture in the Pitti Palace. In fact, its first design was to give Mr. Kenyon an idea of that picture, a copy of which the poet could not send him. In this aspect the poem is a vivid success. The painter and his wife are in talk over a letter which she holds. His hand is on her shoulder, and he is looking into her face, while she looks away from him. She is cold and masterful, he loving and submissive. By her beauty, as by her self-will, she rules him. That is the picture. Turn to the poem. It is evening. The painter is weary, and wants to rest. The twilight soothes him as he looks towards "sober, pleasant Fiesole," and he wishes his wife to stay with him kindly for a little. It will help him, and he will do the picture she wishes. Her beauty has done much for him, as her figure in so many of his works proves; her love would do more. But he knows that he pleads vainly; she is her own, not his, yet "very dear no less." She smiles coldly as he pleads. He feels the charm, but also the want of ardour and hope, the greyness of everything in his life and work. All is toned down to the tint of the autumn evening, and he accepts it for its harmony and quiet. It is God's will too; for nature and circumstances are destiny, and men are not free. And if it be not the best, it is many ways good and fit for him, with his defects and limits. He knows his powers, the artistic value of his work, but also its want of force and depth. His work is exact and adequate to its themes. The work of others, who are and see more than he does, is for that reason less exact and perfect. The low pulse gives a steady hand, but it is the craftsman's, and truth and vital beauty are more felt in the work of the others less skilful than he is.

This clear self-consciousness and technical mastery are good as means; but the gain is loss when they become ends. There is no progress, and can be no future for any art that is without spiritual effort and suggestiveness, however placid and perfect it may be within its own limits. The future is to those who see more than they as yet express.

And why has he not done greater work? for, though he can see Rafael's faults, he feels that Rafael's work is greater than his own. Is it because his wife has not given him love, and has cared for the money, not for the work? But neither Rafael nor Agnolo were so helped, and the true incentives to all creative work must come from the mind itself. Is it, then, a law of life that gifts be parted—executive power to one, and passion and insight to another? It may seem so. Yet he too had days of passion and a fire of souls about him once, when in France; and he thinks of those days, but only to fall quickly into his mood of acquiescence. Yet he is not quite satisfied, for perhaps he might have done more.

27

He calls to mind Agnolo's remark about him.
Then he frankly allows he could not have made
Rafael's work. Still, what more was possible he
has given up for his wife, and he tries to find in
that a gain for all loss, and an incentive, not to
better work, but to work that will make more
money.

It is dusk now, and they go in. She is in
haste to go to a certain "cousin." He wishes
her to stay this evening, if only that he may
dream of one great picture—"a virgin, not his
wife this time"—that should justify the praise of
Agnolo, and after that he will find her the money
she wants. But no; he will never, he sees, do
better work here. Will he anywhere take his
place with the great ones? He does not know;
he knows only the bondage he cannot break.

In "Andrea del Sarto," then, we have a study
of character, and of art as qualified by character.
The study of character is both exact and gentle.
Candid self-judgment is the quality of men like
Andrea. He describes himself and his work
frankly, touching the source of evils in life and
art. He is weak, and his art is limited. His
love for a selfish, worldly woman has been a
hindrance; but a radical and insuperable hindrance
lay in himself. He has not the passion or stuff
of the higher minds; their power and their divine
necessity are both wanting to him. He can
express well what is in him, and there is nothing
in him he cannot express; but his mastery and
expression are adequate just because his thoughts

are inadequate to the life of man and the meaning of the world. His technical perfection results from his limitation. That perfection is not the highest note of art. In the highest art a certain incompleteness may be the result of greatness, and great work is often true and suggestive, because of that incompleteness which conveys the artist's sense of the greatness of his theme—or even Fra Lippo's sense of the wonder and beauty of the world, and of man's life in it.

Then these poems, taken together, touch *certain ideas in the history of art*. The early masters went beyond Greek art, so far as they expressed the Christian ideal. But they missed truth and greatness in art, not only for technical reasons, but because of their ascetic view of the Christian ideal. With the Renaissance came a new impulse and idea—the impulse of free enjoyment and the antique idea of life and beauty. These ideals could not, as then seen, be combined; and not only did art fail for that reason, but life had become worldly and corrupt, and the old motives and ideas had lost their inspiring power and sincerity, as the temper and work of Andrea clearly show.

And, taken with "Pictor Ignotus," which is put with them, these poems are studies of *unfulfilled lives*. Lippi through circumstances, Andrea through moral defects, and the unknown painter through moral sensibility and ascetic ardour, fail to grasp and unfold an idea they see; and the fact is very general, so general that it must be

accounted for, which this poet does by regarding
life with reference to the "soul," and by taking
fidelity and aspiration rather than achievement
and finish as its proper measure.

And there are, it will be seen, implicit or
expressed in Browning's criticism of art other
leading principles of his criticism of life, his
idealism, his value for personality, his care always
for life itself.

He has we have said a very cordial care for art,
but of art apart from all other interests in life he
knows nothing. "Art for art's sake" was no
notion of his. Art as the chief interest and
consolation of life would not have consoled him,
would have touched his sense of humour somewhat keenly. His care for man was too robust,
his intuition of man's proper good was too large,
to allow him to mistake any means for that end.
And as he did not believe that that good could
be summed up in any quality or form of pleasure
merely, he held that the pleasure given by art was
not the last question about it ; that in fact behind
that question for the artist was its bearing on life ;
and, behind the question of the ideal of beauty
itself, the question of its relation to the truth of
things and the good of man.

And it is here we see broadly the bearing of
these art poems, so full as they are of interest in
art, and still fuller of interest in life as they are,
on the poet's criticism of life. In art, as in every
form of human activity, he insists on the value of
personality and its rights. Knowledge, experience,

art, character, faith are all individual, and are of
value and of interest as they are the true fruits of
personality.   As with the " Grammarian " and
knowledge, as with " Aben Ezra " and character,
so is it with the artist and art.   Combining the
intuition of the " Old Pictures " and " Andrea "
with that of the poems just named it would appear
that neither knowledge, nor life, nor work, nor the
thought of the artist can ever be " made perfect."
The conditions of personality as well as the conditions of life are against that.   And yet the idea
of the perfect and the passion of beauty hold
every sincere artist and every earnest man.   We
never reach our ideal, and yet we rest only in
the consciousness of an honest approach to it.
No life is complete nor can be, and no work ever
satisfies the ideal of the true artist.   And that is
because art and life alike are at their best, not in
partial fulfilments, but in resolute aspiration and
faithful advance.   The end is growth.   The condition and law of all good is the ceaseless progress
of the spirit itself.   The poorest and most futile
work is the work that is complacent, self-satisfied.
Honourable failure is better than that.   Time and
circumstance may appear to be against us. Yet work
and circumstance are adequate to those who will
take circumstance and work the right way.   Since
all work and service are of worth not absolutely,
but with reference to the progress of men towards
truth, beauty, goodness, it is the spirit in which and
the aim with which the work is wrought and not the
work itself that in the long-run count and endure.

Circumstance and work our poet holds are always equal to this. There are three grand mistakes— (1) To be indifferent, inert, as the duke and the lady in the "Statue and the Bust"; (2) to be eager for absolute attainment, as "Paracelsus," or so caught in a dreamy ideal as not to care for action, which must always be partial, as "Sordello" was; (3) to be complacent and worldly, as "Andrea del Sarto." In life and work we must put ourselves forth, and put our best into both. We cannot have the perfect. "Earth is not heaven." But the perfect is not only the goal, it is the law and element of our lives. We must be "realists" —we must work under the conditions and at the task set us. We must be "idealists"—we must work at all points in "the light that never was on sea or land." We must value all things, works, duties even, as they bear towards the truth and power of soul and will.

CHAPTER XVI

POEMS ON ART: POETS AND POETRY

BROWNING has shared our age's romantic interest in art. He has also shared its interest in art theories, and most of his poems on art have a critical quality. It is matter of regret to some that since Goethe's days our artists have been so often occupied with these points. They hold that art should be instinctive, and think it has been made self-conscious by all this criticism. It is, to a great extent, a result of the intellectual and inward quality of our interests and work— our self-consciousness has produced the criticism, if it has also been increased by it.

And since the days of " Sordello," which so strongly expressed the poet's theoretic and ethical interest in art, he has touched these things with power and strong sense. The poems on art we have still to consider are mainly of this critical kind, and if their ideas should not seem, after all our criticism, original, they throw light on the poet's mind and aims, and put forcibly his ideas about his own art.

1. We take a group dealing with *the conditions of art* in the lives of the artists. The story of the

sculptor in " Pippa Passes " bears finely on this.
The love into which he has been entrapped reveals
to him a principle higher than he had yet known,
shows him how helpful love is, how it is the true
principle of life and work. True work must rest
on the true spirit and the right relation to men
—must be made in a spirit of pure service.

" Youth and Art " has the same truth. Two
artists, one a woman and a singer, the other a
man and a sculptor, lived in their early days of
struggle in opposite garrets. They had something
more than kindness for each other, and might
have helped each other. But, with fame and
fortune to make, they had no room in their lives
for simple love. They have made, not all they
wished, but some part of what they hoped of
both now, yet she feels something lost never to
be gained. They are worldly and cold, and you
feel that their art is less because they are so.
With more of the heart, and less of the world,
their lives had been happier and their art higher.

" Pictor Ignotus " touches the above point, and
the next to be considered. As the poet has put
this poem, made in 1845, with his " Men and
Women," and in the Renaissance series, he meant
it as a study of the meeting of the older, religious,
and free popular art. The work and breath of a
new time were round the painter—breath of popular interest and work of popular appeal. He
would gladly have made such work, and had the
joy of the fuller passion and the wider service.
Why not make the work, then ? Because he

saw that popular work must reflect and gratify the popular mind.   He would not degrade his art to that.   And so he made his choice—the cloister with its seclusion and its integrity.   He has missed fame, but he has kept his aims true, his heart pure.   With his proud self-respect and severe conscience this was his only course, and though he feels the loss of influence, and feels too the narrow scope, the cold and shadowy quality of his art, he rests in the conviction that it could not have been other than it is without loss of that inward honour which to such as he is more than life.

" The Lost Leader " is indirectly a criticism of the conditions of good and strong art in the life of the artist.   Your best singer will be a ' leader," perhaps must be.   In life and in art he will stand on the side of the high things and the " forward " causes.   The great ones are there. But this poet has foregone his privilege and lost his place, and the battle goes without him hence-forth, or sets us, who still fight in the van and with the freemen, against him.   We lose, he far more, and in the hour of glad victory we forgive him.   These verses with their vivid energy of phrase and rhythm had Wordsworth primarily in view, and his defection from the progressive and democratic cause.   But the verses in that reference ran quite beyond fact and justice, and Browning wrote them with a wider reference, and let them stand for that reference.   They are typical, not personal, and their point is, that pure fidelity to

generous causes and to the service of man is
better for a poet's influence and genius than those
rewards which, as he implies sarcastically, the
world gives but sparingly even to those poets who
desert to its side.

The poem called "Shop," with its blunt phrase
and tone, bears on life, but touches the artist as
well as the merchant. Its main point is the folly
and essential poverty of those who have no life
or interest except in their trade or calling; who
starve and crush the man into a hole behind the
"shop." There are writers who have no life
except in their books, artists to whom nothing
has interest except their pictures. The man and
the work both suffer in such cases. The best
work requires a man's free soul and true life
behind it, and a fine interest in many things.

2. Our next group is one dealing with the
relations of the *popular judgment* to art. And
first "Respectability." This is its theme. A
artist and his wife have had a free ramble i
Paris, with picturesque views of the city's life
But what would the world, or, in George Eliot
phrase, "the world's wife," say if she saw then
if she knew their freedom used in other ways
Be severe and condemn, of course. But tho
who would depict life must see it and keep
touch with it. There are many gains for the fre
Life and experience, and the world of men, a
more for the artist than any conventions.

"Popularity" deals with popular relations
the true artist in another way. You may ta

the poet himself as speaker, and John Keats as the case he had most in his mind. And he thinks how the public ignored Keats until he lay in his Roman grave. Yet, never mind; he is " dear to God and the coming ages " for the work he did and the genius he proved, and a few knew him. And what happens when he is gone? Others take his secret, copy his art, popularise and vulgarise it, grow famous, and, it may be, rich by doing so. He found the " Tyrian dye, blue as Astarte's eyes." Hobbs, Nobbs, Nokes, and Stokes get all the " profit " of it—and the good-natured scorn of our poet.

" How it Strikes a Contemporary " deals with *popular mistakes* about the poet. It begins—

> I only knew one poet in my life :
> And this, or something like it, was his way.

He was a man of mark, though not after the style or for the uses of the world. His dress and bearing made you aware of that. He mixed in and noted the world, quiet, withdrawn, but full of eyes. He saw every one, stared at no one. You stared at him, and though he barely looked at you, he knew you and took your gaze as a thing of course. Not knowing what these "ways" meant, yet sure they must have some " use," people said he was the king's " spy," and they could quote cases that seemed to be explained by it. And they mistook his private life as much as they did his public function. The poet lived in the simplest way, but the public thought he lived in a voluptuous style. The speaker's father, a man of

sense, saw in him the true Corregidor, " censor "
of men's ways. The poem ends with the poet's
death, and the simple dignity and honour of the
close crown his worth—

> Here had been ——, the general-in-chief,
> Thro' a whole campaign of the world's life and death,
> Doing the King's work all the dim day long.

The " scene " is Spanish. Was there thought o
Cervantes, and his way of life when he made
Don Quixote, and proved his place among the
world's great poets ?

3. We come now to the most interesting
group of the poems dealing with poetic art —
those in which we have more or less of a *personal*
expression.

And first of these we recur to *the digression*
in " Sordello." There the poet pauses at a crisis
of Sordello's story to give account of his own
art and its aims. It opens with the distinction
between Eglamor's and Sordello's art—the first
able to put all his heart and soul into his work
and to make his songs complete, because his
theme is small and his art the whole of his life;
the other feeling his work but part of his life,
with greater themes, and work that shows in its
very manner, purpose, and passion outreaching.
The latter is the true poet. The former is an
artist, or at most a troubadour. Beyond all his
work the poet feels a life great and free, and his
true mind has no sooner made any work than he
" strikes sail, cuts cable," and is away again upon
the broad and open sea. And this distinct

gives a clue to his choice of Sordello's story.
Other themes occur as he muses in Venice, but
he seeks some theme that shall give the realities
and scope of human life, in the hope of serving
mankind through the spiritual interest of his work.
And what is humanity? and how can he help
it in its need? He sees it vividly through what
he sees in Venice; sees its sin and weakness and
suffering, as of some erring woman. But can
he explain such a life, or help to clear it up for
these "warped souls and bodies" that he sees?
Life seems the grand teacher, through a very
maze of lies guiding by some thread or core of
truth, and through all the evil and pain working
a way to good. Such life seems, and we have to
master its method and purpose if we would help
men through it. How do this? By clever verses,
by pretence of knowledge, by laborious science?
By none of these, as it seems to him, but by
the living waters that flow from the rock of truth;
and this rock the poet must smite at his peril,
that the waters may flow forth for men. Some
poets only "see," and some reveal, the truth of
life, and "the best impart the gift of seeing to
the rest"; but insight is the basis, and truth the
bearing, of all their work, and the work must be
done with courage and devotion. These were the
principles our poet grasped, the aims he took, in
his early manhood, risking the ugly name of
"metaphysical poet," and other perils too.

The peculiar poem, "A Light Woman" connects with part of the above passage, that in

which he sees the " lost ones " of mankind as
first claiming his help.   The theme of the poem
is an imaginary subject from life, and its design
is to show, through the case put, how complex
men's motives may be, and how hard it is often
to reach a judgment that shall include and explain the facts of conduct ; only those who have
the power of getting behind apparent facts and
to the heart can hope to do so, and they have
often to pause, and even to fall back on the facts
as the best they can do.   Here is the problem
There are two friends.   The younger and weaker
falls into the " net " of a " light woman " ;   the
other, to free him, makes love to the woman on
his own account, and the woman loves him.   What
is he to do ?   Quite misunderstood by his friend
and by the woman, he scarcely knows what to
think of himself, and certainly does not know
what to do.   The problem is handed over to the
dramatic poet as one he ought to be able to deal
with, and in any case the pity of it !

" Transcendentalism " is a piece of advice to
a poet not yet up to all the secrets of his art
—to the poet of "Sordello" say (its date is 1855)
Its burden is, that the poet speaks and does not
sing; that he puts forth his thoughts solid and
bare, not draped in the folds of imagery and
metre.   The thoughts are good, but to give out
this kind of things as poetry is too bad.   Better
throw the harp away, get a Swiss horn, and shout
his " great thoughts" for all Europe to hear.   But
he may say, grown men want thoughts, not verses

truths, not images. They ought to, perhaps, but they really do not. They spend years in spelling out the meaning of things through science and philosophy, and find life's summer gone, and the "meaning" still to seek. How help them? What do they need? Another book, tough and dark too! No; they want some mage or poet, to give them hold of the things in their inner meaning and beauty; to give them life in its glow and its zest; to make them young again, and "pour heaven into this shut house of life." That were worth doing. Try song that way. Sing from the heart, and put the life of that into your song. You are a poem, though all the poetry you make as yet is nought. *Was this mockery of his critics, or self-criticism?* Poetry is not magic, and the poet is no magician, as the vulgar conceive it. Yet poetry ought to do something of this kind for us, by its thoughts, its images, its verses, its emotion and influx of the poet's soul.

The last sections of " Pacchiarotto, and How he Worked in Distemper" (xxiv.–xxix.) also deal with his critics and with poetry. In the former parts he thinks he has given them something to their taste, something simple and direct, with none of the " harsh analytics " they have so often charged him with giving, and he greets them in a spirit of frolic fit for the season, May day. One of them explains that the good critics have only swept his chimney for him, and that really he ought to consume his own smoke, and not let so much of it forth to become a public offence—a hit at that

labour and learning which may go to poetic work,
but ought not to give trouble to readers in it.
And he retorts with rough good humour that they
" bring more filth into his house than ever they
found there "—the offences they grumble at come
rather from their own minds and methods than
from his work, but since it would seem they are
made that way he is " pious " and will take them
as they are, and try to please them for once.
Hence this poem and the pitch of it, which he
calls whistling not singing. Having thus looked
at the critics and their " case " he dismisses them
with further banter to resume his work in his own
way, and appeals at the close to Euripides, whose
approval goes for much more with him than the
judgments of those who would cut down literature
to the quality and measure of some " Banjo-
Byron " or " Quilp, Hop o' my thumb."

" At the ' Mermaid ' " (" Pacchiarotto," 1876) is
a monologue imagined for Shakespeare, and spoken
at the tavern that was the rendezvous of Eliza
bethan wits. It deals with the true relation o
the dramatist to his work. It may be regarded
as a protest against certain recent criticism o
Shakespeare, and against an easy kind of criticism
that every dramatic poet is open to. It mock
the notion that the poet puts himself and his lif
into his work for all the world to find.

The speaker says he has no wish to take th
kingly place some would give him ; it is enoug
to have done the work. But the work is not th
whole of life or all the man, and he wishes to liv

a man's life with his fellows, cheerful, free, kindly,
independent. He has not sold his soul for the
world's praise, or made life's good turn on that.
He has kept his soul safe and clear within, and
wishes his work to stand by itself. By the work
let him be judged, without vain curiosity as to the
life. He has made no vain display of feelings or
of " morals," and if any seek a poetry of gloom
and discontent, he has none such to give. Life
has been and is good to him, and heaven " blue,
not grim," and men have been friendly on the
whole, while a few, honest to the core, have loved
him well. Nor of women has he had the sad
experience some like in their verse. Not " world-
smart," but friendly enjoyment, has, in fact, been
his note.

Now, despite its drift, what relation has this
to Browning ? It was not made for or of Shakespeare only, though much of it is fit for him.
The dramatist cannot keep his work clear of
himself in the way here implied ; not even
Shakespeare could, if he even deliberately wished,
which is doubtful. To find the dramatist through
his dramas is indeed a task of much delicacy,
and can only be done by those who respect
the principles of dramatic art; but it can be
done more than this poem implies. And the
poem itself we may surely take in evidence, for
Browning is distinctly here in these notes of it—
the appeal to the work, the reserve of the heart,
the self-reliance, the cheerfulness and frank enjoyment, the manly value for life as the more essential

28

good, the scorn of sentimental art and of melancholy as a poetic mood.

The poem that follows, named "House," suggested, perhaps, by certain "Lives" and the public curiosity in that matter, denies of even Shakespeare's sonnets their directly autobiographic quality. If Shakespeare did unlock his heart so, he was not the man or the poet some of us have thought. An author may give the public a peep through his window, but only an earthquake can be an apology for destroying the privacy of a house by throwing its whole front down. The public has no right to such exposure of the whole "interior," and if it be made it only leads to blunders and perversions. The intimate facts of life are for those eyes only that have "the spirit sense," and these can find what is of moment without any vulgar exposure.

The "Epilogue" in the same volume is, of course, personal; an expression of the poet's views about his own work. Poets, it is said, should give us wine, to gladden the inward sense, and they ought. But neither poetry nor wine can combine in one all the virtues. A certain kind of sweetness cannot be united with real strength. But is it not the very business of the poet to give us the "impossible," "body and bouquet in one"? There is such wine of poetry in the world, mighty and mellow. Pindar and Æschylus, Shakespeare and Milton, though those who loudly demand this quality from living poets take no great draught of it out of these poets. So let them talk. And as to his own work. He "brews stiff drink," strong rather than sweet. But, like wine, poetry grows mellow with age, if only it have strength. Anyhow, he gives his best, with zeal and without sparing. And his vineyard is earth, "man's thoughts, loves, and hates." But why not give it a lyrical, emotional, flavour? Because he will not "strip his meadows of the cowslips and the daisies." He keeps the tender and private emotions for the health and good of his own heart.

The Epilogue at the close of "Dramatic Idyls" (second series) has the same note. It contrasts two kinds of poets, the one emotional, superficial; the other with thought and depth of soul. Song in the one flows lightly, on the least impulse; in the other more slowly, but from fuller power. And strength is the soil for song; the power of a nature not lightly moved, but capable of strong passion, thought, and will, and whose work grows as the pine, because, like the pine, its roots are in the rock.

The prologues to "Pacchiarotto" and "Jocoseria" give other notes and aims. In the first, the sight of a garden wall, and the thought of the life beyond it, tell how often "wall upon wall are between us." Song should remove the walls, and bring heart to heart. It is the spirit that unites men, and the poet has put his hopes on that "subtle thing."

The lyric in "Jocoseria," "Wanting is—what?" like the prologue and epilogue to "The Two Poets of Croisic," turns on the power of love. The last of the three will serve best to put the idea as regards poetry. At an ancient contest for the prize of song, a poet was singing so that it seemed certain the prize would fall to him, when one of the strings of his lyre snapped. But all was not lost, for a " mad thing " of a cricket, " with its heart on fire," came to his help. Lighting on the lyre, it gave the missing note, " low and sweet," and he won the prize. A parable—Love was the cricket that replaced the broken string, and gave its sweetness to the song.

The conclusion of " The Two Poets of Croisic " (1878), all we can here speak of, has bearing on the criticism of poetry. One of the poets, after a brief blaze of fame, withdrew to the rustic quiet of Croisic, and put verse aside. He did so because he thought he had once had " direct dealing with God." The other found a brief fame, and then sank into neglect. The poem puts dramatic explanation of both cases. Then, in view of both, the poet asks, *By what tests shall we try poets*? In the spirit of Scott and Wordsworth he offers this test, " Which one led a happy life ? " The man's worth, and life's value to him, must be taken as our final test. The strong because joyful man, who stands master over his passions, using brightly his acquist of power and experience, is victor in every sphere, and nothing can make up to any man for the lack of this.

Then there is a further aspect of our poet's work, and another group of his poems, to which brief reference must be made in relation to his

criticism of poetic art. We allude to his poems
on Greek subjects, and his value for Greek poetry.
It has seemed to many that the complexity and
obscurity of Browning's characteristic work put a
classical standard wholly out of the question in
his mind, and in the expression of his genius.
Yet that is by no means the case, and a true
appreciation of his poetry has to comprehend the
fact, that our poet's conception of his art, and of
its subject and method, are such as to embrace a
Greek principle with a romantic scope. His interest in Greek art was early, and it was genial
and lasting. It appears in "Pauline." It is still
fresh and strong in the "Parleyings." And there
was appreciation, not interest only. He seldom
used the Greek manner, but he could use it, as
Landor recognised. And his translations from
the Greek, mostly from Euripides, render spirit
and style with sympathy and accuracy. We
have found him in "Pacchiarotto" appealing from
the critics, who were so ready to "dust his jacket"
without mastering his work, to Euripides, sure of
the sympathy of that old master of the truth and
poetry of human life. And this regard for the
poet of the "Alkestis" and the "Elektra," who
was a favourite also with Milton, was an old
affection. As early as the "Dramatic Lyrics" of
1841 we find it. "Artemis Prologizes," one of
that series, marks thus early his sympathy with
Greek imagination and his interest in the work of
Euripides. The theme of that poem was suggested by one of the dramas of Euripides, but is

taken up at the point where the old dramatist
stopped in the story of Hippolutos.   Artemis
speaks because the centre of interest is in her
mind.   Hippolutos, indifferent to Venus and
honouring Artemis, is lying wounded to death
through the malice of Venus.   Artemis, in honour
of her pure votary, has carried him from the
funeral pyre itself to her forest depths, and is,
with help of Asclepios, bringing him again to
life.   She tells the story of the love and lie of
Phaidra, and all that followed, and now she
watches while the healer's skill restores Hippolutos.
He lies as one asleep, and will come back.   She
waits, in silence from this point, the event.   There
the matter ends.   It is a mere fragment.   Its
interest is its Greek theme and its Greek manner,
its blank verse, and its dramatic-lyric quality.   It
may be that it could scarcely as conceived have
made part of a drama.   It may well be that there
was not matter in the myth for that.   But the
dramatic situation is finely stated from the point
of view chosen, and the story fitly told.   It reminds one of " Cleon," with simpler theme and
phrasing, and the poet has put it with the series
of " Men and Women."   Much of his matter
was unfit for this type of poetry, but thus early
our poet had skill in this manner.   And the
poem has the interest besides of being his first
dramatic monologue in blank verse, and of this
length.

In " Balaustion's Adventure " we have not only
a sympathetic version of the " Alkestis," but a

praise of the fine interest and human power of the author of that "strange, sad, sweet song." It tells how Balaustion, a Rhodian girl, charmed the Syracusans by reciting the touching drama, and won a lover too. She is a creation of the poet, and the qualities he gives her, her very name, are a tribute to the dramatist, whose work she knows so well and loves so much.

In Balaustion's second adventure, which is given in " Aristophanes' Apology," we have our heroine of the first poem set to defend her and Browning's favourite dramatist against the great comic writer, Aristophanes, and we thus get Browning's defence of Euripides against his greatest contemporary critic. It is the night when news of the death of Euripides was brought to Athens, and Aristophanes is returning from a feast held over one of his own triumphs. He comes to the house of Balaustion, where the dead poet is honoured, and he defends himself and comedy, against tragedy and Euripides. The tragedian was austere, rational, antagonistic to the old principles and life of Greece. He has been genial, conservative, lashing the follies of his fellow-citizens but upholding good old principles. Balaustion, in turn, argues that his defence is much too favourable, and does not, besides, agree with results. And then she turns to defend Euripides for his humanity, his love of truth, and ends by reading in proof of his quality the " Herakles " (" Hercules Furens "). The great comedian listened, but at the close returned to his " Apology "—a defence now of his *naturalism* against the *moralism* of Euripides, though he is made further to suggest that a greater poet than either may come—one who shall unite their gifts and points of view in a fuller and more completely human art.

The knowledge of Aristophanes and of Greek things shown in the "Apology" is great. The genius of the Greek master of comedy is fairly indicated. But the chief thing in the "Apology" is the ways in which it shows how distinctly Browning had considered the principles raised by the later drama of Greece, and how deliberately he preferred Euripidean art and aims to Aristophanic naturalism. He likes the human and ethical standpoint, the serious and truth-loving spirit of the tragic, rather than the "pure Hellenism," of the comic poet; while the "Apology" suggests, as we have seen, a broader spirit and a larger view, an art that unites the realism of the one with the higher interests of the other—delight in and free study of the world, with ideal aims and spiritual truth.

And is not this *the aim of his own art*? Let me answer that question very briefly by a simple statement of leading principles. Art may and ought to deal with all the significant facts of human nature and life. It should be commensurate with the world and spirit of man as man's thought and passion have grasped them. And the medium of art should correspond with this view of its matter. In selection and subjects and treatment art should be free, rational. It should not be restrained by theories based on past ex-

perience only, or by the conventions of custom
and pleasure. The poet must trust his own
genius and insight in his choice of themes, and
must establish his "rights" by his mastery and
vital power. The substance and power of the
work are primary; its style and form secondary.
Truth, not beauty only, is required in art. The art
that is made with an exclusive regard for beauty
is as inadequate to life as it is false to the higher
thought of man. That emphasis on beauty and
music, which is part of our inheritance from the
classical revival, is narrow as art and untrue as an
"image of life." If the poet is to give men the
contact and power of life as he sees it—the impulse of that vital thought and passion in which
the world and the soul are truly expressed—he
must use a fuller medium. To represent life, art
must deal frankly with experience, and, so dealing,
must not be afraid of the facts of pain and sorrow
Its image of life and its image of man must both
be frank and adequate. This vital adequacy and
truth of art is a ruling principle, and essential to
its higher functions; for art is not an end so much
as a means. It should serve the life of man, not
in the interest of any types or theories, whether
of culture or belief, but as promoting the fullest
expression and the freest development of man;
and this it may do only by using the poet's
imagination, passion, and delight, and all the
means and powers of art and song, to give the
world of man's life in its "higher reality."

CHAPTER XVII

POEMS ON ART : MUSIC

OF Browning's poems on art there remain those dealing with music. In the other arts we have found enjoyment and insight—the grasp of a mind dealing vitally with matters proper to it. The music-poems show even greater power. In these the poet has fuller value and originality as an interpreter. The poet's heartiness and breadth of sympathy with the arts has led to a question whether he might not have found expression for his genius in some other art. And in the dedication of " Men and Women " he hints at the possibility of such expression. If there be another art in which this might have been done most congenially, we should say it was music.

Browning has gathered much knowledge — some of it quaint and remote, and, as part of it, there must be much knowledge of music and musicians. The composers to whom he refers, the technical mastery implied in his criticism, and in the statement of his ideas in the poems on music, prove this ; while his power to interpret musical ideas, and to express the very soul of music, show how full is his sympathy with the art and its modern aims.

And this care for music means much more than "ear" and sensibility to sound. It speaks of the poet's large and subtle passion, and of his spiritual sense of things. It is, in truth, fit that the poet of "the soul" should prove his power and scope by his relation to that art by which so much of the modern mind, with its large ideas and desires, has been expressed.

We have *three poems of this class*, two dealing with special kinds of music and views of life suggested; the third with the general power of music to express the passion and life of the soul itself, and that world for which large suggestive expression is best.

The first and lightest of the three is on a "Toccata of Galuppi." It is spoken by some one listening to the music, who has a basis of conscience and purpose, and feels that life must be looked at in the light of these. And it puts a train of images and thoughts suggested by the music—a train of thoughts and images that give the meaning of the music itself by interpreting the emotions in which it took its rise and to which its appeal was made. You may, of course, object that this can only be dramatically true; that by reading music this way you get a purely subjective interpretation of it; and the poet meets the objection by making his poem from that point of view, though he would not say that such criticism has a merely personal value.

Baldassare Gallupi was a Venetian composer (1706–1785). Starting as an organist, he made himself famous as a writer of operas, producing fifty-four of these. He also wrote for the harpsichord, and church music too. He wrote easily, it seems, and his music is light and melodious. But Dr. Burney, who met him in Venice in 1770 (*cf*. Grove, *Dictionary of Music*), speaks of "the fire and imagination" of the composer; of "the novelty, delicacy, and spirit" of his music. His works were very popular, but, with all earlier operatic writers, were thrown into the shade by Rossini, and he has long been a name only known to the learned.

But the life and meaning of the poem depend simply on its force and truth as an image of one piece of his music. The speaker has been listening to a toccata of Galuppi—a light, simple kind of music, and as he listens the past returns. He sees the musician and Venice (though he never was there), and the men and women who used and loved this music, and, through the music they loved, the lives they lived and the quality of their hearts. And what he sees is not cheerful, now that death has cast its solemn shadow over the picture. Light was their music and gay their lives, bright women and careless men ; merriment their key, and pleasure their good. They wore the days out, and the nights too, and themselves also, in balls and masks, while our genial musician made fit music for them at the harpsichord. I was all bright and graceful, and they would pause at times as Galuppi's music fell on their ears, and

in a light way put questions the music lightly
touched. A plaintive passage would hint, " Must
we die ? "—for even such life is touched at times
by the sadness of the close. Yet, though it could
not avoid the question, it did not let the mind
dwell on it. It whispered hope, if only the
delusive sort which comes from putting cer-
tainties out of sight. "And are we happy?"
it would ask, and persuade them they were,
though men never are so when they put the
question that way, and it could not disguise the
fact that their hearts were unsatisfied. So they
listened, and then left him for their pleasures
until death put an end to it all. And as we
listen now to the cold, shallow music, death seems
the proper, not the casual, close of such lives.
Life with no more in it must end. Immortality
is fit where you have undying principle and purpose ; where no soul can be found, it were out of
place. But these, too, were men and women,
and to think of them as the music makes you
think is not only to feel the pathos of death, but
a chill of doubt cast on more serious lives, and on
the value of man.

" Master Hugues of Saxe-Gotha " is a study
and, from a certain point of view, criticism of the
fugue as a form of music. It gives the effect of
the fugue from the standpoint and through the
mood of the speaker, and the life it would be the
image of, and in the interest of life sets it aside
for a better music.

" Master Hugues " (given by fugue ?) is not in

the dictionaries, and has no " Life." He is an invention of the poet—the genius of the fugue. And what is the fugue? It is a form of music in which the parts seem to answer and pursue each other over and over, intricately, elaborately, until they may seem to lose themselves in the " hot debate," and all without " result." From one or two simple themes a great structure of sounds may be evolved and built, as Bach does in his great fugues. Such music has largely and in many instances technical meaning and value. It gives scope for ingenious construction and masterly execution. It is the mathematics and the mechanism of the art; it is the form more than the poetry or the passion of music.

The speaker here is an organist who has been playing certain great fugues. He has mastered them, and is satisfied so far. But now that it is all done, he would like to be clear as to the good of this sort of music. What relation has it to the reasonable ends of life? The question may seem beside the mark, and it does not occur to him that such music may be made simply for itself. In his present mood he thinks that even our master of the fugues must have had thoughts and passions, and that his music must have had meaning for him in relation to these. He has seen this old master in the loft while he played, come from the dead with his quaint face to listen to his own music, and he wishes to talk the matter over with him, as circumstances are most favourable for doing so.

And so the question is discussed from section xii. The structure and drift of the fugue are described. You begin with your phrase. There isn't much in that—a brief series of single notes. It is answered, though there seemed really nothing to answer. Thus two have started. Then another is added, and another, until five are going, the wrangle getting faster and faster, and not one of them with anything to say. A listener, who is not a musician, soon gets lost; the whole thing turns to a maze, with no order or result; and the musician even may tire of it.

But it may be this is its *design* and proper result? The master meant to land us on this very moral. This is his image of life; life is a fugue, a web simple yet subtle and intricately woven, but aimless and resultless, full of impotent striving towards nothing, and without real conclusion — not ended, but cut short by death. Over us, indeed, are nature and truth, but by vain habits and customs we keep ourselves quite from them. We even make a body of laws on purpose to bar our way to them; we take opinion and usage without wisdom and without reality, and put those for life. Nay, " the nothings grow something"; we get to believe in their reality, and so " close the earnest eye of heaven "—life's fact and the soul's truth—and in the end have " no glimpse of the far land at all." We take the fashions and the traditions for the secret and the substance. We are even wilfully blind. We argue down our souls, and whoever may see.

Our fathers were wise and *knew*—all we need; and so the folly goes on. To keep the " web " whole becomes the great point, and we neither live nor get any true hold of things.

It was his meaning, then, to have no meaning, because he saw that life and conduct have none. Ah ! most wise master, so you knew life well, and your music is worth playing, because by its combined difficulty and futility it gives a forcible sense of what men make of their lives. So far he interprets and seems to agree, but now you find he has been ironical; he has been bringing the matter to the point of absurdity. This is not the whole of life, though very much in men's lives is like that ; there is a better view, and he throws the fugue aside for a music that is closer to the right view and spirit. Clear off your fugues, and give us Palestrina with the full power of the organ, a music with natural passion and depth, and vital, not only technical, result. It is our fault that life is not better. Truth is near us, and we can touch nature if we will.

But his light dips and goes out, and the poet leaves him in lines that are the metrical echo of the noise he must have made rattling downstairs in the dark church. The humour of the piece is delightful, and the verse fits it. Its conception and estimate of the fugue are questioned. But the poet is not seriously concerned there. It may be taken as the utterance of a mood, or of this particular organist. It is in any case, we should say, rather a criticism of a certain quality of

art and view of life, than a serious criticism
of the great fugues as a musical form.

The last of the three poems, " Abt Vogler," is
the poet's fullest word on music. In verse and
thought it is one of his finest poems, and as an
interpretation of the scope and power of music
as it is now made and felt, it is, perhaps, quite
unique. Both verse and diction have a noble
fulness and fitness. The long roll of its Alex-
andrines seems to carry those tides of emotion
which the organ stirs and sustains. And the
imagery is expressive as the verse, and so is the
range of noble ideas. It is in truth a masterly
essay on the part of one always deeply moved by
great music to suggest the inexpressible reach
and power of the art. None of our poets, save
Milton and Shakespeare, have shown a similar
power of interpreting music through poetry.

The musician from whom the poem is named
is to a great extent a symbol of the art in its
modern scope. But a few facts of the abbé's
life, as told by M. Nisard, will make some points
clearer. (I take those facts from an analysis
made by Miss Marx.) Vogler was born at
Würzburg in 1749. He early showed his power
in music, and was sent by the Elector Palatine
to study under Martini at Bologna. He tired of
Martini in six weeks, and went on to Padua to
study under Valotti, on whose system of harmony
he based his own. He also studied theology,
and was ordained a priest at Rome in 1773, and
was well patronised by the Pope. Returning to

Mannheim in 1775, he opened a school of music
there, and published his " Theory of Music and
Composition." Later, he made a " Miserere,"
and wrote operas at Munich without success.
He went to Paris and produced an opera there,
which failed. Having travelled in the East, he
settled for a time in Sweden, and there invented
his " Orchestrion." His organ is described by
Grove (*Dictionary of Music*) as a very compact instrument with four key-boards of five
octaves each, and a pedal board of thirty-six
keys, with swell complete. With his organ he
gave concerts in London in 1790, which were a
success, and this seems to have been the turning-
point in the abbé's career. He went back to
Sweden, and was there until 1799, and after that
visited the chief cities of Germany. At Darm-
stadt he had Weber and Meyerbeer as pupils,
and was much valued by them. His mastery of
his art was original and thoughtful, and his devotion to it full of zeal. His organ and powers
of extemporisation made him famous, and these,
with his serious interest in his art, made him most
suitable for our poet's purpose.

The poem is a *monologue*, and so the abbé is
free to speak his ecstasy, and the moment is fit.
He has been extemporising on his organ—putting
all his passion into it—and he wishes the music,
with all its meaning, would last. He has built a
palace, magically as Solomon, for the princess he
loved, only in the legend the palace remained,
while his fairer palace of the sounds is fleeting as

the clouds and subtle as the air. Yet what power and beauty were in it! and how nobly built!—deep as the roots of things and high as heaven, and with a light upon it beyond the glory of Rome on a festal night.

He has said Rome and in sight; but that is not half the truth as to his city built of sounds and for the soul. It rests on the deepest and soars to the highest, and it does much more both ways. It brings heaven to earth. If his passion sought to scale the sky, heaven yearned down to crown his aspiration. Music not only makes the soul alive and aware, it gives life the height and hope and glow of heaven. The ideal of man's highest passion is brought near, made real for the time in the soul, so as to light up every point of man's effort.

Nor is that all. As it kindles the soul with its passion, music makes us aware of the universal. The free scope of life is felt, its depths and springs are opened. We are with the ages past and to come; free of our limits, we catch the meanings and see the unity of the system from its simplest to its highest parts. An intuition and sympathy vaster than thought seem to comprehend things, making their law clear, and the divine good in and for them all.

This music achieves, or say music and the soul acting as one. And what other art can do this for us? Painting cannot, for there means and method too are seen. In music only you have an art that is above art; you have creative power and beauty, and the mystery that belongs essentially to these—law, certainly, but the hidden Power that is behind all law. And the wonder is greater as we see how simple are the elements of music. By itself each tone of the scale is nothing, and you can do nothing with it except make it loud or soft. But the musician takes it, and what then? He finds the chord (the fundamental chord, which is the basis of harmony, a tone, its third and its fifth), unites the tone " with two in his thought," and of the three makes not a fourth sound, but a wonder before unguessed—" a star of the eternal sky," whose beauty and power we cannot explain.

So he built his golden palace on the impulse of the moment. But it is gone. Such music is in its nature momentary, and never to be brought back; other great combinations may be, not this, for all its life and glory. A better may be, but that does not take away the sadness of this loss. It seems part of himself gone. It belongs to his soul to cling to all that has been fair, to the whole self, to the eternity of all good. And the music seems to say that good things may pass away.

But can that be so? Can any good be so transitory as the music seems to have been? It cannot be; and he falls back on the soul and its faith in the divine eternity to correct his impression; and then music becomes a subtle and splendid suggestion of the way in which this may happen. His course of thought seems to be this—the transience of the music, which a minute

ago filled his whole soul, reminds him vividly of
that law of change and loss which plays so great
a part in life. Everything is for a moment only,
then seems to fade into a past that never comes
again. But surely the very joy of music, its sense
of beauty and wonder and resource in the universe,
proves that this " law of loss " is an illusion. The
permanence of good must be the true law, for that
is the orderly result of the divine eternity. The
eternal God is the Maker, the universe is His
palace. Being what He is, His work must stand.
Fear of change is thus out of place in a world
which He has made and *makes*. If he expand
the soul, it is to fill it. Our ideals are the instinct
of His designs. All good endures in ever fuller
good. It is evil that passes—is nought, or is on
its way to reach and be good. It is a mistake to
go by what is now seen; earth is part of which
heaven gives the whole.

And so music, the amplest and most spiritual
expression of the heart, becomes symbolic, prophetic. Its longing and dreaming are not a hint
only, but a promise of what is to be. All
aspiration is prayer to the Eternal, our souls
seeking the good meant to be ours. And all the
effort and passion of human life that had good
for their aim are " music sent up to God," which,
by the law of things, reaches its goal.

It is the musician, then, who has a true hold of
life's order. He best feels its hidden law. The
very principles of his art, the way in which all
tones and pauses make his work, and in which

even discords can be used to reach the full harmony, give him an intuition of God's method and its "far-off divine event." Thinkers reach a timid and partial solution of the problem; musicians hold the secret and know.

But these hours, when insight seems to grasp the heart of things, pass. Their vivid glory "fades into the light of common day." "Silence resumes her reign" as the great extemporisation closes. This, too, is part of experience. We cannot *fill* life with the harmony or the passion of music and keep it so. Things are as they are. It is earth now, though heaven may be to come. There is defect and there is evil, and for the present we cannot but think of evil as evil. He will, however, hold by music's great assurance of complex harmony as the result of the whole. He will be patient and proud therefore, and return faithfully, hopefully, to the levels of life and duty. To descend from the heights to which music has carried him, and get well back to those levels of the every-day life, is for most a hard task—to the master it is an occasion for mastery. And so, by a series of bold movements, he seeks his way back, and finds his resting-place at length on "the C major of this life," on sober acquiescence tempered by enthusiasm and insight.

This is how Browning read the meaning of music through the soul of the Abbé Vogler, in one of his hours of inspiration. Is the poem "true" only in that way? or does it, in a measure, say what the poet himself felt about an art that had for him too rich power and meaning? We must think that the poem says in its own terms very much what great music often said to the poet. It depicts that world of high emotion into which music carries the soul. It suggests that sphere of the ideal and the universal which music has the power to suggest. Whether its suggestions be as hopeful and definite as those of the abbé must depend on the mind set in motion by the music; but music commands a sphere of emotion such as this, and interprets the soul by its power over it. All that is meant by this world of sublime and subtle emotion neither thought nor music can tell us, and the soul itself, in all the fulness of its life, must be our final interpreter.

CHAPTER XVIII

DRAMATIC ROMANCES AND BALLADS

AMONG the poems Browning made between 1845 and 1855 was a group called "dramatic romances," and these, with certain others of the same kind, were set together in vol. v. of the final edition of the poet's works as issued by himself in 1888–89. When the group is examined to ascertain what is meant by a "dramatic romance" it becomes clear that it is a poem in which the matter and incidents are for the most part imagined, "invented," and in which such fact as there may be is construed with a view to certain ends of the imagination; and they are called "dramatic" because they are devised from the standpoint and through the *persona* of one of the "actors." The "Grammarian's Funeral" is a "romance," and so are "The Boy and the Angel" and "The Statue and the Bust." But some of the poems set finally among the romances were at first described as "dramatic lyrics," *e.g.* "Waring," and "Porphyria's Lover." What is the difference? It seems to be that the "lyric" is imagined more strictly in the sphere of emotion, of the mind itself, while the "romance" is imagined in the sphere of event,

action, or it may be of *vision*, as in the case of
" Childe Roland," and we presume in that of
" Porphyria's Lover." In both " romance " and
" lyric " one would say the poet is at work to
present a dramatic statement of his theme and
his thought, only in the case of the " romances "
it takes the form of story or of vision, and
becomes, as in " Childe Roland," a kind of
dramatic picture, as we may call it, of his thought.

Yet why, it may still be asked, should the
poem, " How they Brought the Good News from
Ghent to Aix," be classed as a " lyric," while
" Porphyria's Lover " is put with the " romances " ?
Neither ever happened, and surely the latter has
quite as lyrical and a more visionary quality than
the former.

The fact is that the lines of distinction cannot
be very sharply drawn, and the poet's own
classification may in one or two instances be
fairly questioned. Some of these poems were
suggested by fact, others rest on fact taken as
typical, not actual, and both of these groups are
shaped in the medium of facts and events, while
others of the class are purely imaginary, and are
wrought in a medium of images and emotions.

The first groups include—(1) Certain poems that
are a kind of " ballads," dramatically presented,
g. " Incident of the French Camp," " How they
Brought the Good News from Ghent to Aix " ;
while akin are the riding song called " Boot and
Saddle " (one of the " Cavalier Tunes "), and that
other riding song, " Through the Metidja to

Abd-el-Kadr," though Browning has only made one great ballad in the stricter sense, " Hervé Riel"; (2) such poems as " The Patriot: an Old Story," and " Instans Tyrannus," " Count Gismond," and (3) " The Glove"; (4) a group which we may call the romances proper, " The Flight of the Duchess" and " Childe Roland," which are pure inventions, though not of the same quality, the latter being intensely visionary, the former, though strongly coloured in the great parts by the " passionate invention" of the poet, being more in the nature of a romance of event and character.

First, then, are those we have called a kind of ballads, and the great ballad of " Hervé Riel." These poems show well certain of the poet's qualities, his fine sympathy with heroic deeds, and an energy of conception and movement unsurpassed in English verse. The " Incident of the French Camp" lays hold of an event that happened in the Napoleonic wars to give it a more vivid life. The boy of the poem, a French soldier, in fact, planted the French flag over the market place of Ratisbon, was fatally wounded but bore news of the capture of the town to the emperor. Seeing him hold himself erect with difficulty, Napoleon said, " You're wounded." " Killed, sire," said the boy proudly, and fell in the glory of the soldier's last honour.

The " Ride from Ghent to Aix" is surely a dramatic romance. It is a fancy piece and never happened. The poet had been at sea for some time, and filled the poem, which was made by the side of the ship, off the African coast, with his longing for a good gallop on a favourite horse. And the verse gallops well until the speaker's horse, last of three that set out, drops exhausted in Aix, the rider saying that the glory of bringing news of the pacification of Ghent (the supposed news) belongs to the noble horse, not to him.

"Through the Metidja," also anapæstic, every line chiming with "ride," is a clever feat of verse, and a capital riding song. Abd-el-Kadr was an Arab chief who led his people in a sacred struggle for their country when the French invaded Algiers, and kept it up for some years.

"Boot and Saddle," built again on a single rhyme, and chiming with "away," is supposed sung by a cavalier as he gallops off to relieve his castle, defended in his absence by his "wife, Gertrude."

"Hervé Riel" is, we have said, a true ballad, and it is a noble lyric, one of our noblest heroic ballads, with strong grasp of the situation and the hero, in lines that honour both. It is the story of the simple Breton sailor who saved the French fleet, pursued by the English after the battle of La Hogue, by the skill and coolness with which he led the ships through the narrows of the Rance "at slackest ebb of tide," to where, "'neath rampired Solidor," past Grève, they might ride safely, and then, when offered reward for such service to France, asked only for a whole holiday to go to Croisic and see his wife, whom he proudly calls "the Belle Aurore." As France has no way honoured him, Browning will. It was a tale got at Croisic on a holiday visit in 1867, and written there. It was published in the *Cornhill Magazine* in March 1871, during the Franco-German war and the distresses of France ; and the sum got for the poem was sent by the poet to the Paris Relief Fund, a fine touch of sympathy with a country in which his later writings had shown much interest.

" The Patriot" and " Instans Tyrannus," taken before in another relation, show in different degrees the poet's imaginative treatment of fact in these romances. The facts are chosen, and the poems are fashioned, to be the " image" of their " morals "—to shape them, as we say, in terms of life ; the first to show what " patriots " may often expect and get, and to hint the law behind ; the second to show how the strange passions and evil wills of men, though they may too long have their way, are in the last resort checked by a moral power that is the " last nature" of men, and of things as well.

" Count Gismond " is a tale of chivalry, imagined to present the same emotion at a time when the supreme appeal was to ordeal of battle. The story is thrilled with memory of a past event, and yet quieted by a sense of years of happy peace intervening. It is told by the lady who was the heroine of the event. She was an orphan, hated by two cousins for her beauty. A certain Gauthier, set by them to do it, alleges her dishonour and unfitness to preside over a tournament. It was a lie that could only be refuted in one way. That way was opened by Count Gismond. He took up the lady's cause and smote her accuser, compelling him before his death to take back his lie, and then claiming her as his wife in still further vindication. The lady's entire confidence in her cause and her champion are finely expressed, and the whole story lives with the life of its time and of the human heart.

"The Glove" is an old story retold in the poet's own way, and we may say with his moral. Leigh Hunt had told the old story in smooth verses. Browning devises a fresh story in verses that express by their double rhymes the humour in which he regards the story and the Court of Francis I. The lady threw her glove among the lions to test her lover, and lost him and the approval of the Court. Browning held the loss in both cases good and the lady right. She was tired of this trivial and make-believe chivalry. She desired a true knight for a lover, and for the rest fact that should answer to words. She has not succumbed to the quality of her time and the Court. That is gay, pleasure-seeking, trivial. Her face has purpose in it and a care for reality. For them life is brief and sweet, and not to be risked at all. She is weary of the self-love and emptiness and shows of the life they are living, and, provoked by her lover's fine words, she sets him a task to strike the note of real daring through the shows. He does it, urged by fear of laughter, but resents it, and insults the lady by flinging her glove in her face. He did not look to be taken at his word. She had thought as much, and knew now the hollowness of their tournaments and their phrases.

And the sequel fits this reading of the story. De Lorge, her lover that was, famous through his double deed, easily won the finest beauty of the Court, who loved him as such will in such places. The lady of the glove had a better fate. A young knight, who saw her quality and loved her, took her from the Court and married her. His "calm fervour" matches her firm sincerity.

Pierre Ronsard it is who tells the story, and fitly, since he is more interested in human nature and more genial than Clement Marot. Ronsard's part is told with humour, in double rhymes except in the lady's speech to him, and the learning is that of the Pléiade, while the opening speech of Francis with its frivolous weariness is a touch of local colour. It was the age of "The Field of the Cloth of Gold."

Two "romances," that follow "The Glove" in the poet's last issue, give in other ways the quality of the class. "Time's Revenges" imagines a situation, clues to the tragic humour of which are given in the title, and in the closing couplet. "There may be heaven; there must be hell; there is our earth here." The speaker has a friend devoted to him, would do any service for him, he values his work so much, while he, on his part, just barely likes his friend. And he is madly devoted to a lady who does not even like him, but would see him suffer anything if only that "would compass her desire" to get an invitation to "the famous ball to-morrow night." And he

tense spring of the verse gives the passion and the self-mastery of the lover in the poem.

But two of the romances have a visionary and spiritual, or, as some think, allegorical quality of their own, and may be called *the* Romances. We refer, of course, to the "Flight of the Duchess" and "Childe Roland to the Dark Tower Came."

The first of these in point of time is "The Flight of the Duchess." It is also nearer the others in manner. To some it seems a flight of fantasy. It is, like others of the romances, an invention of the poet. Its first suggestion, we are told (*Academy*, 5th May 1883), was a line in an old song Browning heard sung when a boy, "Following the Queen of the Gipsies, O." And that, it seems, started the first part, as we may call it (sections i.–ix.) of the poem, published in *Hood's Magazine*, April 1845. Then a phrase heard at a friend's house in the country afterwards, when some one, to show how early and sharp the winter was likely to be, told how "the deer had already to break the ice in the pond," appears to have started the poet's mind afresh on the track of invention, and he wrote the remaining sections of the poem. The "story" is simple. The speaker is a huntsman, whose family has long been in the service of the duke, and much valued. This man tells the story so far as he understood it, and, like all stories of years past that have made a deep impression on the simple but intense imagination of such people, it has grown to a romantic legend. The style is meant to suggest the speech and tone of the peasant, and verse and phrase are such as to give his mode. You may, indeed, demur to so rude a transcript, and most of all to the rhymes; but if you accept the dramatic intention, you must allow some freedom to the humour of the speaker.

And the character of the huntsman is one of the "successes" of the poem. His bluff, hearty, vivid nature; his simple yet deep and generous heart; his shrewd sense and brusque realism, with what you find in these natures, a strong vein of poetry and ardour, and a truly chivalrous temper, make him the very man to tell the story here told.

The story is told thirty years after the event. Its period is that of decadent feudalism, in a country where old fashions linger long. The poem opens with a picture of the country. It is a great, wide, wild land, bounded by mountains with solemn pine woods on their slopes, opening on a wider and wilder land bounded by the sea. The old duke was a strong baron, fit to rule such a land and enjoy its life. The young duke is of another kind and for another sphere. The sturdy baron died, and left his young son to his wife's care. She was a sickly, sour, masterful woman, from another country, and of obscure origin. The son is like her, and, to make him more fully to her mind, she takes him to her own country to be educated. So the old hall was dull and empty for years, and when they came back the results of descent and training were too plain. The young duke was pert, full of his

travels, full of himself, scornful towards his own
rough northern land, and full of Parisian notions.

And one of these ideas was a fantastic and
shallow regard for his own country and its past.
It was rough, but stood nearer picturesque
"heroic" times, and was full of crude poetry. So
he set himself to "restore" the past; to set up
again its dead forms, and make an idle show of
them. Having nothing solid to do, and no life
in himself, he plays at living the life his fathers
really lived. Such a spirit is a double falsehood.
The past has no meaning to it, and the present
no use. There is no reality; all is shadow and
make-believe. The honest huntsman knows this;
sees the thing so hollow that it gets its value
even for the duke from the impression it makes
on others. And the very horse he rides, "all
legs and length," is a type of the sham it is.

But soulless as is the duke, he must marry.
So he brought a lady to his castle to be duchess,
not wife, as part of his ceremonial, for no moral
object. She was from a convent; a very little
lady, but quick, fervid, and full of life and enjoyment, so much so she "might have been made in
a piece of nature's madness"—a woman, frank,
vivid, and natural, with interest in everything,
longing to live, with heart in every tone, meaning in every look, fascinating and friendly to all.
What a contrast! The stiff, self-conscious, dead-
alive formalist, all affectation and pride, beside
this woman! And worse still the mother! Her
very first tone and glance chilled the girlish

heart and took the light from her face. The
duke did not know her, did not affect to love
her. Such things were not in his plan. Yet it
had been better if in this case they had been.
The very retainers see the situation. The lady
got over her first shock, and meant to make the
best of so stupid a life. She would live the life
there was, and take her part in it. But that was
not the duke's idea. She was for show, not use,
and, being "his," must take his way, "sit, stand,
see, and be seen," just when required, and "die
away the life between." And when she tried to
give her help, she was treated as a child whose
opinions matter so little that they are simply
ignored.

She now saw where she was, and lost hope.
Chilled and frustrated, she grew sad and ill. The
duke saw this, and thought it done to spite him.
Any illness springing from the soul he could not
conceive. But he will bring her to reason, and
arranges a great hunting-party, in which she is to
take her part. The part gave much trouble to
find, and when it had been found she would not
fulfil it. The duke and the mother did their
worst to bring her to terms, but the lady kept
her purpose.

The hunting went without her help. The duke,
angry with her, left the castle by sunrise. Just
outside he came on a troop of gipsies. It was a
land, set between the civilised and ruder peoples
and cultures, where gipsies seemed native, and
showed their full powers. In the troop was one

who might be the very oldest gipsy above ground,
skilled in all their lore, well known in and knowing the country well. She begged the duke she
might go and pay her duty to the duchess; and
he, thinking to show the duchess what life and
sorrow might bring a woman to, and so teach
her submission, let the crone go, sending our
huntsman with her.

The gipsy had heard the lady's story from the
duke, and she had skill in the "cure of souls," if
he had not. So she went with zeal. She no
sooner left the duke than her mien and face
changed. She grew taller, brighter, younger.
Her eyes grew "live and aware"; her soul and
aim shone through her. And in the presence of
the duchess she became the very genius of a
great message and a great deliverance. Life's
pure fire seemed to flow with magnetic power
from her speech and spirit. Words, we are told,
failed to convey what was done and given, but
the substance is this. Crushed under the dead
weight of the life about her, and weary of its
vanity, the lady had revealed to her, with mystic
passion and promise, the vision of a true, keen,
full life—a life of free activity, of heroic deeds
and generous passions and sustaining love. Her
soul had longed for this. She found new life in
the mere vision, sprang to meet it, threw off the
vain life about her, and left it for ever.

Only part of the message that had this great
result is given, music being the medium for the
rest. These are the ideas that got into words. She

finds her race, proves her power and her right to
share in its tasks, is taken to its heart, and made
one with it in love, honour, and duty. She sees
that love, the love of those who live for great
common ends, is the only good in the world.
She sees that it is power as well—power so
great that if any two hearts and wilis were to
become really one, and alive with some true purpose, they would do more than has yet been
done in the world. And in this new life she is
offered just and warm regards, praise and blame,
never indifference. And when age comes, rich
in memories, and the past is reviewed, and all its
goods gathered at the last, another life will dawn
beyond the dark, and the soul pass to the scope
of that. Then the words cease.

This is the heart of the romance. And you
ask, did it ever happen? or was the soul its
sphere, and moral passion its medium? What
matters? This was and is the " way of life," the
only way of escape from a life that has gone to
formality, worship of custom, selfish sentiment-
alism, pride, and show of sense, and that has no
love, service, or sacrifice in it.

The story does not go much farther. The
lady left the castle, beautiful and glad now, and
the huntsman, as if enchanted, helped her to go,
and in going, with the frank humanity that had
won him from the first, she left him a plait of her
hair. He has heard nothing of her since, and yet
her memory has been the romance of his life,
more so than his love and marriage; and in his

last years, his wife and children being dead, he
is going to seek her.

The combination in the poem of the mystical
and the grotesque makes it a trial to some
readers, but is very characteristic of its author.
He opens the way for the homely by choosing
his *persona*, and the strain of mediæval fancy is
in the story. Browning's usual resource for the
homely and the comic, his clever use of rhymes,
double and even treble, is turned to much account;
and other resources of his genius and his talent
are freely employed, as if the particular romantic
form used here gave scope for it. It is a constant
stroke of humour to tell such a story through the
mind of such a "person," and the point of view
thus got, and the effects thus secured, were part
of the plan. It gives the "older" type, and
shows how the fashions and qualities of the new
type and régime looked to such men.

But now, is this poem an *allegory*? or a
romance without moral design? a study, say, of
certain types of character in romantic forms of
them, and in circumstances fitted for them? I
should not call it an allegory—that is not Browning's mode; and yet, if we say that dramatic
statement of spiritual truth has been a mode of
his art, the difference is not great. The characters are types, we must admit, and the poem
becomes quite mystical, and even the peasant
hears a wondrous music. He stands for common
sense, the duke for false culture, and the duchess
for the higher spirit and passion—so some have

read it. It seems to us that this goes beyond the design of the poet, and the matter of the poem. We have above indicated certain dramatic and moral points of the poem, and need only add that it contrasts the free yet earnest life, a life at once natural and spiritual, with a formal, external life, a life of pompous and selfish routine and isolation. The lady, by nature and race, is formed to hate the one and seek the other; the duke to do the contrary. All experience and the rich promise of life are to the first, death in life to the other. And it may be that the poet had an eye to certain " revivals " and " mediævalisms " that were making a vain effort to become a " way of life " to Englishmen about the date of this poem (1845), in setting his moral thus.

"Childe Roland" was first published in 1855, and has, I believe, been a puzzle to most readers since. A study of madness, says an injured reader, with some tendency to produce it.

Shall we, then, regard the poem as a pure fantasy, and nothing more? If we do, how shall we take it, and what value could it have? Much still, we should say, as the expression of a series of emotions, or the invention of a series of images that depict these, and so suggest certain experiences of the soul. But how is this? It is hard, we judge, for most of us to understand how a poet may express himself in images and metres simply, stating his emotions and perceptions in concrete imagery. The poet has spoken of " Childe Roland " as a pure romance made in that sense, and we shall take it first in that way.

But how did the poem arise in the poet's fancy? and what were its primary suggestions? First, there is the line from Edgar's song in "Lear"—a line that seems to have haunted the poet's mind, insisting on interpretation: "Childe Rowland to the dark tower came." That line is from an old ballad, and takes us back dimly to heroic times—to heroic legends and within the charmed circle of Arthurian story. It is possible that the line in "Lear" is from the ballad of "Childe Rowland and Burd Ellen." And that was a tale of the feats of Rowland, son of Arthur, in bringing back his sister, "the fair Burd Ellen," from the castle of the King of Elfland, where she was helplessly enchanted. It was a long and weary journey to Elfland, and worse than the journey were the risks of the soft twilight land and the hall of the king. But the undaunted Rowland went, and brought back his sister and his two brothers, who had tried and failed, and this he did with help of the good sword Excalibur and Merlin's wisdom. Such at least is one form of the old romance, of which there are only fragments, though a similar ballad is found in several northern languages.

Then one would think that the tragic scenery and situation of "Lear" in that great part of the drama also wrought on the poet's imagination. Edgar sings that song in the awful silence on the heath and before the hovel. King Lear is

his Childe Rowland, and the tower, both blind
and dark, was the madness to which Lear was
coming. Other points in the picture, and things
entering into its composition, are mentioned by
Dr. Furnivall—the gaunt figure of a red horse
on a piece of tapestry in Mr. Browning's house,
which kept staring at him, and a picture seen at
Paris. As to the tower, two statements are made
—Corfe Castle, and a tower among certain mountains in Italy. None of these items may seem
of much importance, but they give a clue to the
nature of the poem through its elements and
composition. And as you read the poem you
will see how these images, with the emotions
they touched, have formed a striking picture.

The hero of the adventure is the speaker, so he
has survived "the dark tower." As a knight, he
had gone round the world to carry out the task
laid on him. Many had tried and failed, and
that seems likely to be his fate. He has even
got to a point at which failure would be a relief.
It is the dull twilight of a dreary day. He comes
on a hoary cripple, with a look of malice, who
points out a path. He has no confidence that
the path is right, but takes it, caring only that
somehow his quest should end. He is in such
weariness that he seems cut off even from those
who have failed, and left to seek vainly alone
And the whole scene looks the shadow of his
despair. The very sun "leers" at him as it sets
But so much he knows—the "tower" is some
where in the tract. So he took the plain, and

as soon as he had done so the path behind
seemed gone, and he was bound to his fate; he
must go on if only because there was nothing
else to do. And on he went, through a scene
starved, base, and dead, hardly a blade and not
a creature, save "one stiff blind horse, with every
bone astare." This horse seemed so wretched he
could not help hating it; it must be wicked to be
in such misery. It was all so bad he shut his
eyes to seek comfort out of memory and the past,
but there was no comfort that way. All those
once with him who have failed come back to him,
and to avoid the past he takes the path again. It
grew darker, drearier, and all seemed so dead that
he longed for anything—an owl or a bat, even,
if only it had life or motion. He came on something in motion—a restless, spiteful little river,
that seemed a curse to everything near it, and
whose presence only gave new horror to the
scenery. It was a relief to get away from it.
Surely something better must come. But no; a
worse tract, full of horrid, shadowy struggle, like
"wild-cats in a red-hot iron cage," base, cruel,
vain. And the very ground was evil; not only
waste, but hideous. This to bear, and the end
far off as ever, and neither desire nor aim left!
But there came another crisis. A great black
bird went past, and as he looked up, thinking
even that might be a guide in so strange a land,
he saw mountains shut him in on every side. It
all seemed a horrid dream; and now both escape
and progress seemed cut off, and he was giving

all up, when he heard a sound as of a trap closing,
and knew the time and place to which all the
years had led. And there in the midst was the
tower—

> The round squat turret, blind as the fool's heart,
> Built of brown stone, without a counterpart
> In the whole world.

It came on him *unawares*, after years of training
and quest. As he saw it the dying sun shone
out, and the hills lay on watch for his fate, and
all who had failed seemed there to see him fail.
The woe of years was pressed into a moment.
But the passion of years turned to instant purpose. To win or lose, he threw himself on his
task, and blew his knightly challenge.

Such is the poem. Have its images and incidents any meaning or result? Is it a dream
without coherence or aim? Is it a symbol of a
whole class of experiences? or of some definite
conflict of the soul—some chapter of a " Pilgrim's
Progress," or adventure of a " Faerie Knight"?

It will be readily believed that the " riddle " of
Childe Rowland and his tower have been variously
read by those who have seen a riddle in it. The
" riddles " of the poets, when they set them, have
many sides, and give scope for guessing. So some
see in the poem a parable of the search for truth
found only after infinite, weary, disheartening toil
and as if by chance at length. Others find in the
romance an image of death, and all the vain fear
that gather and darken in that waste land of sunset. And others read it of any troubled crisis i

life, or of life itself, with its many fears and illusions, which are chiefly shadows and moods of
the soul itself.

Mrs. Orr holds that the poet had no "meaning"—did not work with ethical purpose at all,
but in the medium and with the elements of pure
fantasy. And yet she speaks of the poet as
aware of, and as touching the ideal aspect of, his
marvellous picture. There can, we think, be no
doubt that the poem is the most purely romantic
and fantastic of all Browning's works, that that is
its predominant aspect. He could not have been
the strong romanticist he was without sensibility
and power of this kind, and the "suggestions" we
have referred to had curiously stimulated fantasy
in this instance. But being the poet he was in
other respects, he could scarcely avoid touching
his knight's intense adventure with ideal suggestion, and certain phrases of the poem appear to
bear this out, while even dreams have relation to
life, and express mind, not brain only. The poet
had no design, and the poem is a vivid romance;
but his romance is some image of experience all
the same. And so at the risk of adding another
fancy to those this haunting and singularly expressive and Dantesque poem has provoked, let
us indicate the "ideal aspect" it suggests to us.

It seems to me a romance of the soul in one of
its hardest tasks—the task of keeping true to
itself against itself; the task of keeping on when
the fire of life burns low, and experience looks not
so much painful as hideous and futile. It is a

romance of that high courage which hardly knows itself as courage or purpose, but which fights down the depressions and terrors that crowd round one when years of zeal and effort seem to have gone for nothing; when duty looks so dull and uncertain that disaster, or any change to break up the vanity of things, seems desirable. To conceive high aims and enter the knightly course is not so hard; but to carry these through the years against weariness and temptation requires that high virtue—tenacity and fidelity of the very soul. Childe Roland has no foes to fight; that may be past. His critical fight is, we said, in the soul, and against the whole appearance of things. And life often seems a conspiracy, not so much for defeating high purpose as for dragging it down, making it seem foolish and out of place; and the worst of all our doubts at times is the doubt whether our best aims be not absurd. Childe Roland had not failed. He had kept on till it hardly seemed worth while to succeed, and in the dreary dusk everything took shape and colour from his own apathetic moods, and the whole of heroism had sunk down to going on because there was nothing better to do. This, we said, may be the last trial of some, and it asks more of virtue than tasks that seem far more heroic.

And if any say, "that or some similar series of ideas and emotions," we do not object. A great passage of music says one thing to one mind and other things to other minds; and there is nothing wrong with interpreter or music when it is so.

Poetry, cannot, of course, have the suggestive power and freedom of music. Yet as all true poetry has a power of suggestion reaching past its mere words, so there may be poems made of the elements and in the sphere where the art is most concrete and simply suggestive. In this class is " Childe Roland," with some of the romantic work of Coleridge, in spite of its marked difference of tone and texture.

And this reference might very well raise, could we here follow it up, two questions—(1) As to the principle of this class of imaginative literature, of which there are so few instances; (2) why Browning working so strikingly here did only " Childe Roland." We can only suggest as to the first, that such work appears to be a kind of dream work, with a sharpness and energy dreams seldom reach. And Browning has shown something of the intense visionary power in not a few places of his work, though only here, and with differences in " The Flight of the Duchess " and " Porphyria," giving scope to it.

CHAPTER XIX

THE LOVE POEMS

BEFORE anything gets into song it must have risen to a good degree of interest and charm in life. Literature is the record of these interests as they reach power in the lives of men. And one point made clear by the historic method of literary study is, that ideas and sentiments that seem primitive and simple are really complex and of late growth.

Love poetry is an instance of this. Love, it may seem, is a theme old as song, and old as the heart of man. But the fact is not so. War and adventure, the brave deeds and braver sufferings of men, valour and danger, man's power and heroism, and the pathos of man's fate,—these are the old themes and springs of song.

But though not primitive, love, it may be thought, must, as passion and song, be ancient. Again the fact is not so. Love as we conceive it is modern—had its rise in the Middle Ages. The union of Christian and Teutonic ideas with feudal institutions and the temper of chivalry led to its rise and fixed its quality. The Christian idea of woman's worth, with the Teutonic idea of her place and honour in the home, gave her a new dignity and a higher position. The rise of the feudal castle and knightly service, and the place of the lady in the castle—her relations and duties towards the youth there for knightly training— gave her new and special influence. The leisure of the Middle Age, with its romantic dreaming, and the mystical fervours of the time which wrought the ideals of the Church on that of knighthood, gave a higher quality to feeling. And the worship of "the Mother of God," with its honour of woman and its standard of womanhood, told greatly in the same direction.

Through such causes chivalry developed a new emotion, fixed it in human life, and gave it power among the motives of men. It may be, as Vernon Lee holds, that mediæval love was in many cases ignoble; but, as she allows, whatever its precise origin, the sentiment grew to a strange depth and fervour, created a high code of honour, led to romantic devotion, and produced the first liter-ature of love for love's sake.

The "Vita Nuova" of Dante is the expression of the mediæval sentiment at its best, the first great expression of love as ideal passion—a passion of the soul, pure, austere, and grand. Petrarch, in a lower key, and one nearer the hearts of men, made the sentiment the possession of culture and the fashion of verse. To English verse the im-pulse came from Petrarch, and first in the work of Wyatt and Surrey, but better in that of Sidney and Spenser, found utterance. In Spenser "all

31

the loveliness of love and beauty " are realised in
verse fit for them. Romantic love is the theme
of Shakespeare's poetry, and the leading interest
of some of his plays, while the beauty and honour
of his women have *embodied* the visionary glory
of Spenser. The songs of the dramatists touch
the theme with beauty, and the seventeenth-
century lyrists keep the song with less passion
but more art. It dies out after the Restoration
and during the eighteenth century; but with the
revival of deeper passion and ideas at that century's
close, and with the romantic movement of the early
nineteenth century, the true love-song is found
again. Shelley and Coleridge touched its finest
notes, and Rossetti, with inspiration and intensity
of Dante, has given a fervour and ideality to the
poetry of love at once Elizabethan and Italian.

But why go so far to get to Browning's love
poetry? Because Browning's work of this class
grasps strongly, and interprets with poignant
passion, the love-motives of the modern mind from
Dante to Shelley. It may seem indeed unlikely
that Browning should handle this of all themes
well; but if he be a genuine singer of love, it will
be allowed that the fact must throw light on his
general power as a poet. And if there be special
quality and power in this part of his work, elements
of original passion and insight, it will not only give
interest to this part of his poetry, but bear on our
estimate of the poet in other ways.

And here, as we glance at the kinds and motives
of love-poetry to ascertain the quality and scope

of Browning's, we shall find the use of the survey
above made. The poetry of love may spring
from and express delight in several aspects and
qualities of its subject. Physical beauty and
charm is an obvious theme; beauty and interest
of character, grace and charm of manner and
mind is another theme, implying higher interests
and feelings. The attraction and sentiment of
womanhood enters into both—gives sweetness
and force to both. And there is a still higher
level and strain—the attraction of mind for mind,
of soul for soul, of the man in his ideal desires for
the woman in her ideal qualities and promise.
In other words, love-poetry may be a poetry of
pleasure, of beauty, or of social sentiment, and it
may be a poetry of spiritual passion. It may be
made for the grace and wit of it; it may deal with
love in its place among the stimulating incidents
and joys of life; or it may be taken in its relation
to the deeper life of men and women, and as a
study of the heart's essential power and bias.

Now, some will think that love does not get to
that depth, and that in such a view we recur, not
merely to the passion, but to the dogma of Dante,
and yet it may be that the ideal and scope are the
heart's own. Browning certainly reads it so. The
mysticism of Dante, the ideality of Shelley, the
passion and depth of Rossetti, are *truer* to him
than any prosaic views or feeling. His characteristic love-poetry is not only poignant,—it is inward,
ideal. Its passion carries the life with it, and goes
forth to grasp the life of what is loved; it seeks

what is intimate and vital in heart and mind.
Such love comes from and concerns the whole life;
it tells not only what has been won, but what is
desired; tells not of aspiration only, but of scope
—that bent and power of the soul which fixes the
orbit of each life. Every soul is on an eternal
way. The way it is on and the ends it is capable
of are best seen in its higher and deeper passions.
True passion is deeper, fuller than thought. Love
is greater than knowledge; and all we have really
loved of beauty and of good we shall yet be. Our
ideals that carry the life and power of our best
passions in them are promises. Life's powers are
not only best seen in, they are best quickened
by, the higher love. The soul is best developed
through its most powerful and vital emotions, and
in the play of such emotions through spiritual
love it is not only on the way to, but is even now
realising, its full and proper life.

From this point of view, and on these principles,
the first section of Browning's love poems may be
read; and first of them, "Rudel to the Lady of
Tripoli." It is a story of that Rudel, the troubadour, who from the shores of southern France
yearned towards the far-off dream of the lady of
Tripoli. He had not seen her; she is a figure
of fancy only, but with power over him passing
reality and sense. He finds a pilgrim going East,
and to him he tells his love, that he may tell it
everywhere in the East, that it may come to his
lady's ears. He has taken as his device a sun-
flower, because, as the flower follows ever and

cares only for the sun, so he turns ever eastward to catch one look of love's sun across the far sad waters. And his songs and fame are as little to him compared with love as the things about the flower are to the flower, which cares the day through only for the sun. Here is the passion of love for love's sake alone—the soul's passion towards an ideal of its own creation—an ideal made and maintained of its own forces and needs —its need to love nobly and wholly.

"Cristina" is a higher statement of the same passion. Published in 1842, it was then named "Queen Worship." The queen was Cristina of Spain, and the hero of the story loved her without hope, yet so passionately that he went mad over it. Where is the interest, and what is the meaning, the poet seems to suggest, of such love, into which without earthly hope the soul puts its life? The poem is a dramatic answer to that question.

The youth is one of sensitive and ardent soul, essentially sincere and faithful. He meets the queen; she meets his glance as if she knew and cared for him. Love springs up instant, complete, final; and such love is right. Life is dark enough, and men blunder much, but there are gleams of heavenly light which disperse the illusions and disclose the realities. Such passion is one of these, lighting up the past of the soul and its future, and making life's meaning plain. The lady, it may be, felt this, but put it aside, let the world and its vanities rush in, and ignoring the soul through contempt of love she missed life here.

But the man found and held life's substance and secret in his love. The use of life he saw was to grasp clearly love's ideal, and carry it beyond earth into that sphere of better scope and surer results, where ideals may be realised. That this will happen he has no doubt, for such passion has in it the power and promise of an " endless life," and love assures its goal. Such love is its own reward; it abides all earthly loss, and the life beyond is but the realisation of the life within.

"Evelyn Hope" is a more striking expression of the same ideal; one of the most tender and beautiful of love-poems, blending in one moment of passion the pathos of death and the victory of a deathless love. The form is dramatic-lyric. The lover is by the dead girl. She has not loved him —she did not even know him, and it was not her time to love—but in her he saw the lady of his finest passion and hope. And by her dead form, though earth has given him nothing but this knowledge, he is satisfied that he must some time find what his soul worships and needs, else life stands on illusions, not on truth, and the soul itself is the worst of its vanities. A large argument over a matter of love! How are we to take it? As the language of passion resenting death and this life's woeful incompleteness? or as a pre-vision of the soul in a moment of intensest life? The latter is the assurance of passion, of course, and the past sympathises with it. This lover has searched life, has tried the ages and the gains of men, and has passed through a quest of fifty years

unsatisfied——without finding the ideal and harmon-
ising principle he sought. In "Evelyn Hope,"
"made of spirit, fire, and dew," that principle was
present, that ideal of nature's special grace was
vitally expressed, and as "God creates the love
to reward the love"——makes soul to complete
soul——he leaves in her hand a token of the union
that must come though there should be worlds to
traverse and lives to wait for it. But this, it will
be said, is no poetry of love, only of mystical
passion for an ideal, suggested, it may be, by its
object, but not given in it. Yet again, is not the
ideality the heart's own, and is not that largely the
quality of modern love from the "Vita Nuova" to
"Faust," from Shakespeare to Rossetti?

"Love in a Life" and "Life in a Love" are
variations under their own images of the same
theme. In the first the lover seeks through all
the "rooms," through all the ways and experiences
of life, for the loved one, and does not find, but
keeps on seeking, in the faith that love is ever to
find, and cannot be baffled. In the second, the
lover finds the loved one bent on escaping, but
that only adds zest to the pursuit and meaning
to life itself, whose law is search, not rest. "Two
in the Campagna" as a love-poem has the same
idea. Love is ever to seek because it is ideal,
and the heart is restless because passion is infinite,
while satisfaction is and must be finite.

And so this poetry is romantic and passionate,
rendering not merely the force but the mystery of
passion. "Poetry," said Börne, "gives us what

nature denies," and yet what it gives is also a
part of nature, and our hearts respond because it
interprets them, as well by its scope as by its
intensity. That must still be our point of view
as we read such poems as " A Woman's Last
Word," "A Lovers' Quarrel," and "Numpholeptos."
The first expresses, at the close of a disagreement
that words cannot heal, the heart's longing to
keep love whole even at the cost of surrender and
illusion. Over something, or over nothing most
likely, there has been strife, and the woman gives
way, though she keeps her thoughts. Differences
are nothing beside love's ideal and the heart's
agreement. She clings to the Eden of entire
trust, and will throw even truth over to keep it.
A moment of weariness, or fear of disillusion, you
think ; but a paradise into which doubt has come
is paradise no more ? Can it be regained ?
Some answer to that question will be found in
" A Lovers' Quarrel." The difference in this case
has been greater and has gone much further. It
is the man who speaks, and he is alone. There
had been days of love that made the bleak winter
bright, but parting came of a mere idle word, and
now the spring days are a pain and a discord.
But the heart's one wish is re-union, and he were
well satisfied that winter and storm should make
life bare as a crypt, if only it forced his love back
to the only place that can never change or grow
unkind. She will come back, he is sure, if not till
the night is late and the storm at its worst, and he
will take her home, and love will be whole for ever.

And our poet is not afraid of romantic notes when the fidelity and absoluteness of love is the theme. In " Misconceptions " the mere fact that one who is loved had leant on her lover's heart, using it as the bird may use the spray on its way to the treetop, is taken as enough for honour and joy. In " The Lost Mistress " we find the same note of surrender and loyalty. One who has loved is resigning love for friendship; yet is so frankly true to love's heart, so purely kind to love's dream, that he begs warmest friendship for love's sake. To such hearts, devoted to love and not to self, love is all, and simple love enough. So in the fine lyric " Natural Magic," love is the magician working all the wonders, with ample power to clothe the bare walls of life with the beauty of June, and fill its blankest hours with music and all its spaces with flowers,—its powers in this way a mystery and yet a fact! This poetry of love in life is seen from another point of view in " Magical Nature," which is an instance of our poet's point and power in this sort of brief lyric. The loved one is conceived as a flower for delicate beauty, as a jewel for changeful un-changing loveliness—the magic thus in her nature. " In Three Days " is thrilled with longing and hope, with quick desire that makes the time feel long, and ardent hope that makes it seem short until the lovers meet—only " three days and one short night " hence. In quite another key, wistful minor the strain of it, and set to a measure that expresses the strain, is " In a Year." It is full of

the strange sadness of love's disappointment and
decay as it touches the woman's heart still loving,
and wondering why it has happened, and whether,
when "the cold clay clod" that "was a man's
heart" has turned to dust, the true life will then
begin—"what comes next? Is it God?"

Dealing with disappointment of another kind,
and raising certain ethical points in the relations
of love, while putting its magic and ideality very
strikingly, is the poem "Numpholeptos" (nymph-
caught, entranced). It is a kind of dream started
by the myths of nymphs too etherial and perfect
for mortal life, yet fascinating the hearts of mortal
men. The lover sees the loved one in that form.
She is above him, out of his sphere even, and yet
the vision attracts, impels him to seek, and gives
him hope. He may win her, but only when he
reaches the white light of a full yet stainless
manhood. He woos her again and again, but is
sent back to life for some fault or defect, with a
calm, pitying, yet unyielding smile. He is at the
point to resent the severity of the ideal, but its
beauty and power command him, and the quest is
renewed. Is that love's part, then, to reward the
victor only? or is it also to cheer and help the
struggle? Both certainly. Yet love is often the
sternest of idealists, exacting the best, and that
for love's sake. And the lover yields and clings
and hopes for ever.

Other notes of ideal or tragic passion we have
in other poems in all periods of the poet's work,
showing both his knowledge of the heart and his

firm and subtle mastery of the lyrical measures
fitted to the various themes and phases of love he
has dealt with. "In a Gondola" has been referred to in other relations, but must be named
here for the pure intensity of its conception of
love and its ardent satisfaction with love as the
lover's only reward—the note of "Romeo and
Juliet." So with "The Last Ride." There, we
have seen, the lover is aware of questions and facts
beyond his hour of present joy, but in his pure
abandonment to this hour of love he shuts them
out, and realises only that this is heaven. And
if this be near tragic passion, Browning has finely
given the depth of such passion in poems like
"St. Martin's Summer" and "Too Late." "St.
Martin's Summer" gives the glow of a dead love
kindled later in life and not known at first for
what it is, but recognised at the point described
in the poem. A man loves a woman, and he and
she think the love is for her, but he comes to see
that the charm is woven by the ghost of an old
love. She has revived that and no more. To
build a "mansion" for love, then, were to build
it by love's grave, and find it haunted by a ghost.
He describes the situation in vivid phrase, with
tragic emotion, and begs her to leave and avoid
him, that the ghost may be laid and the past left
where the years have buried it. It is one of the
finest and strongest of these love-lyrics, dramatically and poetically keen and strong as Elizabethan work. "Too Late" is a tragedy of another
sort. It is the forlorn lament of one who feels

that he has lost the best thing life had for him.
He loved a woman, but did not seek her. She
married another and never knew his love. But
now she is dead, and for this life, at least, the
matter ends utterly. But this end is a new
beginning, for death sets her free and binds his
heart again purely to the dead. The husband
may tag her epitaph in his cold way, but in the
grave she is her lover's, and in the after life she
will be. So he turns his back on the world, with
remorse for the past, with resolve to pay all the
heart's debt and make his days one sacred ritual
of love and memory.

These are romantic notes, it was said, but the
poet has other notes too in this part of his poetry
—notes humorous and masculine, though always
frankly passionate. " Love among the Ruins " is
mainly a picture of a wide, quiet, landscape, en-
closing the remains of an old capital. And there,
amid the ruins of the once busy city, two lovers
are to meet in the evening. One of them waits
and meditates. The noisy city is gone like a
dream, its very ruins almost gone, but love abides,
and renews itself for ever in human hearts, and
love's quiet hour is worth, it may be, all the
centuries of noise and glory. " Meeting at
night" and " Parting at Morning" are also
pictures with love for motive—the glad meeting at the day's close — and the parting with
morning when the need for action and for a
world of men returns.

" One Way of Love" and " Another Way of

Love" are complementary, and humorous. In the first the lover has been stripping June of all its roses to express his love. In the second, too, the lover has done a good deal that way, but has got tired of it, and in reaction from it feels some scorn of himself for his folly, and some malice towards the lady whose charms have befooled him. So he asks, half-sighing, a smile in a yawn, "If I tire of your June will she greatly care?" The poem is the lady's reply. She knows how men tire of love, and find the June with its wealth of roses a bore. Let them change then, only let them know that as June has her light-nings that vary the weather and her perfection, so gentle ladies have means to change the monotony.

"Women and Roses" is a lyric of much beauty, in a mood our energetic poet hardly ever allows himself. It deals dreamily with the theme of unreturned love, and in verse and imagery of fine fitness expresses the loveliness of beauty apart from the ordinary sentiment of love. He dreams of a rose-tree with three roses, about each of which gathers mystically the beautiful women of the past, the present, and the future. But the dreamer is out of the magic circles. They will have nothing to say to him. They will not "for once girdle" him, and yet the beauty of the rose-tree is his too.

"The Flower's Name" is akin, we may say, to "Natural Magic," its note that of love, which gives beauty and value to all associated with it, to the garden where it has been, to the flowers it has touched, and even to a soft meandering Spanish flower-name it has used.

"My Star" gives the intimacy of true love, and the insight that comes of it. A certain star darts red and blue——to the lover, to no others. Others see Saturn, not "my star."

In "Song" the lover challenges all to admiration and praise; knowing men's way of praising, and their need to admire, he offers them this theme.

"Earth's Immortalities" is in another key, and of a quality this poet seldom writes,——sentimental it may seem, though there are *facts* of this order. Fame is immortal, and yet your poet's grave is neglected and his name is being covered with grey lichens. And love's "for ever" has been known to last less than a single season.

"Confessions" is in its way another humorous love-poem——quaint and vivid. The speaker is dying, and the parson by his bed asks him whether he has not found life a vale of tears. He says bluntly "No," while his mind runs back to his love-days long ago, and he lives it over once more, so keenly that the things about his bed, his very physic bottles, become parts of a picture of the place where he met his lover in "the old June weather," by "the rose-wreathed gate." Glad for what has been, and free of cant he would gladly have his life again, and most of all for love's sake.

There remain two classes of the love-poems,
those of a personal nature, and the poems of
wedded-love. Of the first class there are only
two, for this poet keeps his life, though not his
personality, well behind his work. In "One
Word More" the poet gives his "Men and
Women," the first-fruits of their years of married
life, to his wife. And for his design the theme
is fit and expressive. Dante, wishing to show
in a special way his love of Beatrice, so the story
runs, made not poetry his usual work, but a
painting. And Raphael, with the same motive,
made poetry, not painting. Such special work
has unique value and beauty—the work by which
a man is famous is for all—this is for *one*. So
the poet here does other than his usual work, to
mark his love. Poetry, he says, is all he can do
in this life, though in other lives he hopes for
other tasks in other arts, and "*all* the gifts" in
all the lives for his wife. But he can make
another than his usual kind of verse, and he
makes this lyric, that he may speak in his own
voice, and from his heart, to her only. "Prospice"
looks forward to the last fight set for men. The
poet would meet that fight with clear eye and
soul, would face all the pain and the darkness,
"the press of the storm and the fear of the foe."
And this he would do to fare as the heroes of his
race, and to taste the *whole* of life; but, above all,
because he knows that beyond the fight comes
the meeting that will pay for all the pain—for in
the storm will come peace, and then still light,

and then the union of soul with soul in love's
eternal life.

> First a peace out of pain,
> Then a light, then thy breast,
> O thou soul of my soul! I shall clasp thee again,
> And with God be the rest.

From such poems it is fit to pass to the others
named above; for it is one of the distinctions of
Browning's poetry that it has sung the " prosaic
and hazardous " theme of wedded-love.   In fact,
two of his most subtle and original love-poems
are in this class.   This is not a new thing in
literature.   There are poems on the theme, while
Thackeray brought it within his art.   But the
theme has been rare, and few have given it such
depth and beauty.   Both choice and treatment
of this theme stand in relation without doubt to
the poet's life,—and, indeed, the words of one of
the poems in question make that clear.   Those
words, twice said in " By the Fireside " (and
other words there too)—" the great brow with
the spirit's small hand propping it"—surely speak
of its inspiration, and make it right to say what
is here said.

" By the Fireside " is a little hard to read.
Its hardness comes from its point of view and
construction, and from the way in which story
and description are worked in with and delay
the main theme.   The speaker looks forward to
the autumn evenings, and to the November of
life, and thinks what he will do then.   He will
sit by the fireside with some great book, Greek

and prose, not reading, but thinking on the
past, on his early days of love, and all the
days that came after. He sees, as he thinks
of it, the little chapel among the Alps, where
his heart first spoke out its love and found
the life that has been so good. Then in stanza
xxi., as he recalls the place and the years
since, and sees his wife by the fire, he dwells
on all they have become to each other. And so
he asks her too to go back to that place and
time, that they may live it again, and, in the
light and consciousness of the years that have
grown out of it, realise its meaning. That, as he
now sees, was his spiritual birth-hour, the crisis
of his life. By the choice and event of that time
he found his soul's faculty and meaning; he took
his right place in life's order with motive and
power to fill it.

So the poem depicts the quality and influence
of masculine love, enriched by years of growth,
and matured by the experiences of life. Love
began then. All that went before, and that
poets have mostly sung, was a prelude only.
The rich and happy years that have come of
that hour and choice make the years of youth
look barren and poor. The union then begun
has grown until the two souls are as one soul—
the streams of their lives a single stream, and he
cannot now imagine any life for them apart.
What will happen when " earth breaks up and
heaven expands " he does not know; but he
knows that his wife must share and help in

whatever life may be—" see, and make him see,
new depths of the Divine."

He did not know, we have said, the meaning
of what took place that evening among the Alps
by the Alpine chapel, nor did the motives of the
time forecast the results of it. Both love and
life have deepened, and he gathers its meaning
now with a sense of glad surprise. As he does
so, that moment, " one yet infinite," seems to
blend with the evening and the scene, giving
and getting depth and colour. The intense twilight, followed by the tender evening, the one
star, the sense of the two souls near each other
and far from all besides, the lights and shadows
of sky and woods, the stir and trouble of hope
and fear, the crisis of speech, the gentle-hearted
acceptance, and the moment after when the night
fell, and they knew their hearts one—all these he
now sees belong to the supreme hour when his
soul made the choice that has been its life—a life
that age and death fulfil, and in which the best is
yet to be.

" Any Wife to Any Husband " is another
theme of married life—the pathos of the change
death may make in a man's love. The wife
knows his love true, and yet she foresees that
when left alone he will seek other faces, other
hearts. For this there are excuses, good as the
world goes, but which do not leave love's heart
whole and pure. She feels that in like circumstances, though in most ways weaker than her
husband, she could have been faithful. It seems

strange, and feels bitter as she thinks of it, and most pitiable, in that it seems a wrong done his own soul. Yet she forgives him, because their past life and her own love tell her that he is and must remain hers, and will return to the place she keeps for him in her heart for ever. Only, why should he come stained by unfaithfulness or weakness? Pride might keep him true, and the faith of the life beyond. But he will fail, and she accepts what she foresees, in the certain hope of that final union which love claims and assures. Thus does love ignore death, and seek a home "where the eternal are."

"Earth's Immortalities," above referred to, may give us here part of the *sentiment* of this poetry of love. These are apt, indeed, to be illusive; Love changes or forgets, Fame turns to the fading memory of a name, Death conquers and bears all away in the end. Yet love asks and affirms deathless constancy, and condemns the vanity of life apart from such elements of spiritual permanence. Again the note of infinite passion and the pain of hearts that feel and resent the bonds of finite life!

"James Lee's Wife," a series of dramatic lyrics, is another "study" of married life. In this case the love—the constancy, at least—is on the wife's side again, and by her love she feels driven to leave her husband to his own devices, and the light such a crisis may bring. He loved her once, or he liked her, but he did not know or really esteem her. The ignorance was in degree mutual. Differences were accentuated and increased by marriage and daily life, and they could not come to a compromise. The woman is the more restless and ardent of the two, more capable and active. She has sensibilities and ideas, longings and ideals; poetry and art are her way, and she wishes life to have the quality of the one and the beauty of the other. James Lee, we infer, is prosaic, solid, and it may be stolid. His wife has "fancies." They don't hurt him, if they amuse her; but if she insists on his sharing them, that will be another matter. When she took him she knew the state, if not the stuff or the limits, of his nature, but she had *hopes*, and it may be the hopes were part of her reasons for taking him. Love would improve him. But he has no wish to be improved her way, and what with her designs on him, and her demands from him, and her moral discontent, he feels bored. To love, and mutually admire and stimulate, as she fancies, would only be to hug the chains of a life of bondage; so he thinks. He won't have it. She is disappointed, and lets it be seen that she is, which, of course, makes him still less disposed for culture or conciliation. And they are living too much alone—living in a quiet, simple way in a little house on the French coast, idyllic and picturesque, no doubt, but just the situation to find out the weak places in their union, and throw up the discords of their characters. Then she is a plain woman, and her husband is by her account manly and handsome; and he is not unkind, only rather cold, reserved, self-sufficient. Altogether their relations are strained; the situation is unsafe. It breaks down, and the wife, in despair of any other solution of a problem she has chiefly raised, leaves the French coast and James Lee.

The situation and story, so far as we can get at matters, are presented only by the wife. We have never a word from James Lee. We could have done with his version of the tragedy, but he was not likely to have given it, nor would it as given by him have been poetic. His story would have been brief—his wife's "folly and conceit" the main part of it. Yet at first the series was called "James Lee," and some think it ought to be so. The later title is fairer to James Lee, and true to the dramatic point of view, and as nearly all there was to tell took place in the mind and heart of the wife, it takes its title fitly from her.

The course and factors of the drama need care, as you have these only through the wife's thoughts and feelings. The first poem is spoken "At the Window." The husband is coming home after a short absence, and the wife longs to greet him. It is the turn of the season, and shadows of "the fall" are seen and felt. The sense of change in nature hints a fear of change in the things of her life—in the old and dear things of love. But, no; such change can't fall there. True, James Lee is only a man, but she is his wife, and that bond should hold them true.

So for the time her fear is set aside; but the fear and the hint, only "a man," and the self-consciousness, are ominous.

They are next "By the Fireside," and the fire of driftwood gathered on that bitter coast of France speaks of the deadly risks of the sea, and the fatal chances of life. It is night, and the sailor, seeing their lighted window, will think how warm and bright all is within, not knowing how ships and hearts may rust and rot in the harbour, and that is worse than all the sea's perils. Note the boding heart, the spirit of revolt, the sharper sense of facts; with James Lee beside her she feels the change and "the hell opening under her."

In the third poem she is looking from "The Doorway." The autumn darkens, and with it her mood. The swallows are about to go, the sea is stormy, and threatens change and disaster, and she hears the wail of the wind. The trees suffer, and her heart with them. But she argues for content, and rouses herself with the thought that the soul, made with divine range and power, should be above outward things, and able to give them what they lack—to give, not to get. So she will love and bear. But her place and tone are lonelier, and love is not made whole by arguments.

So in the next poem the accent of difference is more emphatic. She is "On the Beach," and talking matters over to her husband, who may be with her, though her speech has the effect of a soliloquy, and seems to come as the hopeless end of other talk. She reasons, but it is to show him why he is wrong. He asked her love; she gave it—gave it rather for what she hoped from than found in him. She knew him " mere earth, with much waste and many a weed "; she hoped for richer soil and better things. She has waited with her love and her care, and the better things are still to seek. And still she waits, set on her task and wedded to her hope, with praise for him and blame, and most of all, love. But he is offended by her candour and by her expectations, and the pity of it is that his annoyance is as natural as her discontent. Her tone and her ideas first bore, then vex him.

But she does not give up hope yet, and when we find her " On the Cliff," she is trying hope again. The turf is dry and dead, the rock low and bare—" death's altar by the lone shore." A grasshopper springs on the turf, and a butterfly settles on the rock. The life and beauty of these change the face of both. Cannot love, settling on the " low and bare " natures of men, change them so ? She has, you see, much candour and a little hope. But the separation grows. James Lee is not on the cliff, if he was on the beach.

Hope is gone, and change certain, as she reads " Under the Cliff," a poem made to interpret that tone of " the wind with its wants and its infinite wail," which had struck her before. The poem does not, she feels, interpret that note of the autumn wind which touches the heart so strangely as the mystic echo of all sorrows that have ever been. (The poem is Browning's own, made in 1836, though put as quoted. It is not quite in tune with the series, but raises well the question of this part.) The poem is youthful, she thinks, and does not get to the depth of its theme. The young cannot know that. They play with failure and sorrow as sentiments only. It takes years of both to mature the heart, and give it touch of the larger reality—of the pathos of man and the world. What, then, means that mystic wail of the wind? It is nature's lament over her own changes, over all that has been and never can be again. All things pass away—that is life's wrong and the world's woe. It may bring us the perfect; it takes from us what is good and dear. Yet, if it be the law, let us fall in with it, and move with it to that fuller good to which it urges us. But is that really the drift of all the changes that make life? We cannot be sure of that. God alone knows. Our part is to endure God's act, and move onward. Only, made as we are, there is pain in the process. Loss and change may be part of a law of divine fulfilments; for us they are sorrows. And so, with a sense of coming change in her own life, the wife of James Lee feels it. She sees the law, but not yet its good.

Does she in the next part? "Among the Rocks" she speaks of a "doctrine simple, ancient, true," but what is it? It is now a bright autumn morning, and nature in this season of change basks with broad smile in the sun. Why so? Is it that the law, being universal, must be good? or is it that acceptance is any way our duty? Put it thus: Change is the law, and love is subject to it; but change is God's way to something better than we at first choose. If we love what is not worthy, or what is not enough, we need to find this out, and our pain should rouse us to raise the lower nature in others, and rise above it in ourselves.

By "the Drawing-Board" she learns a further lesson, hints of which came to her among the rocks. Her last thoughts there seem to be that it may be good to forego happiness here, and that the higher aims find their satisfaction only after much waiting and denial. Now her question is as to duty, and this is how she finds her answer: she recalls a saying (original here, we guess), " As like as one hand to another." How absurd, she thinks, as she compares a cast by Da Vinci with the hand of a peasant who sits for her as a model —how perfect the first, how coarse the other! But then, thinking how Da Vinci made the cast, she sees that to reach such beauty all the artist's mastery of the lines and secrets of the body were required. Life, then, is the basis of the right art, the way to the true beauty; and long study and love are needed for it, and the surrender of one's own fancies. But life is bigger than art, and harder too, and in life use is more and more lasting than beauty. Let her learn patience, regard for reality, other aims than such as are self-pleasing, and, since love is denied her, let duty take its place. No changes can affect that, or narrow its scope.

Being found next "On Deck," she may seem, in leaving James Lee, to be neglecting the lessons she has learned. She is, in fact, carrying them out, as she sees it. Having resigned love and its hopes, she seeks a larger world of duty and service. The heart of James Lee is closed for the time. He has made her feel all she cannot be to him. Yet her love for him is strong as ever. She bears away in her heart and brain his every tone and look. And her hope is that his love for her may now revive until she be in his eyes what he is in hers. Love can make both equally fair and dear, and if to unite them love should make him "fade to a thing like her," she would not know or care, since all care would be lost in the joy of a true union.

But with such a love the separation may look impossible. Yet it is not so. James Lee had taken, it is clear, a hard and bitter tone. His soul was "locked fast." He had made his wife feel her defects, her very love a bondage, her best things an offence. She must, then, to save his soul and her own, set him free. It is better so, for love and for duty. Some think hard things of her for acting thus, holding that it can never be right. The poet has, of course, nothing to do with that question. He is right if the lady would have done what he makes her do. The situation had become intolerable to her, and she cut

the knot, not meanly.   What other way had she?
Tame submission that might have ended worse?

There is, we believe, sympathy with James Lee
at other points.   His wife is, it seems, too serious
and moral, and the handsome and sensible husband
was right to resent a view of married life which
made it a spiritual education.   But Browning has
written love-poems that insist even more strongly
on that idea.   In " Dîs Aliter Visum," or " Le
Byron de nos Jours," he " argues " that love is no
matter of pleasure or convenience, but a power
and opportunity for the higher uses of life, and
for the fulfilment of what is best in each.   The
first title is ironical ; the second suggests the true
quality of the choice made.   It is the woman
who speaks, and she is speaking to the man who
was the other actor in the drama, and in circumstances that give an edge to her irony and point
to her moral.   They have met in a Parisian draw-
ing-room.   They had met ten years before, when
the woman was young, her career to make, her
character to fashion.   They were drawn to each
other.   Love sprang upon the woman's side (for
that is the point of view of the poem surely), and
a little on the man's.   But he was elderly, worldly,
prudent, and he drew back.   And what has come
of it now ; as she sees it?   She has married, but
never loved ; he has neither loved nor married,
and though famous as a poet is meanly entangled with a woman he does not esteem,
and so she says bluntly, what rhythm and
phrase, and the irony and candour of her whole

utterance enforce, that through his cynical mistake
"four souls" have found life worse and less than
they ought to have found it. Their whole idea
of life has been false, and all their work poor.
To make worldly success primary is to deny the
soul and miss the scope of life. The love and
conflict, the high aims, the failures that let us
through into "eternity," are best for us. "Sweet
in sad and sad in sweet" is our proper food—a
life that keeps us from low content, and braces us
to divine passion and effort.

"Bifurcation" presents again, in another way,
the situation of "By the Fireside," of "Dîs Aliter
Visum," and of "Numpholeptos" too—the situation
and the problem of opportunity thus arising.
But in this case it is the woman who postpones
love for what she takes to be duties. The man,
with warmer soul, in harder circumstances, fails.

Who is to blame? Love could have given the
help needed, and ought to have given it. Through
such help love's ideal is reached, and life's too.
The harder, richer way of love is the right way in
such cases, and this "moral" in different ways
each of the poems above referred to seems to
point.

"The Worst of It" is a tragedy of married love,
and such a problem of passion in one of the crises
of the heart as this poet likes, tracking the heart's
way when both thought and feeling are alert
and intense. It is the man who speaks, and his
wife has fallen and deceived him, and the worst
of it is that he feels he owes all his good to her,

and she part of her evil to him. He prays her to return to purer ways for her own sake. He would shield and excuse her wholly, and take the blame—and the pain too, if he could. He feels how harsh the law of society is on women. He makes nothing of the wrong done him. He only feels pity and a strange new tenderness, such that should they meet in paradise he would pass her without claim, and without reproach, grateful only for all her love in the past had given and done for him. It is indeed strong and keen, with noble, gentle passion, and the verse is high-strung as the sentiment is.

One other tragedy of love and marriage Browning has given among his later dramatic lyrics. It is that named "A Forgiveness"; and in grasp of passion, as in keen, strong present-ment of tragic situation, it is one of the finest of the lyrics of this class. The swift and compact statement of the poem, its fine dramatic combination and expression, with its intensity of suppressed emotion, make it indeed remarkable even among these lyrics. The moment chosen is one singularly fitted to present the inner and outer climax of the tragedy. The husband is telling the story of his love and his misery to the man who wronged him—he is at the confessional, and the man behind the grate is the other man concerned in the "action," which is the theme of the poem. The story is of tragic misconceptions, entangled by jealousy, embittered by scorn, darkened by hate, brought to a crisis by revenge, followed by forgiveness, and then, when misconceptions are cleared, and all is seen as it was, in retrospect, by tragic love, with desire to punish the man who had partly been the instrument of the wrong. The husband, who really loved his wife, was devoted to public business, in part from the interest of an able man in affairs, largely to prove his love for his wife, and to reward her love through his success and honours. She thought he cared more for " affairs," for " power and place," than for her, and was unhappy. Full of his own scheme and motives, and self-centred rather, as such men are, he did not notice her feeling. She sought to provoke and rouse him to love by showing that another sought her love. He, returning home sooner than usual one day, and entering by the " postern gate," found that other in his grounds. He could not at first guess the meaning of the matter. But as the man skulked off, his wife stepped forth to take the whole blame of his being there on herself. So the husband hardened to contempt, thinking he knew the whole event and its meaning, and her device of a heart desiring love was vain. For three years they lived a public life that was an empty form, and a private life that was a virtual separation, and chill as death. Shut within his iron scorn, he did not see what was going on in his wife— how she was dying by the situation she had created, and he perverted and embittered. But one night, after they had been honoured by a visit from the king, and their public life seemed at its height, she asked him for a word in " the room that was his." They withdrew thither, bitter and sad, and she told him now the truth. She had loved him, and sought his love, even in what she had done, but now she wished to die, his cold hardness having shown a side of him she had not known. Her confession turns his scorn to hate, and kindles a desire for revenge. He insists on her writing her statement in a form he dictates. She is willing, and will do it in her own blood. He gives a dainty poignard from the land of spices and poisons to do it with. She does it, sick at heart. He knows she will die, and his hate now turns to forgiveness as he sees the issue. She dies in the night, and then his eyes opened, he sees all, and love is reborn with remorse. And afterwards, with complex passion and revenge, remorse and love, he comes to the very church in which " she sleeps, as erst beloved," and to the father who hears confessions there to stab him through the grate for his part in the tragedy of his life. The story, we said, is finely and strongly told, and he who tells it has its quality of strength, and the faults of pride, self-will, and one-sided masculinity which made the tragedy of his wife's fate and his own possible.

It is thus clear that Browning gives love ample energy and value. He put his own keenness, force, and tenderness of passion into it. He holds by the duty of a frank and full development through the proper play of life's most powerful and vital emotions. He seizes the interest of love for the dramatic poet—its interest in itself and in the light it throws on man. And he is frank and positive in his dealings with love, as with life. Browning's love poetry has, of course, the quality and scope of his work as a whole—it is intellectual, subtle, rarely in the simple sense lyrical; but with qualities of genius so marked as his, and with a " criticism of life " so valuable in all its phases, even those of his readers who may prefer other types of this poetry ought to see the fine value of the above poems.

CHAPTER XX

BROWNING'S HUMOUR

WE come now to consider Browning's humour, and the work in which it is more especially exemplified. Humour, it has been said, is the test of a man, and of his power to see the world justly, and no work dealing with human life can have large application or be really great without it. Our greatest poets are our finest humorists, and in such a world as this, humour is, for very obvious reasons, a part of wisdom. No dramatic poet can be without it, and all " criticism of life " from which it is absent must be partial, if not futile.

Browning has this power, and no study of his art, no survey of his work, can omit his humour. The recognition of it has been present, we trust, in most parts of our study so far; for our poet's dramatic expression and his thoughts are constantly modified by it, and neither his art nor his ethics can be rightly judged apart from it. This pervasive humour has, in fact, drawn not a few readers to Browning : some, it may be, read him for that alone. They like his matter-of-fact temper, his strong sense, his fine bluntness of manner, his curious types of men ; and they feel behind his work a shrewd reality and manliness of mind. Such readers are often impatient with other things and qualities of his work. Yet it is just his combination of principles that gives his humour its special quality, as his humour gives special interest and value to other sides and parts of his work—his power to depict man and life, and his larger views of both.

It is very hard to define humour—it is subtle, penetrating, a temper, a point of view, a balance or reserve of judgment. It is hard to define it even in single cases of it. The latter is all we try here. And to the inquiry, What are the notes of Browning's humour ? most readers would reply, a bias for the grotesque ; those who have got deeper would say a realistic mode and style of art, and a casuistic subtlety and many - sided quality of mind ; and a few that his humour is best seen in his dramatic breadth and power, and in the fact that all he has to say of man and life is said from a dramatic point of view, in that subtlest and largest medium of humour which comes from the necessary differences and partial agreements of men, owing to the fact that the bias and standpoint of each are his own ; and a few, carrying the analysis to even more subtle points, might add that Browning's sharp sense of facts and steady regard for them, united with his spiritual passion and thoughtfulness, give a rare element and interest to his humour.

And this humour, arising from strong and varied qualities, and pervading his work, shows there in

many ways. It is felt in his wide, free, and curious
interest in men. It is seen in the mixed and
curious characters he chooses to depict, and presents with such zest and enjoyment. It shows in
his quick eye for the incongruities and contradictions of life, " the masses of absurd detail and
comic fact that lie about in history and the world."
His rhymes and metres, his words and images, his
rhythm, pitch, and style, all reflect it. With the
exception of Butler, he is our greatest master of
comic tone and grotesque suggestion by these
means. His copious mastery and easy abundance of comic rhymes, of double and even treble
rhymes, his command of comic diction, and over
the sounds and associations that express his kind
of satire, his skill in expressing the comic or the
grotesque by his very rhythm and pitch, and
indicating dramatic estimate simply by that means,
—these are no small part of his resources as a comic
poet, and these, little as they may seem to agree
with other gifts and parts of his genius, are a
distinctive and almost unique part of that genius.
And his power to depict fierce and strong passions,
grotesque situations and types of character, is a
further and eminent proof of his humour.

Browning's power of grotesque is, in truth,
great. His taste for and use of it are part of
the man, with caprice in it at times ; but mainly
it conveys the image and emotion of life as the
poet sees it — its follies, defects, surprises, its
amusing ugliness. As to the rights of the grotesque to a place in art, little need be said, though

Browning's work raises the question certainly, and
to some his use of the grotesque seems part of his
disregard of beauty.   It is rarely absent even from
his serious work.   You are never " safe " from it
—by one or other of the means named it breaks
upon you, apparently without ethical pertinence or
æsthetic function.   And yet on examination, apart
from quite occasional *tours de force*, it will be
found that his use of the grotesque is significant.

And Browning has a broad and subtle humour
of characterisation, the power to present character
with its lights and shades, its limits and defects,
its generous errors and conceits, its powers of self-
delusion, and set all in the broader field of virtue
and reason.   This breadth, vigour, and freedom in
the appreciation and interpretation of character
appears early and runs through his work.   It
shows in the appreciation of " Agricola," and the
handling of " Waring."   It is felt strongly in the
study of " Lippi."   The humour of " Master
Hugues " is good part of its pleasure.   The large
and subtle appreciation of " Blougram," and the
rough yet genial treatment of " Sludge," show the
same quality.   It is felt strongly in the broad and
vigorous development of "The Ring and the Book."
Even in poems like " A Grammarian's Funeral "
the humour of the poet qualifies both the estimate
of character and the criticism of life.   And in
" Fifine at the Fair " the humour of the mind at
work is as clear as its energy and its subtlety.
The criticism of " Hohenstiel-Schwangau " has the
same quality, and so has "Aristophanes' Apology."

Browning's intellect and emotions never, in fact, work apart from this spirit of humour. There is a strong background of humour in " Christmas Eve." It runs right through the " Flight of the Duchess," romantic as that is, and it is in the vivid expressive realism of " Childe Roland."

The purely humorous poems are not a numerous group, but what a group they are ! from the " Pied Piper " and the " Spanish Cloister " and " Holy Cross Day " to " Pacchiarotto " or " Ned Bratts " ! What end of poetry is served by such pieces as these ? They are vigorously told, and give pleasure by their energy and by the light they flash on certain facts of life. The significance of all moral facts is part of this poet's creed, and if such poems " purge the mind by pity or pain," the poet is right. And the art that presents life, and the modes of man's emotion and intelligence in relation to it, must find place for strong rough humour.

But the bearings of the poems of this group on these and other matters will be seen by a glance at the poems themselves. Almost the first of them was " The Pied Piper of Hamelin." It was done in mere sport for the son of Macready, the actor, and thrown in to fill up Part iii. of the " Bells and Pomegranates." But the special humour and picturesque quality of the poem, its " unromantic romance," its naïve realism and simplicity have made it a pleasure to " children of all ages."

In the same group of early dramatic lyrics was the " Soliloquy of the Spanish Cloister." It is one of the poems of fierce and sarcastic passion that

our poet had a gift for, and whose " storm-sweep "
he liked. It is the speech of a monk, who has
to live daily beside one so wholly unlike himself
and all he values or cares for, that he hates him
heartily, and pours grotesque abuse on the very
thought of him. At a distance he might have
felt amused tolerance or impatient scorn for
" Brother Lawrence," but as they are he breaks
out in aversion and disgust at all the man does
and is. He is a burly lover of " the world and
the flesh," while Lawrence is a simple monk; and
in the mood here expressed he would like to
catch his so innocent brother in Belial's or the
devil's grip, to punish him for being an irritating
simpleton. So great the differences of men ! and
nature to answer for both ? Such the wrong of
a system that forces men like these into such
close contact, with so little to do !

Two other poems of the same quality and
similar power were done a little later, " The
Laboratory " (1844), and " The Confessional "
(1845). The first is an utterance of passionate
intensity in a situation that gives passion scope. It
depicts the ruthless jealousy of one who is taking a
cruel pleasure in watching behind a mask every
detail of the preparation of a deadly poison for one
who is her rival in love, who has " snared " her
lover. She is impatient till it be ready, and will
give all she has for it. Every line and phrase is
keen with bitter fire, and tense with eager hate.

" The Confessional " has a fuller if less intense
emotion. It pours forth the sorrow and scorn and

loathing of a girl, who has been deceived by the Church into betraying her lover to his death, for the inhuman policy and lies of that Church. She is in prison because her revolt against those who deceived her would declare itself, but unsubdued she intensifies her loathing of their system—she will have neither " their heaven nor their hell."

" The Tomb at St. Praxed's " (also 1845, and renamed later " The Bishop Orders his Tomb at St. Praxed's Church "), with its broad and genial appreciation of that bishop of the Renaissance, is a masterly piece of humorous depiction, as rich as it is accurate, as just as it is vivid and strong. Here you find all the virtues and vices of the Renaissance ecclesiastic drawn to the life by one who knows " both sides of the account."

" Sibrandus Schnafnaburgensis " (published in *Hood's Magazine* in 1844) is a hearty laugh at pedants and pedantry. Bored with a dull book, the reader pitched it into the hollow of a tree. A month later he found it in a queer state, it having been the sport of the elements, and of all those living things that are found busy in such places. And now he sees plainly that the author is too deadly dry and dull for such a spot. Let him go to the only fit place for such—the topmost shelf, where dry-rot consumes.

" The Glove " is a humorous handling of an old story, from the point of view of one interested in human nature, and both point of view and pitch give a humorous tone to a romantic interpretation—a turn our poet likes well.

" Up at a Villa—Down in the City " (1855)
is a broadly humorous contrast of the dulness of
the country and the liveliness and interest of the
town, from the point of view of rustic discontent,
a mood in which the speaker sees all in the country
on its worst, and all in the town on its best side
—the fun of it being that he does not know the
town, the pity of it that he cannot afford to live
there.

" A Serenade at a Villa " (1855) is fine as a
lyric, but has the note of humorous exaggeration,
and frankly suggests the point of view of the lady
who would rather have " the taskmaster's curse,"
and the stillness of the " thick, hot " midnight,
than such music as that made by the serenader
and his lute in her garden.   The intensity of the
poem, and its keenly cut phrases, are from the
lover's point of view the day after, with note of
reaction.

" Old Pictures in Florence," in its banter of the
old masters, who are not taking due care of their
pictures, and above all in its ironic criticism even
of a leading principle of the poet's thought in the
poem, gives us his attitude of humour towards his
own convictions and preferences.

His special power and quality in grim humour,
satiric description, and ironic suggestion are best
seen in two other poems of the " Men and
Women " series, " The Heretic's Tragedy " and
" Holy Cross Day."   The former is called " A
Middle Age Interlude," and describes in lines
of strong irony, and with grotesque detail that

deepens the ironic force of the poem, and expresses aversion and disgust, one of these scenes of the Middle Ages when religious passion trod every principle of humanity and reason under foot. It gives the death of Jacques du Bourg-Molay, who was burned at Paris, 1314, in the form of an " interlude," supposed sung at festivals long after. The poet suggests that it is " distorted" in consequence, but the fact of such an event being gloated over two centuries after increases our horror of such passions. It is mainly " sung " by one who is supposed to have shared in the scene on the side of faith, and he is backed by a chorus. The unshrinking realism of the piece drives home its point, and presents the spirit of such scenes with power, while implying the poet's aversion.

" Holy Cross Day" is a similar theme, artistically and ethically. It turns on the mediæval custom of compelling the Jews to hear one Christian sermon during the year, and that on September 14, known as " Holy Cross Day." It purports to give, as against the cant of a certain bishop's secretary, what the Jews really " said " (amongst themselves) on being thus driven to church. From this point of view it depicts most forcibly the evil and futility of such a proceeding, and of Middle Age conduct towards Jews, giving broadly besides a sense of its absurdity. The poem positively throbs with hate and contempt for the Christians and their creed ; and with an extraordinary command of diction and rhythm to express it in abrupt and grotesque words and lines, whose force is heightened by the time and place at which they are supposed spoken, it makes the soul of the Jew, and the strange scene of which he is part, live. Then the storm of hate falls quiet, and you see the deeper mind of the Jew, the strain of old religion, the hope of a Messiah kept fresh by bitter wrongs, a hope so sure of God it appeals to Christ (if He be Messiah) against the Christians.

" Filippo Baldinucci " (" Pacchiarotto ") is the story of another Jew, who took his revenge for one of many wrongs done his nation. A fresco of the Virgin had been so put as to overlook the Jewish burying-ground at Florence. The Jews paid for its removal, only to find a " Crucifixion " in its place. Their remedy failing, a young Jew went and bought the original of the Virgin, and bore it off, not the least for its value, but to place it among his pagan pictures. It is a story of a later time, when the pious old days have gone by. The note of sympathy is again with the Jews, and the humour of the poet is used on their behalf, for the conclusion of the story which brings the powerful young Jew on the scene to frighten the painter, and discomfit the author of the insult, is Browning's. The first part of the story is to be found in the life of Buti as given in Baldinucci's *History of Painters*. The force of the " moral " is increased by the fact that the story is told by the farmer to his son as a warning. It pleased the poet to think of the means nature provides for foiling bigots, and his sympathy is strong with the bold young Jew.

"Pacchiarotto" is another Italian theme to the poet's mind, in its grotesquerie and in its moral. Giacomo Pacchiarotto was a painter of Siena in the sixteenth century. He had been a strong reformer, one of a society known as the Bardotti (the "spare horses," who walk by the waggon, and tell how all ought to be done, but do nothing). But criticism proved thankless and reform impossible, so he gave it up and took to improving a company of figures he had drawn on the walls of a room in his own house. This went well —at least he had his way and all the oratory he wished. But men and affairs are not so abstract and docile as that. Famine fell on Siena, and our good painter, with his passion for reform, and his confidence in his own ideas, was drawn away from his imaginary audience to real affairs. The Bardotti thought they knew how by revolution to put matters right—turn things "upside down" and they would be "right side up." And so thought the painter. But when in his enthusiasm for the cause and for his own powers he hinted that he was the right leader, the other "radicals" were down on him. He fled, hid in the first place that offered—a tomb with small room for two, and in two days he came out much the worse for his quaint lodging in some ways, but well rid of his crude radicalism. He now saw the wisdom of sensible acceptance and slow progress, of minding his own business, and respecting the conditions of life and the laws of the world.

"Caliban" and "Sludge," which are earlier

work than the foregoing, show a subtle intellectual humour, with notes too of the broader humour. The theology of Caliban and his circumstances—the method, the ground, and the details of his view of things—could only have been developed by a true humorist, only such a mind could track the ways, catch the associations, shape the imagery, and vitalise the workings of so quaint and primitive a nature as that of Caliban. And the apology of Sludge is a larger and of course a subtler piece of humour — no mere " advocate's plea " for the medium, but such a study of the man amid his conditions, in his principles and passions, and in the curious and tangled ways of these, and in his by-play with reference to other minds and the weaknesses of these, as only a strong humorist could have given. It is an " apology " for, an exposure of more than Sludge, of human nature in its play among the temptations and cravings of human life, and in face of its limits. Some have thought of Browning that he was only too capable of " arguments." They have not seen how such " arguments " as these are wrought, not merely of matter of intellect, but of matter of character. So it is anyhow.

" Blougram's Apology," too, where the matter and scope of the " argument " are more intellectual, is finely humorous throughout. And it is so, not only in the dramatic quality of the " argument," the monologue, which is a defence and a reply, and not only in putting Blougram and

Gigadibs well on " the stage," but in the way in which the whole statement implies the subsidiary place of arguments in such cases, and suggests the richer humanity and strength of the bishop as against his critic. It sets the real defence of Blougram broadly in the field of life and nature —among the facts and conditions of life, and the instincts and needs of human nature. The bishop is a *man* with the need of a world of men ; more obviously it may seem he is a worldling with the need of a world. And he is a shrewd critic of men, with a considerable knowledge of that sphere of fears and hopes and cravings which is called the heart. He measures Gigadibs in himself, and in relation to the world and man, and his irony towards him is a complex of principles and judg- ments that draw more from the large world of thought and passion than from any direct argu- ments he feels it necessary to offer against his critic. Gigadibs will not carry the world he knows, and his thin criticism does not greatly affect the bishop, but it pleases Blougram's strong mind to put a case that shall meet him, while he suggests that better argument which he indicates but does not present, and could not answer.

" Protus," put with the " Dramatic Romances " beside " Holy Cross Day," is a sketch of the strange humours of fate, and of the contrasts of life. It is a study of busts with " records " to throw light on them—first Protus, the fair baby face, with violets in the hair ; and then John, the blacksmith's son, with his rough hammered head and great jaw. And the point is that the fair face, born in the porphyry chamber, with queens round it, and so many hopes, was thrust aside into utter obscurity by this other of the " griped lips " and the rough head.

" A Likeness," among the " Dramatis Personæ," is a humorous account of remarks people make on pictures, not knowing the associations, to their owners. A man owns an etching so like a certain face, that to him it is of touching value, and a friend glances at it with a word of faint praise. Such are the risks of sentiment, even with friends !

" Confessions " has a simple humour and a pleasant sincerity. It is the story of an old love affair, vividly recalled and told by a dying man to the parson, who has been talking the commonplaces of such times. And the frank temper of it, waking up the past and brushing aside empty talk with a smile, has the poet's sympathy.

In the same group is the curious theme, humorously set for its quaint comment on human nature. " Gold Hair : A Story of Pornic." It is a story the poet heard in the little Breton town. A girl, simple and saintly, hid thirty gold pieces in golden hair of which she was vain, and carried both to the grave, the gold pieces being her secret, found years after—a case of the weakness found in all hearts, and proof surely of the truth of the Christian doctrine of " original sin."

" Pambo " is another quaint instance of the

poet's humour. It turns on an old story, and applies it bluntly to a modern case. One Pambo, as the story is told in old Church history, went to St. Anthony to learn a psalm, and the saint gave him Ps. xxxix. 1, " I will give heed to my ways, that I offend not with my tongue." And being a simple man he took only the first part, declaring it enough, and after many years, says the old historian, it was still enough for Pambo. With a change Browning makes it apply to himself. He takes it that the monk thought the latter more than he could do, and for himself it would seem, his critics being judges, he has found it too much —he has " looked to his ways " for years, still he " offends with his tongue." It has to be borne now !

" Ned Bratts " (" Dramatic Idyls," first series) is an example of the humour of the poet's later manner. It is from a quarry containing much honest but crude matter of human nature—the writings of John Bunyan. It is based on the story of " Old Tod " in " The Life and Death of Mr. Badman." It is a rough and vivid picture of the hero and the scene. Into the packed court at Bedford, on a broiling June day, one Ned Bratts, a thorough ruffian, broke, to confess his crimes and ask instant execution. Under influence of John Bunyan, then in prison, he had become deeply penitent, and his only fear now was lest he should have time to change to his old mind and ways. He tells the story of his life to an amazed court, and gets his wish. He and his wife are hanged, and that way escape further crimes, and, let us hope, " the City of Destruction." It is a grotesque story and scene, given with much force and humour, suggesting the question of " Halbert and Hob " as to the reason in nature for such ruffians, and pointing to the Power " above nature " that can soften even these hard hearts.

This poem may indeed serve to bring out points of style and design in its class. In metre and words it is a kind of transcript of the facts, and may seem a clear instance of that harsh realism, without beauty or imaginative suggestion, that is alleged against most of the " humorous " poems, and so many others in Browning. And yet is it so even in " Ned Bratts " ? Leaving the question of metre and words, which are from the poet's truthfulness and dramatic sincerity, the spirit and drift of the poem are on the side of beauty and humanity. It is not very clear what forces led to the penitence of Ned Bratts, or how far it would have stood the test ; but the poet leaves an impression of thorough earnestness on the part of, and of hope in regard to this rough pair of converts.

In this and other ways " Ned Bratts," on which the poet himself it seems put much value, may suggest what else needs saying of Browning's use of the grotesque, and of his humour as a whole. Why does our poet use his powers to depict so much that is " unpleasing " ? Why so much rough reality, such ready and amused ac-

ceptance of ugliness, villainy, and pain as parts of
the world? Why bring these with a kind of
delight in them into the world of art? These
questions are put, and they are fair. What
answers are suggested by our study of Browning's work in this aspect, in these parts of it?
It comes in part from his frank attitude, and
from the clearness and vigour of his perception
of life. He will not dwell on facts of beauty and
goodness only or long. The world is his field,
and he would know as much of it as he can.
He feels how the facts in question add to the
force and interest of life. And he is drawn to
the problem these facts raise. For him they
indicate the path and drift of great laws. He
sees how they work towards a higher life, and
illustrate his great idea of the balance and co-
operation of all moral factors as the law of
development. These facts as elements of the
general situation are cosmic, not chaotic. They
are very amusing, and give life a variety it would
not otherwise have. And besides they have high
uses, and are good in the long-run.

And so laughter with Browning rests on the
goodness rather than the evil and disorder of
things. His humour is not energetic only, it is
friendly, kindly. It sees much to laugh at, and
it has variety of laughter, but even its satire and
its irony are generous and manly, friendly to the
failings, patient of the follies, and hopeful of the
slow gains of men, though caustic towards their
meaner vices, and severe towards every form of

34

cruelty and selfishness. The crimes of bigotry move him to indignation and ironic exposure. He has frank appreciation for the manifestations of power and of strong character, but he detests the abuses of such power, whatever infringes the rights or reduces the good of men. He has pathos for the humour of tragic errors, though only at times does he touch that note, and anger at times for tragic wrongs, but his general note as a humorist is a kindly realism and optimism of temper which can laugh at the mixed quality of experience, and the defects of men and things, without egoistic or fanatic reactions, without didactic or reforming urgency and passion, and wholly without cynical emotions or confusions. His humour, in a word, is a part of his health and his wisdom, and, let us add, of his faith and his hope.

CHAPTER XXI

NATURE POETRY IN BROWNING

THERE is one aspect of Browning's work we have scarcely touched, so far, or only incidentally—his relation as poet to the life and beauty of nature. In a century so deeply interested in the order and life of nature, and so much engaged with the nature sentiment as ours has been in many ways, it were strange to find a poet, frankly in sympathy with the life of his age, without this sentiment and interest. And yet the general impression is, that such was the case as regards the mind, and as regards the work of Browning in this relation. Nature poetry and the modern nature senti-ment are, it is thought, " conspicuous by their absence " in Browning, in the century that saw the rise and rich development of a great nature art.

And there is, without doubt, a general and a significant truth in this impression. Neither the modern scientific nor the modern æsthetic interest in nature are found in the poetry of Browning, as they are in that of some of his contemporaries. Tennyson's steady interest in the larger facts and ideas of science, and closer study of one or two sciences (cf. *Memoir*, vol. i. pp. 298, 299, etc.), and his life-long love of English landscapes, scarcely show in Browning. And what has been said of Matthew Arnold (*Letters*, vol. i. p. 9), that he could never live long away from the presence and peace of nature, would not have been said of Browning. Mrs. Orr indeed quotes a remark of the poet made in reply to the question of a friend, " You have not a great love for nature, have you? " . . . " Yes, I have, but I love men and women better." Such a remark does not throw much light on our question. Wordsworth might and would have said that, and Tennyson and Arnold. But Mrs. Orr seems to say, on her own account (*Life of Browning*, pp. 316, 317), that the poet's love of nature, " inanimate nature " is her phrase, was rather a late growth than a life-long feeling and interest. He was always fond of animals, and flowers pleased him by their perfume ; but nature at large interested him more as " the prefigurement or the echo " of human nature than for itself, until his closing years, when he found increasing pleasure in the mountain beauties and air and sunshine of the southern slopes of the Alps. In his letters of this time there is even, Mrs. Orr says, "a ring of enthusiasm" in his enjoyment of nature, and this enthusiasm "deepens as the years advance."

Now the general truth in the matter is, and all his work seems evidence of it, that in part from his pre-occupation, and in part from his temperament, Browning shows less interest in nature than most men of culture and sensibility have shown during the Victorian age. He is so much and so steadily occupied with man and human life, that nature at large—the nature that so many influences and circumstances have been drawing so many of us to love, since Wordsworth and Scott in their different ways took us to nature—the nature of the hills and the sea, of the woods and the fields, of the clouds and the sky;—this nature, and our sentiment about it, had no great interest for him. And his active temperament and energetic passion, untouched by the moods of Arnold or the sentiment of Tennyson, moods and sentiments that yet belong to so many of us, did not make the life, the quiet, the large order and beauty of nature the emotional comfort or necessity to him, as man or as poet, that they have been to many of us.

And yet there is fine nature poetry in Browning. It is small in amount compared with the sum of his work, and it is occasional, but it is in his work from the first. And as much from its freshness and force as from its distinctive quality, caught from his genius, or reflected from his standpoint, it is well worthy of distinct and careful consideration in our studies of his poetry.

His dominant interest in human passion and thought, in the life of personality, are found as early as "Pauline." But even in "Pauline" we found fine touches of nature poetry, and a zest both of youthful and romantic appreciation of certain facts of nature, e.g. and to quote phrases only, "the black thorn boughs . . . were white

with coming buds," p. 5 ; "climbing plants heavy
with bloom and dew," p. 8. Or take this from
p. 26—

> . . . the late glow of life, like change on clouds,
> Proved not the morn-blush widening into day,
> But eve faint-coloured by the dying sun
> While darkness hastens quickly.

Or the passage, too long to give here, on pp.
33, 34, and others that might be quoted.

It seems clear from "Pauline" that the young
poet had felt the attraction of the modern sentiment of nature, as it touched certain poets before
him. He depicts the *persona* of the poem, as
drawn to identify his life with that of nature
(*cf.* p. 32); and in "Sordello" we shall find him
return to that idea, as one conception of the
poetic relation to nature, but only to set it aside
on behalf of one much more independent and far
more characteristic of his own mind.

In a remarkable passage of "Paracelsus" he
has described the place of man, and the meaning
of man's nature in relation to the other nature.
As he thinks of it there, man is the apex of the
great order. The appearance of man within it
gives it a new meaning, or rather brings out its
true meaning for the first time. Epitome, and as
it seems climax, of the natural life, man is, through
his thought and emotion, the clue to nature (*vid*
the closing speech of Paracelsus, pp. 165–176
This speech sums up, as we have seen, the gain
of the life of Paracelsus. Its great principle
that of spiritual evolution—rooted in, unfolded b

the supreme Spirit, and working towards "ends" that mind alone rightly interprets (*cf.* especially on our present point, pp. 170, 171).

And Browning took the results of this poetically and ethically. The winds become voices. The pines of the deep wood commune together. The peerless cup of the lake lily is an urn upborne by a nymph. Morning has enterprise, and the glory of the sunset an emotion of triumph, and the deep night a solemn quiet.

Nor is this, as the poet conceived, "the pathetic fallacy." It is just interpretation, for nature is alive, and in her inmost life spiritual. In a noble passage, which precedes that just referred to, nature is set before us as thrilled with a mystic joy, with life, love, and beauty, wherein the indwelling God "renews his ancient rapture" spring after spring, and age by age.

Now this may seem the antique mythopœic fancy, touched by the imagination and principle of Wordsworth. But even here the leading interest is ethical, as we have seen, and the poet makes little use of the principle here grasped, so far as the forms and life of nature go.

Towards the passive imagination, and any brooding over sensuous nature, Browning is quite opposed. To the nature love of Aprile, and the nature poetry of Eglamor, he was quite averse. They make nature too much a ministry of sensations, or at best of emotions (*cf* "Paracelsus," p. 58, "Sordello," pp. 99, 100, *cf.* pp. 106–108), and so Eglamor is described as "the copier," not the

" protoplast " dealing with surfaces and fancies without hold of the creative principle and meaning of things.

" Sordello " has not a few fine descriptions, and among them, descriptions of nature. This for example, on p. 54—

> . . . That autumn eve was stilled :
> A last remains of sunset dimly burned
> O'er the far forests, like a torch-flame turned
> By the wind back on the bearer's hand
> In one long flare of crimson ; as a brand,
> The woods beneath lay black.

Or those on pp. 87 and 91, or on pp. 134, 135. But " Sordello " is little engaged with matters of this kind. The drift of the " argument " is in fact on the other side. Sordello begins with the love of nature " in a drowsy paradise," but is woke up by the touch of life to a better interest in human life. He read his own life into nature in idle fancy or mere sentiment, and the first touch of actual life and passion broke up the vanity of that dream-life. After his failure he returned to nature again, but only to discover how different nature is from man, how inadequate by herself for man, and to be recalled by the mightier interests of human life.

At the opening of " Pippa Passes " is a sunrise, romantically touched—

> O'er night's brim, day boils at last ;
> Boils pure gold, o'er the cloud-cup's brim.

And in one of its strongest scenes, Elizabethan in its nervous force, is the thunderstorm so vividly

given in the words, from the situation and with the
feeling of Ottima (*cf.* pp. 22, 23).——

> . . . Buried in woods we lay, . . . ;
> Swift ran the searching tempest overhead ;
> And ever and anon some bright white shaft
> Burned through the pine-tree roof, here burned and there,
> As if God's messenger thro' the close wood screen
> Plunged and replunged his weapon at a venture,
> Feeling for guilty thee and me ; then broke
> The thunder like a whole sea overhead.

From the point of view of the guilty lovers,
that is powerfully done ; and the contrast in the
simple morning song of Pippa that follows, with
its note of birds and its freshness of dewy dawn,
is well conceived——

> The year's at the spring
> And day's at the morn ;
> Morning's at seven ;
> The hill-side's dew-pearled ;
> The lark's on the wing ;
> The snail's on the thorn :
> God's in His heaven——
> All's right with the world.

Quick glimpses of landscapes, and rapid descriptions of natural facts, occur frequently in Browning, and they are good, though quite subordinate.
In not a few of the dramatic lyrics you find these,
sometimes in a phrase only, or a line, but fresh,
and to the life. You have such in "The Ride
from Ghent to Aix," and in "A Lovers' Quarrel,"
"The Lost Mistress," "Up at a Villa," and others
of this group. In "Meeting at Night" the
scenery is given in swift touches, that make
simply for the meeting of the lovers, we may say.

But in others of these lyrics, and certain of the dramatic romances, the scenery is more, and it is more fully given. "Love among the Ruins" has a picture, quickly drawn, yet distinctly seen, the picture of a large pastoral landscape in the level evening light, with the sheep moving across it, and the tinkle of sheep bells. It is simple, but good, and is heightened by the suggestion of the bustling noisy city that was once there, but is gone, only its ruins left now, with the tints of the quiet evening on them. Love and nature endure.

"Home-Thoughts from Abroad" is the picture of an English spring, the lines made firmer and warmer by the fact that it is drawn from a distance—a picture of spring in England, with its song of birds, its blossoms and dew-drops, its clover and buttercups, "the children's dower"—

> The wise thrush; he sings each song twice over,
> Lest you should think he never could recapture
> The first fine careless rapture.

In "Saul" the appreciation of nature, and of all the interest and good of the natural life of man, is large and cordial, and there are vivid pictures of both, fit for the shepherd poet of passionate soul and frank humanities—

> How good is man's life, the mere living! How fit to employ
> All the heart, and the soul, and the senses for ever in joy!

That is its note as regards nature and the healthy life of men with nature, even while it rises to the life of spirit.

Many lines we might quote from " Saul,"—only these we can—

. . . slow pallid sunsets in autumn, ye watch from the shore,
At their sad level gaze o'er the ocean—a sun's slow decline
Over hills which, resolved in stern silence, o'erlap and entwine
Base with base to knit strength more intensely.

The description of Florence in the spring morning is well etched in " Old Pictures," and the landscape in " Two in the Campagna" is made to suggest and symbolise, though it does not create, the mood of the lyric ; its spaces, its wide ocean of air, its great stretch of sky, are symbols of that immensity of desire, whose spring he has touched, whose satisfaction is to seek.

The warm breath and sweetness of the spring night give charm to and bring out the temper and meaning of "Fra Lippo Lippi"; and the twilight of Florence, with its grey tone, its dreamy peace, fits the pitch of " Andrea del Sarto "—the pitch of his art, and the temper of his spirit.

The landscape in " By the Fireside " is also of the neighbourhood of Florence ; and it is not only well described, as in " Andrea del Sarto," but the scenery of the twilight hour are inwrought with the mood of the lovers, in a way Browning does not often use. The landscape acts on feeling, qualifies passion, becomes a part of its fellowship, and thus fixes itself in the heart, we may say, not only in association, but in sympathy for a lifetime.

The scenery of " James Lee's Wife," also, seems to us related to the stages and moods of that series of dramatic lyrics. It was composed at a "wild little place in Brittany," a lonely place, with "a soft and a mournful wind." And the description of the dawn in one of the series (vi.), and of the bright autumn morning in another (vii.), are good examples of the kind of nature art our poet did in association with his dramatic work.

The noble description of the double lunar rainbow in "Christmas Eve," besides fitting well its dramatic purpose in the poem, is a masterly piece of nature work. And so in another sort, though still of the sky and its splendours, more purely imaginative, is the part of "Easter Day" which describes the awful dawn of judgment from the heart of the midnight. Space forbids us to quote either passage. They can easily be referred to, "Christmas Eve" (iv.), and "Easter Day" (xv.).

In the Romances, we said there is more landscape. But there is one of the lyrics that has a fine bit of work of that kind, we would refer to before glancing at the romances. The night scene in "A Serenade at the Villa," in dramatic sympathy with the lover's passion and with his situation, serenading on such a night, gives in bold romantic phrases the storm and the excitement of the lover, in reminiscence.

> Earth turned in her sleep with pain,
>   Sultrily suspired for proof:
> In at heaven and out again,
>   Lightning !—where it broke the roof,
> Bloodlike, some few drops of rain.

That is of a piece with the storm in "Pippa Passes," and would have pleased Webster.

The Venetian landscape in "In a Gondola," with its rows of lighted houses and level canals, its stillness yet passion, is well suggested.

So is the spring, given in "Waring," when in the Kent country " 'tis cherry time," and

> All God's creatures crave their boon,
> All at once and all in tune,
> And get it,

through the bounty and the beauty of nature at that fair time.

There are two poems almost purely descriptive, and both of them occupied chiefly with Italian landscape, "De Gustibus" and "The Englishman in Italy." In the first, called a lyric, the differences between English and Italian scenery are drawn out; England with its trees and cornfields, its towers and song of blackbirds, Italy with its

> Castle precipice encurled
> In a gash of the wind-grieved Apennine.

Or—

> A seaside house to the farther south,

with its single cypress, standing sharply out, and the

> Great opaque blue breadth of sea without a break

beyond—such are the contrasts.

In the second, called a romance, there is description in bright verse, and in a happy vein, of Italian life in the country, and of the scenery of the plain of Sorrento. It is told to a girl who is sheltering in a cottage from a rainstorm brought by the sirocco. The Englishman is turning her attention from the terrifying storm by telling her of the things he has seen and done since yesterday, especially he tells her of a visit to the mountains and what he saw thence—looking far over the soft plain and the sea, with the isles of the sirens in the fair blue waters, and " the infinite movement of the mountains," and overhead the depths of the sky. It is all very brightly done, but, like this poet, the human interest is strong, the interest of the child to whom it is told, and of the peasant life described in the early part of the poem, and our interest in the speaker too.

The landscape in " The Flight of the Duchess " fits the people and culture of the dukedom, and is broadly drawn. It is a great wild country, with cornfields and vineyards, but much of it sheepwalk, cattle-tract, and open chase bounded by pine-clad hills; and beyond, a greater, rougher country, a dreary, burnt-up plain, bounded by the salt sandy shore of the great sea. It is a country of farmers and huntsmen and old retainers, where gipsies haunt, and the crude past lingers ; and in which, because of these elements, strange and romantic things are possible. The rude background, thus given in the opening landscape, is kept, we may say, in the pitch and chime of the verse, except, of course, where the romance takes that higher flight before described. It is as characteristic of the descriptive power as of the humour and fancy of the poet.

But " Childe Roland " is the most remarkable

of the romances from our present point of view, though one scarcely knows whether to call the wonderful scenery of this romance " landscape " at all. As we have before suggested, the scenes that follow each other, each bleaker and harsher than the other, up to the crisis, have a quality of intense realism, a kind of startling sharpness and vividness, like Dante's " visions " of hell ; and yet the whole seems to belong to an awful region of dreams, its elements borrowed from earth but combined and transformed at the bidding of emotion and in the service of imagination. Bleaker than the bleakest moorland, and wilder than the barren mountains, with a silence and loneliness of the land of death, and tints as of the last sunset over a dead world, the poem is perhaps unique in its quality and force of scenic embodiment, and it is strongly dramatic in the power with which it realises the emotions of the speaker right through its course.

There is good description in " The Ring and the Book," but little description of nature. What there is marks the poet's memory and love of Italian scenes and scenery of the years spent in the land with his wife, for " The Ring and the Book " was written when all that was past. Parts of the monologue of Pompilia and the speech of Caponsacchi contain brief scenes of this kind.

Speaking generally, one would say that the later poetry of Browning shows less sympathy with, and attention to, nature than the earlier work—the poet is more fully absorbed by the

special themes of his own art. But parts of
"Fifine" and parts of "Red Cotton Night-Cap
Country," and certain of the "Dramatic Idyls"
give a little work of this kind.

It follows of course, from the dominant interest
of the poet, that in his work landscape should be
subordinated to the other and stronger interest.
And there are instances of a fine subordination of
nature to dramatic feeling and purpose. We
have already referred to "Andrea del Sarto" and
"Fra Lippo Lippi" as cases. The soft twilight
tone of "Pompilia" is another instance. And
from remote periods of the poet's work we may
cite two others, "Porphyria's Lover" and "Ned
Bratts"; the beating rain and the sullen wind of
the one, and the broiling weather and the stifling
court of the other, give the mood and atmosphere
of each poem.

We have said that in Browning's later poetry
nature is even less than in the earlier work. But
in the "Parleyings," as if to show his sympathy
with the art of the painter and his power in that
kind of conception, his power too in a certain
kind of nature art, and his sympathy with Greek
art, with his sense of its limits, he sets himself in
his colloquy with the Dutch painter, Gerard de
Lairesse, to present a series of subjects for paint-
ings, in association with different times of the day.
They are in part studies of nature, from before
the dawn till after the sunset, more particularly
studies of Greek myths, in association with nature.
Through a dim thunderous dawn Prometheus is

seen chained to his rock. When day has broken, Artemis, goddess of nature, is seen in the clear daylight, the huntress-queen, pure as snow, with tint of the apple-blossom, but pitiless and proud. With the noon-glow he gives in the forest depths the satyr, that loved Lyda and was despised by her, gazing on the nymph asleep. At sunset he describes the preparations of Darius and Alexander for battle, so typifying the solemn hush of eve. And when night has fallen he sees as end of all the glories of the day only a ghost, "voiceless with deprecating hands"—bewailing the dead day and expecting no morrow — the Greek view of life. The themes are thus Greek, and the outline and style Greek, such as Landor would have approved. And the aim is in part to give the quality of Greek imagination, and its interpretation of life. In part it is to affirm characteristically the law of progress in art and life—to discard, in the very spirit of "Old Pictures," the art which clings to the past for that which includes the future, the art whose very idealisation is sensuous for that whose scope is spiritual, leaving the sad school of Hades for that of Christian hope, whose type is the eternal springtide.

It thus appears, on survey of those parts of his poetry touching the matter, that Browning was no "worshipper of nature" in any of the senses that familiar phrase has borne during the century. He did not find in nature the chief companion or consoler of man. He did not regard nature as greater or "more divine" than man. Neither the

35

æsthetic nor the scientific worship of nature
found the response in his mind that it has found
in so many. He is in truth sarcastic regarding
sentimental attitudes towards nature—towards
what he took to be Byronism in this matter, as
towards the sentiment of physicism. He will
neither cower in self-pity before the often terrible
and impassive greatness of nature, nor is he over-
mastered and awed by her physical extent and
splendours. He places himself firmly beside the
out-nature as greater and more significant than it
—as sharing more of the highest nature.

His attitude and feeling in this respect are well,
if roughly and anti-sentimentally expressed, in
these lines, the allusion being to the famous
closing passage of " Childe Harold " (*cf.* Epilogue
to " Pacchiarotto," stanza xx.).

> " O littleness of man," deplores the bard ;
> And then, for fear the Powers should punish him,
> " O grandeur of the visible universe
> Our human littleness contrasts withal ;
> O sun, O moon, ye mountains and thou sea,
> Thou emblem of immensity, thou this,
> That, and the other,—what impertinence
> In man to eat and drink and walk about,
> And have his little notions of his own,
> The while some wave sheds foam upon the shore."

The worship of material immensities, however it
might justify itself to sensuous imagination, he
regarded as poor poetry and bad ethics—as a
misapprehension of values and a derogation from
self-respect.

It is a proof of the slight stress he has put on

the poetry of nature that it is impossible to place him in any of the " schools " of nature art since Scott and Wordsworth. He would respond to the sentiment of " Tintern Abbey," though scarcely to that of Arnold's " Resignation." He was too active and too intensely human to dwell in Wordsworth's or in Arnold's way on the life of nature. He feels nature as she responds to or repels man in hours of sensibility. He has sense of the surpassing beauty of moments and scenes of her life. And he has sense of her grandeur and terror, and of her peace. But nature is secondary, almost never primary. She is kept subordinate to dramatic purpose and quality. Browning rarely dwells on nature for herself. He never broods on nature, and never seeks through her the principle of beauty or the secret of peace. He is more disposed to read nature through mind than mind through nature.

And so when we sum up the points and qualities of his nature work we find that he gives strong and rapid description, swift strokes and broad effects, without detail. He is not much interested in romantic nature for itself, but his appreciation is often romantic, his phrases keenly cut and well coloured, with an Elizabethan, and at times a pre-Raphaelite, quality. And chiefly we find that all in his thought and in his art has been subservient to his study and expression of the things of man's mind.

EPILOGUE

WE have now brought under review, and considered somewhat closely, all sections and aspects of Browning's work, and in fact no small part of the whole of that work. Let us pause for a little at the close to gather up and bring well together, if we may, certain points that come out on survey thus made—(1) As regards the manner of Browning's work, his art, and what to many has seemed his lack of art, and the difficulties thence arising; (2) as regards the matter of the poet's work, his leading ideas as a poetic thinker and master of life, what is often called the "Message" of the poet, and how that is to be construed through the work itself considered as a whole.

As regards the poet's art and manner, a question that rises early and lingers late with many readers, it will have been seen long ago, by any who have come so far with us, that we hold no brief for the perfect satisfactoriness of these.

That the poet is great here we hold of course.
He could not be the poet he is, or have the
power he has in the realm of poetry, were he not
so. But both his qualities and his defects have
stood, and stand even yet, in the way of readers.
And in certain cases, it may well be, they will
strike out works on which he spent no little
labour and time, from the abiding possessions of
English poetry. It is said that even his works
of the best period are often too long, and that
his works of the other periods are constantly so.
Tennyson speaks of him as the largest-brained
poet of his time, and the richest in thought, but
with emphasis on "brain" and "thought." The
late Master of Balliol wrote, even in 1887,
(Tennyson's *Memoir*, vol ii. p. 344): "Browning's
thought, feeling, and knowledge are generally out
of all proportion to his powers of expression.
Since I have been ill I have been reading a good
deal of his poems, and have come to like him,
and in some measure to understand him." And
Edward Fitzgerald, who had a very true if not
catholic taste in poetry, found the larger part of
Browning quite impossible.

Now it goes without saying, that when men
such as these find Browning difficult or distaste-
ful, even after he had established his place in the
literature of his age, that there are reasons in
matter and manner, in temper of mind and form
of work, for the friction and dislike referred to.
And reasons are easily found, especially by such
as seek to justify a distaste they do not care to

get over. The ways of this poetry are hard for a time, and in parts they remain so. It goes often through new country, and the poet has scarcely cared to select or present it so that the prospects please on first acquaintance, however much they may interest on fuller knowledge. The poet himself said to Tennyson, late in his career (*Memoir*, vol ii. p. 230): " I cannot change myself—people must take me as they find me"; in other words, he had become fully aware of the defects of his qualities, of the undue energy of certain virtues of his genius.

And much of the friction and the difficulty is just there, no doubt. Tennyson was dwelling on his dictum (vide *Memoir*), that an artist should make his work as perfect as possible; but that was not Browning's bias nor his way—dramatist, thinker, searcher of the soul, singer from passionate interest in human hearts, he did not care to finish his work as Tennyson did—he could not have done it. He gave himself to his subjects. He put himself into his work with zest and power, and the qualities of the mind thus at work, as well as the quality and form of the work itself, have been a source of difficulty. It has often been said that his basis and quality are too intellectual for poetry. And there is force in the criticism. His intellectuality, his energy and tenacity of argument and research, his interior quality, his steady handling of psychical and ethical fact, his study not of actions but of thought and motive, and the springs of action, have taxed the attention of most and mastered the patience of many. His quality of passion too, rather than emotion or sentiment, is unpleasing for many. And so is the intellectual rather than the sensuous construction of his work. His set on matter rather than manner, and his indifference or insensibility to the minor graces and lesser virtues of mood and style, goes with a strenuousness and actuality that wearies some. There is even a certain nervous restlessness of mind and manner, a certain vigour and stringency of temper and purpose, that tire those who go to poetry for a play of emotions. Besides, he has often the air, shall we say, of composing in the thick and stress of working a subject out, rather than in the mood of tranquil imagination that should ensue on its mastery. And he moves at a speed that many will never follow, and carries an amount of matter they will not bear, and not only sees too many things, but seems to see things from several points of view at the same time. And he not only puts a broad grasp on his subjects as wholes, but insists on their being so grasped by his readers before they can understand him; while there is the large fact that, as dramatic lyrist and thinker, he essays new themes and interests, he breaks up new ground for poetry, and must ask the kind of discipline, the quality of study, that are required for the mastery of such work. He recovers, as we have said, the impulse of the Elizabethans for psychical presentment, and for psychical explanations, in

a modern quality and in a field they scarcely
entered.

These then, let us say, are some chief reasons
for the difficulty of Browning, and for his alleged
obscurity—his themes, and certain strongly individual qualities of the work and of the workman. With
his method and dramatic principle we have already
dealt. But there is no doubt that these are a
leading cause of difficulty with readers, until they
have grasped them. The poet's theme and sphere
are the hearts and minds of men, and through
these the heart and mind of man—significant
moments and crises of the lives of men, and the
scope and meaning of passion and the soul.
And his *principle* is what we have called the
principle of dramatic individuality, his *method*
what we have called dramatic monologue, his
form the dramatic - lyric. His presentment is
always individual; and dealing with the inner life
of his persons, it is intensely so. He starts from
the point of view of the person speaking. He
assumes a knowledge of the circumstances and
history, and of the situation of the speaker; you
are thus plunged into the very heart of the circumstances and of the speaker. You must listen,
and go through with it, and then construe the
whole, backwards and forwards, so to speak,
before you know the *persona*, or the situation and
problem. And that is not all, for the poet's use
of his method, as we have seen, is not simple, it
is complex. It is not meditation you have, nor
one *persona*. Several minds and characters are

often involved, much play of thought and passion, and many circumstances, in complex presentment, though all from the standpoint and through the mind of one person. Nor is that all; for in the work you have, further, the mind of the poet himself presenting his drama, and busy too with his larger sphere and his deeper problem—the nature of man, the scope and meaning of passion, thought and will, of what he calls the soul. It is necessary to see all this, and not easy to follow it; but as the method is fit for the matter, so the presentment is such in its intimacy, individuality, and fulness, that the gain is more than worth the trouble.

Then the dramatic quality and vivid individuality of the poet's conception and work go far to account for, if they do not justify, his faults, his details, his changes, his light thrown here and there, his speed, his broken style, his references to out-of-the-way matters, his neglect of narration, his rash and his often undue condensation,—they come from the dramatic posture and animation of his mind, and are part of his vehicle of expression. That they run to excess, and with his humour carry him into extravagances and mannerisms we must hold. Most of these have been duly analysed long ago,—his strange constructions, his ellipses, his freaks of condensation, his packed description, his grotesque diction,—and we have no need, nor have we space, to dwell upon them here.

And when it is said that Browning is indifferent to art, and to the music and rhythm and colour of phrase and verse, to the beauty and supreme harmonies of great and pure art, as Shakespeare and Milton and Keats have felt and fashioned them, it will be seen that we partly allow this. Yet this comes, we have said, in part from his dramatic realism ; and many parts of his work, regard being had to its dramatic quality and aim, have strong excellence and fine value as art. His style is strong, nervous, varied, direct, copious, humorous, drawn from the great sources of style— life and the elder masters of English. His gifts in the matter of verse are good. He is facile and even copious here. He makes blank verse of fine strength for his work, and his lyrical verse has verve, energy, subtlety. His lyrical measures indeed, fitted to his different *personæ* and themes, have unusual variety and a supple and passionate vigour. His gift for rhyming verse, we have seen, is extraordinary, liable to abuse, but of exceptional and quite graphic force often, in its command of double and even treble rhymes.

When it is urged, that for a poet the intellectual energies are too strong in Browning, that for poetry the play of intellectual interests and activities is too great in his work, and that Browning often and at times ruthlessly sacrifices the requirements and effects of art for the expression of thought, that though he "refreshes the heart he tires the brain," we should admit this with regard to a good deal of the work of the third period. We should allow that this is the side to which he leans generally, but still hold that, though to many his intellectual quality and energy may well seem excessive, yet in great part of his work, and that of course his best, the passion of the poet and his kind of imagination are just as fresh and powerful as the intellectual force and subtlety are keen and abundant.

And now returning from "allowances, qualifications, and criticisms," to the merits, gifts, and value of the poet, we need add little here to all that has been already said in this book, except what may seem further necessary to indicate Browning's place and worth among Victorian poets. Grasp his method, get at his point of view and way of thought, put your mind in frank touch with his poetic mode and interest, and you find him a rich and generous giver. In knowledge of human nature, in his kind of dramatic power, in energy and subtlety of thought and of passion, in spiritual range, in breadth of interest in and free sympathy with the nature and history of man, and in a certain stimulating and cordial vital influence, he is great. In his dramatic studies, and in his love poems, in depicting the crises of character and thought, and in presenting the crises of passion, he has shown not only great power but variety and versatility. His studies of motive and of the "approaches to action," and of character in action, have given a new depth to our dramatic literature. His character studies and his love lyrics, which are also dramatic, show a greater wealth of character, situation, and passion, and even of metrical form and force, than are shown by any poet of his time. His lyrical power is fresh and keen; his humour is broad and strong; his satire is frank and friendly; his talent for grotesque is forceful and distinctive; his pity and pathos are true if rare; his criticism of life is at once thoughtful and healthy, broad and sound, and at the same time loftily ideal. His interpretation of religious passion and faith is the most penetrating and significant criticism of religion our age has had from any poet. And the personality of the poet, in wealth and health and vigour of thought and feeling, in frank and generous response to all high and good human things, is felt through all his work. The charm of Tennyson, and the different charm of Arnold, the romantic beauty of Rossetti, the colour and grace of Morris, the lyrical music of Swinburne, are not Browning's; but for his own things and by his own gifts he stands nobly and securely with the best.

And this brings us to certain further points that we feel it necessary to deal with here—points arising out of the interpretation of the poet's leading ideas, or what is sometimes called his "message." It is very wrong of a poet to have such ideas—so some think—though it is singularly clear, from the recent *Memoir* of Tennyson, that he had them too, and not only valued them highly, but used literature as a medium for them. Browning had such ideas, and constantly expressed them through his various *personæ* and as parts of his study of life. A critical estimate of them as a whole, and an examination of them in the larger field of literature and of philosophy, would demand far more space than we can now give. We have, within the limits of these studies, aimed rather at exposition than at critical estimate and comparison. But in view of what has been said, and of certain criticism that has been made of this side of Browning's poetry, we wish to set down here, however briefly and simply, our judgment on some points that have been raised. Mrs. Orr has dealt with certain of the larger aspects of Browning's criticism of belief in her *Life* of the poet, and Professor H. Jones, in an able and interesting book on *Browning as a Teacher*, has subjected the poet to a somewhat elaborate examination from the point of view of his own philosophic method and principles. The standpoint and principles of the critics are widely different on the matter of philosophy, but their criticism of the poet shows a general agreement on a leading point: they both hold the poet to have been agnostic on the fundamental questions; the one to agree, the other to disagree with the agnosticism; the one to approve the poet's criticism of knowledge and belief because of its agnostic basis; the other to condemn the teaching and so far the poetry, on the ground of its agnosticism. Professor Jones condemns what he takes to be the poet's praise of the heart at the expense of the head, his praise of love to the discredit of knowledge; while Mrs. Orr, from her own basis of thought, reads the poet also in an agnostic sense, and agrees with him. Professor Jones argues that Browning's whole view of things rests ultimately on an absolute distrust of knowledge and an absolute faith in love. And Mrs. Orr says that the poet's ultimate intellectual attitude towards Christian theism was one of admitted ignorance.

The point has been touched several times in the course of these studies, but could not be dealt with at large, nor can it now. A few sentences only may be given to it. As respects the criticism of Professor Jones, we have touched the main point of that in our study of " Paracelsus," and elsewhere. We should largely agree with the philosophic teaching of the book. We cannot agree with its criticism of Browning on this matter. And it seems to us that Professor Jones cuts the ground from under this part of his book, as criticism of the deeper drift of the poet, by the admission virtually made in the chapter on " Heart and Head." It comes to this, surely, that no thinker who was also a poet, and a master of human nature, could by love mean only feeling. He really means the total view of things won from the standpoint and in the spirit and relation of love. Love's intuition, in fact, is not emotion only, but the insight of all the powers of one's nature, qualified and stimulated by love. We entirely agree with Professor Jones, that when doubts arise, because theory lags behind experience, there is no way out of the wood then save a fuller and better theory, and then love may be one of the powers urging forward a larger solution. Love as such is not light, let us say, but it is the fine medium of Light on the great questions of life.

And if it still be said that the poet when philosophising was agnostic, and, as Mrs. Orr tells us, spoke, in the terms of a certain type of Kantianism, of the hopeless contradictions of the logical understanding on the greatest matters, even then certain things might well be urged in deprecation of Professor Jones' critical condemnation. We might appeal from the " abstract thinker " to the larger thought of the poet. Or we might appeal to the philosophers themselves, and compare the positions say of Mr. Bradley and Professor Seth with that of Professor Jones, allowing the poet the advantage of such comparison, and the rights of a somewhat different philosophic position.

We here, in fact, raise broadly the question, not of agnosticism, but of the place and part of doubt in human life. Browning does recognise, in frank sympathy with the spirit of his age, the limits and uncertainties of knowledge in relation to the great points of belief and the higher interpretation of things, but holds that this uncertainty, and the doubts that arise under stress of experience, belong to the wholesome conditions of human education, and are indeed essential to it. We know in part, and proceed to ever fuller and clearer constructions of experience. This partial knowledge is a condition of progress, and throws us on our highest principles. To some this may seem a compromise with experience. It is not in any case agnosticism, for by the conditions of the problem our knowledge is enough for its moral function, while as science it is constantly being carried to fuller power and better clearness.

Browning applies his principle to the doctrine and growth of Christianity in "A Death in the Desert"; and in "Karshish" and "La Saisiaz" he brings it to bear on our faith in a future life, and on the degree of uncertainty that attaches to any science of that matter. And his conclusion is, that our experience and the state of the question in regard to both is such as was to be expected, keeping in view the nature of the questions and the discipline of human life itself.

But, says Mrs. Orr, the poet's attitude and inner mind, on such questions, was really one of doubt and confessed ignorance. His attitude towards historical Christianity was, she would say, one of ethical and spiritual response, but of large intellectual uncertainty (cf. *Life and Letters*, pp. 318, 319, 436). "Christ was a mystery, and a message of Divine Love, but no messenger of Divine intention." And further it is said, that "no one knew better than He that every act and motive which we attribute to a Superior Being is a virtual negation of His existence." And yet we are told Browning "believed that such a Being exists, and accepted His reflexion in the mirror of the human mind as a necessarily false image, but one that bears witness to the Truth." The words are curious, and show the straits to which a certain type of "agnosticism

with faith" is reduced—"necessarily false," yet
bearing "witness to the Truth"! Are we to take
the words as an instance of the contradictions
into which "logical understanding" falls, whenever
it has the temerity to deal with or speak of these
high things? This is, of course, a question of
philosophy, and it seems to us that the philosophy
here is quite unsatisfactory. But setting that
aside, as unfit for our present discussion, one or
two obvious reflections surely occur. And as
they seem to us important in their bearing on the
attitude of the poet on the questions we are
considering, we shall beg permission to set them
down at this point, and in view of Mrs. Orr's
interpretation of the poet's thought and "teaching." And one obvious remark surely is, that the
reflexion of Deity in human mind can scarcely be
"necessarily false" if it bear witness in any
degree to truth, to reality. Partial, defective,
it may be, and is, but not "false." Then, further,
Mrs. Orr says that "his works rarely" show this
state of "feeling," and his conversation did so very
seldom. She then adds, that "the faith which he
had contingently accepted became absolute for him,
from all practical points of view," on the ground,
we presume, of moral argument, and, Mrs. Orr adds,
of "transcendental imagination, and the acknow-
ledged limits of Reason." And then leaving
philosophical criticism of belief, whether adequate
or not, Mrs. Orr (*vide* p. 437 of *Life*) gives her
view of what remains. She holds that the poet's
testimony to the value of the higher beliefs is then

36

" most powerful when least explicit "—and most valid when it is " the unconscious testimony of creative genius to the marvel of conscious life— through the passionate affirmation of the poetic and human nature, not only of the beauty and goodness of that life, but of its reality and persistence."

This is well said, and one agrees with it, but how stand criticism and argument then ? and what is this worth as " argument for faith " ? What Mrs. Orr has to say of the " transcendental imagination " and of the " limits of reason," as grounds of belief somehow regarding matters that we do not really know, might, indeed, draw one aside to philosophy, especially as one recalls the unphilosophic uses such conceptions and terms have been put to; but, setting aside the questions of philosophy as such, let us try the matter on the broader and simpler ground that belongs to us here. And when we do so, is not this what it comes to ? When leaving metaphysics, good or bad, we put the argument as Mrs. Orr has put it in the words quoted, and make our appeal to interpretation of human nature and human experience, as these are read through the grasp and insight of the poet as a master of both, we are plainly taking our stand on the ground, not of psychological religion merely, but of a large ethical and human construction of things—not in the light of our needs only, but of our natures and our highest principles. And this surely is a ground, not of ignorance but of knowledge, and of valid though modest constructions of human mind and of human life. And this is the right, as it is the strong ground when dealing with a poet, and with poetry, as we have before said and repeated.

This interpretation of things, and of man in relation to them, is, of course, from the scientific point of view, a large hypothesis, rather than a completed truth; but it is a hypothesis whose fundamental principles belong to the core of our poet's intuition of man and of life. It is interesting, it is important no doubt, to know what a poet, who was a strong thinker, held when critically reflecting on the great final questions, and the conditions of our knowledge of these,—it is more important to read rightly what he grasped and felt when working with his whole mind as a poet, as seer, as interpreter of the things of man, and, through his grasp and mastery of these, as interpreter of the things of the world.

The further question raised by Mrs. Orr's criticism of the poet's religious position, his exact attitude to Christianity as an "Absolute Revelation" of the existence and character of God, and of the destiny of man, we do not feel called upon to discuss, or only so far as it comes up within the works of the poet, and in that relation but slightly. No historical "Revelation," we presume, can be "absolute," either as to its contents or its "evidences," though it may be morally adequate; Browning certainly did not conceive that such a "Revelation" had been made, or was desirable. And if he held, as he certainly held, that our knowledge of the greater things

is never complete, he held still more strongly that
this incompleteness is essential to human life.
Life is progress, and he conceived that a perfectly
clear and full knowledge of the great things would
bring both discipline and progress to an end.
At the same time, as we read him, he saw in history
and experience a stimulating and practically sufficient revelation of the nature and law of Life ; and
with the most generous faith and insistence he
urges men to live heartily in the light of a high
and noble conviction as to that supreme matter.

And he is Christian, we have said, not only
because he sees in the Christian spirit the purest
and highest ethic, and in the Christian standard
the fairest ideal of life, but because he recognised
the spiritual supremacy of the Founder of the
Christian faith and spirit, and because he held by
the sweet and noble reasonableness of the Christian
idea of God. We have argued indeed, justly it
still seems to us, that Browning's interpretation of
the Christian religion as a life of the spirit, and as
a theory of life that lifts life to a plane where all
its facts gain high uses and a divine meaning, is
one of the great things he has done as a poet.

And at this point, and on this ground, let us
say, we reach the last of the aims we set ourselves
in this part of these studies—that is, a summary
and interpretation of Browning's principles as a
religious and ethical teacher, though simply to
gather up and indicate the due construction of the
foregoing expositions. It has been shown that
the poet is idealist, in sympathy with Plato and

Shelley, and most of his work down to the " Bells
and Pomegranates " has this quality. But with
the stress on the dramatic interest, and the development of the " dramatic lyric," and at length
with the adoption of that as the form of his work,
what has been called the realistic side of his
mind was brought strongly out. Only let us be
clear what this realism is. By recurring to the
principle of his dramatic form and the scope of
his dramatic art we get at it. That principle we
have defined as the principle of dramatic individuality, and that scope the embodiment of such
individuality in unique expression. And here we
catch the meaning of what has been further called
Browning's real - idealism. As poet, he sees
things from the point of view, through the mind,
and in terms of the experience of persons. Thus
for him, as the dramatic interpreter of life, the
" real " is the " soul," and experience is a construction, always from the point of view and
through the minds of persons. His realism then
lies largely in his intense apprehension and vivid
presentment of all that makes life for " souls," for
persons ; while his idealism consists, not only in
his grasping this basis, but in his affirming, through
his art and in his thought, the ideal quality and
range of emotion and thought——the full depth and
height and scope of life——the quest, the passion,
the effort, the aspiration of the soul. The development of the " soul " is the sphere and interest of
art, and the development of the " soul " is the
scope and meaning of life——the proper fruit of all

experience. That is the issue of education in
"Rabbi Ben Ezra." It is, he conceives, the end
of this life and the goal of every other. The
evolution of spirit, he imagines, is the cosmical
goal, and is the only conception we can frame on
that great matter. This is his moral frequently,
his principle always. It is the result of "Paracelsus" and "Sordello"; it is the moral of "The
Grammarian's Funeral," of "The Statue and the
Bust," and of "Andrea del Sarto."

And when Browning speaks of spiritual development as the proper fruit of experience and our
goal of life, it is well to see how, by his art as by
his thought, he stands on and works out life's
facts. For him the spiritual is the full human
fact seen in its due relation to the whole of life,
and development of the "soul" is development of
the man in the just balance and unity of his
powers and relations. This is the spiritual and
at the same time real ethics of "Rabbi Ben Ezra"
—the due subjection of all the parts and aims of
life to the law of the whole, securing the integrity
and harmony of life, and an equal development of
its powers towards the highest service each is
capable of. The spirituality of life and the reach
and quality of human aims and passions we have
found further indicated in "The Grammarian,"
and more largely, more explicitly in "Easter
Day," while the quality and reach life must have
to satisfy the "soul" is given in other ways in
"Karshish" and "Cleon." The Grammarian's
quest is for the whole of knowledge, for the "per-

fect" that way. The *persona* of " Easter Day" finds
all things, the best things of life, lose their worth
when they become " finite." Cleon has found the
same under Greek culture and in Greek life.
Only a divine beauty and depth in things—only
a truly spiritual reach in life—gives things and
life enduring value for the mind and heart of man.
And this is got by setting things in their place
and in divine relations, and by keeping them to
their true function — the development of the
" soul." A wholesome concreteness with his
ideality we have noted in our poet, and this is
seen here by his sharp sense of the defect of
types like Lazarus, and by his firm grasp of the
principle of the good Rabbi Ben Ezra, and of all
that is covered by his parable of " The Boy and
the Angel," in relation to our present question.

And this is his clue to the discipline as it is his
idea of the function of life. The test of life in
that aspect also is still spiritual result—development of the man. And this he conceives is the
test of all circumstances and of all experiences.
They are good as they enrich and unfold the life
within—wisdom and power and good there—as
" they propel the soul on its way." They are
poor and null, or bad and hurtful, as they make
men miss that, or mar their progress in it. And
seeing that the scope of the soul, of mind, and will
in man, is spiritual and so infinite, that life is the
best, the most " successful," which is moving freely,
and with fullest, steadiest grasp of its law and
principle towards the ideal.

And the "way of the soul," the element and sphere of this ideal, it will be seen, after what has been above said, is the way of the actual life. The world of human relations, tasks, circumstances, difficulties, defects, sorrows, limits, losses, is, Browning conceives, the very world wherein to work our problem out and get well started towards our ideal. By his principle, indeed, we not only use but master environment towards spiritual ends. Positive and cordial he would make even the losses and defects, even the hindrances and sufferings of life, serve to unfold life, moving strenuously and gratefully forward to that only end which seems to justify and consecrate all experience—an ever greater fulness, strength, and gentleness of heart and will, a riper wisdom and a richer power of the whole man.

He thus accepts the law of moral evolution with its consequences. He holds by good, but is not afraid of evil. He uses struggle and error as a way to good, crisis and profound disturbance as a means of education and high deliverance. Life is perfected through many experiences, belief through doubt, faith and hope through fear and effort. His faith in the other life is a faith in life; his faith in God a faith in the living Good, manifest in life and in the soul. And the key-stone, we should say, of his art and of his thought is the value, not merely the interest, of the soul. His art, his ethic, his faith, are all drawn from this source; and partly because of his reverence for souls, and partly because of his supreme and strenuous faith in Good, he is able to face the worst and hope the best, and urge life always onwards.

Here we touch again, at the close of these studies, though only for a moment, the question of the specifically religious idea as it is presented in Browning—the question, that is, of the theistic idea and interpretation. We saw in our opening chapter how, by his mode of thought as by his ruling interest, Browning was disposed to take man as his clue to the true nature of things, and to take moral power and spiritual quality as his clue to the value and meaning of man, and this gave him his approach to, his principle for, the matter now in hand—it gave him indeed, as essential to his highest idea, a principle of conscience, and a ground of reason. And this mode of conception is part also of what we have called his dramatic concreteness, his sense of and faith in personality, and his way of taking and presenting things always dramatically. For it is, as it seems to us, one result of his intensely dramatic mode of thought that Browning uses the terms of theism, often with great force and vividness, at times with fine freshness and beauty, to express his ultimate idea of the nature and law of life— " the high and true nature of Reality."

In " Saul," in " Karshish," and in the Pope's speech in " The Ring and the Book," particularly, the moral and human power of the idea in its Christian form and quality are nobly set forth. It is thus freshly and touchingly put in the " Epistle of Karshish "—

> So, the All-Great, were the All-Loving too—
> So, through the thunder comes a human voice
> Saying, "O heart I made, a heart beats here!
> Face, my hands fashioned, see it in myself!
> Thou hast no power nor may'st conceive of mine,
> But love I gave thee, with myself to love."

And in " A Death in the Desert," parts of which have close and important bearing on our present point, the poet says, and presumably more from his own thought, that having reached the higher conception of will, and of supreme personality, with regard to the ultimate nature, we cannot fall away or be driven from these, through our very need of them. And he says further, in that poem (*cf.* vol. vii. p. 130), that—

> . . Life, with all it yields of joy and woe,
> And hope and fear . . .
> Is just our chance o' the prize of learning love,
> How love might be, hath been indeed, and is.

But, say certain good critics regarding all such passages, these are dramatic utterances and figures of speech, and we must not take our strong poet as attributing " human emotions " to the Deity. As to that, " Saul " surely says, that unless we conceive the Deity as animated by love we have not conceived the Highest. And to it the Pope would say that, given that conception of the Highest, we have got a clue to the best and deepest things in ourselves, and to all things in life. And that we take it was broadly the poet's own view. Love is no mere " human emotion," but the greatest principle, as it is the purest activity of our natures. And if we may not think our highest thoughts, and attribute our purest and loftiest principles to Deity, we are ignorant indeed. But the Pope may answer that, and this must be our last word on a matter whose scope and importance demand much more, our finest, and our brightest light of reason, and of goodness, may be but a star in the infinite sky; but our "spark had for its source the sun," and of the central sun itself it bears, and must bear, true witness.

It is not only in deep agreement with our poet's principles, but their necessary fruit, that he should encourage and require a large freedom of interpretation. The "Epilogue" to "Dramatis Personæ," and the main argument of "A Death in the Desert," give the vital grounds of this freedom. The true faith is for him a living construction of experience, besides being "soul of the soul, and mind of the mind" of a man. But it did not enter into his imagination to conceive a "religion of the future" which could transcend, not to say traverse, the noblest Christian idea of God. That idea has difficulties, but it draws from our highest, and finds room for heart and soul and mind. And if with Renan (Preface to *Feuilles Détachées*), our poet would have agreed that "all religions are vain," with Renan he would more strongly have said that "Religion is great, eternal." For the drift of his thought, and the fashion of his art, tend nobly to reconcile these two positions, so characteristic of the mind of our time, by showing how "the eternal, the universal" manifest themselves in the forms of human character and human mind.

Life is—to wake not sleep,
　　Rise and not rest, but press
From earth's level where blindly creep
　　Things perfected, more or less,
To the heaven's height, far and steep.
Reverie.

Let a man contend to the uttermost
For his life's set prize, be it what it will!
　.　　.　　.　　.　　.　　.　　.
The sin I impute to each frustrate ghost
Is—the unlit lamp and the ungirt loin.
The Statue and the Bust.

. . . man knows partly but conceives beside,
Creeps ever on from fancies to the fact,
And in this striving, . . .
Finds progress, man's distinctive mark alone.
A Death in the Desert.

　　Our times are in His hand
　　Who saith, "A whole I planned,
. . . Trust God: see all, nor be afraid!"
Rabbi Ben Ezra.

From the first, Power was—I knew.
　　Life has made clear to me
That, strive but for closer view,
　　Love were as plain to see.
Reverie.

INDEX

573

PRINTED BY MORRISON AND GIBB LIMITED EDINBURGH

THIS BOOK MAY BE KEPT

14 Days

may be renewed if not called for by
someone else.

per day is charged if the book
the last date stamped below.

DUE	DUE
9 '65	MAR 3 '78
MAR	APR 10 '78
	NOV 3 '79
JAN	NOV 1 3 '79
	MAR 6 '79
	'80
	MAR
	MAY
	2006

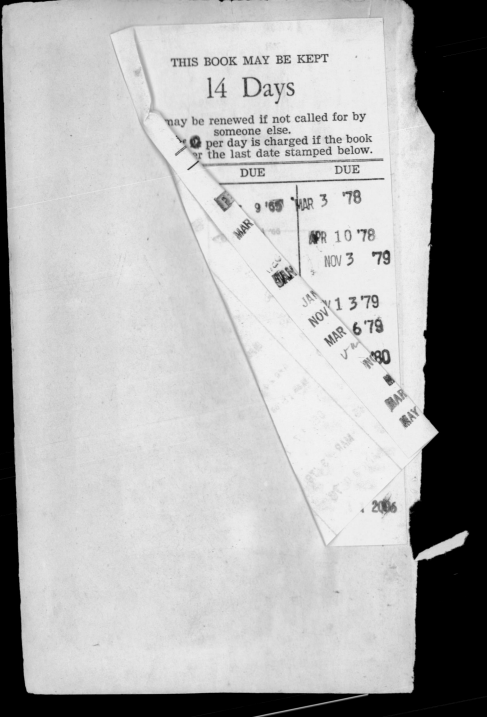